Brutal Campaign

Brutal Campaign

How the 1988 Election Set the Stage for Twenty-First-Century American Politics

Robert L. Fleegler

THE UNIVERSITY OF NORTH CAROLINA PRESS

Chapel Hill

This book was published with the assistance of the Luther H. Hodges Sr. and Luther H. Hodges Jr. Fund of the University of North Carolina Press.

© 2023 Robert Fleegler
All rights reserved
Designed by Richard Hendel

Typeset in Utopia and The Sans
by codeMantra
Manufactured in the United States of America

Cover art: (top) *Presidential Candidate Michael Dukakis on the Campaign Trail during the New Hampshire Primaries in February 1988* (Brian Harris / Alamy Stock Photo); (bottom) *President Bush Waves from the Back of the Train during His Re-election Campaign in Bowling Green, Ohio, September 26, 1992* (Everett Historical Collection / Alamy Stock Photo)

Library of Congress Cataloging-in-Publication Data
Names: Fleegler, Robert L., author.
Title: Brutal campaign : how the 1988 election set the stage for twenty-first-century American politics / Robert L. Fleegler.
Description: Chapel Hill : University of North Carolina Press, [2023] | Includes bibliographical references and index.
Identifiers: LCCN 2022042606 | ISBN 9781469673363 (cloth ; alk. paper) | ISBN 9781469673370 (paperback ; alk. paper) | ISBN 9781469673387 (ebook)
Subjects: LCSH: Bush, George, 1924–2018. | Dukakis, Michael S. (Michael Stanley), 1933– | Presidents—United States—Election—1988. | Political campaigns—United States—History—20th century. | Advertising, Political—Social aspects—United States. | Television in politics—United States—History—20th century.
Classification: LCC JK526 1988 .F54 2023 | DDC 324.973/0929—dc23/eng/20221021
LC record available at https://lccn.loc.gov/2022042606

Contents

List of Illustrations / vi

Acknowledgments / vii

Introduction / 1

Chapter 1. THE STAGE IS SET: 1984–1986 / 9

Chapter 2. THE SCANDALS / 32

Chapter 3. DUKAKIS'S TRIUMPH / 64

Chapter 4. BUSH'S TRIUMPH / 94

Chapter 5. THE FIGHT BEGINS / 132

Chapter 6. COMING OUT OF REAGAN'S SHADOW / 159

Chapter 7. THE DEBATES TAKE CENTER STAGE / 188

Chapter 8. ONE FINAL CHARGE / 224

Epilogue: THE LEGACY OF 1988 / 252

Notes / 269

Bibliography / 323

Index / 331

Illustrations

FIGURES

Gary Hart press conference / 44

Image of the "Seven Dwarfs" / 47

Joe Biden withdraws / 55

Newsweek cover of Jesse Jackson / 82

Newsweek cover of George H. W. Bush / 105

Pat Robertson in Iowa / 119

The Republican field / 123

Michael Dukakis at the Democratic convention / 155

Bill Clinton with Johnny Carson / 162

Dan Quayle introduction / 171

George H. W. Bush acceptance speech / 184

Dukakis in a tank / 200

Lloyd Bentsen / 213

Second Bush-Dukakis debate / 219

Newsweek cover about the negative campaign / 237

Bush takes the oath of office / 253

MAP

1988 Electoral College votes by state / 243

Acknowledgments

It will be hard to list all of the people who helped in this endeavor, as writing a second book proved more challenging than the first one in many ways. I researched and wrote most of this book while a non-tenure-track faculty member at the University of Mississippi. As a result, I am deeply indebted to three history department chairs—Joe Ward, Jeff Watt, and Noell Wilson—because they all strongly supported my research while I was in a teaching-oriented position. In particular, Jeff and Noell arranged for me to have a significant teaching reduction for a semester so I could write the bulk of the manuscript. Very special thanks also go to Rick Gregory, the director of my regional campus in Southaven, Mississippi, for supporting this quasi sabbatical, and especially for his instrumental assistance in my promotion to a tenured position.

Several friends and colleagues read over all or portions of the manuscript. Aram Goudsouzian and Andrew Huebner reviewed early drafts of the book and offered vital input. My sister, Melissa Fleegler, and my brother-in-law, Reed Vawter, read later versions of the entire text, providing very helpful comments. Dan Williams gave key advice on chapter 4, assisting me with his considerable expertise on the religious right.

At the outset of the project, my graduate adviser, James Patterson, offered comments on a skeleton prospectus, as did Don Critchlow. Jeff Watt provided comments on the final prospectus I sent to the University of North Carolina (UNC) Press, and Charles Eagles gave helpful advice on conducting oral history. Curtis Wilkie, a former *Boston Globe* reporter who now teaches at the University of Mississippi, helped in a number of different ways.

I spent six weeks researching Michael Dukakis's papers in Boston. Many thanks to everyone at Northeastern University Archives and Special Collections, especially Michelle Romero and Dominque Medal. Also thanks to the archivists at the George H. W. Bush Library in College Station, Texas, who helped find some important documents that were not listed in the regular finding aid. These sources greatly enhanced the book. Thanks also to archivists at the Seeley G. Mudd Manuscript Library at Princeton University, the Dolph Briscoe Center for American History at the University of Texas, and the Vanderbilt Television Archive.

I also must thank everyone involved in the 1988 presidential campaign who agreed to do an interview with me for the book, but in particular

Governor Michael Dukakis. He gave me two hours of his time for an in-person interview and gave unvarnished, frank responses. The book is so much better because of his willingness to discuss the campaign.

I'd also like to thank Brandon Proia, my editor at UNC Press, who endeavored to get the book published despite multiple delays due to the difficult conditions of 2020–21.

Finally and most importantly, I must thank my parents, Bruce and Ruth Fleegler, whose moral and financial backing gave me the ability to get a PhD, write a first book, and now publish a second one. Their support was unstinting during a publication process that was elongated and emotionally draining because of COVID-19.

Brutal Campaign

Introduction

At 8:00 P.M. eastern time on election night 1988, NBC anchor Tom Brokaw informed Americans that they would soon know more about the outcome of "one of the longest and bloodiest presidential campaigns that anyone [could] remember." A little more than an hour later, ABC and CBS declared that Vice President George H. W. Bush had defeated Massachusetts governor Michael Dukakis to become the forty-first president of the United States. After the polls closed on the West Coast, Dukakis conceded, and a few minutes later, Bush came out to deliver his victory speech. "We can now speak the most majestic words a democracy has to offer: the people have spoken," declared the president-elect. The first vice president to succeed his president by electoral means since Martin Van Buren in 1836, he thanked President Reagan "for turning [the] country around and for being [his] friend, and for going the extra mile on the hustings." Seeking conciliation after a brutal campaign that had infuriated many on the other side of the aisle, Bush added, "To those who supported me, I will try to be worthy of your trust, and to those who did not, I will try to earn it, and my hand is out to you and I want to be your President, too." He ended by thanking New Hampshire, where his comeback primary victory over Kansas senator Bob Dole the previous winter had been so key to his march to the nomination and the presidency.[1]

A few months afterward, the *New York Times*' E. J. Dionne and *U.S. News and World Report*'s David Gergen elaborated on Brokaw's election-night remarks, observing, "America has suffered through nasty presidential campaigns in the past; it has endured more than its share of shallow campaigns; it has frequently watched with some embarrassment as one candidate has pummeled another against the ropes and there has been no referee to leap in and stop the fight." They concluded, "Rarely have all of those elements come together in the same campaign, as they did in 1988."[2] With these words, Dionne and Gergen succinctly summarized most Americans' feelings regarding the recently concluded presidential race, which many felt had set new lows in terms of a lack of substance and the degree of negative campaigning. In the end, Bush rode the peace and prosperity of the 1980s to win forty states in a landslide victory. Dukakis would return to his job as governor and leave politics for good when his third term ended in 1991. After one largely unremarkable term as president, Bush would lose his bid for reelection four years later to Bill Clinton. Though his reputation would rise over the years, Bush would be overshadowed in history by the man who made him vice president, the man who defeated him, and even by his own son.

And so the 1988 presidential race would quickly recede into history, largely to be forgotten. It brought no "realignment," as many say occurred in 1896 and 1932.[3] It did not produce a historically consequential president as 1980 did with Ronald Reagan, or 2008 did with Barack Obama. There would be no disputed outcome as in 1876 or 2000.

Reporters produced several books in the immediate aftermath, mostly focusing on the same theme of the highly negative and superficial nature of the campaign.[4] Jack Germond and Jules Witcover, who had assumed Teddy White's role as the chief journalistic chroniclers of the nation's elections, titled their book *Whose Broad Stripes and Bright Stars? The Trivial Pursuit of the Presidency 1988*. "The plain fact was from the outset George Bush ran a campaign distinguished by a degree of negativism and intensity that had never been seen in presidential politics in the television age," wrote the two authors. The journalists called the Republican candidate's quest for the White House "a campaign that appealed to the lowest common denominator in the electorate."[5] Thirty years later, a leading history survey textbook read much the same way, with Eric Foner explaining that "the 1988 election seemed to show politics sinking to new lows."[6] The virtually universal encomiums for the forty-first president when he died in 2018 stressed his personal decency and modesty while acknowledging that the 1988 campaign was a dramatic exception to that rule. "He was not above rough politics," wrote Dan Balz in the *Washington Post*, adding, "His [Bush's] 1988 campaign will be remembered as one in which he pushed the envelope with tactics and issues—the Pledge of Allegiance and prison furloughs—that put his opponent, Michael Dukakis, on the defensive and left Democrats crying foul."[7]

While no academic wrote a book on the subject for thirty years, a few documentarians revisited the election a generation after its conclusion with one singular emphasis—Dukakis failed to respond to Bush's attacks, allowing the vice president to define him.[8] "The key lesson that political consultants learned from 1988 was that you cannot let an attack go unrebutted," comments Professor Kathleen Hall Jamieson in one film. "If an attack has substantial air time behind it, if it synergizes with news, it's going to be believed."[9] The lesson is clear: any politician has to fire back when fired on.

With the perspective of three-and-a-half decades, however, we can more clearly understand the importance of the election and its place in history. Notably, key long-term social, economic, and cultural trends that began in the 1960s, 1970s, and 1980s came to fruition in the 1988 race, revealing the roots of modern American politics as it illustrated and demonstrated structural forces that would influence the country's path for the following thirty years. In particular, key groups within and across the two political parties emerged stronger, reshaping both the Republicans and the Democrats in the years since 1988, while national politics settled on new ideological positioning. Furthermore, the structure of the media changed, as a more confrontational and intrusive press scrutinized new aspects of candidates' lives while the decline of the traditional media gatekeepers began.

The 1988 presidential election deserves the attention of scholars who have largely ignored it in the intervening years. Using archival sources now available and interviews I conducted with those involved in the campaign, including Governor Dukakis, I am able to outline the contest's centrality in late twentieth-century and early twenty-first-century U.S. political history.

So many key trends that would deeply influence American politics from 1988 onward began or dramatically accelerated during the fateful campaign. In addition, Bush's victorious tactics clearly illustrated the strategies and issues that enabled the Republicans to win five of six elections between 1968 and 1988, dominating the White House for that period. The election also clearly revealed the nature of political practice in the late twentieth century, as well as its sharp difference from the way politics would be conducted in the early twenty-first century. Finally, the legacy of the Bush-Dukakis election would be felt for years, with Bill Clinton, Joe Biden, and Donald Trump all launching their national political careers during the 1988 cycle.

These changes in politics began to be seen in the very early days of the campaign, as the combination of the growing aggressiveness of the post-Watergate media and the rise of second-wave feminism precipitated a closer examination of the personal lives of politicians. This led to Democratic front-runner Gary Hart's implosion over a sex scandal, previewing the "personal is political" scandals that would dominate the 1990s and beyond. Unlike the days of FDR and JFK, in this era adultery and other aspects of a contender's private behavior were now clearly fair game.

The rise of new video technology and cable television meant that candidates were now constantly monitored on the trail, and any small stumble could damage their bid. As a result, Joe Biden's first presidential campaign—launched thirty-four years before his inauguration as the forty-sixth president in 2021—ended when cameras caught the Delaware senator copying language from the British opposition leader, putting politicians on notice that their every utterance could be used for or against them in the court of public opinion.

The growing gap between rich and poor and the decline of industrial jobs in the 1980s threatened the living standards of non–college educated workers. Many blamed the growing globalization of the American economy and the rise of foreign economic competition for the travails of this group. Missouri congressman Dick Gephardt's populist antitrade campaign tapped into this growing anxiety, and while it did not propel him to the Democratic nomination, it foreshadowed a generation of politicians in both parties who would pursue white working-class voters using that message.

A generation after the civil rights movement but two decades before President Obama was elected, the Black community had attained enough power within the Democratic Party to propel an African American candidate into contention for the presidential nomination. While contemporary pundits declared that no Black candidate could be elected president in 1988, for a brief moment Jesse Jackson seemed to have the chance to become the first African American nominee from a major party. Though he came up short, Jackson's alliance of Black and highly educated white voters laid an important part of the foundation for Barack Obama's breakthrough two decades later.

While Jackson tried to pull the party leftward with his progressive message, it was Michael Dukakis's neoliberal approach that won the Democratic nomination in the end. Though caricatured as an out-of-the-mainstream liberal in the general election, Dukakis articulated a technocratic center-left philosophy in line with the post-1960s attempts to reform the Democratic Party. And he anticipated many of the moderate themes Bill Clinton would espouse in the 1990s.

A similar dynamic played out on the Republican side, as Bush and Dole both tried to soften the edges of Reagan-era conservatism, another precursor to the Clintonian centrism that would prevail in the following decade. With prosperity restored after the malaise of the 1970s, the antigovernment tide receded slightly. Bush and Dole pledged to support a greater role for the federal government in education and the environment, and to help those who hadn't benefited from the economic growth of the 1980s. While the Republican Party had shifted sharply to the right during the Reagan years, moderate conservatives and suburban voters still retained significant power during this era, especially when compared with later years. In fact, while historians often focus on the rise of conservatism in the period from

1964 to 1980, it should be noted that the tide had ebbed a bit by the end of the Reagan years.[10]

At the same time, Christian conservatives—who had first arrived as a force during the Reagan years—continued their ascendancy into the upper echelons of the Republican Party. Pat Robertson's surprisingly successful campaign demonstrated the growing strength of the religious right in the GOP, paving the way for the emergence of the Christian Coalition in the 1990s. Social conservatives would garner even greater power within the party in the upcoming years.

The 1980s witnessed the emergence of a new entrepreneurial class, and no one symbolized it more than Donald Trump, who briefly toyed with a Republican presidential run of his own. In the midst of his first brush with national fame, he attacked American allies as free riders and called for the nation's leaders to take a tougher line with U.S. trading partners. Though he didn't enter the race in the end, Trump first laid out the themes he would use in his unlikely presidential triumph three decades later.

More trends became clear during the general election cycle, as Bill Clinton made his national debut with a speech at the Democratic convention. He nearly destroyed his presidential prospects with long-winded remarks that only received applause when he said, "In closing." But he also recovered with a charismatic appearance on *The Tonight Show Starring Johnny Carson*, inaugurating a long history of self-inflicted setbacks and impressive comebacks that would mark his career. And the success of Clinton's performance on an entertainment show like Carson's foreshadowed the growing importance of nontraditional programming to presidential campaigns, as well as the beginning of the decline of the established media gatekeepers.

The Democrats also debated Palestinian self-determination at that convention, marking the first time a major American political party seriously broached the topic. The discussion revealed the emerging division among liberals over the Israeli-Palestinian conflict, which would lead to greater partisan differences over the issue in the early twenty-first century.

Exploiting a loophole in the campaign-finance system constructed after Watergate, the Dukakis campaign truly popularized the use of soft money— virtually unlimited donations to the political parties—to fund presidential races. By going around the giving limits enacted by Congress in the 1970s, Dukakis's team helped pave the way for the gutting of the post-Watergate system of public financing of campaigns. Eventually, the rise of soft money would lead to major scandals in the 1990s, followed by another round of reform.

Bush's choice of Indiana senator Dan Quayle as vice president—a candidate with little national name recognition—placed the first baby boomer on a national ticket, signaling the political coming of age of that influential generation. Quayle's possible avoidance of combat in the Vietnam War immediately became the center of controversy and introduced questions about Vietnam-era military service to presidential politics, something that would become a quadrennial ritual for baby-boomer politicians. From this point forward, the question, "What did you do in the war?" would plague nominees from Clinton to Trump. The controversy over the relatively unknown Quayle's selection also brought about a more cautious approach to vice-presidential picks by both parties that lasted at least two decades.

Less dramatically, in another example of the growing importance of nontraditional news sources, *Saturday Night Live* political sketches became a fixture of American life. Global warming also become part of the presidential discussion for the first time.

In the end, Dukakis lost by a wide margin to Bush in the popular vote, but showed his party an Electoral College path out of the wilderness Democrats had wandered in since the age of Aquarius. Winning important states on both coasts while coming close to victory in a number of key midwestern states, Dukakis's campaign laid the groundwork for the "Blue Wall" of states that would pave the way for Clinton's and Obama's two-term presidencies, as well as Biden's victory in 2020.

Finally, violent crime rose dramatically during the crack-cocaine epidemic of the 1980s and became a central issue in the race. Dukakis's opposition to the death penalty and perceived weakness in that regard provided a lesson to all politicians to avoid being seen as soft on the issue. Consequently, the reaction to the Bush campaign's use of William Horton—a Massachusetts felon who committed serious crimes while out on a furlough—contributed to bipartisan support for tougher sentencing policies that impacted criminal-justice policy well into the twenty-first century.

The ideological battles seen in the 1988 race can be traced to the turbulence of the 1960s, as the divisions in the country over civil rights and the Vietnam War produced cultural splits that never truly healed. The civil rights movement produced historic gains for African Americans, with the Civil Rights Act of 1964 and the Voting Rights Act of 1965 burying legal Jim Crow in its grave. However, the movement also precipitated a white backlash, first in the South and then in the North, when its focus shifted to economic issues. Crime rose dramatically during the decade and combined with major urban riots in Watts, Detroit, and Newark to make "law and order" a national cry. The Americanization of the war in Vietnam and the concomitant rise in antiwar sentiment split the nation as nothing had since the Civil War.

These disputes over race and patriotism laid the groundwork for the contemporary gap between red states and blue states, as Republicans took advantage of such divisions to paint Democrats as out of the mainstream.[11] In 1968, Richard Nixon defeated Hubert Humphrey, calling for "law and order" while suggesting a slower approach to civil rights. Nixon also criticized antiwar student protesters who he claimed didn't respect American traditions. Running as a third-party candidate, Alabama governor George Wallace delivered an even more uninhibited version of this message, saying, "The overwhelming majority of all races in this country are against this breakdown of law and order as much as those who are assembled here tonight. It's a few anarchists, a few activists, a few militants, a few revolutionaries, and a few Communists."[12] In Nixon's acceptance speech at the Republican National Convention, he claimed to represent "the voice of the great majority of Americans, the forgotten Americans, the non-shouters, the nondemonstrators."[13] Once he came into office, this group of working-class ethnics in the North and whites in the South became known as the "silent majority."

Going further in his reelection bid in 1972, Nixon tried to link George McGovern to the excesses of the 1960s counterculture, calling him the candidate of "acid, amnesty, and abortion," while declaring the antiwar senator weak on defense. Cultural and race-based appeals on the "wedge" issues of crime, welfare, relations with the Soviet Union, and a permissive approach to values also played a key role in Reagan's triumphs in 1980 and 1984, and Democrats who responded to this message evolved from the silent majority to become "Reagan Democrats."

Scholars debate how important racial splits and cultural divisions were in bringing about conservative dominance in the 1970s and 1980s. Some view this disunity as absolutely central to the rise of the GOP as part of both a "Southern Strategy" to garner the support of estranged white southerners frustrated by racial change, and part of an appeal to white ethnic voters in the North concerned about similar issues. Others contend that a more race-neutral ideology focused on middle-class voters defending their newly earned privileges in the burgeoning suburbs was the primary driver behind the move to the right, or that social issues such as abortion undermined the New Deal coalition. Regardless, there can be no question that the GOP placed Democrats on the defensive on issues such as crime and national security, thereby controlling the White House for all but Jimmy Carter's term from 1968 to 1988.[14]

This strategy reached its apotheosis in 1988, as Bush and his surrogates appealed to Reagan Democrats by repeatedly labeling Dukakis an extreme

1960s liberal, while often comparing him to McGovern and explicitly portraying him as "out of the mainstream." Citing Dukakis's veto of a bill mandating that teachers lead students in reciting the Pledge of Allegiance, the Bush campaign claimed the governor was insufficiently patriotic. Using the case of William Horton, a prisoner who committed crimes while out on furlough, Republicans suggested Bush's opponent was soft on crime. In the last election of the Cold War, they claimed Dukakis opposed key military programs and would undermine the national defense.

The Bush-Dukakis race also revealed the nature of American politics in the late twentieth century and how it differed from politics in the first two decades of the twenty-first century, when the parties became more ideologically homogenous, and national politics became more polarized. Twenty-first-century candidates have primarily focused on revving up their respective bases. Yet in 1988 the vice president and the governor sought to seize the middle, lavishing attention on the Reagan Democrats, working-class swing voters who had backed the Gipper twice but who might be convinced to return to their ancestral homes. In an attempt to win over centrists, Bush pledged to be the education and environmental president, while Dukakis claimed the mantle of fiscal conservative and welfare reformer. Given the larger number of persuadable voters, both candidates held seventeen-point leads at one time, something virtually impossible to imagine given the stronger partisan attachments of the early twenty-first century. Moreover, both sides ran national elections with a majority of states in play at one point, as opposed to simply battling over a relatively small number of swing states. Finally, in an era before talk radio, the internet, and social media, network television ruled; the battle over evening-news sound bites and thirty-second commercial spots was the primary determinant of electoral success.

On Election Day 1988, Dionne wrote in the *New York Times*, "Thus ended one of the longest, most expensive, and most bitter campaigns the country has ever experienced," laying the groundwork for the conventional wisdom about the race.[15] By the time the presidential race had ended, however, American politics had been significantly altered by the events of the previous eighteen months, which created an impact that would be felt for decades. But before the election battle could start, the framework for the contest would have to be laid in the first two years of the second term of the man who dominated American politics in the 1980s—Ronald Reagan.

1 The Stage Is Set 1984–1986

As the election returns came in on November 6, 1984, it was clear President Ronald Reagan was cruising to a historic landslide reelection victory over former vice president Walter Mondale. Reagan won forty-nine states, while Mondale clung to a narrow victory in his home state of Minnesota. In winning the popular vote by a margin of 59 percent to 41 percent, the incumbent triumphed in every age group, every region, and every income group except voters making under $12,500 a year.[1] "It was the night Ronald Wilson Reagan became Mr. America," wrote Walter Shapiro in *Newsweek*, adding, "Rarely has America seen so all-encompassing a landslide."[2]

Such an outcome was by no means certain two years earlier when House Republicans had lost twenty-six seats in the midterm elections in the midst of the worst recession since the Great Depression. To purge the high inflation of the 1970s, Federal Reserve chairman Paul Volcker implemented tight money policies and other anti-inflationary measures that produced the highest unemployment levels since the 1930s. Reagan's popularity plummeted as his approval rating reached a low of 35 percent in January 1983.[3] Eventually inflation subsided, Volcker lowered interest rates, and unemployment fell from a postwar high of 10.8 percent in December 1982 to 7.2 percent by November 1984.[4] Reagan's campaign promoted the economic recovery, declaring it "Morning in America" in a famous political ad. Nearly 60 percent of voters agreed, believing the economy was better off than it had been four years earlier, with those voters supporting Reagan by a margin of six to one.[5]

The outlook, however, would not seem as bright a mere two years later. Republicans lost control of the Senate, leading many to suggest that the "Reagan Revolution" was over and that the nation's politics were moving back toward the center. Meanwhile, the Democrats worked to learn the lessons from Mondale's defeat as well as their other losses over the previous two decades, shifting their policies and ideology in the hopes of appealing to this new middle. And the biggest scandal since Watergate would imperil Reagan's second term, his legacy, and the chances for his vice president to succeed him.

From 1932 to 1968, the New Deal political coalition forged by Franklin D. Roosevelt during the Great Depression dominated American politics, paving the way for FDR's four terms in office, as well as the elections of Harry S. Truman, John F. Kennedy, and Lyndon B. Johnson. The alliance of white southerners, African Americans, northern white ethnics, labor unions, and intellectuals made the Democrats the majority party in the country, allowing them to control the White House for twenty-eight out of thirty-six years during this period. And after LBJ's landslide win over Arizona senator Barry Goldwater in 1964, some believed the GOP was finished as a national political party.

But the turmoil of the 1960s broke up the Democratic coalition. Many southern whites left the party once Kennedy and Johnson embraced the civil rights movement. Some southern whites became more affluent, moving into the GOP as they became more receptive to Republicans' conservative economic message. The cultural changes of the 1960s, with the rise of the counterculture and the anti–Vietnam War movement, alienated working-class whites in the North. Many believed the Democrats flirted with unpatriotic elements of the country. The dramatic growth in street crime, along with urban riots, which liberals diagnosed as a response to poverty and discrimination, led some to see their ancestral political home as soft on crime. Others believed that Johnson's War on Poverty had been ineffectual, increasing dependency on government and worsening the problems of the cities. Richard Nixon harnessed these disaffected voters in his victorious campaigns in 1968 and 1972.

Some of these trends accelerated in the 1970s as more upper-middle-class suburban voters became Democrats after the McGovern campaign of 1972, and the party increasingly embraced the cultural liberalism of the feminist and gay rights movements. In the aftermath of Vietnam, the party moved away from the Cold War liberalism of Truman and Kennedy, and Republicans eagerly critiqued the Democrats as not tough enough in foreign policy and weak on containing communism.

But it was not just the Democrats' flaws that were the problem—Republicans developed new institutions to strengthen their cause. To counter what they perceived as the liberal dominance of the culture, the Right started to build journals, think tanks, lobbies, and other organizations to advance the conservative message. Republicans also developed new intellectual analyses delineating how the welfare state, government regulation, and taxation could slow economic growth. And party conservatives, who had been left for dead after Goldwater's defeat, increasingly challenged the moderate establishment that controlled the GOP.

Following Watergate, Jimmy Carter reassembled the New Deal coalition to some extent to win back the White House in 1976, shifting to the center by emphasizing balancing the budget and calling for a stronger defense. But this success proved to be short-lived. Carter's shortcomings in handling the multiple crises of his presidency, like the Iran hostage crisis and the Soviet invasion of Afghanistan, weakened his support and further damaged the Democrats' credibility in foreign policy. Also, Carter's more centrist politics alienated progressives in his party, and he had to beat back a primary challenge in 1980 from Senator Edward Kennedy of Massachusetts, the leading torchbearer of traditional liberalism.

In addition to the Left's frustration with Carter, many moderates held Democratic policies responsible for the economic stagnation of the 1970s. High oil prices and long gas lines ensued after the Iranian Revolution, and the chronic inflation that plagued the decade pushed many Americans into higher tax brackets. The latter development precipitated a national tax revolt embodied by the passage of Proposition 13 by popular initiative in California; the measure dramatically cut property taxes. The simultaneous appearance of high unemployment and high inflation—known as stagflation—along with double-digit interest rates, created frustration in the country that Carter tried to address in the summer of 1979 with a nationally televised speech. But instead of focusing on those day-to-day concerns, the president sermonized about the spiritual crisis and loss of confidence in America. These remarks became known as the "malaise" speech, which became a metaphor for the difficulties of his term.

Stagflation also weakened the credibility of Keynesian economic theory, which had held sway for most of the postwar period. This created an ideological vacuum, opening the door for supply-side economics. This new economic theory promoted by conservatives suggested that tax cuts could accelerate saving and growth to the point that deficits would not ensue.

Moreover, broader cultural shifts worked against Carter and in favor of the GOP. After the *Roe v. Wade* decision in 1973, the Democrats gradually became the pro-choice party, and the Republicans become the pro-life party, leading many social conservatives in the South and elsewhere to change their allegiance after supporting their fellow evangelical Carter. Others were alienated by Democratic support for the Equal Rights Amendment (ERA) and the social changes of the 1960s and 1970s. The religious right's emergence in the late 1970s—symbolized by the creation of Jerry Falwell's Moral Majority in 1979—organized these voters into a key part of the Republican Party, as Reagan openly embraced them. These forces all helped to lead to Reagan's defeat of Carter in 1980.

After his first two years in office, however, Reagan looked vulnerable, with unemployment rates reaching double digits in 1982. As the Democrats prepared to challenge Reagan in 1984, the party establishment unified behind Carter's vice president, Walter Mondale of Minnesota.[6] Key elected officials and interest groups, most notably organized labor, endorsed him in overwhelming numbers, making him the heavy favorite for the nomination. Among the other contenders, Ohio senator John Glenn—a more centrist former astronaut who had been the first American to orbit the earth two decades earlier—seemed the most likely to give Mondale a fight.

Glenn's campaign, however, never gained traction, and Colorado senator Gary Hart emerged as the strongest threat to the front-runner. Running on the theme of "new ideas," Hart presented a contrast to Mondale's traditional New Deal philosophy and appealed to suburban and younger voters. Noting the former vice president's backing from the AFL-CIO and other traditional liberal constituencies, Hart repeatedly criticized Mondale for being the candidate of special interests.

Though Mondale carried the first contest in Iowa by a large margin, Hart's surprise second-place finish generated huge media attention, allowing him to build momentum. He then proceeded to win New Hampshire, launching himself further into the national spotlight. A marathon race between the two men ensued throughout the winter and spring of 1984, and Hart at times seemed to wither under the lights. "Where's the beef?" asked Mondale in regard to the senator's new ideas in a television debate, referencing a famous Wendy's ad of the time. "Many party pros think his performance in the primaries displayed a political glass jaw," wrote *Newsweek*'s Tom Morganthau about Hart, noting "his arrogance, his impatience, and his inability to project warmth."[7]

In the meantime, the Reverend Jesse Jackson ran the first major African American presidential campaign. Though most Black elected leaders lined up with the establishment behind Mondale, Jackson energized African American voters, carrying three-quarters of the Black vote while winning five contests. Running on a platform to the left of Mondale and Hart, he finished third in votes and delegates, establishing himself as a force to be reckoned with inside the Democratic Party as well as in national politics.

After finally defeating Hart at the end of the primary process in June, Mondale turned his attention toward the general election. Trailing badly in the polls and looking for a dramatic step to shake up the race, the former vice president nominated Geraldine Ferraro, a three-term congresswoman from Queens, as his running mate, making her the first woman ever to run on a major-party national ticket. Though the selection of the first woman was history making, Ferraro also noted her immigrant background in her acceptance speech in San Francisco. Previewing Dukakis's discussion of his own heritage four years later, she declared, "Tonight, the daughter of an immigrant from Italy has been chosen to run for [vice] president in the new land my father came to love."[8] Similarly, New York governor Mario Cuomo did the same in his keynote address, stating, "We will have a new president of the United States, a Democrat born not to the blood of kings but to the blood of pioneers and immigrants. And we will have America's first woman vice president, the child of immigrants!"[9]

Though throughout his career he had largely governed as a New Deal liberal in the mold of his mentor, fellow Minnesotan and vice president Hubert Humphrey, Mondale—as many post-LBJ Democrats did—tried to show that the party had evolved and learned from the shortcomings of the Great Society era of the 1960s. In his acceptance speech, Mondale proclaimed, "So tonight we come to you with a new realism: ready for the future, and recapturing the best in our tradition." He elaborated, "Look at our platform. There are no defense cuts that weaken our security; no business taxes that weaken our economy; no laundry lists that raid our treasury."[10] Most notably, Mondale touted himself as a fiscal conservative who would honestly confront the large budget deficits resulting from the Reagan tax cuts and defense buildup. "We are living on borrowed money and borrowed time," explained the vice president. He continued, "These deficits hike interest rates, clobber exports, stunt investment, kill jobs, undermine growth, cheat our kids, and shrink our future." Promising to cut the deficit by two-thirds, Mondale declared, "Let's tell the truth. That must be done—it must be done. Mr. Reagan will raise your taxes. He won't tell you. I just did."[11]

Reagan's advisers pronounced themselves thrilled at Mondale's promise. Deputy campaign manager Lee Atwater thought he was dreaming upon hearing the speech, asking, "Did he just say what I thought he said?" Though Mondale thought he was demonstrating fiscal responsibility, the opposition believed otherwise, with Reagan pollster Bob Teeter commenting, "It was perfect. It just did for us what we couldn't have done with advertising. . . . He just proved himself to be the classic, big-spending, liberal, New Deal, old-time Democrat."[12]

Reagan and his consultants came down hard on Mondale for pledging to raise taxes. Interestingly, though, Bush initially left the door slightly ajar to a tax increase, saying, "Any president should keep his options open." But Reagan made the contrast clear, declaring, "My opponent has spent his political life raising more taxes and more spending. For him, raising taxes is a first resort. For me it is a last resort."[13]

Attacks on the tax issue continued throughout the fall campaign. One ad for Reagan contrasts the two candidates' economic philosophies; the narrator says, "With Reaganomics you cut taxes. With Mondalenomics, you raise taxes. Reaganomics you cut deficits through growth and less government spending. Mondalenomics you raise taxes. They both work," the commercial concludes, "[but] the difference is Reaganomics works for you. Mondalenomics works against you."[14]

Reagan also stressed his toughness vis-à-vis the Soviet Union. The USSR had often been referred to as the "bear" during the Cold War, and one Reagan ad shows a bear prowling while the narrator observes, "There is a bear in the woods. For some people, the bear is easy to see. Others don't see it at all. Some people say the bear is tame. Others say it's vicious and dangerous. Since no one can really be sure who's right, isn't it smart to be as strong as the bear? If there is a bear." The end of the ad shows a man—presumably Reagan—seemingly taming the bear.[15] Attacks on Democrats' supposed softness on national defense and eagerness to raise taxes had been Republican staples since 1968, and they would return again in 1988.

Though Mondale's campaign is often remembered as a textbook example of failed liberalism, his ads—like the convention speech—repeatedly stress the need for fiscal responsibility. Criticizing Reagan for the rising deficits and the national debt, one ad's text reads, "Mondale Deficit Reduction Package: Cut Spending, Close Tax Loopholes, Trust Fund," spelling out the fact that Mondale would "put new taxes in a trust fund to pay off Reagan's debt." Another commercial shows a roller coaster going down, and the voice-over says that Reaganomics had plunged the economy into a severe recession in 1982. Then, as the spot continues, the roller coaster starts going up again. The ad's narrator agrees with President Reagan when he says the economy is on an upward trend in 1984. But the narrator elaborates, "It is. Up on a mountain of a debt and record Reagan deficits. More borrowing than all the other presidents in history combined. That'll drive interest rates up, slow the economy down." The coaster then starts going down dramatically.[16]

The public, however, rejected Mondale's gloomier outlook in favor of Reagan's optimistic rhetoric, embodied by the legendary "Morning in America" ad, which resonated because of the economy's strong recovery from the 1981–82 recession. "It's morning again in America. Today more men and women will go to work than ever before in our country's history," the narrator declares as viewers watch images of ordinary Americans going about their daily lives. "It's morning again in America, and under the leadership of President Reagan, our country is prouder and stronger and better," the narrator then concludes, asking, "Why would we ever want to return to where we were less than four short years ago?"[17] The memory of the malaise of the Carter years would again be invoked by Reagan's vice president four years later.

Mondale and his advisers thought they had a brief opening after the president stumbled and appeared confused in the first debate, raising the issue of his age and mental acuity, but this opportunity quickly faded when Reagan came back strongly in the second debate. When asked whether his age might be a problem, the seventy-three-year-old adroitly responded, "I will not make an age an issue in this campaign. I am not going to exploit, for political purposes, my opponent's youth and inexperience."[18] Mondale laughed along with the audience in response, but he recalled that he knew the campaign was over then.[19]

Yet despite the GOP's overwhelming victory in 1984, many pundits believed the Republican Party had fallen short of achieving the historical breakthrough it sought. A week before the election, Richard Wirthlin, Reagan's lead pollster, declared that he saw "the seeds of realignment" in his candidate's polling advantage, adding that the 1984 results might provide the Republicans with "an edge it hadn't had for 50 years."[20] The GOP, however, lost seats in the Senate and made only marginal gains in the House. "It could in fact be the death knell for the Democratic majority forged during the New Deal. But does it herald a new era of Republican dominance?" asked *Time*'s Evan Thomas.[21] That remained to be seen.

After suffering their fourth defeat in five presidential elections and the second presidential contest where they only won one state, Democrats engaged in serious soul-searching about whether Reagan's victory was merely due to a strong economy and the president's personal appeal, or whether it was a signal to fundamentally change their message. Former secretary of defense and longtime Democratic elder Clark Clifford opted for the first position, declaring, "It was a victory of personality far more than party."[22] Democratic pollster Peter Hart agreed, comparing Reagan's win to Ike's reelection in 1956: "There were five P's in this election, and Reagan clearly won four of them—peace, prosperity, popularity and pride. The fifth one is policy, and that's an open question. That's what saved the Democrats in the House and the Senate."[23]

Others were less sanguine. "This party is in the worst shape of my lifetime. The worst since the Civil War!" exclaimed one Democratic strategist.[24] Of particular concern were the party's continued losses among white southerners and blue-collar whites in the North, as the Democrats' support among these once-upon-a-time pillars of the New Deal coalition had declined precipitously during the 1970s and 1980s. In 1985, pollster Stanley

Greenberg's survey of working-class whites in Macomb County, Michigan, a suburb outside Detroit, revealed that many labor Democrats had left the party over the previous two decades because they now believed its programs largely benefited African Americans and other minorities rather than the middle class.[25] If the New Deal coalition was still alive in 1984, it was clearly on life support.

Some blamed the loss on the failure of the Democrats to modernize ideologically, arguing that Mondale was an old-school New Dealer out of step with politics in the 1980s. Mondale's attempt to break with Democratic orthodoxy and espouse a message of fiscal responsibility only seemed to deepen his image as a traditional liberal. In addition, organized labor's unstinting support opened him up to accusations that he was too close to special interests. Others thought that labor and other interest groups, such as feminists, teacher unions, etc., appeared to control the party agenda. "There is a feeling that our party has become not a party of the whole but simply a collection of special interests that are narrower than the national interest," commented Virginia governor Charles Robb.[26] Many of Robb's fellow moderate Democrats shared his concern.

Many observers also cited television, still viewed by some as a relatively new force in American politics, as the culprit in Mondale's demise. The former vice president bemoaned the fact that the small screen was now central to politics, admitting, "I think you know I've never really warmed up to television, and in fairness to television, it's never really warmed up to me."[27] Crediting television for much of Reagan's success, *New York Times* columnist Tom Wicker wrote, "The remarkable size of his victory, in my judgement, owes much to the way in which that preference was reinforced by his and his managers' mastery of television—the new reality of American politics, the eye through which voters now see most of what they know about a Presidential campaign."[28]

As attention began to turn to 1988, pundits and political strategists name-dropped numerous Democratic contenders, with Hart and Cuomo garnering the most attention. Cuomo electrified the 1984 Democratic convention in San Francisco with his keynote speech, and one political consultant said Republicans would "tell you the one guy they're afraid of is Mario Cuomo." Still, others saw Cuomo as simply carrying the same flickering ideological torch as previous failed Democratic nominees. "Cuomo," said political analyst Richard Scammon, "is just a Mondale with charm."[29]

By the 1980s, the Democrats had split into several loosely organized factions. Some, like Speaker of the House Tip O'Neill of Massachusetts and Cuomo, still pledged fealty to the old New Deal faith. Many southern

Democrats had broken with the segregationist policies of their ancestors to assemble biracial coalitions with moderate stances on social and economic questions. Another group of moderates mostly from outside the South—often referred to as "Atari Democrats" or "neoliberals"—sought to move beyond the top-down government policies of the New Deal and Great Society and achieve the party's traditional goals by applying new and more market-oriented policies, including alliances with business.

Historically, "neoliberal" described a free-market libertarian economics inspired by conservative intellectuals such as Austrian economist Friedrich Hayek and American economist Milton Friedman. In the context of the United States in the 1980s, however, it meant a belief in a new kind of liberalism that merged a different kind of government activism with more pro-business policies. *Washington Monthly*'s Charlie Peters, who coined the term "neoliberalism" for this period, explained this philosophy and its divergence with conventional liberalism: "[Its adherents'] primary concerns are community, democracy, and prosperity. Of them, economic growth is most important now, because it is essential to almost everything else we want to achieve. We want to encourage the entrepreneur not with Reaganite politics that make the rich richer, but with laws designed to help attract investors and customers."[30]

Hart was a central member of the neoliberal group, and he suggested a break with Democratic orthodoxy that was echoed by many in the party, especially those who had been elected from suburban constituencies after the 1960s. Having emerged from the social movements of the 1960s, like the women's, environmental, civil rights, and antiwar movements, these Democrats were more likely to focus on quality-of-life issues than economics. They tended to be less supportive of organized labor, which they had come to see as part of the political establishment during the Vietnam era. In the aftermath of Watergate, government reform became a central focus for these officeholders, especially the large Democratic congressional class elected in the 1974 midterm elections shortly after Nixon's resignation. This faction also tended to be more fiscally conservative because its members' political philosophy had been molded by the prosperity of the 1950s, as opposed to the privations of the 1930s. They did not adhere to the bread-and-butter labor economics of Mondale and O'Neill.

And like many Democrats who emerged in the 1970s and 1980s, Hart challenged certain aspects of liberal conventional wisdom. He spoke of the need to update traditional Democratic thinking by moving more toward a free-market philosophy while using the government to promote high-tech industries.[31] After Coloradans elected him to the Senate in 1974, he described his evolving ideology, as well that of many of his fellow class of 1974 "Watergate babies," when he memorably declared, "We're not a bunch of little Hubert Humphreys." With this remark, Hart distanced himself and his colleagues from one of the iconic figures of New Deal and Great Society politics.³²

Beyond Hart, a new breed of leadership was ready to take charge, and in the Senate, New Jersey's Bill Bradley, Delaware's Joe Biden, and Arkansas's Dale Bumpers drew mention. Reformers also thrived on the state level, where Democrats still controlled an overwhelming majority of the nation's governorships. John Herbers wrote in the *New York Times* of this suggestion from the DNC's party spokesman: "There was now a strong belief among Democrats that power must shift to those in the party who believe [that] the American people want a continuation of many of the social programs[,] but that delivery of them must be reformed and decentralized along the lines favored by a number of Democratic governors," including "Bruce Babbit of Arizona, Michael S. Dukakis of Massachusetts, and Robert Graham of Florida."³³

On the Republican side, conservatives had largely taken over the party during the previous two decades, as the center of gravity of the GOP shifted from the Northeast and Midwest to the South and West. During the first two decades after World War II, liberals like New York governor Nelson Rockefeller and moderates like Kansas's Dwight Eisenhower, who accepted the New Deal and supported a degree of modest activist government, held the upper hand in the party. Ideological conservatives like Ohio senator Robert Taft and Goldwater, who believed in dramatically rolling back the scope of the federal government, remained in the minority. But starting with Goldwater's 1964 presidential campaign, the right wing of the party gradually gained power. While the Arizona senator lost badly to Johnson, Ronald Reagan, then an actor, gained national notoriety for speaking on Goldwater's behalf in a nationally televised speech shortly before the election. The address launched Reagan on his way to becoming governor of California in 1966. Activists who worked for the Goldwater campaign, like Pat Buchanan and Phyllis Schlafly, also began to push the GOP in a more conservative direction. Having maintained a foot in both moderate and conservative camps, Nixon held the factions together in 1968 and also won over voters who supported George Wallace that year to win in a landslide in 1972. But after Watergate, Reagan nearly defeated the more establishment Gerald Ford in a primary challenge in 1976, making him the inheritor of Goldwater's mantle and paving the way for his win in 1980, cementing conservative control of the GOP.

As part of this process, the party's ideology transformed, as its economic agenda shifted from a focus on balancing the budget and compromising with the welfare state to an emphasis on cutting taxes and reducing government spending. With the rise of religious conservatives, the GOP moved from cultural moderation to a platform that opposed ERA and the right to choose. In relations with the Soviet Union, Republicans abandoned the détente policy promoted by Nixon and Ford in favor of the more militant anticommunism espoused by Reagan.

Though conservatives were now clearly in control, the moderate wing of the party—the Rockefeller Republicans—still maintained a significant presence. A considerable number of pro-choice representatives and traditional fiscal conservatives remained in the party, especially when compared with their near extinction come the early twenty-first century.

Vice President George H. W. Bush stood poised to take up the Reagan mantle. But some were worried that he was not up to the challenge. Despite an impressive resume that included service as a decorated World War II pilot, as well as stints as UN ambassador, chairman of the Republican National Committee, and director of the CIA, Bush had achieved limited success in electoral politics. He had lost a race for the Senate in 1964 in Texas, won a House seat in 1966 in the Houston area, and then lost another race for the Senate in 1970.

Moreover, Bush was held in suspicion by conservatives. Despite his years in business and politics in Texas, he had grown up in Connecticut and had the bearing of a New England Yankee. Many on the right viewed him as a Rockefeller Republican who had derided Reagan's supply side economic program as "voodoo economics" in his 1980 run for president. Loyal service to Reagan had won Bush some affection from the party base, but it was clear that he would have to work to earn those constituents' enthusiastic support. "We've always been able to know who our favorite was at the end of each election—starting with Taft, then Nixon, Goldwater, and Reagan," noted Richard Viguerie, a key conservative leader. "That's not so now. I don't know of anybody among us who has firmly settled on a candidate."[34]

Finally, the vice presidency itself posed obstacles to Bush's presidential ambitions. His unstinting support for Reagan made him seem like less of a leader and drew derision from some quarters. The political cartoon *Doonesbury* suggested that Bush had placed "his manhood in a blind trust." Observers believed he had to break from Reagan at some point to show his own political independence and identity. "He doesn't have to disagree before 1986," said one of Bush's aides to *Newsweek*, "[but] he might have to after that."³⁵ Indeed, no sitting vice president had won election to succeed his president since Martin Van Buren had followed Andrew Jackson in 1836.

Following Reagan's reelection, Bush began putting his team together. During Christmas 1984, Bush asked Atwater, whom he'd first met when he was chairman of the RNC in the early 1970s and the latter was executive director of the national College Republicans, to serve as his campaign manager.³⁶ Atwater had honed his considerable skills in the no-holds-barred world of South Carolina politics, working for future governor Carroll Campbell and legendary senator Strom Thurmond in the 1970s, then moving on to Reagan's primary campaign in 1980. In the process, he developed a reputation for his willingness to do virtually anything to win an election. Among the many charges Atwater's opponents leveled at him was that he had arranged for a third-party candidate in a 1978 House race to attack a more viable Jewish opponent for not believing in Christ as his savior. Atwater himself criticized another foe who had undergone electroshock treatment for having been "hooked up to jumper cables." He moved on to work in the Reagan White House in the Office of Political Affairs and served as deputy manager of the president's reelection campaign in 1984. Atwater, along with future Fox News founder Roger Ailes, would prove critical in pushing Bush to be tougher and more negative on the campaign trail during the primaries and the general election.³⁷

Others were waiting in the wings in the event Bush stumbled. The Senate minority leader, Bob Dole of Kansas, had presidential ambitions and could run as a moderate conservative with a similar ideological profile to Bush. Jack Kemp, a congressman from upstate New York and former star professional quarterback, had stronger conservative credentials than Bush. Kemp could appeal to the right wing of the party as a longtime supporter of supply-side economics and cosponsor of the Kemp-Roth tax cuts that were the centerpiece of the Reagan economic program of 1981.

Of course, Reagan still had a second term to govern, and a successful finish to his presidency would be essential to Bush's chances or to those of any other GOP nominee in 1988. Reagan, Bush, and his supporters hoped the fortieth president could avoid the "second term curse" that had plagued so many modern presidencies. For example, FDR followed his 1936 landslide with the unpopular court-packing plan, while Richard Nixon got caught up in the mire of Watergate after his own forty-nine-state triumph in 1972. Post-Reagan presidents such as Bill Clinton and George W. Bush suffered similar travails.³⁸

The first two years of Reagan's second term saw some major legislative successes. In domestic policy, Reagan worked with Senator Bradley and Congressman Richard Gephardt (D) of Missouri to produce the Tax Reform Act of 1986, which lowered marginal tax rates while broadening the tax base by closing key loopholes. Congress also passed and Reagan signed the Immigration Reform and Control Act of 1986 (IRCA), also known as Simpson-Mazzoli. While providing a path to citizenship for some who had entered the country illegally, the legislation mandated sanctions on employers who hired undocumented workers in the future.

Furthermore, Reagan held his first two summit meetings with the new Soviet leader Mikhail Gorbachev in Geneva and Reykjavik, beginning the process of reducing Cold War tensions, which had reached their most dangerous point since the early 1960s. Gorbachev, who came to power in 1985, began his dual policies of glasnost (political openness) and perestroika (economic liberalization) to try to reform his stagnant country. Reagan had won two elections on a platform of getting tougher on the USSR, and he referred to the country as the "evil empire" during his first term. Yet he reached out to test the genuineness of Gorbachev's overtures despite the suspicions of some of his advisers. In doing so, Reagan established the basis for the most important achievements of his administration. As we will see, however, trouble was on the horizon for his presidency.

During this period, moderate and conservative Democrats formed the Democratic Leadership Council (DLC) in the hopes of moving the party back to the center. The legislators went forward despite resistance from Democratic National Committee (DNC) chairman Paul Kirk, believing it was urgent that the party make significant changes following the Reagan landslide. "There is a perception our party moved away from mainstream America in the 1970's," commented Senator Sam Nunn of Georgia, a leading conservative Democrat and possible 1988 presidential contender.[39] Other prominent elected officials who were incumbent members included Senator Lawton Chiles of Florida, Governor Robb, Governor Babbit, and Representative Gephardt.

With Governor Graham (D) of Florida declaring, "The cavalry is on its way," DLC members took their show on the road for their "first grass-roots" outing in Florida in May 1985. Traveling to Tallahassee, Tampa, and Gainesville to meet elected officials, businesspeople, and students, Nunn clarified the organization's mission: "We're not talking about abandoning the values of the Democratic Party. We're talking about re-examining its programs." From the outset, many criticized the DLC's lack of diversity, as it featured only two Blacks and no women at its inception.[40] Graham talked of the need for a southern primary in mid-March because he believed this would enhance the importance of "mainstream voters" to the nomination process and reduce the influence of the usual interest groups.[41]

Plans for such a primary dated back to the 1970s, when Jimmy Carter recommended its creation while he was governor of Georgia. The Southern Legislative Conference (SLC), a four-decades-old organization of southern state representatives, worked to develop one for the 1984 cycle, but the effort began too late. Many southern Democrats were then frustrated when Glenn's moderate candidacy ran out of steam before their region voted.[42]

The conference succeeded in creating the southern primary in 1985–86, with John Trager, a Texas state senator who chaired the SLC, declaring, "We've had more cooperation on this than anything since the Confederacy." The intent was clear. "Many Democrats, northern as well as southern," wrote James R. Dickenson in the *Washington Post*, "hope a southern regional primary would force their party to nominate a moderate candidate who could win in the South, and break the Republicans' recent lock on Sun Belt electoral votes." One southerner even called the new primary "the Fritz Mondale Memorial Southern Regional Super Tuesday."[43] Though many DLC members like Graham were ardent backers of the change, the organization did not have a formal role in the process.[44] Some warned, however, that a southern primary might backfire and boost Jackson if he ran again because he could win an overwhelming percentage of the Black vote, while several moderate candidates might split the remainder of the electorate.[45]

Southern Republicans went along with the change for a number of reasons, including wanting to have a bigger say in their own party's nomination in 1988.[46] But they also believed they could attract conservative Democrats—who had been trending Republican in any case—to vote in their primaries. Future RNC chairman and Mississippi governor Haley Barbour, then a GOP strategist, started the Southern Primary Republican Project to accomplish this end.[47]

Regardless of the ideological debates between the Democrats' various factions, Republicans faced a stiff political challenge in the 1986 midterms. Traditionally, the party that holds the White House loses seats in off-year elections and especially in the second term of a two-term presidency, when the "six-year itch" can cause difficulties. Democrats had controlled the House since the 1950s, but the GOP gained twelve seats in Reagan's first landslide in 1980 to take control of the Senate for the first time in twenty-six years.[48] In addition to the twelve seats gained, four new Republicans were elected in seats already held by the GOP. By 1986, the Republicans had an advantage of fifty-three to forty-seven in the Senate, but twenty-two of the thirty-four senators up for reelection were Republicans.[49] The sixteen freshmen elected in 1980 rode Reagan's coattails to victory, some of them by narrow margins, with seven garnering 51 percent or less of the vote.[50] Without the president on the ballot, they faced an uphill battle to win their first reelection.

In the plus column for the Republicans, Reagan maintained high approval ratings throughout most of 1986, with Gallup showing him above 60 percent in every poll but one.[51] In an attempt to transfer his popularity to Republican candidates, Reagan campaigned 25,000 miles through twenty-two states, waging "the most vigorous midterm campaign ever in an effort to save the endangered class of Republicans Senators he had carried into office in 1980," according to Jacob Lamar of *Time*. Lamar added, "A vote for these candidates, he [Reagan] said over and over, was a vote to preserve the revolution."[52] Reagan went on the offensive against the opposition, declaring, "The changes of the last six years were not an accident. We are bringing America back, but now Democratic leaders who were in charge in 1980 want to be put back in charge again."[53]

In the end, Reagan's efforts were not enough, as the Democrats gained eight seats to retake the Senate by a margin of fifty-five to forty-five. Coming a mere two years after the disastrous Mondale loss, Democratic leaders were ecstatic. "[I] can say it all in four words, the Democrats are back," asserted Kirk.[54] Though Republicans only suffered minimal losses in the House and gained eight governorships, the president admitted defeat, calling the results "not the outcome we wanted."[55] Although he also said that he and his allies would "complete the revolution that we have all so well begun."[56]

The media interpreted the loss of the Senate as a defeat for Reagan. "Democrats won control of the Senate yesterday," wrote E. J. Dionne Jr. in the *New York Times*, "dealing a major blow to President Reagan, who had crisscrossed the country pleading for a Republican victory."[57] A *Time* article headline screamed, "The Teflon President's Teflon Coattails."[58]

Democrats went for the jugular, arguing that the results represented a repudiation of the president's policies. O'Neill, Reagan's longtime foil, declared, "If there was a Reagan Revolution, it's over." New York senator Daniel Patrick Moynihan called the election the beginning of a "new era in American politics" where a more centrist philosophy would hold sway.[59]

The White House countered, emphasizing the fact that the races focused on local issues rather than the president and his agenda. "We saw a collection of personal contests, as opposed to a party election," responded Mitch Daniels, Reagan's political director. "[It was] certainly not a referendum on the President because we know the result of that one." Daniels noted that Democratic candidates avoided attacking Reagan directly.[60] In winning his race in Louisiana, for example, incoming senator John Breaux referred to the president as "a very nice gentleman who gets bad advice."[61]

In an era of greater ticket splitting and relatively heterogeneous political parties, many who supported Reagan also backed Senate Democrats. According to a *New York Times* / CBS News exit poll, more than a third of those who approved of Reagan's performance in office voted for Democratic Senate candidates.[62] "In eleven states, voters chose Senators and Governors from different parties," noted Lamar in *Time*.[63] In these times, while the Democrats regaining control of the upper house was quite significant, it didn't necessarily mean as dramatic a shift as it would have in the twenty-first century, as both parties formed more diverse coalitions than they would a generation later. Ideological divisions between the sides were not as great. Only 25 percent of Americans believed there was "a great deal" of difference between the two major parties in 1987, a number that would double over the next three decades, reaching 54 percent by 2019.[64] The level of racial resentment among non-Hispanic whites in the two parties was virtually the same, whereas by 2016 the level was much greater among Republicans.[65] The parties' constituents even held relatively similar views on abortion rights, a sharp contrast to the twenty-first-century split on the subject.[66]

Reflecting these trends, both parties remained fairly big tents in the first few decades after World War II. The Democratic Party in the Congress held majorities composed of northern liberals such as Humphrey and Mondale, who served alongside conservative southern Democrats like Herman Talmadge of Georgia and James Eastland of Mississippi. At the same time, the Republican caucus was made up of northeastern liberals like Senator Jacob Javits of New York, and moderate midwestern conservatives like longtime Senate minority leader Everett Dirksen of Illinois, as well as ideological conservatives like Goldwater.

In the years after the passage of the Civil Rights Act of 1964 and the Voting Rights Act of 1965, the parties began to fracture along regional lines. After the Democrats embraced civil rights and as the South grew more affluent, the region gradually shifted toward the Republicans on the presidential level. But many southern Democrats remained in Congress at this time, using their incumbency and seniority to deliver resources back home to maintain their seats. As the GOP grew more conservative, northern liberals and moderates began to fade but still remained a force. By the twenty-first century, northeastern GOP centrists and conservative southern Democrats had virtually disappeared. This process, however, had not yet taken its course by the mid-1980s.[67] Reflecting this dynamic, the Senate Democratic caucus could still stretch from Ted Kennedy of Massachusetts on the left to segregationist John Stennis of Mississippi on the right, while the Republicans ran the gamut from liberal gadfly Lowell Weicker of Connecticut to conservative hero Jesse Helms of North Carolina.

Of course, a major question emerging out of the midterms was how the results might impact the 1988 presidential race. "Winning back the Senate did give the Democrats a vital shot in the arm," wrote the *Washington Post*'s David Broder, the dean of Beltway political reporters, concluding, "They were so trapped in self-doubt after the 1984 reverse landslide that another loss might have sunk them." But, he added, it did not eliminate the serious problems that had kept the Democrats out of the Oval Office for most of the previous two decades, notably their weakness across the South and West. Indeed, starting in 1968, Republican presidential candidates had won twenty-three states in every one of the last five elections, which would give them 202 of the 270 votes necessary to win the Electoral College in 1988. Only the District of Columbia had supported Democrats in each of the previous five elections. Given this history, many believed that Republicans had developed a virtually insurmountable "lock" on the Electoral College that made it extremely difficult—if not impossible—for Democrats to reclaim the White House.[68]

With regard to the Democratic hopefuls for 1988, some suggested Cuomo and Nunn were the big winners. Cuomo won a landslide reelection for a second term as governor but also raised doubts because of his angry exchanges with reporters.[69] *Time* suggested Nunn's new post as head of the Armed Services Committee would heighten his profile. Meanwhile, the magazine also noted that Massachusetts governor Michael Dukakis had won a big reelection victory, observing, "His innovative initiatives and strong stance against nuclear power would make him a contender in the New Hampshire primary, especially if Cuomo falters."[70] Early national polls of Democratic voters showed Hart leading with 26 percent of the vote, followed by Cuomo with 20 percent, then the Reverend Jesse Jackson at 7 percent, with other candidates at 2 percent or less.[71]

Some said that the loss of the Senate revealed Reagan's inability to transfer his popularity to others, which could present a real problem for Bush.[72] Republican strategist Kevin Phillips, who had famously forecast a national Republican majority back in 1969, explained why he believed Bush should be concerned: "This election suggests that the Federal tide is moving away from what Bush and Reagan represent. It moves both parties into the post-Reagan era and into a spirited competition for the center of American politics."[73] Bush's advisers understood this, and in an early memorandum from the campaign in November 1986, they wrote, "There is an *inescapable conclusion* we can draw from the 1986 elections: *the pendulum is swinging back—slowly—to the left.*" As the counsellors rhetorically asked, "The country voted for lower taxes, less government, and more defense in 1980. Does *anybody* think that the voters in 1988 will vote for *even lower* taxes, *even less* government, and *even more* defense? The voters' signal was *loud* and *clear.*"[74] Though the midterm outcome certainly impacted the shape of the presidential race, the real shock that would upend everything was about to come.

In the summer of 1985, Reagan made the fateful decision to sell arms to Iran despite the existence of an arms embargo on the Islamic Republic. He and some of his advisers hoped to strengthen moderate elements in Iran, as well to gain the release of American hostages held by Iranian proxies in Lebanon. In direct contradiction of rhetoric by the president and others that they would never negotiate with terrorists, the administration sent the first arms to Iran in August 1985, and shipments continued throughout 1986 despite the objections of Secretary of State George Schultz and Secretary of Defense Caspar Weinberger. American hostages were released, though new ones were taken as well. The vice president clearly supported the policy, and his knowledge and judgment regarding the Iran initiative would become a major issue during the 1988 campaign.

Unbeknownst to both Reagan and Bush, national security adviser John Poindexter and another member of the National Security Council (NSC) staff, Lt. Col. Oliver North, were using the proceeds from the Iranian sales to arm the Nicaraguan rebels, the contras. The contras were fighting against Nicaragua's leftist Sandinista government, which had allied itself with Cuba and the Soviet Union in the Cold War after overthrowing the pro-American dictatorship of Anastasio Somoza in 1979. Reagan wanted to support the contra opposition as part of his policy of supporting anticommunist insurgencies throughout the world, which became known as the "Reagan Doctrine." Congress, however, had forbidden such assistance through two amendments sponsored by Congressman Edward Boland (D) of Massachusetts. The diversion of funds to the contras laid the groundwork for the biggest political scandal since Watergate.

The Iran-Contra story emerged in two waves in November 1986. First, a Lebanese weekly magazine, *Al Shiraa*, exposed the story of the United States selling arms to Iran, and then the revelation moved into the American press. After a week of criticism, Reagan addressed the country from the Oval Office on November 13, acknowledging the weapon sales but denying that there was any quid pro quo to facilitate the release of the hostages. The president explained that his aim had been to "send a signal that the United States was prepared to replace the animosity... with a new relationship," adding, "We did not, repeat, did not trade weapons or anything else for hostages—nor will we." Nevertheless, at one point Reagan noted that he had hoped Iran would use its influence to gain the release of the hostages in Lebanon.[75] The speech and a nationally televised press conference a week later did little to quell the controversy. During the latter, Reagan stated that "to eliminate the widespread but mistaken perception that we [were] exchanging arms for hostages," he planned to cease the weapon sales to Iran.[76] Nevertheless, many still doubted Reagan's denials of a direct exchange.

The other shoe dropped a week later on November 25, when Attorney General Ed Meese discovered that some of the funds from the Iranian arms sales had been diverted to the contras. When Meese personally informed Reagan of the diversion, White House chief of staff Don Regan noted that the president's expression of shock clearly revealed his lack of awareness.[77] At a press conference, Meese told the nation that "somewhere between $10 and $30 million" of the receipts from the arms deal had been placed in Swiss bank accounts for the contras at the direction of North.[78] North was relieved of his duties at the NSC, and Poindexter resigned as national security adviser. The following day Reagan named a three-member panel headed by former Texas senator John Tower to investigate the scandal, with former Maine senator and secretary of state Edmund Muskie of Maine and former national security adviser Brent Scowcroft rounding out the commission.[79] Congressional investigations were clearly on the horizon as well.[80]

Though the full impact of the scandal was not yet certain, anything that had the potential to damage or even prematurely end the Reagan presidency was very bad news for George Bush. Craig Fuller, the vice president's chief of staff, believed his boss immediately understood the gravity of the situation. After finding out about the diversion from Meese, Fuller recalled that "the vice president just kind of slumped in his chair wondering whether all he had worked for had suddenly been for naught, and seriously wondered whether he could actually be successful in the election."[81]

Bush's fears were justified—Reagan's popularity plummeted, and the vice president suffered damage as well. Gallup showed the president's approval rating falling from 64 percent in early October to 47 percent a week after the revelations of the diversion.[82] As Bush went to New Hampshire for his first major speech of the campaign, local Republicans recognized the changed environment, with the Concord Republican chairman saying. "It used to be George Bush's playing field. Now it's a whole new ball game." Polls showed Dole closing a thirty-point deficit to Bush in national surveys to seventeen points.[83]

While Iran-Contra did not have an immediate impact on the opposition party's race, one Democratic contender's interest was clearly piqued by the scandal. "I never ever given running for the presidency a second's worth of thought," recalled Michael Dukakis, saying he wanted to get reelected and serve one more term as governor of Massachusetts. He continued, "And then something called Iran-Contra hits and we got the spectacle of the president and the vice president lying to the Congress, documents being shredded in the basement of the White House, the administration deliberately violating the law by trying to secretly get arms to the contras when Congress has said in no uncertain terms legislatively that is no longer going to be permitted." After the scandal and his big reelection victory, people began to suggest he run.[84]

Indeed, the day after his reelection, John Sasso, Dukakis's chief of staff and right-hand man, delivered him a memo outlining why he should make the run. Sasso wrote that Dukakis would be able to raise the funds for a national race, and that his record of achievement in Massachusetts would give meaning to his campaign promises. Finally, he told his boss that he had the right makeup to endure the rigors of a presidential campaign.[85] Dukakis began to mull it over.[86]

As the Tower Commission investigated, the early contours of the race began to take shape. Polls continued to show Bush leading the Republican field nationally, but privately some questioned Bush's front-runner status as a secret ballot of Washington insiders split thirty-five to thirty-five between the vice president and Dole, with ten guessing Kemp as the eventual victor.[87] Danger potentially loomed in Iowa, where Iran-Contra and the troubled farm economy made the vice president's links to President Reagan more of a liability than elsewhere in a GOP contest. Dole, who hailed from neighboring Kansas, led Bush in the polls for the opening caucus 28 percent to 25 percent. In what would become a recurring trend, though, analysts questioned how quickly Dole was putting together a national organization.[88]

The race for the Democratic nomination was clearly open. While Hart maintained a significant lead over Cuomo and the other Democratic challengers, his support seemed to rely heavily on the name identification from his strong 1984 effort, as only one-sixth of his backers said they were firmly behind him.[89] Cuomo's decision not to enter the race a month later, though, cemented Hart's status as the front-runner among Democrats. The New York governor's choice also opened the door to the lesser-known candidates in the field who were fighting to be considered as the main alternatives, especially Biden and Dukakis.[90] Moreover, Dionne noted in the *New York*

Times that it meant the race would largely be "fought among a generation of Democrats who [question] the party's orthodox liberal themes and sought to push the debate within their party in new directions."[91]

And the nomination seemed to be very much a prize worth having in early 1987. Though the GOP had won four of the last five presidential elections, there now appeared to be an opening for Democrats to regain the White House. Hart and Bush were essentially tied among registered voters in general election surveys, with Hart leading Bush 49 percent to 41 percent among those who had strong knowledge of both men.[92] Some analysts thought long-term historical forces also weighed in the Democrats' favor. Arthur Schlesinger Jr., historian and longtime adviser to Democrats, published a book called *The Cycles of American History* in 1986.[93] In *Cycles*, Schlesinger theorized that American politics consistently moves back and forth between periods of public purpose and private purpose. Arguing that people adopt the values of the period when they attain political consciousness, he hypothesized that a new era of liberalism would succeed the conservative Reagan period when those who came of age under Presidents John Kennedy and Lyndon Johnson during the 1960s came to political power. "At some point, shortly before or after the year 1990," Schlesinger wrote, "there should come a sharp change in the national mood and direction—a change comparable to those bursts of innovation and reform that followed the accessions to office of Theodore Roosevelt in 1901, of Franklin Roosevelt in 1933 and of John Kennedy in 1961."[94]

More mundane trends might also benefit the Democrats. For the first time since 1968, there would be no incumbent on the ballot, and the party out of power usually gains an advantage from the natural fatigue with a two-term presidency. No national party had won three straight presidential elections since the FDR-Truman era in the 1940s. As a result, an opening existed for Hart or the ultimate Democratic nominee, and Bush's advisers were well aware of the difficulty of winning a third term. "We thought about it a lot," remembered Fuller.[95]

Meanwhile, the Tower Commission delivered its report on February 26, and it was very critical of the president and his management style. Among its other conclusions, the commission explained, "The N.S.C. system will not work unless the President makes it work," adding, "The President did not force his policy to undergo the most critical review of which the N.S.C. participants and the process were capable."[96] Steven Roberts of the *New York Times* wrote, "The report said Reagan's management style generally leaves operational details to others," and he elaborated on the document's findings: "At such a critical and risky moment, the report added, the President should have been more diligent in forcing reviews of the policy and insisting upon accountability among subordinates."[97]

Democrats joined in this critique of the Reagan administration's competence. The administration "was so devoted to contra aid," declared Hart, "that American laws and traditions were abandoned." Nunn, Gephardt, and others weighed in with attacks of their own. Summarizing the Democratic commentary, Dionne presciently wrote, "They [Democratic politicians] also said it was more likely to make technical competence, as distinct from philosophical predisposition, a central concern for voters in the 1988 Presidential campaign."[98] The eventual Democratic nominee would use language very close to this in his acceptance speech for the nomination eighteen months later.

Some Republicans also strongly criticized the president. While Dole said that Reagan wanted "the truth out," he added, "It does indicate that blunders were made of colossal proportions and the President didn't adopt a hands-on approach toward the National Security Council." The twin quotes show how Dole had to carefully walk the line between supporting a president popular with Republican primary voters and taking advantage of the opening the scandal created for him. Congressman Newt Gingrich of Georgia, then an insurgent backbencher in the House, was typically more direct: "He will never again be the Reagan he was before he blew it. He is not going to regain our trust and faith easily."[99]

The vice president accepted the Tower Commission's findings, acknowledging that mistakes were made while maintaining his loyal defense of Reagan. He noted that the report stated Reagan had been motivated by compassion for the plight of the hostages and had not been aware of the diversion of funds to the contras. Bush rejected allegations that Reagan was not in charge or was weakened by age or illness: "Please do not accept the view of some critics that the President is not on top of things—he is." The vice president also believed the commission exonerated him, pointing out that Muskie had said at the press conference that there had been too few meetings of the NSC for Bush to have played a major role.[100] Thus likely began Bush's defense that he was "out of the loop" with regard to Iran-Contra.[101] Bush's advisers knew what a threat the scandal posed to his electoral chances and since it was part of the vice president's official work. "We would try to keep everybody else away from the story and not have them talk about it except me," Fuller recalled. "It was very disruptive when it came. Thankfully it kind of came early in the process."[102]

Reagan, who had not discussed the scandal with the country for three months, delivered another nationally televised address from the White

House on March 4, 1987. As he prepared to do so, polls showed his approval rating had fallen to 42 percent following the release of the Tower Commission's report. The rating had reached its lowest point in four years, with the last low occurring when the country was still in the early stages of recovery from the recession.[103] In the speech, the president took full responsibility for Iran-Contra, even though he maintained that he had not been aware of certain aspects of it. With regard to the Nicaraguan part of the story, Reagan admitted, "As personally distasteful as I find secret bank accounts and diverted funds, well, as the Navy would say, this happened on my watch." As far as quid pro quo for the hostages went, the president offered this explanation: "A few months ago I told the American people I did not trade arms for hostages. My heart and my best intentions still tell me that is true, but the facts and the evidence tell me it is not."[104]

The speech was well received, drawing bipartisan approval. "The Gipper's back," declared Senator Dan Quayle (R) of Indiana. Dole praised the speech as well but added, "Let's face it, the Iran affair is not over." Dionne noted that, unlike other Republicans, Dole did not declare the matter closed. "We must commend him [Reagan] for it," remarked Hart, "But more than a single speech is required to restore the public's trust in our government."[105]

The groundwork seemed to be laid for a Democratic return to the White House following the midterm results and Iran-Contra. Many, including Bush's own advisers, thought the country was moving away from Reagan-era conservatism and turning back toward the political center. Polls showed that the percentage of people who would vote for a Democratic presidential candidate in 1988 had risen from 32 percent in October to 41 percent at the end of February, while the same numbers for Republicans had fallen from 33 percent to 26 percent.[106] While some warned that Republican scandal would not be enough to guarantee a victory if Democrats did not espouse a clear message on economics and other issues, optimism was very high.[107] As *Newsweek* recalled in its postelection issue, "For a fleeting passage in Reagan's second term, 1988 had seemed to them [Democrats] as pink and gold with promise as a sunrise. The administration was waist deep in scandals of policy and money, some touching the president's innermost circle of counselors and friends. The economy had the swollen look of a balloon about to burst. An unpopular proxy war in Nicaragua was wakening the ghosts of Vietnam."[108]

But the ghost of Democratic shortcomings of the past would prove to be the party's Achilles' heel.

2   The Scandals

Few races for the nomination of either political party have been more eventful, featured more ups and downs, and seen more candidates play a role than the 1988 campaign for the Democratic nomination. It witnessed everything from multiple scandals to frequently changing front-runners. A virtual who's who of late twentieth-century and early twenty-first-century Democratic politics was involved, including a future president in Joe Biden, a future vice president and party nominee in Al Gore, a future House majority leader in Dick Gephardt, and key consultants such as Bob Shrum and David Axelrod. In the end, Massachusetts governor Michael Dukakis emerged as the party's nominee after a marathon struggle, but before anyone had even cast a vote, the campaign illustrated major shifts in the way politics would be practiced in the 1990s and onward.

First came the scandals. Gary Hart started out as the leader but was felled when the media caught him allegedly having an affair with a model. Once upon a time, the press would have ignored such a dalliance, as reporters had not seen fit to concern themselves with JFK's extramarital activities a quarter century earlier. But the emergence of the women's movement created a greater stigma on such activities, and Richard Nixon's character defects prompted a closer examination of the private behavior of politicians. The controversy over Hart showed that the post-Watergate media had evolved from an era when politicians' private lives were ignored. In this new period, officials would be routinely subjected to strict scrutiny, previewing the "personal is political" scandals of the Clinton era and beyond.

Though the three traditional networks still dominated the airwaves in the late 1980s, the structure of the media was changing, and the emergence of cable television created new challenges for American politicians. C-SPAN followed candidates wherever they went along the campaign trail, capturing their every utterance for posterity. Network cameras caught Joe Biden using the same language as a British politician without attribution in a debate, as well as exaggerating his own academic record. In an earlier time, his gaffes might have gone unnoticed. But in 1987, now-ubiquitous video technology caught virtually any comment made by an American officeholder, knocking out Biden and creating a chronic issue for politicians in the future. When the year ended, the two scandals left the Democratic race up for grabs while American politics had been significantly altered.

Michael Dukakis's long journey to the Democratic nomination began when his parents emigrated from Greece to the United States during the Ellis Island wave of immigration in the early twentieth century, a part of his biography that would eventually become central to his political career. His father, Panos, arrived in 1912, with his mother coming the following year. Panos went on to become the first Greek to attend Harvard Medical School, propelling him to a long and successful career as an obstetrician in the Boston area.[1] His son followed in his father's footsteps of academic excellence, graduating from Swarthmore College in 1955 with highest honors, then from Harvard Law School in 1960. The younger Dukakis served in the U.S. Army in South Korea in between earning these degrees.

Ideologically, Dukakis came of age during the McCarthy era, which shaped his views on the role of government in privacy issues. While in the Washington semester program in college, he watched approvingly from the gallery as the Senate censured the junior senator from Wisconsin in 1954. When Dukakis entered the army a year later, a personnel specialist confronted him with a file containing information on his political activities while at Swarthmore, including his organizing a fundraiser for the American Civil Liberties Union (ACLU). He attributed such discoveries to an FBI tap on the college switchboard. "I'm a fierce civil liberties guy. When it comes to that I want the government to get the hell out of my way," remarked Dukakis, adding, "You couldn't live through McCarthy and not be influenced by that thing. It was terrible."[2]

Motivated to clean up the commonwealth's notoriously corrupt state government, Dukakis entered politics as a reform Democrat from suburban Brookline, first winning election as a town-meeting member in 1959, then serving in the Massachusetts state legislature from 1963 to 1971. Dukakis and his good-government allies represented yet another generation in a long history of suburban reformers who had tried to curb the excesses of the urban machine politicians on Beacon Hill.

With a slogan of "Mike Dukakis Should Be Governor," he defeated GOP incumbent Francis Sargent in 1974, running as a fiscal conservative focused on balancing the budget. James Dorsey of United Press International (UPI) wrote that Dukakis would deliver a "staid management-oriented administration," not for the last time describing him as having a "technocratic" style. While Dorsey noted that the newly elected governor was expected to continue the spending programs of his predecessor, he also stated, "Dukakis will do so with the bottom line in mind—how much is it going to cost and can we afford to do without it?"³

Dukakis's victory demonstrated the ongoing shift of the heart of the Democratic Party from labor unions and blue-collar workers to the suburban knowledge class and white-collar workers.⁴ Beginning in the 1930s, unions had formed the heart of the New Deal coalition, but they began to decline after their membership peaked in the 1950s. Shortly thereafter, many suburban voters moved into the Democratic Party through the social movements of the 1960s and embraced a politics more focused on cultural issues than bread-and-butter economic concerns. This became clearly visible during George McGovern's 1972 campaign, in which these constituencies became prominent. Though the South Dakota senator lost in a landslide to Nixon in 1972, he won college towns and did better with white-collar professionals than Humphrey had four years earlier.⁵

Like a lot of post-1960s "neoliberal" Democrats who emerged from the suburbs, Dukakis embraced a combination of fiscal conservatism and social moderation. He questioned certain aspects of the New Deal / Great Society conventional wisdom, stressing the need to modernize the activist-government philosophy that characterized the Democratic Party. In 1975, he told the National Democratic Issues Convention, "Much of what government has tried to do in the last 15 years has failed."⁶ Writing about the convention in a 1976 piece for the *Washington Monthly* called "Last Hurrahs for the New Deal," Alan Ehrenhalt discussed Dukakis and other Democrats questioning traditional liberal nostrums. "Dukakis has attracted attention during his first year in office for his skeptical attitude toward government expansion," wrote Ehrenhalt. But he noted that Dukakis faced a budget deficit at this time: "Give the governor a little money, it is said, and you will find him as orthodox a liberal as anyone else. Michael Dukakis is Hubert Humphrey with a payroll to meet."⁷

Humphrey himself disagreed, seeing stark differences between his politics and Dukakis's. According to longtime Democratic consultant Bob Shrum, the liberal icon responded sharply to criticism from Dukakis in the mid-1970s. While having lunch with Shrum and McGovern, the former vice president minced no words: "I tell you the difference between Dukakis and me. He wants the pipeline to be nice and clean and shiny, and as long as it is, he doesn't care if shit comes out the other end. I don't care if the pipeline's messy and even shitty at times as long as the right result comes out the end."⁸

Dukakis rejected the idea that he was breaking with traditional liberalism. "Look I'm a guy that believes that government has an active role to play . . .

especially when you're dealing with communities or regions which are in deep trouble economically," he said. "I mean you're not going to turn them around with the free market." He added, "I'm not somebody who wants to regulate for regulation's sake. I mean who wants to regulate if you don't have to?"[9]

When he assumed the governorship in 1975, Massachusetts "was in desperate shape," according to Dukakis. Some old industrial towns reached 20 percent unemployment because of the long-term loss of industrial jobs and the 1974–75 national recession.[10] Having campaigned on a "lead pipe" guarantee not to increase taxes, the governor initially resisted a hike when facing a fiscal crisis, instead trying to pare the budget with spending cuts, which pushed 18,000 people off of welfare. But the following year, he implemented a 7.5 percent income-tax surcharge, which some referred to as "the Dukakis tax," and raised the sales tax from 3 to 5 percent. Cashiers told their patrons the increase was "2 cents more for the Duke," precipitating a populist backlash in the midst of the national tax revolt.[11]

Dukakis also faced trouble on other fronts, acknowledging, "My legislative relations were terrible in my first term." Indeed, that term was marked by the governor's extremely contentious relationships with legislative leaders. "I truthfully practically didn't speak to him at all," said Speaker of the House Tommy McGee. "We might have been there and we might have been talking, but a lot of the things I was saying, he wasn't hearing." In particular, the Speaker had been furious when Dukakis ruled that summer jobs could no longer be used as political patronage, and he said the thought of a second term for the governor made him want to "throw up."[12]

Progressives were disappointed with Dukakis as well, including future congressman Barney Frank, then a state legislator and a leader of the liberal wing of the party in Massachusetts. Frank, who referred to the governor as a "political ingrate" at one point, endorsed the liberal mayor of Cambridge as a primary challenger to Dukakis in 1978.[13] In addition, Frank recalled that some journalists saw what he didn't, which was that "Dukakis's liberalism was at its strongest when it came to 'reform' issues like cleaning up elections. It was not as pronounced in areas of economic policy or the regulation of personal behavior (for example, he later opposed the adoption of children by gay men and lesbians)."[14] Though Frank later regretted not supporting Dukakis, his critique offered a revealing window into Dukakis's political priorities.[15]

Despite a huge polling lead early on, Dukakis lost his reelection bid in the Democratic primary in 1978 to former Massachusetts Port Authority director Ed King. "By 1978, we had the state economy turned around—unemployment was dropping. I thought we'd turned a corner, but I guess first impressions are the ones that count," said Dukakis.[16] Massachusetts

Democrats put the blame squarely on the exiting governor, and the loss was a tremendous personal blow that Kitty Dukakis called akin to a "public death." "I figured that's it in terms of my political career," thought Michael, who moved on to teach at the Kennedy School at Harvard.[17]

In 1980, John Sasso, whom Dukakis had first met shortly after his primary defeat, came on board and became his political alter ego, masterminding his comeback.[18] Running to regain the governorship in 1982, Dukakis stressed his heritage more, running an ad detailing his parents' immigrant story. Therein he describes himself as having always been a Democrat because it's "the party that gave a couple of Greek immigrants a chance to succeed in America."[19] Continuing his career-long focus on clean government, Dukakis attacked his successor's administration as corrupt, running on a slogan of "honest and effective leadership."[20] He won a rematch with King in the primary, profusely thanking the voters for "giving [him] something that one rarely gets in American politics—a second chance," and then defeated his Republican opponent in the general election.[21]

Ensconced on Beacon Hill yet again, Dukakis tried to correct the mistakes of his first term. "I was a much better governor the second time around. . . . I was a helluva lot better at consensus building and reaching out," he asserted.[22] Some called his second term "Duke II." Like many neoliberals of the era, the governor improved his relations with the business community, using public-private partnerships to rebuild distressed communities as part of a quasi-industrial policy.[23]

In line with this ideology, Dukakis also implemented a welfare reform program that offered extensive support services to enable recipients to attain employment. Called Employment and Training Choices (ET Choices), the program provided training, day care, and transportation to assist the transition from welfare to work.[24] He would repeatedly mention ET throughout the 1988 campaign, regularly returning to the story of Ruby Sampson, a single mother who had been on Aid for Families with Dependent Children (AFDC) and then used the ET program to move off public assistance and into stable employment. "What we did was put together a welfare to work program that was not workfare, and wasn't picking up sticks along the highway, it was providing the kind of training that made it possible for these overwhelmingly single mothers to get and keep good jobs to move up," explained Dukakis. "If you go back to the New Deal and you look at Roosevelt's stuff that was exactly what Roosevelt was saying in the 30s. People would kind of say well you guys are different. . . . It's a question of helping people to become independent and self-sufficient in a way that's not only good for them it's great for their kids."[25]

This did reflect some change in thinking, though, as Dukakis broke with some of the 1960s-era dogma to demand greater personal responsibility from recipients of public assistance—with the hopes of assuaging working-class whites frustrated with the welfare system.[26] Though the Republicans would attack Dukakis as an out-of-the-mainstream liberal in the general election, his policies had much in common with Clinton and the "New Democrats" of the 1990s.

As Dukakis cruised to a landslide reelection in 1986 with 69 percent of the vote, the state's economy was booming, with unemployment at 4 percent and employers facing labor shortages.[27] High-tech industries had moved in along Route 128 outside Boston, helped by the highway's proximity to intellectual centers such as Harvard and MIT, as well as the Reagan defense buildup. Some referred to the Bay State's renaissance as the "Massachusetts Miracle," which would become a centerpiece of Dukakis's presidential campaign. His fellow chief executives rated him the most effective governor in the country.[28]

Safely reelected, Dukakis debated whether to run for president. At the beginning, he thought the odds were nine to one against, and the governor spent three months talking the matter over with advisers and asking people how a campaign might work.[29] When he mused to a *Boston Globe* columnist about whether he could do the job, the columnist cautioned him that presidential candidates usually don't express such doubts. Dukakis retorted that such people were either "kidding" the reporter or "kidding themselves."[30] He talked about the decision with his family members, telling them their lives would never be the same again, and letting his daughters know they wouldn't be able to go on dates without Secret Service protection. But in spite of such warnings, Dukakis recalled, "My family was a good deal more enthusiastic about it [a presidential campaign] than I was."[31]

Dukakis's advisers also strongly pushed for him to run. "I was working for Mondale and you know Dukakis was a surrogate and people really liked him. That's I think when the sort of thought got planted in our heads that he could be a national candidate," remembered Jack Corrigan, who eventually served as the governor's director of campaign operations.[32] Sasso, who became Dukakis's chief of staff and had taken some time off to run Ferraro's vice-presidential campaign, was also very eager. "The only reason Michael decided to run was because John told him he could win," one Dukakis adviser concluded.[33] By February 1987 Dukakis had made his decision, telling his wife Kitty, "Well I guess we're going to do it." But Dukakis's son, John, held some reservations, fearing that the family and the governor's staff may have put their own ambitions above his father's desires.[34]

Having made up his mind to run, Dukakis announced his plans at a news conference on March 16, claiming he had "the experience to manage" and "the values to lead." His early rhetoric revealed many of the key themes of the coming campaign, as well as their strengths and weaknesses. Like Ferraro had four years earlier, Dukakis emphasized his Ellis Island–era heritage, speaking of himself as "a son of Greek immigrants," and he returned to the immigrant story again when he made his formal declaration at the Boston Common on April 29. Along with describing a series of governing principles, Dukakis stated, "A son of Greek immigrants named Mike Dukakis declares his candidacy for President of the United States."[35] He concluded the speech by paraphrasing the Athenian oath and alluded to his immigrant background five times in a thirteen-minute speech.[36] Reporting for PBS's *MacNeil/Lehrer NewsHour*, Judy Woodruff reiterated this identity, observing, "With his Greek background, Dukakis is known as an ethnic politician."[37] When asked about the repeated references to his heritage, the governor explained, "I thought it was important that people have a sense of where I'm coming from. Who am I and how I have gotten here and why do I feel so strongly about this."[38]

With regard to the role of government, Dukakis told Woodruff, "I'm not talking about a heavy hand in Washington, I'm talking about a helping hand." The same news program featured a separate segment on a trade amendment sponsored by rival candidate Gephardt, who had been the first Democrat to officially declare for president.[39] The divide between Dukakis's support for free trade and Gephardt's economic nationalism would become an important point of debate during the primary.

Dukakis made his management skills and the "Massachusetts Miracle" centerpieces of his campaign. From the beginning, the media and his primary opponents questioned his role in the state's resurgence, suggesting that military spending and broader economic forces might be more responsible. Shortly after Dukakis entered the race, *NBC Nightly News* aired a segment stating, "Defense contracts are up 60 percent over the last seven years [in Massachusetts]." The piece noted that those funds created Raytheon and GE jobs for missiles and aircraft engines. "Governor there's a lot of talk about the Massachusetts economic miracle," observed Tom Brokaw, the program's anchor. He then asked, "What would happen to Massachusetts, for example, if there had not been the Reagan military buildup in the last six years?" Rejecting the idea that defense spending was key, Dukakis responded, "We were really moving even before the buildup. I think it's a great mistake to suggest that Massachusetts' success these days depends on the defense budget."[40]

At the first announcement, Dukakis confessed, "The odds against winning are very long."[41] He began with little national name recognition, though a poll in February showed him in second place behind Hart (41 percent to 28 percent) in New Hampshire, where Dukakis would be expected to perform strongly given his status as a neighboring-state governor.[42] Another poll in April showed that 70 percent of likely Democratic primary voters in New Hampshire had a favorable opinion of him, second only to Hart's 73 percent.[43] But Dukakis recalled later, "I didn't think there was any big challenger," suggesting that Hart's lead was largely based on name recognition. "When I started really getting out into the field in Iowa," Dukakis said, "in other places, Hart wasn't any stronger than anybody else. He hadn't really kept up out there he hadn't continued any organization of any kind."[44]

Soon Hart, who had left the Senate to focus on running for president, was going to face a much bigger challenge than a weak organization. He carried a debt from his 1984 campaign, but Walter Shapiro of *Time* pointed out an even larger problem: "Potentially far more serious for Hart, are the lingering echoes from what is potentially called the character issue." In addition to generating years of rumors about womanizing dating to his time as campaign manager for George McGovern's presidential run in 1972, the former Colorado senator had changed his name to "Hart" from "Hartpence" and misstated the year of his birth.[45] Hart had also earned relatively little support from Democratic insiders during the so-called invisible primary—the time before actual voting when candidates seek the backing of elected officials, fundraisers, activists, and interest groups. The *Washington Post* headline "Politicians Refuse Rides on Hart's Bandwagon" was followed by a story referring to the senator as "a lonesome front runner."[46] Labor was especially unenthusiastic given Hart's attacks in 1984, as well as his attempts to distance himself from traditional liberalism; as an Iowa union official observed, "The name Hart doesn't come up among our rank in file."[47] Noting the candidate's lack of institutional support, Susan Casey of the Hart campaign commented that "there was never a sense in those early days, despite the polls, that it was his race, that he was indeed the front-runner, because he wasn't in a lot of ways."[48]

Still, Hart was about to be caught in the confluence of two key structural changes in American politics and life. In the two decades following World War II, most Americans trusted their public officials; three-quarters of citizens believed that the federal government did the "right thing" all or most of the time. Members of the Washington press corps often had a clubby relationship with the politicians they covered, but starting with Lyndon Johnson's lies about Vietnam, a "credibility gap" began to emerge, and distrust of the federal government grew. By the mid-1970s, only about one-third of Americans trusted the federal government as Richard Nixon's deceptions and cover-up of his Watergate crimes further exacerbated the chasm.[49] The media played a key role in his downfall, as the reporting of the *Washington Post*'s Bob Woodward and Carl Bernstein kept the story alive in the scandal's early months.

The press's behavior then changed as a new generation of college-educated, baby-boomer reporters—inspired by Woodward and Bernstein and their heroic portrayal in the hit film *All the President's Men* (1976)—emerged and took a much more confrontational approach than their forebears.[50] These investigative journalists aggressively explored the public behavior of politicians, hoping to expose the next major scandal. But they also began to explore officeholders' personal lives. For example, in his famously disastrous 1979 interview with Roger Mudd, where he flubbed a question about why he wanted to be president, Ted Kennedy also responded to queries about the state of his marriage—something his older brothers would have been unlikely to face.[51]

At the same time, the feminist movement gained momentum during the 1970s, and the fight over the passage of the Equal Rights Amendment (ERA) represented one of the signature battles of the era. The cultural changes that came along brought about more egalitarian relationships between the sexes, and thus a greater stigma on adultery. While FDR's and JFK's extramarital liaisons had been seen as virtually irrelevant to their fitness for office, by the 1980s, many believed that "the personal is political." A candidate's personal treatment of women became a public concern. More now saw this behavior as a relevant part of a candidate's life to explore—as opposed to a private matter—and potentially disqualifying.[52]

Hart's fall began in March 1987, when he and a friend, Billy Broadhurst, took a trip from Miami to the island of Bimini in the Bahamas. They traveled on a yacht with the unfortunate name of *Monkey Business* and were accompanied by two young women, Donna Rice and Lynn Armandt. Hart had first met Rice at a party the previous December at the house of pop star Don Henley, the former lead singer of the Eagles. The four of them spent the night in the Bahamas, though they claimed the two women slept on the yacht while Hart and Broadhurst retired to the latter's fishing boat. Hart said he thought they needed to remain on the island overnight because they didn't have the necessary permission from Bahamian customs officials to return. However, the government denied such permission was required. They four went back to Miami the following day.[53]

With the official launch of Hart's campaign imminent, Howard Fineman wrote a feature about him for *Newsweek* in early April. As he often did, Hart expressed disdain for the more personalized approach to politics that now prevailed, observing, "People didn't examine Franklin Roosevelt, or even John Kennedy, the way they examine us today." Fineman discussed Hart's conservative upbringing as well as his marital difficulties, noting that the former senator and his wife, Lee, had twice been separated. And in a key observation, John McEvoy, who had advised Hart's 1984 campaign, said, "He's always in jeopardy of having the sex issue raised if he can't keep his pants on," a comment many believed opened the door to a closer look at Hart's personal life.[54]

On April 13, Hart officially declared that he was running for the presidency again. In a speech in Colorado, he outlined some of the same reform themes he had campaigned on in 1984 and throughout his career. Criticizing the influence of special interests, Hart declared, "We've increasingly let narrow single interests finance our campaigns and control our political process." He downplayed ideological labels, saying, "This election in 1988 is not a question of whether our country should move left or right. It's an issue of recapturing our basic principles, beliefs and values, and, as we did in 1932 and 1960, moving this country forward." A poll taken two weeks earlier had shown him leading the Democratic field with 38 percent of the vote, with Jesse Jackson placing a distant second at 9 percent.[55]

Meanwhile, the *Miami Herald* received a tip that Hart was involved with a young woman. "Gary Hart is having an affair with a friend of mine," said the woman who called *Herald* political editor Tom Fiedler. "We don't need another president who lies like that," she added. The anonymous caller first spoke to Fiedler on April 27 and eventually provided him with information about when the woman was traveling to Washington to meet Hart.[56] Years later it was revealed that the caller was Dana Weems, a friend of Rice's who might have been jealous of her.[57] On May 1, *Herald* reporter Jim McGee flew from Miami to Washington to check out the tip, and by coincidence he took the same Eastern Airlines flight as the woman in question. After arriving in D.C., he saw the same woman emerge from Hart's house; though she was unknown to him at the time, it was Rice. McGee then called Fiedler in the hopes of getting more assistance for the stakeout, but there were no more flights to Washington that night. McGee and another former *Herald* reporter, now with Knight Ridder, watched the house during the night and didn't see Rice leave after she and the senator returned to his townhouse that evening. Yet Hart would claim she left ten or fifteen minutes later.[58] The thoroughness of the *Herald*'s surveillance, however, would soon become a bone of contention.

Fiedler, another reporter, and a photographer flew up the next morning to help. During their flight, Fiedler read a passage from an advance copy of Sunday's *New York Times Magazine* where Hart famously—or infamously—told E. J. Dionne, "Follow me around. I don't care." He continued, "I'm serious. If anybody wants to put a tail on me, go ahead. They'd be very bored."[59] Dionne said later that he didn't think Hart's challenge was serious, and while the journalists cited the candidate's statement to justify their surveillance in their initial story, the *Herald*'s reporters began following him prior to reading that quote.[60] The five-man team continued to monitor Hart's house during the day and saw him leave with Rice again on Saturday evening. Probably recognizing McGee from the previous night, Hart realized he was being followed and quickly went back into his townhouse with Rice. Emerging alone a few minutes later, Hart got into his car, drove a few blocks, and parked, then began walking back toward his townhouse, passing Fiedler and McGee's car and going into a nearby alley. The *Herald* reporters made the decision to approach the candidate and engaged in an impromptu interview with him in the alley. The journalists questioned Hart about his relationship with the woman, and he explained, "I'm not involved in any relationship" and "She is not staying with me." Yet he admitted to calling her several times recently while on the campaign trail.[61] McGee asked the final question, inquiring whether Hart had had sex with the woman, and the former senator responded, "The answer is no. I'm not going to get into all that."[62]

The next day, Sunday, May 3, the *Herald* published a story that began, "Gary Hart, the Democratic presidential candidate who has dismissed allegations of womanizing, spent Friday night and most of Saturday in his Capitol Hill townhouse with a young woman who flew from Miami and met him. Hart denied any impropriety."[63] The *Herald* did not name the woman in question, but Hart's campaign manager identified her as Rice.[64] What followed was what the *Herald* called "one of the fastest, most shocking unravelings of a presidential campaign in American history."[65]

Some in the media harshly attacked the *Herald*'s conduct. "When I read about the *Miami Herald* story on Gary Hart, I felt degraded in my profession," declared Anthony Lewis, longtime liberal columnist for the *New York Times*. "Is that what journalism is about, hiding out in a van outside a politician's home?" he asked.[66] His colleague Tom Wicker agreed, alleging that "police agencies" using the same tactics "would be denounced by the *Herald* and most other press organs."[67]

The editorial page of their paper sharply disagreed, however, saying, "Reporters once treated candidates 'personal indiscretions' discreetly. No longer and that's to the good. Mr. Hart's judgement was already in doubt. This new episode deepens those doubts."[68] Another story noted that even though most journalists believed the reporters' behavior would "have violated journalistic rules only 15 years ago, it [was] warranted—even essential—in today's climate of political campaigns based on carefully constructed images that [might] obscure the real person."[69] Vietnam and Watergate had changed norms, creating a press much more skeptical of politicians and more concerned about their private foibles. On ABC's *This Week with David Brinkley*, Sam Donaldson offered what would become the most common line of criticism, declaring, "If in fact he [Hart] was dumb enough to go ahead with conduct that if discovered would be inimical to his campaign, he should be disqualified for stupidity."[70]

Hart's campaign went into full damage-control mode to save his candidacy. Staffers questioned the thoroughness of the *Herald*'s stakeout, and the reporters acknowledged gaps in their monitoring of Hart's house that were not in the initial article. In a summary published after the end of the scandal, the *Herald* wrote that "no one was watching the townhouse from 3 a.m. to 5 a.m., the back entrance wasn't covered at all times, and the view of the front door was sometimes blocked."[71] Hart's campaign explained that Rice had left through a rear door when the reporters were not looking, which investigations editor James Savage acknowledged was possible.[72]

On Monday, May 4, Rice told news organizations about the Bimini trip.[73] On Tuesday, Hart spoke to the American Newspaper Publishers Association in New York City and addressed the controversy: "This story was written by reporters who, by their own admission, undertook a spotty surveillance, who reached inaccurate conclusions based on incomplete facts, who, after publishing a false story, now concede they may have gotten it wrong." He did, however, admit to erring: "Did I make a mistake by putting myself in circumstances that could be misconstrued? Of course I did. That goes without saying. Did I do anything immoral? I absolutely did not."[74]

The speech didn't stop the bleeding, and Hart's aides urged him to make an already-planned trip to New Hampshire.[75] During a press conference at Dartmouth College, Hart again admitted mistakes and suggested that if he actually had been engaged in an improper relationship with Rice, he would have been more circumspect. One reporter said a new poll showed him falling behind Dukakis in New Hampshire and asked Hart whether the scandal was going to damage his campaign. "I think the impact will be short term," responded the candidate, in what proved to be a poor assessment.[76]

Gary Hart answers questions from the media regarding his personal life on May 6, 1987, a few days after the *Miami Herald* published its story about his relationship with Donna Rice. (AP Photo / Jim Cole)

After he again denied any sexual relationship with Rice, Paul Taylor of the *Washington Post* asked Hart point-blank, "Have you ever committed adultery?" The candidate responded, "I do not have to answer that question." Taylor then inquired whether he and his wife had an understanding that they could have relationships with other people, which Hart denied as well. Tom Oliphant of the *Boston Globe* followed up, asking whether Hart's marriage had been monogamous when he and his wife were not separated, and Hart again said that he did not need to respond. Another reporter asked Hart whether he would take risks as president similar to those he took as a candidate. E. J. Dionne offered the final question, recounting Hart's interactions with Rice and then saying, "How can you convince us, or anyone, that your story is true? What can you tell us that will?" "I can just tell you the facts and leave it up to you and the public to believe me," responded Hart. "If you don't believe me there's nothing I can do about it."[77] The press conference was virtually unprecedented in content, with Dionne writing that "it was almost certainly the first time a candidate was questioned in an open room about his marital fidelity," previewing the tenor of the politics of the 1990s and the "personal is political" sexual scandals of the Clinton era.[78]

Interestingly, the eventual nominees expressed diametrically opposed views regarding Hart's predicament. Thirty years later, Dukakis was unsympathetic, saying he tells his students who want to go into public service, "[There are] two rules you got to follow. First plan to live moderately. If you want to make a lot of money don't go into public life. And secondly have a good but conventional sex life."[79] On the other hand, Bush disapproved of the media's behavior, writing in his diary, "I must confess, I am rooting for Hart. I think the journalists have gone way too far this time."[80]

The final blow to Hart likely came when the *Washington Post* told his campaign Wednesday night that reporters had information regarding his relationship with a woman in Washington. With his poll numbers falling and all-important fundraising drying up, the new accusations "accelerated the inevitable," observed one of Hart's aides.[81] By Thursday, Hart had decided to withdraw and scheduled an announcement for Friday, May 8.

In his speech, Hart sounded notes of defiance. He began by saying he had planned to make a brief statement about leaving the race, but he then declared, "[After] tossing and turning all night, as I have for the last three or four nights, I woke up about four or five this morning with a start. And I said to myself, hell no."[82] The crowd of staffers and supporters cheered vociferously, believing he was going to stay in the contest.[83] Hart elaborated that he had never been good at talking about himself and that he understood what had become clear early in the campaign: "I was going to be the issue. Now, I don't want to be the issue. And I cannot be the issue, because that breaks the link between me and the voters." He noted that at his last event in New Hampshire, people had wanted to discuss the issues rather than talk about him. "Whether I changed my name or still own campaign debts may be interesting at least for a while," he remarked, "but for most people in the country that's not what concerns them."[84]

The former Colorado senator then moved to formally announce his withdrawal: "Now clearly under present circumstances, this campaign cannot go on. I refuse to submit my family and my friends and innocent people and myself to further rumors and gossip. It's simply an intolerable situation." Hart declared, "I believe I would have been a successful candidate. And I know I could have been a very good President, particularly for these times. But apparently now we'll never know." He ended with criticism of the media tactics that had brought him down and urged young people to remain involved in the system.[85]

In these days before cable news and the internet were major forces, the old television networks still held sway, and all three broke into their regular programming to show Hart's speech.[86] Afterward, Peter Jennings, then the anchor of *ABC World News Tonight*, asked political director Hal Bruno, "What in the final analysis when you talk to all the politicians this week is Gary Hart being hung for? Is it because he spent time with a woman who wasn't his wife or because he didn't handle it well when it was discovered?" Bruno replied, "I think what he is really being hung for on the part of people in political life is bad judgment. . . . I think among almost all of the political people I talked to, including some who are Gary Hart supporters, the feeling was that he had used incredible [*sic*] bad judgment."[87] The infamous picture of Rice sitting on Hart's lap appeared in the *National Enquirer* a couple of

The Scandals • 45

weeks later.[88] While many think the unveiling of the photo ended the campaign, Hart had already left the race.

Hart's denouement came early in the campaign, but his rapid downfall remains a key part of the legacy of the 1988 election. Once upon a time, the media had ignored FDR's and JFK's liaisons, but Watergate and the rise of feminism and the religious right began to change the standards. "A quarter-century ago, voters presumed their Presidents and their senators to be honorable men (only very occasionally women) who should be accorded the benefit of doubt and the privilege of privacy," wrote R. W. Apple in the *New York Times*. He added, "A relentless succession of disappointments in their leaders suffered by the American people, beginning with the Vietnam War and continuing through the Iran-contra affair, has led them and their surrogates, the press, to believe that they must look more closely at the kinds of people running for high office; that they must examine not only the politicians' policies and accounts of their own lives but also probe deeply into their behavior in all sorts of spheres."[89]

Hart was by no means the first politician whose career was undone by a sex scandal, as the press had already begun examining the private lives of elected officials. In the mid-1970s, for example, police caught Congressman Wilbur Mills (D) of Arkansas with a stripper by the Tidal Basin, leading to the end of his long and powerful reign as chairman of the House Ways and Means Committee.[90] "I think the rules had already changed in terms of what was going to be private and what was going to be public," remarked Corrigan, who had also worked for Ted Kennedy in 1980. Corrigan noted that lingering questions about Chappaquiddick hovered over Kennedy's primary challenge to Jimmy Carter.[91]

Nevertheless, the week that sunk Hart was a key moment in the evolution from a time when the media ignored a politician's peccadillos to a time when those peccadillos became central parts of our politics.[92] It's a direct precursor to the politics of the 1990s, which were rife with questions about the private behavior of presidential candidates. At one point, Bill Clinton's campaign nearly ran aground on the same shoals that Hart did when Gennifer Flowers's allegations of an affair emerged during the 1992 New Hampshire primary. To avoid Hart's fate, Clinton and his wife had to go on *60 Minutes* and answer questions about the state of their marriage on national television. And his presidency was similarly almost undone by his relationship with Monica Lewinsky. Since then, numerous politicians from both sides of the aisle faced similar issues with a wide range of outcomes. As Hart himself recalled in 2016, "When I stepped aside from the race. And that was my choice I wasn't driven out. I said to the assembled journalists if you start

The seven remaining Democrats in the presidential race on June 23, 1987. After Hart dropped out, some in the media referred to the remaining Democrats as the "Seven Dwarfs." (AP Photo / Charles Tasnadi)

down this road you're going to fundamentally change American politics. And I think that's what's happened."[93]

"Once Gary Hart was out, it was a flat field," remembered Susan Estrich, then deputy campaign manager for Dukakis.[94] The media began referring to the Democratic contenders as the "Seven Dwarfs" after Hart's departure left the race without a front-runner, and party leaders did not unite behind one particular candidate.[95] Jackson led in national polls among Democrats, but this was seen as largely due to name recognition and the conventional wisdom was that a major party would not nominate an African American in 1988.

Dick Gephardt took the polling lead in Iowa following Hart's departure.[96] Elected in 1976 from a relatively "conservative, Archie-Bunkerish" district in St. Louis, Gephardt amassed a centrist voting record—including support for the Reagan tax cuts of 1981 and opposition to abortion rights—while ascending to fourth in the House Democratic leadership.[97] Al From, the founder of the DLC, made Gephardt the organization's first chairman because he maintained the strongest rapport with party leaders among its initial members.[98] Indeed, eighty of the congressman's colleagues endorsed his presidential bid, including power brokers such as Ways and Means chairman Dan Rostenkowski of Illinois and Majority Leader Tom Foley of Washington. Both men introduced Gephardt when he became the first Democrat to announce a presidential bid in February.[99] At that time, Dionne noted that Gephardt had developed a reputation as a "negotiator and conciliator." But, in a preview of a line of attack from fellow candidates, Dionne also observed, "[The representative's ability] to sense the direction of the political winds has sometimes subjected him to criticism."[100] Indeed, Gephardt had shifted from his initial pro-life stance to a pro-choice position, as many Democrats with national ambitions did during this time.

The Scandals · 47

The Missouri congressman was campaigning heavily in the Hawkeye State, promoting a tougher stance with trading partners at a time when America's trade deficit and potential loss of economic competitiveness were major issues. For the first three decades after World War II, a rising tide lifted all boats, as poor, middle-class, and rich Americans benefited when the national economy prospered. Non-college educated workers could attain middle-class jobs, with their pay and benefits boosted by the strong unions of the era, especially in mass-production industries like autos and steel. The economic fortunes of blue-collar workers with a high-school education or less, however, began to decline in the 1970s as many entry-level jobs disappeared for this group and manufacturing began to move overseas. Then, despite the renewed economic growth of the 1980s, the income gap between rich and poor grew. The combination of technological change and international competition precipitated a dramatic loss of industrial jobs, as well as falling incomes for less educated Americans.

The gradual weakening of organized labor's power since the 1950s, which accelerated after Reagan fired striking air-traffic controllers in 1981, exacerbated these trends. Furthermore, some believed that Japan and West Germany were surpassing the United States technologically. Of particular concern was the growing market share of Japanese and Asian companies in the auto industry, as well as in high-tech sectors like televisions and VCRs. Many believed that our competitors had abused the international trading system to gain an advantage and damaged the fortunes of less educated workers. Unions embraced protectionist legislation in response, and in 1983, Mondale supported a "domestic content" bill that would have required cars and trucks sold in the United States to contain a percentage of American-made parts.[101] In Iowa and other agricultural regions, the farm economy had suffered as well.

In his announcement speech, Gephardt took up the cause of those who had been hurt by the economic changes of the previous fifteen years and of those who had not shared in the Reagan-era prosperity, declaring, "I know this position will not be popular with everyone, but people sitting in cushy offices, in secure jobs, have no right to tell workers on [an] assembly line that their hopes and their livelihood have to be sacrificed on the altar of a false and rigid free trade ideology." He concluded: "Let's make America first again."[102] According to Bob Shrum, then a speechwriter for Gephardt, "The trade stuff in the campaign came from him. There was a lot of concern on his [Gephardt's] part about what was happening to middle-class folks and working people and trade was a big part of his argument."[103]

Gephardt was following in a long Democratic tradition. Since the Depression, Democrats like FDR, Truman, and Humphrey had employed economic populism to woo the working-class white voters who represented their central constituency from the 1930s to the 1960s. This practice included frequently attacking Republicans as tools of big business. Starting in the late 1960s, however, Republicans like Nixon and Reagan fired back, using cultural populism to attack Democrats for carrying out the social agenda of liberal elites with regard to issues like school integration and feminism. Such arguments often appealed to these same blue-collar voters—who were often socially conservative and economically populist—and they began to switch parties. As time went on, though, politicians in both parties had to address the financial travails of these workers if they wanted their support, especially given how the economic winds had shifted against them in the 1970s and 1980s, in part due to the impact of globalization.

While it appealed to many in Iowa and organized labor, Gephardt's protectionism hurt his fundraising and drew the ire of the establishment media. "Emotional economics and discredited protectionism drive Richard Gephardt's Presidential campaign," editorialized the *New York Times*, attacking the Missouri congressman for oversimplifying America's economic challenges.[104] Debates over the sources of the nation's economic problems would prove an important dividing line between Gephardt and Dukakis.

In New Hampshire, Dukakis seemed likely to benefit most from Hart's exit. Coming from a neighboring state, the Massachusetts governor had the highest name recognition of any remaining candidate, while his opposition to the Seabrook nuclear power plant boosted his support among Democratic primary voters.[105] A manager of another Democratic campaign explained the only downside for the candidate: "Expectations are going to be very high for Dukakis in New Hampshire. Maybe too high to meet."[106]

Meanwhile, the establishment tentatively began to rally around Dukakis. In the aftermath of the Hart scandal, his clean image became a bigger asset.[107] Many of Hart's supporters also moved to back the governor because of the contrast between his pro-free trade stance and Gephardt's protectionism.[108] Dukakis rose in the national polls and excelled in fundraising, amassing impressive sums in the second quarter from a network that relied heavily on donors from Massachusetts as well as his fellow Greek Americans.[109]

The Democrats held their first primary debate on July 1 in Houston on an edition of conservative icon William F. Buckley's PBS television program *Firing Line*. Though they largely agreed on most issues, the candidates did have key differences over trade, with Biden, now in the race officially, criticizing Gephardt's amendment.[110] Dukakis spoke out strongly for the benefits of free trade, stating, "[There are] six million people in this country who depend on exports for a living," noting that their jobs could be threatened by a trade war. "I'm somebody who believes that more trade is better than less trade. That ought to be our governing policy." Dukakis concluded, "We've got to invest in technology, invest in our people, get that budget deficit down, invest in regional development. That's how we get a competitive America."[111] In doing so, Dukakis sounded themes and policies very similar to those espoused by Bill Clinton four years later.

As he would throughout the race, Dukakis, like Mondale had four years earlier, also stressed his fiscal conservatism, emphasizing the nine budgets he balanced while governor. Buckley challenged his accomplishment, demanding, "What percentage of your budget goes into defense?" Dukakis adroitly responded, "What percentage of my budget goes into defense? None. But a lot of it goes into social services, and education and economic development and that's why today Massachusetts has the lowest unemployment rate of any industrial state in America."[112]

After the debate, a group of Iowans rated Dukakis the victor, with 23 percent saying the Massachusetts governor had won, followed by Gephardt at 21 percent, and Illinois senator Paul Simon at 18 percent.[113] Interestingly, 19 percent of voters said they would support Gephardt prior to the debate, with that number rising to 27 percent afterward, the biggest increase any candidate received. "We went from the Seven Dwarfs to the Magnificent Seven," Gephardt told reporters.[114]

Following Houston, Gephardt, who had criticized Hart on trade in his announcement, now took the same fight to Dukakis. In Iowa, he declared, "The Dukakis trade policy is a little like the Reagan policy—talk about it but don't do anything." Questioning Dukakis's role in the revival of the Massachusetts economy, he said, "To say simply because of his actions—and I think he's a good person and a good governor—but to say that his actions are the sole reason for the miracle of Massachusetts isn't entirely consistent with the facts," noting that military spending was a major factor in the state's recovery as well.[115]

Outlining what would become a major line of argument by populists in both political parties over the next thirty years, Gephardt blamed trade for the shrinking of the American middle class. In a one-on-one debate in Des Moines with Republican presidential contender Jack Kemp, a militant supporter of free trade, the Missouri congressman alleged that the United States was "becoming a modern-day Britain with no middle class" and was "trading in $15-an-hour jobs for $5-an-hour jobs." In a common refrain of the time, Gephardt aimed his fire at Japan, then seen as a rising challenger to American economic leadership, declaring, "The Japanese sold $20 billion worth of cars in the United States this year. The question I've got is, why can't Iowa farmers sell their beef in Japan?"[116]

During the summer, Joe Klein, then of *New York Magazine*, wrote a cover story on Dukakis that would play a significant role in the general election. Klein followed the governor as he campaigned through Iowa, where he made a series of comments that garnered little attention at the time but became a source of controversy the following year. In Sheldon, Iowa, Dukakis defined himself as "a strong Democrat, a liberal Democrat, a progressive Democrat," and in Spencer he referred to himself as "a card-carrying member of the American Civil Liberties Union."[117] The latter seemed an ironic play on the McCarthy-era charge of being "a card-carrying Communist."[118] The Bush campaign's director of research, Jim Pinkerton, found the Klein piece and wrote the quotes down on a three-by-five note card for use in the general election.[119] While this rhetoric might have resonated with left-leaning Democratic primary voters, the same language would be employed promiscuously by Vice President Bush in his attacks on Dukakis in 1988.

By the end of the summer of 1987, Dukakis had emerged as the closest thing to an establishment candidate and the leader in the race for the nomination post-Hart. *Newsweek* anointed him as such in July, and Bill Schneider of the American Enterprise Institute commented in August, "Dukakis is becoming the establishment liberal and Gephardt is becoming the insurgent in the race."[120] Dukakis bested Gephardt in the invisible primary, winning 27 percent of the endorsements in the race to Gephardt's 22 percent.[121] Still, many Democrats remained unsatisfied with the field, desperately yearning for Nunn, Bradley, or Cuomo to enter the proceedings. There was even some talk of Hart returning to the fold.[122]

During the summer, one possible late entry demurred on a presidential run. Though Bill Clinton had been aiming toward the White House his entire adult life and made trips to both Iowa and New Hampshire, Hart's fate gave him serious pause. Rumors of adultery had long surrounded the Arkansas governor, and he and longtime aide Betsy Wright discussed the impact his past might have on a potential candidacy given the new realities. According to Wright, Clinton "wanted to believe and advocated that it [personal behavior] was irrelevant to whether the guy could be a good president." She contended that Hart's behavior was relevant "because it raised questions about his stability." While earlier extramarital activity might not be germane, Wright believed that "to have one [an affair] while he was running was foolhardy." According to Clinton biographer David Maraniss, Clinton "agreed.

Hart, he said, was foolish to flaunt it." At one point, Wright showed Clinton a list of people he had supposedly conducted affairs with and declared, "Now I want you to tell me the truth about every one." After reviewing the list twice with the governor, she recommended he not run. Clinton followed her advice and announced he wouldn't enter the race.[123]

Meanwhile, the Democrats in the race engaged in a debate on economic issues at the Iowa State Fair on August 23, 1987, offering fairly similar arguments about the shortcomings of the Reagan years and the struggles of middle America in the 1980s.[124] In the debate, Dukakis sounded familiar themes about bringing the tactics he had used to facilitate the "Massachusetts Miracle" nationwide, as well as creating "good jobs at good wages." He also emphasized his immigrant experience. But it was Biden, who gave the final closing statement, who would eventually make the most news coming out of this debate. And it would generate another scandal that narrowed the field by yet another candidate while dramatically impacting the fortunes of two others.[125]

Joe Biden's first national campaign seemed very promising at the outset. In February, he delivered a rousing speech to the AFL-CIO's winter meeting.[126] When he officially entered the race in June, the Delaware senator invoked the rhetoric of the Kennedys and pledged to be the candidate for the baby-boomer generation.[127] His early fundraising was strong, and the other campaigns feared him as a rival, with Corrigan reflecting, "Gephardt was the initial focus because he was doing well in Iowa but I always worried about Joe Biden." But by the end of the summer Biden's campaign had stalled, as the senator struggled with his propensity for verbosity on the stump. "Some critics say his campaign seems unable to settle on a message," wrote Robin Toner in the *New York Times*, "shifting from one transcendent theme to another."[128]

Biden's Senate responsibilities also hindered his effort. Associate Justice Lewis Powell, who played a pivotal role as the swing vote on the U.S. Supreme Court, announced his retirement in late June, and President Reagan nominated Robert Bork, a prominent conservative jurist, to replace him in early July.[129] Bork's views on abortion and a wide range of social issues were anathema to liberals, and a vast array of progressive organizations mobilized to defeat his nomination. As chairman of the Senate Judiciary Committee, Biden's position put him front and center in the national debate over the ideological direction of the nation's highest court. This might have concerned the Dukakis camp; as Paul Tully, the governor's national political director, observed, "That's history right in your face, a natural leadership position."[130] Although the hearings offered Biden an opportunity, they also divided his focus. "After the Powell decision, the campaign was highly distracted, without a full-time candidate and plagued by a dual mission," noted Timothy Ridley, Biden's campaign manager.[131] His handling of the Bork hearings, which would begin on September 15, would determine the fate of the senator's presidential bid.[132]

But the campaign faced a crisis prior to the start of the hearings. Three days beforehand, Maureen Dowd of the *New York Times* had written a piece detailing how Biden's closing comments at the Iowa State Fair debate were extraordinarily close to a speech made by Neil Kinnock, the British Labour Party leader. Kinnock's campaign aired these remarks in a commercial during his 1987 campaign for prime minister. "Why am I the first Kinnock in a thousand generations to be able to get to university," he declares in the ad. "Why is Glenys [pointing to his wife] the first woman in her family in a thousand generations to be able to get to university? Was it because all our predecessors were thick?" Biden's closing statement at the Iowa debate appeared remarkably similar: "I started thinking as I was coming over here, why is it that Joe Biden is the first in his family ever to go to a university? Why is it that my wife who is sitting out there in the audience is the first in her family to go to college? Is it because our fathers and mothers were not bright? Is it because I'm the first Biden in a thousand generations to get a college and a graduate degree that I was smarter than the rest?"[133]

The article, which appeared on the front page of the paper, noted that Schneider, who had been in England during the summer, "brought back a tape of the commercial and gave one to his friend Senator Biden, and to people in a couple of other campaigns."[134] The *Des Moines Register*, the biggest newspaper in Iowa, also published a story about the subject, though it ran on page two.[135] David Yepsen, the *Register*'s lead political reporter, wrote, "[Someone from a rival campaign] is circulating a videotape showing a Kinnock commercial followed by Biden's closing remarks using some of the same lines." Yepsen described it as an "attack video" and a "novel use of video technology to try to discredit a candidate."[136] Eventually, the identity of the source who provided the tape to the media would become almost as big an issue as the speeches themselves.

That evening, NBC News ran a piece comparing the videos of the two speeches while acknowledging the Biden camp's contention that a rival campaign was shopping the tape to news organizations. Noting that politicians don't always write their own material, NBC's Ken Bode observed, "The problem here is that Senator Biden told his audience he'd just been thinking about these things and failed to give any credit at all to his famous British speechwriter."[137]

Having first seen the Kinnock speech in July, Biden thought, "That was my argument at heart," adding, "[People] just wanted a little support to help raise them higher. I watched the Kinnock ad once and I never forgot it—partly because it rhymed with my own family experience. Uncle Boo-Boo never let me forget that I was the first *Biden* to go to college. I had ancestors from the coal mining town of Scranton."[138] Biden began using the story on the trail, and as Dowd's piece mentioned, he had credited Kinnock on several previous occasions.[139] He said that he had simply rushed through the account at the end of the debate and that a staffer told him afterward that he had forgotten to mention Kinnock. The campaign thought the media had not picked up on the oversight, but Biden believed he should have corrected the record immediately.[140]

What followed was a political firestorm very similar to the one that had engulfed Hart four months earlier. "It was devastating. It was devastating because it was quintessentially a TV story," noted Ridley, discussing the NBC News report, "When you took those video clips [original Kinnock, Biden in Iowa] and put them side-by-side, it communicated something that hurt the senator beyond all proportion to his simple mistake."[141] After the stories about the Kinnock speech, others emerged detailing how Biden used passages for speeches without attributing them to Robert Kennedy and Hubert Humphrey.[142] Then there was a story that Biden had been disciplined for plagiarism in law school.[143] As the Bork hearing played out simultaneously, many worried "that the troubles plaguing the campaign might inadvertently assure Robert Bork's going to the Supreme Court," observed Ridley.[144]

Biden's problems only got deeper when *Newsweek* published a story about the senator exaggerating his academic record while campaigning in New Hampshire.[145] Caught by a C-SPAN camera in April at a "coffee klatch" in Claremont, Biden claimed that he had gone to Syracuse law school on a "full academic scholarship" and "ended up in the top half of his class." He added that he was "the outstanding student in the political science department" at the University of Delaware and that he had graduated from the school with "three degrees."[146] All of these claims were largely false. A frustrated Biden complained, "I don't understand all this," then swore, adding, "I guess every word I've ever said is going to be dissected now."[147]

On September 23, eleven days after the initial story in the *New York Times*, Biden withdrew from the race. The future president's first foray onto the national stage ended with an ignominious withdrawal before any votes were even cast. Unlike Hart, "Mr. Biden chose to swallow most of his private anger and place the burden for the end of his candidacy on himself," wrote Dionne. The Delaware senator revealed that he needed to focus on the Bork

Senator Joe Biden (D) of Delaware announces the end of his first bid for the presidency with his wife, Jill, by his side. His campaign was short-circuited by allegations of plagiarism. (AP Photo / Ron Edmonds)

fight "to keep the Supreme Court from moving in a direction [he believed] to be truly harmful," and that he might run for president again in the future.[148]

While Biden's withdrawal did not have a major impact on the polls because of his relatively low numbers, it was another sign of how the 1988 election revealed the changing nature of politics in this era—especially the evolution of the media—and previewed future elections.[149] As with Hart, the more aggressive post-Watergate press had been instrumental in Biden's fall, but the future president's fate also reflected other important shifts in the media environment. For the previous thirty years, the ABC, NBC, and CBS nightly news programs, major newspapers like the *New York Times* and *Washington Post*, and weekly news magazines such as *Time* and *Newsweek* had dominated political coverage, setting the terms of the national debate. In addition, the AP and UPI wire services provided national news to the local and regional newspapers, and most Americans received information mediated through these institutions, which served as gatekeepers.[150]

This dynamic began to change when cable emerged in the 1970s and Cable News Network (CNN), the first twenty-four-hour news station, debuted in 1980. C-SPAN, which began in 1979 to show gavel-to-gavel coverage of the House of Representatives, started its *Road to the White House* program for the 1988 election cycle. The show's cameras followed the candidates around Iowa and New Hampshire for months, covering previously obscure campaign events that traditional media had largely ignored. With the arrival of cable and other television outlets bringing near-constant video coverage, little a candidate did or said now would go unnoticed.

In a previous era, the established media institutions might very well have missed the similarities between Biden's and Kinnock's remarks or the Delaware senator's braggadocio concerning his academic record. "The end of Senator Joseph R. Biden Jr.'s Presidential candidacy is a textbook case of a campaign gone sour in an era when television cameras record a candidate's every step," wrote Andrew Rosenthal in the *New York Times*. C-SPAN, CNN, or local news now had cameras at "most campaign events," and "even the smallest events [became] part of the record, available for instant access by the press and by rival politicians."[151]

"Biden was one of the first victims of the video revolution," analyzed Schneider in 1987.[152] The revolution would expand beyond cable news, as cell-phone cameras and YouTube proliferated in the twenty-first century, allowing any individual to cover a candidate. Future politicians would discover this, even if they didn't all pay as severe a price as Biden. In 2004, Massachusetts senator John Kerry's "I actually did vote for the $87 billion dollars before I voted against it" comment on the trail about his support for funding for the Iraq War significantly damaged his presidential bid. Virginia senator George Allen's reelection was tripped up in 2006 when he used the word "macaca" to refer to a campaign worker filming his candidacy for a rival. Mitt Romney's 2012 Republican presidential campaign might have been sunk when a camera at a private event caught him remarking that "47 percent" of voters would vote for President Obama regardless because they were so dependent on government.[153]

However, the full impact of the Biden tape on the 1988 campaign had not been felt yet. Many Democrats were upset that the chairman of the Judiciary Committee had been undermined in the midst of the historically crucial Bork fight. Attention turned to Biden's rivals as the source for the video, with suspicion initially falling on Gephardt, putting his campaign into a tailspin.[154] "We spent 10 days as the unindicted co-conspirator on the Biden tapes," explained Bill Carrick, Gephardt's campaign manager. "In that period we fell from first to second and continued to slide."[155] According to Shrum, *ABC World News Tonight* was at one point going to report that he and his partner David Doak were the source of the story. Doak explicitly denied the allegation to ABC News, and Jennings killed the story for the moment.[156] Eventually, Craig Whitney, the *New York Times*' Washington bureau chief, informed the Associated Press on September 18 that the Gephardt campaign had not given the paper the tape. Whitney, however, did not reveal the *Times*' source.[157]

On Monday, September 28, Dukakis told reporters that his campaign had not been involved, and that he would be "astonished" and "very angry" if one of his staff members had been.[158] Tully also denied the campaign's involvement.[159] But on Tuesday afternoon, Sasso informed the governor that he had given the tape to various media outlets.[160] "I knew it was wrong the minute I did it," he later told a friend. Tully had given a copy to the *Des Moines Register*, and Corrigan had provided one to NBC News, thinking a network should receive a copy because it was a videotape. Sasso offered to resign, but Dukakis suggested he take a two-week leave instead.[161]

On Wednesday, Dukakis held a press conference where he told the media that Sasso had taken responsibility for the tape and that he had rejected Sasso's offer to resign.[162] Then Senators Ted Kennedy and John Kerry suggested that Dukakis fire Sasso, and "statehouse advisers and campaign aides came to Sasso and Dukakis with demands that the campaign manager get out for good."[163] At one point, Estrich went to the statehouse to try to dissuade Dukakis from firing Sasso and Tully. "As usual in my arguments with him [the governor]," she recalled, "I lost.... It became a pattern."[164]

Later on Wednesday, Sasso announced that Dukakis was now accepting his resignation. Tully would also step down because he had denied the campaign's role in the distribution of the tape.[165] It was a dark moment for a presidential bid that had momentum in the polls as well as in fundraising, having raised twice as much as its closest competitor.[166] Corrigan told Dukakis of his involvement after Sasso's resignation but was allowed to stay on with the campaign. Corrigan reflected, "[The] Biden tape was a blow to the campaign in terms of its leadership. In terms of its morale. It was a blow to Dukakis's morale."[167] The loss of Sasso, who had been with the Massachusetts governor since 1980 and had been so central to his political comeback, was as much personal as political. "People say I lost a friend," said Dukakis. "It's worse than that—I lost a brother."[168]

The tape also damaged Dukakis's central message of managerial competence. Having criticized Reagan for not knowing about Iran-Contra, the governor now had to admit he hadn't been aware of behavior within his own campaign. "Dukakis has sold himself as a 'hands-on' CEO, in contrast to Ronald Reagan. Now Dukakis's defense is Reaganesque: nobody told him what was going on," wrote Mickey Kaus in *Newsweek*.[169] Coming on the heels of the Hart and Biden scandals, the Dukakis campaign's misstep also made the Democrats look like they couldn't shoot straight and were blowing their opportunity to reclaim the White House.[170]

Some, however, wondered whether Sasso had truly committed any offense at all. Some Democrats were upset about the timing of the Biden information surrounding the Bork hearings. Yet Rosenthal wrote in the *New York Times*, "Many political operatives and observers are wondering exactly what it is that John Sasso did wrong."[171] In 2017, Estrich reflected, "I don't think he [Sasso] did [behave unethically].... The two tapes were both accurate and true."[172] Dukakis arrived at much the same conclusion: "I think it

The Scandals · 57

was a mistake." Though he said he needed to have a talk with Sasso, Dukakis added, "I really think I overreacted."[173]

The twin troubles of the Gephardt and Dukakis campaigns left an opening for another candidate. According to Corrigan, Dukakis struggled following the scandal: "It inhibited him a great deal because you know he didn't want to say anything bad about anybody. So he was walking around with a fairly bland message."[174] As far as Gephardt went, Shrum recalled, "We just sunk in the polls right after the whole episode."[175]

Paul Simon, running as a traditional New Deal Democrat from neighboring Illinois, moved into this vacuum in Iowa. Elected to the state legislature in 1954 at age twenty-five, he had had a long political career as a reformer from downstate Illinois. He served a term as lieutenant governor from 1969 to 1973 and lost a race for governor in 1972, but he came back to win a House seat in 1974. After spending a decade in the lower chamber, Simon defeated Republican senator Charles Percy to move into the upper house in 1984. When his friend and colleague Senator Dale Bumpers of Arkansas declined to run, Simon decided to enter the fray himself.[176] Even his advisers thought his was a long-shot candidacy. David Axelrod, Simon's media consultant and later Barack Obama's chief campaign strategist in 2008, doubted "America was ready for a jug-eared, bow-tied liberal as president."[177]

When he announced in May, Simon declared, "I stand here as a Democrat, not a neo-anything, as one who is not running away from the Democratic tradition of caring and daring and dreaming."[178] While many of the candidates were trying to nudge the party back toward the center, Simon rejected neoliberalism and unapologetically waved the banner of traditional liberalism. "When people identify me as a Harry Truman Democrat or a Hubert Humphrey Democrat," the senator from Illinois declared, "I say, 'You bet.'"[179] Following in the footsteps of FDR's Works Progress Administration (WPA), he advocated an $8 billion public works program.[180] Campaigning in his signature bow tie, Simon portrayed himself as a nonpolitician who didn't let his consultants tailor his image, and in a race marked by personal scandals, his reformer persona was also a strength. "I think he's Mr. Clean. He's from the Middle West, and I think he knows what it's all about" commented one Iowa farmer.[181] Simon's message resonated with Iowa Democratic caucus-goers, who were more liberal than Democrats at large. By mid-November, he had seized first place from Gephardt in the *Des Moines Register* poll, leading Dukakis 24 percent to 18 percent, with the Missouri congressman falling to third place at 14 percent.[182]

While Simon was making strides among progressives in Iowa in the fall, Tennessee senator Al Gore took the opposite approach, focusing his attention on moderate and conservative Democrats in the South. The son of a senator, Gore—then only thirty-nine years-old—was first elected to the House in 1976. He then moved up to the Senate in 1984, specializing in arms control and the environment.[183] Entering the presidential race late in June, Gore's campaign struggled initially, in part because many centrist Democrats wanted Sam Nunn to carry the flag for southern moderates, and he hadn't decided whether to run. But when Nunn declined to enter the race in August, the future vice president immediately looked to take advantage of the opening left by his absence.[184] "Now that he has decided not to run," declared Gore, "I can say candidly that there are an awful lot of people around the country, in Georgia and across my native South, who've told me that in the event he doesn't run, they're going to look favorably on my candidacy."[185] Some questioned Gore's identification as a southerner; he had spent much of his childhood in Washington, D.C., because his father had served as a senator from Tennessee himself. The younger Gore's record was also relatively liberal for a southern congressman, though he had described himself as a "raging moderate."[186]

Since the Vietnam era, many Democrats had moved away from the Cold War liberalism of Truman and Kennedy to embrace a more isolationist foreign policy. Some opposed military intervention in general in order to prevent "another Vietnam" and strenuously resisted U.S. involvement in Latin America during the 1980s. As a result, some traditional Democrats left the party because they sympathized with the more aggressive anticommunism espoused by Reagan and certain famous intellectuals—particularly those who had been close to Senator Henry "Scoop" Jackson (D) of Washington—who became known as "neoconservatives." Other Democrats inclined to a more interventionist foreign policy, like Nunn and future senator Joe Lieberman of Connecticut, remained in the Democratic camp.[187]

Countering the dovishness of the post-McGovern Democrats, Gore, a Vietnam veteran and DLC member, staked out an ideological niche as a hawkish Democrat in the tradition of Nunn and Jackson. In an October debate on foreign policy sponsored by the DLC in Miami, Gore emphasized a willingness to use military force abroad, attacking his opponents for opposing Reagan's invasion of Grenada in 1983. "Some people learn the wrong lesson from Vietnam," he declared. "We cannot take the attitude that never again can American force be used."[188] Gore took a similar tack at a debate in Washington, D.C., two days later.[189] Some of his rivals countered, claiming his record on national security was more liberal than the image he was now presenting.[190] In an era when Democrats were more diverse ideologically, Gephardt attacked Gore for "pandering to the right wing of [the] party."[191]

Gore was trying to lay the groundwork for a strong showing on Super Tuesday on March 8, when twenty states, including fourteen southern or border states, would hold primaries and caucuses.[192] As noted earlier, blaming their recent electoral failures on a process that produced nominees too liberal to win a general election, the party created the regional primary to enhance the power of moderate and conservative Democrats in the hope of promoting a more centrist candidate.

The new reality was not lost on Gore, who observed, "It's no secret that mine is the only campaign that is not carefully crafting its message to meet all the liberal litmus tests," adding, "Mine is the only campaign that is not jealously guarding its left flank."[193] As he made progress building support in the South, obtaining endorsements from local politicians and matching Jesse Jackson for the lead in a Harris poll, it was clear he was essentially writing off dovish Iowa and other early states. "I have to do well on Super Tuesday," Gore admitted in December.[194]

Also aiming for Super Tuesday was Jackson, who had participated in the early debates but became the last candidate to officially enter the race in October, overcoming last-minute doubts about the impact another campaign would have on his family.[195] Some speculated that despite the attempt to shift the party to the center, Jackson could benefit from the regional primary because he could attain a plurality of the vote in southern primaries by winning overwhelming margins among Black voters.[196] Jackson had cut his teeth in the civil rights movement during the 1960s, eventually becoming one of Dr. King's lieutenants. He marched in Selma in 1965 and worked on King's open-housing campaign in Chicago in 1966, and he was present when King was assassinated in Memphis in 1968. Continuing on with his activism during the 1970s through his organization, Operation PUSH, Jackson became the most prominent leader in the African American community post-King, cementing that status in his first presidential campaign in 1984. "In October 1983, 54 percent of all blacks named him as the most important black figure in America. Now 76 percent of all blacks think he is," wrote Taylor in the *Washington Post* in October 1987.[197] Jackson's grassroots mobilization efforts led to significant increases in voter registration among African Americans, helping Democrats win key southern states in the 1986 Senate elections.[198]

Jackson's candidacies demonstrated the maturation of African American political power both nationally and within the Democratic Party. Though Blacks had moved away from their roots in the Republican "Party of Lincoln" during the New Deal in the 1930s, their loyalty to the Democrats was only completely cemented during the 1964 presidential campaign, when

President Lyndon Johnson signed the Civil Rights Act while GOP nominee Barry Goldwater opposed it. The Voting Rights Act of 1965 further expanded Black political participation, and in the subsequent two decades, African American voters and their progressive white allies elected thousands of Black officials to state legislatures, city halls, and the U.S. Congress, mostly as Democrats. Notable firsts included the elections of Black mayors of Atlanta, Los Angeles, and Chicago, and between 1965 and 1988, the number of Black congressmen grew from a mere six to twenty-three, all Democrats.[199] By the 1980s, African American voters could propel a candidate to significant heights at the local level and, to some extent, within the presidential primary process, as Jackson's stronger-than-expected 1984 showing revealed.

But Jackson hoped to broaden his support from his 1984 run. Then, he had garnered 19 percent of the popular vote in the Democratic primaries, overwhelmingly from Black voters, to finish third behind Mondale and Hart. As he tried, in the words of one adviser, to make the transition from a "protest" candidate to a "message" candidate, he attempted to redefine his image and use economic populism to appeal to working-class whites by denouncing what he called the "economic violence" occurring throughout the country. He called for national health care and major federal spending on education and child care while advocating dramatic cuts in the defense budget. Promoting an economic nationalism similar to Gephardt's, Jackson declared, "The Japanese are making Hondas and Toyotas and Sony and Panasonic VCR's," adding, "President Reagan is making B-1 bombers. We're making what the world's not buying."[200] Summarizing his philosophy, he added, "It's not liberal versus conservative, left versus right, or black versus white. It's the Darwinian ethic of the big eating up the small."[201]

When he declared his run for president, Jackson led among Democrats in the national polls, but most still attributed that margin to name recognition. "Few political analysts expect Mr. Jackson to win the nomination," wrote David Rosenbaum in the *New York Times*, while noting that the contender's base could still propel him to the convention with a major delegate haul or even a lead. While 65 percent of Blacks backed him, only 10 percent of whites did, with Jackson garnering greater support from highly educated whites than from working-class whites.[202] Though he had a stronger and more loyal base of support than the other candidates, Jackson clearly had a lower ceiling, as 42 percent of Democrats "said they would not consider voting for him."[203]

White racism had fallen significantly since the civil rights era and helped to open the door somewhat for an African American presidential candidate. Seventy-nine percent of Americans said they would support a qualified Black candidate for president in 1987, compared with 59 percent in 1965 and only 37 percent when Gallup had first asked the question in 1958.[204] Of course, residual racism still held Jackson back. One in five Americans still wouldn't vote for an African American, and some of those who said they would vote for a Black candidate weren't willing to admit they wouldn't to a pollster. Racism, however, was not Jackson's only major barrier, as his left-wing views on domestic issues and foreign policy and lack of any experience in elective office also hindered his chances. The forty-six-year-old independent socialist mayor of Burlington, Vermont, Bernie Sanders, who would endorse Jackson in a few months, laid out his analysis of the obstacles Jackson faced:

> What Jackson has going against him, in my view, is not primarily that he's black. I mean, there are some people who won't vote for somebody who's black, and that's that. That's a minority. . . . Let me say that one of the nice changes that has taken place in the last 20 or 30 years is that in fact a person like Jesse Jackson can run for president of the United States and be taken seriously. Who would have thought of that 20 years ago? I think the issue is not a racial issue. I think it's a class issue, OK? . . . The real issue is whose side are you on? Are you on the side of workers and poor people, or are you on the side of big money and the corporations? Jackson is on the side of poor people and working people.[205]

Meanwhile, the Dukakis campaign tried to find its footing post-Sasso, with Estrich assuming the reins as manager, becoming the first woman to lead a major presidential campaign.[206] The governor asked her to take the job, telling her that he knew and trusted her, that she could unite the campaign, and it would be great to have a woman in charge. "My focus in those first few months was staying alive," Estrich recalled.[207] Before the hiccup, campaign treasurer Bob Farmer's tactics had already made Dukakis's the best-funded operation, giving him a greater reach than his rivals. The campaign's fundraising prowess gave it "a huge advantage," according to Corrigan, providing Dukakis with the ability to build an organization across a wide range of primary states.[208]

In November, the campaign ran ads promoting the "Massachusetts Miracle," intoning, "What he [Dukakis] did for Massachusetts, he can do for America."[209] Dukakis's opponents questioned his role in the state's success, while some Democrats believed his message was weak. "I think there is a feeling on Cuomo's part," an adviser to the New York governor told the *Washington Post*, "that running for president on the 'Miracle of Massachusetts' and improved tax collection alone is absurd."[210] Sasso realized that communication needed to be retooled, but he left before he had the chance to do so, and the campaign struggled in the following weeks.[211]

On December 1, both parties' candidates participated in a nationally televised debate on NBC moderated by Tom Brokaw. During the debate, Gephardt twice criticized Simon's spending plans, first telling the Illinois senator, "Paul, I think you're not a pay-as-you-go Democrat, you're a promise-as-you-go Democrat. Simonomics is really Reaganomics with a bow tie."[212] Though it fell flat with a group of Iowans judging the debate for the *Des Moines Register*, Axelrod remembered it as a "killer line."[213] Simon's advisers had given him the comeback line of "Dick, nobody knows voodoo like you do," but the Illinois senator failed to deliver it.[214] Later Gephardt did a riff on Mondale's 1984 attack on Hart, asking Simon, "Obviously there's beef here. I gotta ask where's the dough?" Gore also promoted his defense credentials again and attacked Gephardt for his support of the Reagan tax cuts of 1981.[215] Former Arizona governor Bruce Babbitt, who had garnered a lot of positive media running as a fiscal conservative focused on the need to curb the Reagan-era budget deficits, literally stood up at one point and declared that tax increases were necessary.[216] According to those watching for the *Register*, Dukakis gained the most from the debate while Simon lost a bit.[217]

Yet some Democrats still remained unsatisfied with the field. The following day, the *New York Times* published a story indicating that "senior Democratic leaders" unhappy with the current crop were trying to recruit other candidates into the race. "This is the year for Democrats to recapture the White House," declared Senator Bob Graham of Florida, who was part of these discussions. "If we don't do it this year, it looks bleak for the rest of this century."[218]

Not a single vote had been cast, but as 1987 came to a close the 1988 Democratic primary had already been incredibly eventful. The Hart scandal would reverberate for the next three decades, as future candidates competed in a world where their private lives would be fodder for the media and a central part of the American political discussion. Some, like Bill Clinton, were able to survive the scrutiny that Hart experienced, but many others would wither under the pressure. Joe Biden's very long march to the Oval Office began, and his scandal showed that almost nothing a candidate said would go unnoticed anymore, and that videotape would claim its share of victims in the future. As far as the surviving "dwarfs" went, the campaign still looked wide-open. Through his fundraising and polling strength in New Hampshire, Dukakis had emerged as the closest thing to a front-runner. Still, many were still disappointed with what they viewed as a weak field, and the Democratic race remained anybody's game as 1988 began.

3   Dukakis's Triumph

As 1988 began, the race for the Democratic nomination remained fairly wide-open. With Gary Hart and Joe Biden out of the running, Michael Dukakis represented the closest thing to a front-runner, as he led in fundraising as well as in the early polls in New Hampshire. The rumors that Dick Gephardt's campaign had been involved in the release of the Biden tape precipitated a decline in the Iowa polls for the Missouri congressman, and Paul Simon assumed the lead in the Hawkeye State. Meanwhile, Al Gore and Jesse Jackson concentrated their efforts on cultivating different constituencies in the South on Super Tuesday. Dissatisfied with their choices, some Democrats still hoped for a savior like Mario Cuomo or Bill Bradley to enter the race. As with the year preceding Iowa and New Hampshire, the primary campaign would reveal important trends and major changes in American politics that would leave an imprint well beyond 1988.

The gap between rich and poor started growing in the 1980s and beyond to produce something approaching a second Gilded Age. Though the decade saw the economy recover from the stagflation of the 1970s, incomes did not rise for all groups, as they had during the 1950s and 1960s. Technological change and international competition precipitated a dramatic loss of unionized industrial jobs, creating fertile ground for economic nationalism as workers with less than a college degree began to struggle, a trend that would continue into the twenty-first century. Many held Japan and other competitors responsible for deindustrialization, blaming unfair trade practices and cheap labor.

Gephardt's strategy of launching populist attacks on the "establishment" while blaming trade agreements for the declining economic fortunes of American workers appealed to many working-class white Democrats. Though he was unable to sustain his momentum after a win in the opening caucus in Iowa, his campaign paved the way for a generation of politicians in both parties who would use a similar strategy to reach that demographic over the next three decades.

A quarter century after the Voting Rights Act of 1965 dramatically expanded the Black electorate and buoyed by his own voter-registration efforts in the African American community, Jesse Jackson achieved historic electoral success, winning eleven primaries and caucuses while finishing second in delegates and votes. Harnessing some of the same economic frustrations that propelled Gephardt's candidacy, he ran on an unabashedly progressive agenda and reached beyond the African American vote in an attempt to forge a multiracial populist alliance based on common economic interests. As the 1988 campaign got underway, however, the conventional wisdom still held that a Black person couldn't be elected to the nation's highest office. But for a brief moment after Jackson's surprise win in the Michigan caucus, the country seriously considered the possibility of a Black president for the first time in its history. While the moment would be short-lived, Jackson's coalition of African Americans and well-educated whites helped lay the foundation for Barack Obama's breakthrough primary victory over Hillary Clinton in 2008.

Though the divisions in the party were not as great as those over race and Vietnam had been a generation earlier, the Democrats of 1988 were a more ideologically diverse group than the Democrats of the 2020s. The nomination battle eventually narrowed to a three-way fight between Jackson, Dukakis, and Gore. While Jackson represented the progressive wing of the party and Dukakis filled the center, Gore ran as the representative of more moderate southern Democrats who have largely left the party in the intervening years. As Jackson and Gore tried to pull the party further to the left and right, it was Dukakis who slowly but surely won the contest. Sticking to his message of center-left technocratic competence, he pledged to bring the economic prosperity of Massachusetts to the whole country and to create "good jobs at good wages," and he consistently emphasized his immigrant background. Despite a number of setbacks along the way, Dukakis was able to avoid the pitfalls that derailed the rest of the field and emerge from the process as the nominee.

In mid-December 1987, Hart, a candidate few people wanted to return, disrupted the race by reentering the contest. He had first prepared the way by admitting to adultery to Ted Koppel on *Nightline* in September. Friends said Hart was upset at not being part of the national conversation and regretted his decision to drop out.[1] In the first few days, he generated attention as he "dominated the television screens like a Mikhail Gorbachev in cowboy boots," wrote Shapiro. While polls showed Hart immediately retaking the lead nationally, he had substantially less support than when he had left the race in May and very high unfavorable ratings.[2] DNC chairman Kirk said Hart was putting his needs ahead of the party's.[3] The Simon campaign was already dealing with attacks from the other candidates, "and then Gary Hart reentered and things got jumbled up," thought press secretary Terry Michael, adding, "Just at that point in time, Gephardt came in with the Hyundai ad."[4]

As the holidays approached, Dick Gephardt was struggling, having lost the lead in Iowa and fallen behind both Simon and Dukakis in the polls. His team brainstormed about how to explain their trade message clearly, coming up with the idea for a commercial that would demonstrate how expensive a Chrysler K Car was in foreign markets due to various tariff and nontariff barriers. Shrum said the campaign couldn't use Japan as an example because it was the "classic target of anti-trade forces" and would exacerbate the charges of protectionism. Joe Trippi then suggested South Korea. The commercial starts by presenting several images of working-class people in factories while Gephardt says, "They work their hearts out every day trying to make a good product at a decent price." He then alleges that a $10,000 K Car costs $48,000 in South Korea after taxes and tariffs. Emphasizing the need to be tougher on trade, the candidate looks at the camera, declaring, "The Gephardt amendment calls for six months of negotiation. If that doesn't work and I'm president we have to walk away from that table." Saying that the United States would keep its defense treaty obligations to South Korea, Gephardt then remarks, "They'll [South Koreans will] be left asking themselves. How many Americans are going to pay 48,000 dollars for one of their Hyundai's?" The ad concludes with the words "It's your fight too. Vote. Volunteer. Contribute."[5]

The Gephardt campaign, which had not spent money on commercials yet, also filmed a more general biographical ad and decided to go on the air between Christmas and New Year's Day. Some thought Iowans wouldn't see the ads because they'd be vacationing over the holidays, but Shrum said that the candidate's supporters, the "blue-collar, union, and rural Democrats," would certainly be staying home.[6] As a result, Gephardt had the airwaves all to himself for the week, and the impact was almost immediate.[7] Returning from a ski trip with his family, Gephardt called Shrum and told him that after months of having to introduce himself to Iowans, he was now recognized: "I got mobbed in the airport because people had seen these two ads." The advertisements' theme resonated in a state where many had struggled during the 1980s boom, and "the television ads just propelled the campaign," according to Shrum.[8]

Dukakis also retooled his message. Susan Estrich brought in new consultants who suggested the campaign needed more emotion, and they cut ads about homelessness and Latin American policy.[9] The latter particularly resonated with Iowa Democrats, who were more strongly opposed to aid to the contras than Democrats were nationally. The Latin American ads also revealed a more passionate Dukakis, who had strong feelings about the Reagan administration's policy in the region.[10] The new topic of commercials, reflected Corrigan "gave some emotional intensity via advertising, that, you know, frankly we weren't generating in some of his in-person appearances. So it helped boost the campaign."[11]

In order to appeal to Iowa caucus-goers, Dukakis shifted toward a more progressive message. While campaigning in Florida in early January, he said, "Yes we want our government run well and managed well and we don't want money wasted. But we also want a country that's caring and concerned and reaches out to its citizens."[12] By the end of the month, though he denied a shift in tone, his campaign evolved from airing ads about the "Massachusetts Miracle" to broadcasting ads about the homeless and other liberal concerns.[13] In one spot, an audience member asks the governor about the homeless, and Dukakis says, "Let me ask you a question. Eight or nine years ago, did we have this homeless problem in this country?" Later in the ad he says, "Decent and affordable shelter ought to be the birthright of every American." In other commercials, Dukakis talks about protecting Medicare while cutting Star Wars, and in yet another he asks, "Isn't it about time that this nation committed itself to basic health security for every single one of its citizens?"[14]

The campaign also engaged in extensive organizing throughout the Hawkeye State. "I spent 85 campaign days in the state of Iowa," said Dukakis. "I was in every one of the 99 counties. Kitty was in 75 of them. Heavy emphasis on grass-roots stuff."[15] Corrigan elaborated, "We had a candidate who was pretty much an organizer himself and valued organizing," adding that Dukakis had done the same thing while running for governor as well as in his earlier state races.[16]

Meanwhile, Gephardt's campaign had been revitalized. "Welcome to Lazarus Central," declared his Iowa campaign director. Gephardt had pulled ahead of Simon and back into the lead in the polls, with his television ads receiving much of the credit. When a survey asked whether an ad made them more likely to vote for a candidate, 22 percent of respondents cited Gephardt as their preferred contender. Simon came in second, with only 7 percent of respondents choosing him.[17] In debates, Gephardt, though himself a member of the House leadership, railed against the "establishment," asking, "If our party cannot stand up for workers and seniors and farmers, the strength and soul of our country, then what really are we all about?"[18] In *Newsweek*'s January 25 issue, the Conventional Wisdom Watch (CW) feature, which offered a weekly take on the state of the race, awarded the Missouri congressman an up arrow, explaining, "On the move. 'Sharper' populist message, tireless Hyundai-bashing sells in Iowa."[19]

While Gephardt was on the rebound, Hart's comeback quickly short-circuited. Hart led in Iowa polls taken right after New Year's, but with an important catch—his support was strongest among those least likely to attend the time-intensive caucuses.[20] Then he performed weakly in his first debate after returning to the race. "The Hart mystique seemed to evaporate for many voters," wrote Bill Peterson in the *Washington Post*, adding that an internal poll for a rival campaign showed that Hart could finish next to last in the caucus. But the damage to Simon had already been done, as the Colorado senator's return had "halted Simon's momentum and confused the race," according to Peterson. Simultaneously, a new story about financial irregularities in his campaign from none other than the *Miami Herald* cemented Hart's second fall.[21]

Having lost his lead, Simon faced a quandary. He could attack Gephardt, but then he risked losing his reputation as a positive campaigner and a nontraditional politician. While he criticized Gephardt, Simon largely kept his powder dry, much to the chagrin of his advisers. "They would like me to get into a fight every day," Simon said, "[but] that's not my style. I have to be myself."[22] Simon received a boost when the *Des Moines Register* gave him its prize endorsement. "What the record shows is a man who has decent instincts and who sticks by them," the paper editorialized. "Beyond the record, Simon exudes a simple trustworthiness."[23]

With a week to go and a message of "It's your fight, too," Gephardt had become the front-runner in Iowa. His campaign was more worried about Dukakis because he had a much larger organization. Dukakis also appeared to be more of a threat because Simon seemed to be fading.[24] "We were never going to win Iowa," Estrich remembered. With two midwestern candidates from bordering states running in Simon and Gephardt, the Dukakis campaign aimed for a third-place finish. Estrich summarized the thinking of Tubby Harrison, Dukakis's pollster: "We could win New Hampshire so long as we did no worse than third in Iowa. We had to convince New Hampshire voters that we were [a] serious candidate not just a local favorite. . . . And in order to finish third, we basically had to deliver to the caucuses every single human being we've identified in Iowa who's for Dukakis."[25]

Gephardt tried to downplay expectations, saying, "I think the race is very close" and "I don't believe in the polls."[26] The final *Des Moines Register* survey released the following day showed Gephardt in the lead with 25 percent, followed by Simon with 19 percent, and Dukakis with 15 percent. Simon seemed to have recovered a bit and led among those who would definitely attend the caucuses, while Gephardt led among those who were not as certain to attend. The Missouri congressman needed a large turnout to seal a victory.[27]

Gephardt did win the next day, garnering 31 percent of the precinct delegates to Simon's 27 percent.[28] "The Washington insider turned prairie populist, tonight narrowly defeated fellow midwesterner Paul Simon (D-Ill)," wrote Taylor in the *Washington Post*, "as Iowans rendered their first verdict on a Democratic presidential field still largely unknown to much of the nation."[29] In the *New York Times*, reporter E. J. Dionne echoed this analysis: "Mr. Gephardt won on a populist platform that sought to harness economic discontent and anger at what the Missouri Congressman, himself a skilled Washington insider, repeatedly labeled the 'establishment.'"[30] In doing so, Gephardt drew strong backing from relatively conservative Democratic voters without college degrees. Pundits also credited Gephardt's extensive retail politicking for the victory—he had spent 148 days in the state, more than any other candidate.[31]

Though he performed strongly with better-educated voters, Simon's second-place finish was a major disappointment. "We were left in the position of having been a front-runner and having to fight back to be a front-runner once again. We almost did it, coming within a few points in Iowa," observed Michael.[32] Though pundits noted that Simon "did well enough to carry on," his campaign was deep in debt. "A narrow loss on what was viewed as Simon's home turf was enough to doom his candidacy," remembered Axelrod.[33] Nevertheless, Simon continued on to New Hampshire.

Dukakis came in third in Iowa with 22 percent of the vote, but with the start of the Winter Olympics only a few days away, he claimed, "Tonight we won the bronze. Next week, we're going for gold."[34] Senator Ted Kennedy, a Dukakis ally, remarked in good humor, "Only eight years ago I finished second in Iowa and my presidential campaign was finished. This year Mike Dukakis finishes third, and he's on his way to the White House."[35] The governor's result, however, drew mixed reviews from some in the press. Taylor said that "Dukakis had hoped to finish higher than third here," while Shapiro wrote that third place was a "mediocre finish" and a "fitting reward for a fuzzy campaign."[36] Tad Devine, the governor's national field director, sharply disagreed, recalling: "It wasn't disappointing to us. I was thrilled."[37]

Jackson finished a respectable fourth with 9 percent of the vote. The *Washington Post*'s David Broder wrote that "in some ways" Jackson's performance "in a state with very few blacks was more striking" than televangelist

Pat Robertson's shocking second-place finish ahead of Bush on the GOP side.[38] In the *New York Times*, William Safire agreed, opining, "The big Democratic winner in the Iowa caucuses is Jesse Jackson; with over 9 percent of the total delegates in caucuses where only 3 percent of the participants were black, he demonstrated that his anti-establishment appeal goes beyond color lines."[39] Such were the low expectations for a Black candidate twenty years before Barack Obama's victory in the virtually all-white state launched him to the Oval Office. Of course, Jackson was far more polarizing. Hart ended up next to last, behind uncommitted voters and only ahead of Gore, who had pulled out of the state to focus on the South and Super Tuesday.

As the candidates battled it out, however, some observed that the policy differences in the field were not as great as they had been in the nomination battles of the previous two decades. Old fights between southern segregationists and northern civil rights supporters, hawks and doves regarding the Vietnam War, and reformers and big-city machines had sharply diminished since the party's bloody internecine battles in 1968 and 1972.[40]

> Dukakis went into New Hampshire with a twenty-five-point lead in the polls and strengths beyond mere name recognition. "Seabrook was very important up there," said Corrigan, referring to the controversial nuclear power plant under construction in southern New Hampshire. Federal regulations mandated evacuation plans for areas within ten miles of the plant, which included parts of Massachusetts, but Dukakis refused to submit a plan, delaying the facility from going online.[41] Anti-Seabrook people, Corrigan recalled, "loved Dukakis." Dukakis's campaign sent a mailing to New Hampshire voters featuring pictures of citizens talking about the candidate's traditional themes of balancing budgets and opposing contra aid. The mailing added emphasis on regional concerns like opposing an oil-import tariff, something favored by Gephardt. It also included a picture of a high-school teacher saying, "I teach high school two and a half miles from Seabrook. I used to think of the chaos of evacuating 1100 kids in an emergency. Mike Dukakis stopped it. He did what no one else would. He put the power of government on our side."[42]

Gephardt hoped for a polling bounce coming out of Iowa, but he did not get one as large as he desired, because expectations worked against it. "Dick Gephardt was predicted to win in Iowa," said Corrigan. "He got exposure on the national news for two weeks before Iowa and his victory became an afterthought."[43] There were also the distractions on the Republican side, as the media focused on Bush's stunning third-place finish behind Robertson.[44] "That sucked not all the oxygen but a huge percentage of the oxygen out of the victory," recalled Shrum.[45]

Gephardt set out to deliver the same populist message in New Hampshire that he had espoused so successfully in Iowa. Attacking Dukakis for "spouting the Establishment line on trade," he also said the governor was "failing to defend the rights of American workers and businesses."[46] Circumstances were far different in New Hampshire, however, where unemployment was very low and there wasn't the same economic anxiety as in Iowa. When he campaigned in the Granite State in 1987, Gephardt's message of "America in decline" perplexed many voters in the prosperous area.[47]

Gephardt was also battling Simon, who overcame his reluctance to run negative ads against the Missouri congressman. Both campaigns were struggling financially, and given Dukakis's strength, Broder described the "Democratic battle of New Hampshire . . . as a fight to the finish—for second place."[48] Gephardt would not be able to campaign across New Hampshire for months as he had in Iowa, and his advisers feared that other candidates could define him. Simon ran ads suggesting Gephardt supported nuclear power and attacking inconsistencies in his congressional voting record. Gephardt responded, "Enough is enough, and I ask Senator Simon to take these ads off television. And if he doesn't, he ought to take off that bow tie because he's just another politician."[49]

Continuing the tête-à-tête, at a debate in Goffstown, New Hampshire, Simon asked, "Where's the real Dick Gephardt?" Fearing Gephardt's potential strength among moderates in the South, Gore joined in the chorus, remarking, "He hasn't distorted your record. What Paul Simon has done is simply spell out the record." Throughout the week, Dukakis largely remained above the fray while Simon and Gephardt pummeled each other. But the governor did tell the Missouri congressman during the debate, "You can't beat up the establishment and then take their money."[50]

Dukakis went on to achieve his must-win in New Hampshire, garnering 36 percent of the vote. Gephardt emerged victorious in the all-important battle for second place, earning 20 percent to Simon's 17 percent. Dukakis's margin of victory was the biggest by a Democrat in a competitive New Hampshire primary since 1952, and the governor won across all ideological, age, and income groups, according to exit polls.[51] The "Massachusetts Miracle" message worked well in his own backyard; Dukakis's "management ability" was named as a reason to support him by one in four of his voters, with his opposition to Seabrook mentioned by one in three.[52]

As in Iowa, Gephardt performed well with conservative blue-collar voters. A disappointed Simon pledged to continue on to the next week's contests. Jackson received 8 percent of the vote and again earned praise for showing well in an all-white state.[53] The remaining candidates turned partially to the South, with Super Tuesday occurring in three weeks, and partially to the Minnesota caucus and South Dakota primary held the following week.

Relations between the candidates got tense in a debate in Dallas two days later, on February 18. Ironically, the famously wonkish Gore sharply criticized Dukakis for his technocratic message, saying, "We're selecting not just a manager of the Federal bureaucracy, we're selecting a President of the United States." Gore also suggested that the governor "implied it would be all right to have a Soviet client state established in Central America." Dukakis broke in and denied saying such a thing: "Please get your facts straight. If you're going to be President of the United States, you'd better be accurate." In addition, the Tennessee senator attacked Gephardt for supporting "Reaganomics." Firing back, Gephardt claimed Gore's more hawkish defense posture was simply a "political strategy" for the primaries, adding, "You've been sounding more like Al Haig than Al Gore." Gore replied, "That line sounds more like Richard Nixon than Richard Gephardt."[54] Gore's tough—some might say ruthless—tactics in 1988 foreshadowed the sharp elbows he would employ to win his own primary victory over former New Jersey senator Bill Bradley in 2000.

Dukakis initially held a significant lead in South Dakota, but then the Gephardt campaign produced another savvy ad. Using a quote from 1986 in which the governor advised troubled farmers to "grow blueberries, flowers, and Belgian endive," the narrator for the commercial repeated the phrase and then said "Belgian endive" again "quizzically" at its conclusion.[55] "We had the quote and we just sat down and wrote it," Shrum recalled.[56] The ad aired on the Friday before the primary, and when Will Robinson, the Dukakis campaign's deputy political director, saw the ad, he said, "We got trouble."[57] Corrigan recalled, "You could not get into the stations to put anything on in response. So we just took a beating."[58] Polls showed voters who were "leaners" moving away from Dukakis after the ad began to air.[59]

Buoyed by "Belgian endive" as well as an endorsement by popular hometown senator Tom Daschle, Gephardt pulled out a comeback victory to win South Dakota by a margin of 44 percent to 31 percent.[60] The *New York Times* noted that Gephardt "came on late, painting himself as a friend of farmers and portraying Mr. Dukakis, the Governor of Massachusetts, as ignorant of farm problems." The Missouri congressman won by a huge margin among the 40 percent of voters who worked in farming or a field related to it.[61]

Clearly referring to Gephardt, an irritated Dukakis called on his fellow candidates to avoid negative ads and "to run strong, positive campaigns."[62]

Dukakis did win Minnesota that evening, and Estrich labeled it "a very good night" for his campaign. "We gained the most delegates by far," she declared, "and the name of the game is delegates."[63] Again, a combination of the "Massachusetts Miracle" message and focus on Dukakis's Greek background worked well, especially in the hard-pressed Iron Range, where many shared his European heritage.[64] Jackson finished second in the caucus, while Simon, despite pledging fealty to the liberal legacy of hometown icon Hubert Humphrey, finished third. The Illinois senator refused to drop out, however, declaring, "There is no chance I'll get out of the race, absolutely none."[65]

The success of Gephardt's commercials revealed that 1988 might have been the peak of the power of political ads on television. The Missouri congressman's fortunes changed dramatically after his campaign began airing the Hyundai ad in Iowa and the Belgian endive commercial in South Dakota. These spots often got replayed and discussed on the then all-important network evening news. "That was an almost unique phenomenon started in this campaign," Carrick commented. "Paid advertising as news and the unveiling of paid advertising started to drive the nightly news. Everybody's ads were being reported, particularly something new and different and unique."[66] In an era when the three networks still dominated the airwaves, one advertisement could be seen by huge audiences and have a major influence on an election outcome. This trend would also be seen in the general election, when thirty-second spots played a pivotal role. By the 1990s and early twenty-first century, however, competition from cable and the internet had significantly reduced the impact of television commercials.

After South Dakota, *Newsweek* called Gephardt "the smart money pick for the Democratic nomination."[67] He was surging in the polls in the South, and he attacked Dukakis as "the candidate with the most money and the least message."[68] But the Belgian endive ad would change the nature of the campaign. "I've learned my lesson," Dukakis said, taking responsibility for the loss.[69] "Up until that point he had been resistant to negative advertising," observed Estrich, "but when he saw that ad he made the decision—we [the campaign staff] all made the decision—that he had to be ready should it show up again."[70]

Attention now turned to the mostly southern primaries on Super Tuesday, when 30 percent of the delegates would be awarded.[71] Sasso had developed a strategy for his northeastern candidate before he left the campaign. "We wanted to win at the corners," said Dukakis. The candidate further recalled, "The plan from the beginning was that we were going to try to win in Maryland, Florida, Texas, and Washington.... We had four of our best people in those four states for months." Victories in different regions of the country would blunt concerns that the governor was merely a regional candidate.[72] He would also be a heavy favorite in his home state and neighboring Rhode Island, both of which were also holding primaries that day.

The Dukakis campaign targeted areas with the voters that had made up his base throughout his campaign—upscale white liberals.[73] In particular, the governor was counting on strong showings in southern Florida and other areas in the South where there were concentrations of northern transplants. Dukakis also pursued Hispanic votes in Texas, where his fluency in Spanish gave him an edge.[74] With so many states in play, there was little time for the kind of retail politicking seen in Iowa and New Hampshire. Dukakis's superior campaign resources and organization gave him a greater ability to compete in television across expensive states like Florida and Texas, which had several media markets.

Dukakis took aim at Gephardt across the region. "We definitely wanted to knock out Gephardt.... He was the only other candidate that had any momentum at that point," recalled Corrigan. Dukakis had avoided negative campaigning to this point. But "the Belgian endive ad kind of changed that," Corrigan remembered, "and he [the governor] felt legitimate in running ads that were less polite against Gephardt."[75]

In an effort to undermine Gephardt's populist, antiestablishment credentials, the first Dukakis ad begins with the narrator saying, "Dick Gephardt tells us it's your fight too." The voice-over then lists Gephardt's corporate PAC backers and intones, "Kinda makes you wonder—is Dick Gephardt really fighting your fight, or theirs?"[76] The Dukakis campaign followed up with another commercial showing an acrobat doing flips to illustrate the Missouri congressman's changing positions over the years. The "somersault" ad "was brilliant," remembered Shrum. The Dukakis campaign had decided to try to push the Missouri congressman out before he reached the industrial states, where he could threaten the Massachusetts governor.[77]

Gore also targeted Gephardt with ads about his flip-flops. "We did not have the resources to fight back [against both campaigns]," said Shrum, adding that it was "difficult to get money later on because there was real resistance among the people who gave money to the trade message." Protectionism was simply anathema to the major corporate donors and the party establishment who largely benefited from trade economically. Even the young Terry McAuliffe, who would go on to be a prodigious fundraiser for the Clintons in the 1990s and then governor of Virginia, couldn't overcome it. The lack of funds proved especially problematic for Gephardt because he was viewed far more favorably by those who had seen his ads than by those who hadn't.[78] When the Gephardt campaign had less money for television than its rivals, Shrum recalled, he was in a hotel room with the candidate and watching a constant stream of Gore and Dukakis ads attacking him with little response from his own camp.[79]

In addition to going negative against Gephardt, Gore also appropriated his message to some extent by shifting from his hawkish defense strategy and focusing his campaign on working-class economic struggles.[80] In North Carolina, Gore declared, "I've been on the side of the average workingman and -woman," adding, "I've been on the side of small farmers."[81] A new commercial showed him clad in "checked shirt and blue jeans," and he invoked nationalistic themes in another, saying, "The corporations of this nation have to understand they are American corporations and they've got to start investing more money here for a change."[82] Such a populist approach was more in line with Gore's father's politics, as well as the "people versus the powerful" rhetoric that the future vice president used when he ran for president again in 2000. "If Gore wins, it'll be another stunning win for the Gephardt message," mused Joe Trippi, then one of the Missouri congressman's advisers.[83]

From the beginning, Gore and his campaign put everything in the Super Tuesday basket. Since Gore entered the race late, explained Fred Martin, his campaign manager, "the strategy was to try to use the new calendar and take advantage of 20 states casting their votes on the same day, on the 8th of March—two thirds of them in the South—to win a bunch of those states."[84] Gore and his staff saved their money for March, eventually spending $3 million for Super Tuesday, but they of course worried they might lose momentum in the meantime.[85] "We didn't really think Gore was gonna get anywhere," remembered Corrigan. "We thought the strategy of ignoring waiting until Super Tuesday was wrong."[86]

Though he had competed in the previous states, Jesse Jackson focused on Super Tuesday as well. While the Democratic Party designed the regional primary to help a centrist candidate, liberal African American voters were key in the South. Jackson's competitors largely ceded that constituency to him—though Gore looked to cut into his share below the Mason-Dixon Line.[87] Compared with his first campaign in 1984, Jackson had stronger backing from Black elected officials as well as higher support from well-educated, liberal white voters. Moreover, his campaign was more professional the second time around. "Eighty-four was a crusade. This is a real campaign," said Anne Lewis, a Jackson adviser.[88] With these changes, Jackson stood poised to do well across the South and emerge with a delegate total rivaling the leader's.

Television again was central, as the campaigns spent millions of dollars on ads over the last week of the race. Dukakis spent $2 million, Gore spent $3 million, and Gephardt spent $1 million.[89] The relevance of the earlier contests was unclear, as last impressions—rather than momentum—seemed to be of central importance. "Almost a third of the Democrats interviewed as they left the polls said they had made up their minds in the last 72 hours," wrote R. W. Apple in the *New York Times*, "an extraordinarily high figure suggesting that television broadsides may have been the decisive factor for many voters."[90]

When the votes were counted on Super Tuesday, three campaigns could plausibly claim victory. Dukakis won eight states—all "four corners" as planned, as well as Massachusetts, Rhode Island, Idaho, and Hawaii. Jackson carried Alabama, Georgia, Virginia, Louisiana, and Mississippi—all states where Jim Crow had held sway a mere generation earlier—and finished second in eleven others. He had only won two states throughout all of 1984. Gore's southern strategy came together, as he won Arkansas, Kentucky, North Carolina, Oklahoma, and Tennessee, plus the Nevada caucus. The popular vote was extremely close between the three men.[91] Gephardt, who had earlier shifted resources out of the South to compete in Iowa and New Hampshire, was the clear loser, only winning his home state of Missouri. Hart, who had limped on without winning any delegates, dropped out for the second time.

Dukakis had demonstrated national appeal and maintained his lead in delegates, winning 372, with Jackson taking 350 and Gore 346.[92] "We got everything we wanted—Texas, Florida, and Gephardt dead," succinctly summarized one Dukakis adviser.[93] While the other campaigns were all struggling to stay alive financially, the governor's fundraising continued to thrive, setting him up to continue onward. "That's when we started feeling like we were in the lead," observed Estrich.[94]

Jackson expanded his support significantly from four years earlier. After winning 50 percent of the Black vote in Alabama and 61 percent in Georgia in 1984, he won 90 percent in both states in 1988.[95] Overall, exit polls showed him taking roughly 10 percent of the white vote in the South and 96 percent of the African American vote.[96] In fact, he won the plurality of the popular vote on Super Tuesday.[97] "I have a sense of victory and joy," declared Jackson. "It shows that America is getting stronger and better."[98] But there weren't many states left with large Black populations, and most observers still did not view Jackson as a plausible nominee. The Democratic rules, however, allowed candidates to garner delegates without victories, because many states awarded some of their delegates proportionally rather than on a winner-take-all basis. Yet going back to 1984, the Jackson people had been frustrated by various rules that left them with fewer delegates than their proportion of the popular vote, including those provisions that awarded candidates additional delegates for winning congressional districts. The campaign had also been stymied by the power held by party insiders known as "superdelegates." Jackson and his staff pushed for the delegate-awarding process to be changed to a purely proportional basis at the convention. Despite these obstacles, the contender's loyal base of support still allowed him to amass delegates in virtually every contest, giving him a chance to play a major role at the convention.[99]

Gore's shift to the populist message resonated, as he was able to gain the support of many of the conservative Democrats that Gephardt had carried in earlier contests.[100] The thirty-nine-year-old Tennessean, using language reminiscent of Hart's in 1984, declared that he was now in a two-way race with Dukakis and a battle "between the politics of the future and the politics of the past."[101]

Super Tuesday crippled Gephardt's campaign. Running low on funds and facing an onslaught of ads, he simply couldn't get his message out. "We were just spread too thin financially, and we got blown away, particularly as we got caught in the cross fire of negative ads from both Gore and Dukakis," analyzed Carrick.[102] The Missouri congressman said he would skip the next big state, Illinois, and try to make a stand in Michigan, where he hoped his labor support would propel him to a strong finish in the caucus.

Despite the liberal reputation of the 1980s Democratic Party, Super Tuesday and the primary process in general revealed a more ideologically heterogenous party than its twenty-first-century counterpart. "Among Democrats tonight, there is a kind of left, right, and middle. Their names are Jackson, Gore, and Dukakis," noted Tom Brokaw that evening.[103] In 1988, Gore represented the traditional moderate southern Democrats who were still a force to be reckoned with in the party. His strong showing was based on winning 35 percent of the white vote and 39 percent of conservatives in the region.[104] Among his supporters was Rick Perry, then a Democrat and later a conservative Republican governor of Texas and GOP presidential candidate.[105] Indeed, the senator's supporters took a dimmer view of Jackson and were less supportive of laws protecting gays from employment discrimination than Bush backers were.[106] Meanwhile, Dukakis laid claim to the center of the party while Jackson represented the liberal wing.

Though Super Tuesday was supposed to benefit a more conservative candidate in touch with southern Democrats, Dukakis and Jackson had been helped the most, as some had predicted. "They're going to put the guy who thought this up in the wax museum next to the guy who invented the Edsel," remarked Barbour.[107] The regional primary's designers, however, could take some solace from Gore's strong showing. But with no decisive winner, many thought that no candidate would get the necessary 2,082 delegates to win the nomination, fueling speculation about a brokered convention.

As the campaign moved back to the North and into Illinois, Gore tried to present himself as an electable moderate Democrat for the general election. He portrayed Dukakis as another liberal who would go down in a massive defeat in November. "We have been down this road before," alleged the Tennessee senator. "We have lost 49 out of 50 states twice in the last five elections. How long is it going to take for us to learn?"[108] Going forward, however, Gore faced the challenge of winning outside the South.

Simon had stayed in the race, skipping Super Tuesday and planning to make his last stand in his home state. Though some thought he simply wanted to win to give his delegates a chance to attend the convention, he denied such a motivation, saying, "I wouldn't be in this race just to accommodate someone who wants to go to a convention. It's an awful lot of work if you're doing it just for that."[109] Given that he could no longer win the majority of the delegates necessary for the nomination, Simon suggested his constituents support him to give him an opportunity to emerge as the nominee at a brokered convention.[110]

Jackson was also a local favorite, having run Operation PUSH out of Chicago's South Side for many years. Dukakis invested some of his campaign's considerable resources in Illinois, spending more than any other candidate.[111] According to Michael Oreskes of the *New York Times*, Dukakis ran ads portraying "himself as a winner and Senator Simon as part of a cabal to produce a brokered convention," and the day before the primary he declared, "The last thing we need is a brokered convention."[112]

Despite spending no money on television, Simon still won Illinois on March 15, defeating Jackson 42 percent to 32 percent and claimed his campaign was revitalized.[113] Dukakis finished a distant third with 16 percent.[114] "Then I got creamed in Illinois even though we worked very hard there," recalled the governor. "We thought we were going to do better in Illinois."[115] Gephardt's press secretary suggested, "It's not Michael the Inevitable anymore," as the disappointing finish slowed Dukakis's momentum. Hoping to capitalize on his success on Super Tuesday, Gore made an investment in Illinois as well but came up short in what would become a pattern in the North.[116] At this point, Dukakis led with 565 delegates, followed closely by Jackson with 520 and Gore with 411.[117]

Illinois raised the importance of the next major contest in Michigan on March 26. "A poor showing by Mr. Dukakis would be his second consecutive loss and would put him in real trouble," wrote Apple.[118] Jackson hoped to ride support from Detroit's African American community to a strong showing, despite the fact that the city's mayor, Coleman Young, was one of the few Black elected officials not backing him. Gore was still looking for a northern state in which to challenge Dukakis, but he didn't make a major effort in Michigan. Meanwhile, Gephardt made his last stand. He hoped his populist message on trade would resonate with the state's autoworkers, as the Big Three automakers were in the middle of a do-or-die battle with Japanese car companies over market share.

Despite the Illinois loss, the party establishment began to tentatively rally around Dukakis, who still seemed the most likely nominee. "Once we got past Super Tuesday, we began what a front-runner does which is to begin to court the party leaders for endorsements to sort of try to cement your victory and cement your status as front-runner," said Estrich.[119] This process included pursuing the support of many elected officials who would each serve as one of 646 "superdelegates" at the convention in Atlanta. After the disruptions at the 1968 Democratic convention in Chicago, the McGovern-Fraser reforms of the early 1970s shifted the power of the nominating process from the party bosses to voters who chose delegates through primaries and caucuses. Following the victories of outsiders like George McGovern in 1972 and Jimmy Carter in 1976, the party establishment tried to reassert its authority and changed its rules again in 1980. With these adjustments, it became difficult for any candidate to win the nomination without support from superdelegates, who independently decided whom to back. The superdelegates included "all members of the Democratic National Committee, all of the party's Governors, and 80 percent of all its members of Congress."[120] Among those endorsing Dukakis were Senators Barbara Mikulski of Maryland, Patrick Leahy of Vermont, and Chris Dodd of Connecticut. "People like myself and others would like to see this thing put together sooner rather than later," said Dodd.[121] The biggest prize arrived when Bradley endorsed the governor on March 23.[122]

One day before Bradley's endorsement, Dukakis, after a major battle back home, decided to end his opposition to a total ban on furloughs for first-degree murderers.[123] Controversy had ensued after William Horton, an African American man convicted of first-degree murder, had raped a woman and terrorized a couple in Maryland after not returning from a furlough. A local newspaper, the Lawrence *Eagle-Tribune*, had also published a hard-hitting investigative series on the drawbacks of the furlough program, eventually winning a Pulitzer Prize for its work. With the support of the *Boston Globe* editorial page as well as his correction commissioner, Dukakis had opposed a total ban on furloughs for first-degree murderers. He explained his shift to supporting the ban, saying, "I continue to be a strong supporter of the furlough program, and I think in many cases it is an important part of a progressive and successful corrections program."[124] Dukakis added that the citizens of the state and the legislators no longer favored furloughs for first-degree murderers. Though the story gained great attention in Massachusetts, it had barely been an issue in the primary race to this point, despite the fact that the network news had run two stories on Horton and furloughs.[125] While nobody knew it yet, this would turn out to be one of the central issues of the general election.

The campaign for Michigan went on. Dukakis, like Gore before him, picked up elements of the populist trade message, backing a new trade bill sponsored by Michigan senator Donald Riegle (D). Though the measure wasn't the exact same legislation as the Gephardt amendment, the Missouri congressman's camp certainly saw the governor's support for it as a flip-flop from his earlier position that new laws were unnecessary, and as a blatant attempt to curry favor with organized labor.[126]

On the night before the caucus, Greek Americans cheered Dukakis at a fundraiser. Presciently, Coleman Young, who had endorsed the Massachusetts governor, warned, "See how excited these people are about Michael. I got a whole city like that for Jesse."[127] The Dukakis campaign's internal polls showed the candidate with a double-digit lead, while Apple wrote, "[Jackson] is given an outside chance to upset Dukakis."[128]

On the day of the vote, the Dukakis people watched the massive turnout on behalf of Jackson with disbelief. Will Robinson called Corrigan, saying, "There are hundreds of black people turning out. We're gonna get killed."[129] Aided by a caucus system that favored his more energized base, Jackson achieved an impressive victory, defeating the governor 54 percent to 29 percent. Jackson won overwhelmingly among African Americans in Detroit, garnering 95 percent of the vote in certain communities. He also carried roughly 25 to 33 percent of the white vote, winning in university towns like Ann Arbor.[130] In addition, Jackson likely benefited from strong support from Michigan's large Arab American population, which was enthusiastic about his backing for a Palestinian homeland.[131] The media was stunned, as Apple declared the victory "historic, the first ever by a black Presidential candidate in a major state."[132]

"I'm up on Jesse by 15 or something and I lose!" remembered Dukakis. "That was not a great night flying back from Detroit I wanna tell you."[133]

Estrich said someone told her it could turn out to be the best thing that happened to the campaign, but she added, "Believe me, it did not feel like it then."[134] *Newsweek*'s CW watch gave Dukakis a down arrow, saying, "From shoo-in to walking wounded on a single night in Michigan."[135] Pundits claimed the Michigan loss, along with the Illinois defeat, demonstrated the governor's weak support among the blue-collar Democrats in the industrial Midwest who would be essential to victory in the general election.[136]

Gephardt finished third in Michigan and then dropped out to run for reelection to the House. His failure to have more staying power despite his early success reflected the difficulty in winning with a full-throated message of economic nationalism. Though he entered the race as a longtime DLC moderate and performed well among conservative Democrats, Gephardt's rhetoric represented a challenge to the conventional economic wisdom. While the Missouri congressman's approach resonated with certain elements of the grass roots of the party, especially in the labor movement, the Democratic establishment held to more of a neoliberal perspective, which was reflected in his difficulty raising money.

But Gephardt's race left a legacy. Gore and Dukakis picked up parts of his message during the primary, and the governor would go even further in the representative's direction toward the end of the general election. "In some ways I think Dick won the message war but didn't have the resources to win the nomination," explained Shrum.[137] The success of Gephardt's message spotlighted the economic anxieties of blue-collar people during the 1980s. And with white working class voters struggling with stagnant or declining wages in an era of globalization, trade became both a symbol of and an explanation for the economic difficulties faced by workers with less than a college education. And the anxieties that Gephardt tapped into in the late 1980s only grew in importance in subsequent elections, as manufacturing jobs continued to hemorrhage.

Shrum, who worked for Gore in 2000 and Kerry in 2004, reflected, "By 2004, you could hear echoes of Gephardt in every serious Democratic candidate who campaigned against outsourcing."[138] Going forward, Obama and Hillary Clinton both campaigned on revamping NAFTA in the 2008 Democratic primaries, while Bernie Sanders and Clinton both opposed the Trans-Pacific Partnership (TPP) during the 2016 Democratic primaries.[139] And, of course, Donald Trump made opposing NAFTA and other trade agreements a centerpiece of his 2016 campaign as well as his presidency, appealing to the same kind of working-class Democrats who had voted for the Missouri congressman a generation earlier.

After his shocking win in the Michigan caucus in March 1988, the Reverend Jesse Jackson seemed to have a chance to win the Democratic nomination, and the nation seriously contemplated a Black president for the first time. (Photo courtesy of Enveritas Group, Inc.)

Though the exact count was uncertain in the immediate aftermath of the caucus, Jackson's win in Michigan propelled him to either just barely behind or even with Dukakis in delegates. A burst of media attention ensued, as commentators debated whether the nation was ready for a Black nominee of a major party a mere generation after the civil rights movement.[140] In a time when weekly newsmagazines were still very influential, Jackson appeared on the cover of the two most important ones—*Newsweek* and *Time*. "And so, for the first time in the nation's history, a major political party was grappling with one of the biggest what-ifs of all: What if Democratic voters actually nominate a black man for President?" wrote Shapiro in *Time*'s cover story. "Such a nomination would have been unthinkable four years ago. Indeed, it was unthinkable just two weeks ago." Regardless of the final outcome, Shapiro concluded that Jackson had already changed the country's expectations: "For he has already taught white America that a black person is not only nobody, he can be anybody. Even President of the United States."[141]

Electability remained a huge barrier for Jackson, as many liberals continued to be very skeptical of his chances in a general election, even if they admired him to varying degrees. "One, there is unfortunately still racism in the country," analyzed Congressman Barney Frank, a progressive and a Dukakis supporter. "Two, [Jackson's] still to the left of the country, especially on foreign policy," likely referring to the candidate's meetings with Fidel Castro and Yasser Arafat. Though 44 percent of Democrats viewed Jackson favorably, compared to the 29 percent who viewed him unfavorably, only 22 percent of independents viewed him with approval, with 43 percent expressing disapproval. Unsurprisingly, Republicans took an even harsher view of Jackson, with 13 percent of poll respondents approving of him and 58 percent disapproving.[142] Noting his lack of governmental experience, the long-standing concerns about the management of Operation PUSH, and other issues, Anthony Lewis concluded, "Jesse Jackson is not going to be elected president. The notion that he can be is a romantic delusion—one of exactly the same kind that has undermined the Democratic Party in recent years."[143]

Many in the Democratic Party agreed and were frightened by the possibility of a Jackson nomination. As one party pollster put it, "The party is up against an extraordinary end-game. If this guy has more convention votes than anyone else, how can we nominate him? But how can we not nominate him?"[144] Some talked of an effort to draft Cuomo.[145] The New York governor rejected this, declaring, "There should be no draft," though the *New York Times* noted "he did not rule out accepting a convention draft."[146] Dukakis, Estrich, and Corrigan all said they never thought Jackson could win the nomination.[147]

At this time, Jackson gained a new backer, albeit not a Democrat, as Sanders endorsed him. Previewing themes from his own twenty-first century campaigns, Sanders declared, "Jackson alone of all the candidates has raised the issue of the grossly unfair distribution of wealth and power in this country which is clearly the most single important issue which has got to be raised for the future of this country." Going on to applaud Jackson's effort to build a cross-racial alliance, the then mayor declared, "Win, lose, or draw, his candidacy will be remembered as the most significant presidential campaign in at least 50 years in this nation. In attempting to bring working people and poor people and elderly people, and people of all colors together to begin to stand up and fight for their rights and to fight for their dignity."[148]

The two candidates were headed for an important confrontation in Wisconsin, but first Dukakis won an expected victory in Connecticut, which bordered his native state. Despite its considerable success in fundraising and organization, the governor's campaign still faced critiques over what some saw as its weak message. "The heart of Mr. Dukakis' appeal is a solid, unexciting promise of 'good jobs at good wages,' a pledge of economic opportunity from a man who has already shown an ability to deliver it in Massachusetts," wrote Toner in the *New York Times*. "He presents himself as a budget balancer and a job creator, balancing the traditional Democratic concern with economic equity with a pledge of fiscal responsibility. It is a message of moderation, in many ways, and he has yet to find a way of articulating it that stirs voters."[149] *Newsweek*'s CW agreed: "Get this man some Message, and make it snappy."[150]

Jackson tried to carry his momentum into Wisconsin, a state with a small Black population but also a long tradition of supporting progressives, going back to Robert LaFollette in the early twentieth century. If he hoped to win a major primary that was overwhelmingly white, the Badger State offered Jackson his best chance. But it would be a higher-turnout primary as opposed to a lower-turnout caucus like Michigan that favored Jackson's small but more motivated base. Dukakis was trying to recover the front-runner status that had been punctured in Illinois and Michigan. Gore campaigned there as well, hoping to demonstrate success outside the South. Finally, Simon had hung in and hoped he could rejuvenate his campaign in a liberal state adjacent to his native Illinois.

Jackson drew huge crowds throughout Wisconsin and clearly appealed to many highly educated liberals in progressive bastions like Madison, the home of the University of Wisconsin, where the local paper endorsed him.[151] Jackson broke with party conventional wisdom in many ways, concerning both foreign and domestic policy, with his support for gay rights and negotiations with the Palestinian Liberation Organization (PLO). Pushing an economic agenda to the left of Dukakis and Gore as well as a reordering of the government's priorities from the Reagan era, he advocated massive public investments in child care, education, and job training. Jackson claimed these investments would be paid for through major cuts in the defense budget, including the canceling of a number of weapons programs, such as the MX missile and the Stealth bomber. He also proposed raising the top marginal tax rate from 28 percent back to 38.5 percent and increasing the corporate tax rate from 34 percent back to 46 percent. When commentators doubted whether these measures would pay for his programs given the budget deficits of the time, Jackson repeatedly declared, "We cannot afford not to do it."[152]

With his denunciations of "economic violence," attacks on Wall Street, and calls for higher taxes on the wealthy and the passage of national health care, Jackson tried to forge a progressive alliance between working-class whites and Blacks based on common economic interests. During his week of campaigning, Jackson appeared to be achieving some success. "I don't care if he's black or white," declared one factory worker. "He's down to earth and telling it like it is." The *Milwaukee Journal* wrote, "If there's a stereotype that people in these white, 99 percent Democrat working-class neighborhoods don't go for a black man in the White House, consider it shredded." Crowds that gathered to see the candidate even included some people who had voted for segregationist Alabama governor George Wallace in 1968.[153] Jackson's image was changing. As journalist E. J. Dionne noted, "No longer is he a candidate who appeals exclusively to blacks and graduate students and the left. Now he is a phenomenon and a media star who draws support from people who cannot really quite explain why they like him; they just do."[154]

Following a plan developed by Estrich, Dukakis spent a whole week campaigning in Wisconsin and adjusted his message.[155] As he had in Iowa, he attempted to relate to voters in more emotional terms, running an ad about homelessness and declaring, "The human cost of seven years of Republican indifference is staggering."[156] Speaking to union workers in Racine, the governor said, "I know what you've been going through." In doing so, he tried to blunt Jackson's direct appeal to working-class voters, as well as the criticism that he was running as a technocrat.

But the governor also reiterated the message of managerial effectiveness he had pressed throughout the campaign. "I have no interest in being known as the Great Communicator. I want to be known as the Great Builder," declared Dukakis in Milwaukee's Serb Hall. At the University of Wisconsin, he told an audience, "After seven years of charisma, maybe it's time for some competence in the White House."[157] The governor's campaign materials stated his message clearly: "Vote for your job and your future. Vote for Mike Dukakis."[158]

Throughout the week, Dukakis avoided directly attacking Jackson and Gore criticized the governor for his unwillingness to do so. "He's scared to death he'll be misinterpreted," Gore remarked, adding, "If the country is going to mature to the point where we are color-blind and see candidates in terms of their ability and leadership, then we must be prepared to engage in the rough and tumble of politics."[159] The Tennessee senator had already begun to attack Jackson for his positions regarding the Middle East in anticipation of the New York primary on April 19.[160]

On April 5, ten days after the Michigan loss, Dukakis won what Dionne called "the most dramatic showdown yet in this year's Democratic Presidential campaign" by a margin of 48 percent to 28 percent.[161] Jackson's Michigan win had raised the stakes for Wisconsin, and though a majority of whites viewed the reverend favorably, he won votes from only a quarter of them.[162] "I came so close, but was afraid Jackson was not electable this time around," said one voter. Another echoed this sentiment: "I had a hard time deciding. Even three days ago, I thought I would vote for Jackson, but I think he doesn't stand a chance due to the prejudice of other people. We need to vote for someone who can make it in Atlanta."[163] Perhaps reflecting this attitude, Jackson did worse among voters deciding in the last few days before the primary.[164] "Michigan basically doomed us in Wisconsin," recalled Gerald Austin, Jackson's campaign manager, "because people in Wisconsin who would be voting for Jesse sort of as a protest thought wait a second this guy could be president."[165]

Dukakis's win, along with his victories in Connecticut and the Colorado caucus, halted Jackson's charge and made him the clear favorite to win the nomination. According to Dionne, these events gave "the Democratic Party a widely acknowledged front-runner today for the first time in the contorted 1988 Democratic Presidential campaign."[166] Jackson's loss left him without another major primary with a strong chance for victory.[167] Gore, who finished third with 17 percent, had still shown no ability to win anywhere above the Mason-Dixon Line and looked to make a stand in New York. After a dismal fourth-place finish, Simon finally closed up shop.

Jackson would continue on, but Wisconsin ended his long-shot hopes for the nomination. Even so, his campaign left an extremely important legacy.[168] "The world is likely to remember 1988 as the Year of Jackson—the year when, for the first time in American history, a black made a serious bid for the White House and was taken seriously by the electorate," observed Apple. "Jesse Jackson is now a significant power in national politics," declared Mondale, who had campaigned against the minister in 1984. Underscoring the historical nature of Jackson's emergence, the former vice president added, "No black man has been that before."[169]

Eventually, Jackson would finish second overall in delegates, garnering twice the total number of votes he received in 1984. After winning 77 percent of the Black vote in 1984, he completely dominated among African Americans in 1988, taking 92 percent of the vote. In addition, Jackson tripled the number of votes he won among whites, though, despite his attempts to create a biracial populist coalition between Blacks and working-class whites, he did best among whites with a college degree or more education.[170]

Indeed, Jackson's 1988 campaign helped pave the way for the first African American president a generation later, something many speculated about at the time. Duke political science professor James Barber suggested, "[Jackson's success] enables us all to entertain the possibility of having a black President in this country."[171] Richard Hatcher, a Jackson campaign chairman who became one of the first big-city Black mayors in the nation when he was elected in Gary, Indiana, in 1967, added, "I think that it [the reverend's 1988 campaign] moved us a step closer to the day when perhaps the most segregated office in the country—the office of the President—will become integrated."[172]

Jackson's success came at a crucial midway point: twenty-three years after the passage of the Voting Rights Act of 1965 and two decades prior to Obama's triumph in 2008. A generation earlier, Hatcher's election as an African American mayor of a major city had been barrier breaking. Two years earlier, Julian Bond and John Lewis, major icons of the civil rights movement, had fought it out in a Democratic congressional primary in Georgia because that elected office appeared to be the highest to which an African American could aspire.[173] Jackson's campaign demonstrated that white racism had diminished further, and Black political power had grown to the point that a significant Black presidential candidacy was possible. Though the reverend was certainly hindered by the fact that he was a more polarizing figure than Obama, racial liberalism in politics had not yet evolved far enough for the door to greater opportunities to fully open.

Nevertheless, Jackson's overwhelming Black support merged with the kind of well-educated white voters who had entered the Democratic Party since the McGovern campaign, thus previewing the similar formula Barack Obama would employ in his primary victory over Hillary Clinton in 2008. Of course, Obama was able to garner much higher support among white voters, but like Jackson, he did better with whites with college or graduate educations.[174] Also like Jackson, Obama did very well in caucuses and performed best in the states with the highest and lowest Black populations.[175] While campaigning in 2015 in Iowa, Sanders noted, "People forget about this but Barack Obama would not be president if Jesse Jackson didn't come to Iowa. That was a guerilla-type campaign that clearly didn't have resources but had incredible energy."[176] In 2016, Donna Brazile, who had worked for Jackson in 1984 and Gephardt in 1988 and later served in many capacities for the Democratic Party, stressed the reverend's historical importance, saying, "Barack Obama is not the first quote unquote African-American candidate to come close and then of course, win it. Jesse Jackson. Reverend Jackson laid the foundation."[177]

The campaign moved on to New York, where Gore planned on making a final attempt at northern success in two weeks on April 19. The Tennessee senator, however, faced a number of obstacles. Having run as a southern moderate, he faced an ideological challenge. As Jonathan Alter wrote of Gore in *Newsweek*, "He's got the wrong primary for 'moderation.' New

York is not Tennessee. It's one of the three or four most liberal states in the country."[178] Dukakis, with a northeastern background and his ethnic appeal, seemed a better fit for the Empire State. Hoping to end the campaign of the only other plausible nominee remaining, the Dukakis camp worked to defeat Gore. Keeping the message consistent, campaign mailers stressed the same themes the governor had for the past year, noting, "He is the son of Greek immigrants who came to these shores in search of the American dream." In addition, the fliers talked of how Dukakis had rejuvenated the Massachusetts economy and would push for "good jobs at good wages." Tailoring themes for his current audience, they also highlighted his support for Israel and gay rights.[179]

Despite the battle between Gore and Dukakis, Jackson became the major issue in the primary. Jewish voters comprised 23 percent of the primary electorate, and New York City mayor Ed Koch declared that Jews and pro-Israel voters "would have to be crazy to vote" for the reverend.[180] Jackson had a complicated history with the Jewish community, to put it mildly, including previous ties to Nation of Islam leader Louis Farrakhan, who had a long history of vulgar anti-Semitic comments. During the 1984 campaign, Jackson had referred to New York City as "Hymietown" while talking to some reporters. He had also met with and hugged Palestine Liberation Organization leader Yasser Arafat in 1979, when American policy forbade governmental contact with the organization. Jackson had made some efforts to make amends with the Jewish community—"He said things he shouldn't have said and he's apologized," remarked his campaign manager. But he remained an extremely controversial figure among American Jews.[181]

Although few realized it at the time, a pivotal moment in the 1988 election came in an April 12 debate hosted by the *New York Daily News*. Gore raised the furlough program, mentioning that some of the prisoners overstayed their passes and committed crimes. "If you were elected," the Tennessee senator asked Dukakis, "would you advocate a similar program for federal penitentiaries?" Some in the crowd laughed. Dukakis responded, "Al, the difference between you and me is that I have run a criminal justice system and you never have," then added that he was proud of his record on crime. Eventually, the governor did say "Obviously not" as a response to the challenge from Gore, who did not use Horton's name.[182] Dukakis recalled being unsurprised that the subject arose, given his stance against capital punishment: "If you got a furlough program and you've got the kind of attitude I have about the death penalty you expect people to raise it. And he did and I responded. Seemed to kind of disappear as an issue."[183]

But it would come back with a vengeance. Jim Pinkerton, Bush's director of campaign research, read a transcript of the debate and was very surprised to hear about the furlough discussion. "Wow. This is really weird," he said, calling future White House chief of staff Andy Card, a former Republican state legislator in Massachusetts working with the Bush campaign. Card told Pinkerton about the debate in the state regarding the policy. The campaign then Xeroxed copies of articles about furloughs from the Lawrence *Eagle-Tribune* as well as the *Boston Globe*.[184] According to Bush campaign manager Lee Atwater, this was when he first heard about the subject, though someone in the Bush camp had discussed the issue with a reporter a few days earlier.[185]

Gore's aggressive behavior in the debate was part of a desperate Hail Mary pass by his campaign to win New York. Already in debt, he borrowed even more money and spent $1 million on television ads.[186] Hoping to make serious inroads into the Jewish vote, he emphasized his strong support for Israel, even to the point of backing the conservative Israeli government's opposition to Reagan's peace plan for the region. In doing so, Gore criticized a letter thirty senators signed suggesting they were "dismayed" by the current government's unwillingness to trade land for peace.[187]

With Dukakis leading in the polls, however, many New York voters, especially Jews, simply viewed a vote for Gore as a vote for Jackson. One New Yorker said, "I'd vote for Gore—I like the guy. But to beat Jackson you vote for Dukakis."[188] Another declared, "You've got to vote for Dukakis; there's no other way, no matter how you feel about Gore. If you don't, you're voting for Jackson."[189]

After Cuomo finally made a Shermanesque statement ruling out a draft by the party, Koch endorsed Gore five days before the primary.[190] Over the next few days, the mayor seized the spotlight, criticizing Jackson repeatedly and diverting attention away from Gore. Among other things, Koch criticized Jackson's behavior after Dr. King's assassination, when the reverend claimed to have held King while he died and then went on television the next day saying the slain civil rights leader's blood was still on his shirt.[191] The Tennessee senator "became a prisoner of his chief local patron . . . whose vituperative attacks on Jackson further polluted the city's dense ethnic atmosphere and totally obscured Gore's own image," wrote Laurence Barrett in *Time*.[192] In the end, Koch's attacks might have done more harm to his chosen candidate than good.[193]

Though his campaign had fallen short in Wisconsin, Jackson still retained a strong base of support in New York City among African Americans as well as Hispanics, two groups that had not always seen eye to eye politically.

"Politicians noted that Mr. Jackson's campaign had won something that virtually no politician had ever achieved," wrote Michael Oreskes in the *New York Times*, "—the unified support of almost all black and Hispanic leaders."[194] Some progressive unions also backed the reverend, and polls showed him running second, well behind Dukakis but significantly ahead of Gore.[195]

In the end, Dukakis remained above the fray and won a major victory, defeating Jackson 51 percent to 37 percent. Gore trailed the others dramatically, earning 10 percent of the vote. "I love New York," exclaimed the governor on the evening of the win. Dukakis ran up his biggest margins in the suburbs and upstate, while Jackson narrowly beat the Massachusetts governor in the city. Gore's efforts to win Jewish votes failed miserably, as Dukakis beat him 77 percent to 16 percent in that demographic. Exit polls, however, showed that many Dukakis voters were unenthusiastic about him and might have been voting against Jackson as much as they were supporting the governor.[196]

Nevertheless, Gore's third-place finish represented another poor northern showing and led him to suspend his campaign, marking the end for the only other potential nominee. His more moderate message failed to resonate outside his southern base. Even before his loss in New York, many believed Gore's 1988 run had damaged his future national political prospects. Some were even more pessimistic after Gore's departure, with pollster Stanley Greenberg commenting, "I would have thought his purpose in running, given his age, was to position himself for the vice presidency or for a future run. I can't see where either one of his goals was enhanced."[197] The Cassandras, of course, turned out to be quite wrong about Gore.

At the time, however, the most important consequence of New York was that it sealed the nomination for Dukakis. "The object in New York was to see if we could win the thing and get Al out of the race and that happened," the governor recalled. Indeed, the *New York Times* published a headline the day after the primary: "The Look for Fall: Bush vs. Dukakis."[198]

Though Dukakis had essentially wrapped up the nomination, Jackson continued on for the remaining thirteen contests. While he had little chance to win any of them, with the exception of the District of Columbia primary, he hoped to strengthen his hand at the convention, particularly with regard to shaping the party platform.[199] He and his supporters also made noises about Jackson either deserving to be the vice president or at least playing a role in choosing that candidate.[200] Dukakis continued to refrain from criticizing Jackson for fear of alienating his supporters; the governor was going to need their energy and votes to win in November.

In the closing weeks of the primary campaign, Jackson criticized Dukakis for being too centrist. In Ohio, Jackson declared, "We do not need two Republican parties."[201] On May 12, he compared the governor to Bush, alleging, "Both of them brag about being vague, both of them are trying to make bland beautiful. Both of them are running on competence. But the issue is also direction."[202] In a debate in California on May 25, Jackson called Dukakis a conservative.[203] This dichotomy was reflected in the overall primary vote—Dukakis beat Jackson among moderate Democrats 47 percent to 25 percent, while the two candidates split liberals by winning 41 percent of the vote apiece.[204]

It was not simply the comparison to Jackson that made Dukakis appear more centrist. The governor had assembled a relatively moderate economic brain trust, including Larry Summers, Alice Rivlin, Alan Blinder, and Robert Reich. "Michael S. Dukakis is relying on a loose and growing circle of advisers who, like the Governor, have cast aside many of the policies of earlier Democrats that allotted government a major role that required high spending and high taxes," wrote Peter Kilborn in the *New York Times*. While all of these policymakers were certainly committed to activist government, Kilborn noted, "[Dukakis] appears to be making little use of the hard-core, New Deal economists who are close to organized labor and sympathetic to major spending programs like those of President Lyndon B. Johnson's Great Society."[205]

Early general election polls revealed that voters did not view Dukakis as a liberal, though Estrich believed the long-term impact of this perception might have been detrimental. "Looking back, we came out of the primary superficially much stronger than we were. We were the beneficiaries of being the winner every week against Jackson. And, we looked moderate as a result, but we lacked a foundation," she said.[206] Concerning Dukakis being seen as a moderate, Estrich noted that "at some point it made him very vulnerable" to attacks by Republicans defining him as a liberal. She added, "The great failure, I think, of the Dukakis campaign was that we knew certain issues were coming."[207]

As Bush and Dukakis began to tentatively face off rhetorically, with the vice president criticizing the governor's foreign policy experience, polls showed Dukakis leading Bush in the general election.[208] "I didn't know very much about him [Dukakis] at all," Craig Fuller recalled. "We didn't see him as an exceptionally strong candidate; on the other hand he was polling well."[209] Though it was early, Republicans began to show some concern about the deficit, and about the fact that most voters did not perceive Dukakis as a liberal. With his usual hyperbole, Gingrich declared, "If on Election

Day this election is between George Bush and someone who is more liberal than George McGovern we win. If it's an election between two competent leaders, we lose."[210] Though the primaries were not yet over, the Bush campaign's basic line of attack for the fall was already coming into view.

Nevertheless, Dukakis closed out the primary season with another win over Jackson in California on June 7. His overall victory was by no means dominant—his 42 percent of the primary vote put him in the bottom half of nominees from both parties in open races since the McGovern-Fraser reforms had taken effect in 1972.[211] But in the end, none of the other candidates had been able match the breadth of Dukakis's center-left technocratic appeal. Gephardt found some success with his economic populist message, but he ran aground because he couldn't raise enough money due to his trade policy. Simon and Jackson both tried to pull the party leftward toward traditional liberalism. While the historical nature of the latter's candidacy certainly energized African Americans and white progressives, there simply was not a significant enough constituency to carry him to the nomination. Finally, Gore tried to run as a southern moderate and move the party slightly rightward, but he couldn't expand beyond his regional appeal in the end.

Dukakis was able to consolidate establishment support, including the financial resources, to win the race. He achieved this victory despite having a less than compelling message that would hinder him in the general election. But after the long slog, pundits praised the governor for his doggedness and consistency during the year-plus campaign. In a *Washington Post* article titled "The Stubborn Triumph of Michael Dukakis," NPR's Linda Wertheimer wrote that "Dukakis was the candidate who wouldn't be rattled. In a year when other Democratic candidates—Gary Hart, Joe Biden, Dick Gephardt, and Al Gore—seemed to buckle under the intense pressures of the campaign, Dukakis stayed on his feet."[212]

Through its myriad twists and turns, the long Democratic primary of 1988 revealed many of the roots of modern American politics. In their own way, the Hart, Biden, Gephardt, and Jackson campaigns offered windows into the future with regard to how candidates' personal behavior, public comments, messages, and race would impact American politics in the 1990s and early twenty-first century. In the 1988 phase of the primary, Gephardt's trade message foreshadowed a generation of politicians that would use the issue to appeal to working-class whites struggling in a more globalized economy. And Jackson's second-place finish helped lay the foundation for Obama's breakthrough a generation hence.

Finally, this group of Democratic candidates turned out to be far more than the Seven Dwarfs. Gore and Biden both went on to serve as vice president, with Biden becoming president and Gore coming within an inch of reaching the Oval Office himself. Gephardt became House majority leader and came oh so close to being Speaker of the House. But 1988 was Michael Dukakis's year, as he had risen from the ashes of his 1978 gubernatorial reelection loss to become the Democratic nominee for president a decade later. And as the general election began, he led his Republican opponent in the polls. The race, however, was only just beginning.

4 Bush's Triumph

George Bush faced a crucial choice. Since he was struggling in the polls in New Hampshire following a disastrous third-place finish in Iowa, his advisers wanted him to go negative against Bob Dole.

The Kansas senator had won Iowa and was surging in the Granite State, and another Dole victory would likely spell the end of Bush's presidential ambitions. Campaign manager Lee Atwater and media adviser Roger Ailes pushed Bush to approve an ad portraying his rival as having "straddled" on several major issues, including tax increases, which were anathema to the "live free or die" denizens of New Hampshire. Bush hesitated. He—like Dukakis—disdained negative campaigning. His final decision would perhaps be his most important in the entire campaign, as he might never have been closer to losing his dream of the White House than he was in the week between Iowa and New Hampshire.

Despite this key moment, the Republican nomination battle of 1988 would not be as dramatic as its Democratic counterpart. No one would be felled by a major scandal, sexual or otherwise, and the contest would be wrapped up rather quickly by the front-runner, as Bush's ties to Reagan and his organizational strength proved too much for his challengers. But the Republican primary also featured many key players in late twentieth-century and early twenty-first-century politics, including a future president in Bush, a future presidential nominee in Dole, and a future vice-presidential nominee in Kemp.

Further, the race revealed the foundations of the future of American politics. As Dole and Bush battled for the nomination by hewing closer to the middle than Reagan, the nation, at least at the presidential level, began moving toward the center. Scholars have tended to focus on the rightward shift of the country from 1964 to 1980, but the 1988 GOP primary showed that movement was abating a bit at this time. While the two top contenders in 1988 had always had a foot in the conservative camp, however, the right wing of the party saw them as moderate conservatives at best by this point. This divide revealed that while the Republican Party had moved significantly to the right by the late 1980s, it remained a bigger ideological tent than it would be in the early twenty-first century. The suburbs remained Republican redoubts, allowing moderate conservatives to retain power to an extent, with two of them dominating the fight to succeed Reagan.[1]

Yet at the same time, Christian conservatives, who had emerged as a political force following the cultural upheavals of the 1960s and 1970s, enhanced their strength within the party. Having emerged as a key pillar of the Republican coalition during the Reagan years, religious conservatives grew more powerful in 1988 as televangelist Pat Robertson's insurgent campaign energized them. His presidential bid laid the groundwork for the creation of the Christian Coalition, and for an even deeper involvement by evangelicals in GOP politics that would persist for the rest of the twentieth century and into the twenty-first.

And a certain future reality-television star from Queens—who was in the midst of his initial rise to national fame as a symbol of 1980s prosperity—made a cameo appearance. Donald Trump went to New Hampshire in the fall of 1987, criticizing America's military support for its allies and its leaders' weakness on trade policy. His flirtation with a national campaign suggested the GOP might have an appetite for an economic populism that went beyond the cultural appeals that Nixon and Reagan had previously made to blue-collar voters. But this brief foray seemed likely to fade into obscurity—until Trump shockingly became president nearly three decades later.

Unlike Michael Dukakis, George Bush did not need to make a decision to run. He'd been preparing to do so his whole life. Bush came from a wealthy Eastern Establishment family, and his father, Prescott, worked for Brown Brothers Harriman, a prominent Wall Street investment house in New York. Born in Milton, Massachusetts, George grew up in Greenwich, Connecticut, and went to the best schools, attending Phillips Andover for high school.[2] In 1942, he joined the military at age eighteen and became the youngest pilot in the navy at the time, flying fifty-eight missions in the Pacific during World War II. When he was shot down by the Japanese in September 1944, he parachuted out of his plane and was rescued.[3] Returning home following the war, he attended Yale, where he played first base and was captain of the baseball team while graduating Phi Beta Kappa. Eschewing the family business on Wall Street after graduation, George and his wife, Barbara, set off for Texas, where he had a successful career in the oil industry in the 1950s. At the same time, Prescott served as a moderate Republican senator from Connecticut, supporting civil rights and opposing Joe McCarthy.

In the early 1960s, the younger Bush entered politics, becoming Republican Party chairman in Harris County, Texas—the Houston area. This was a daunting task in an era when Democrats still dominated the Lone Star State.

Harris County Republicans, a small group from the Houston country-club set, hoped a moderate Bush would stem the influence of the rising far-right activism of the John Birch Society and other extremist groups. As JFK and then LBJ embraced civil rights, many Democrats in Texas gravitated toward the GOP, especially when Arizona senator Barry Goldwater, who voted against the landmark Civil Rights Act of 1964, became the Republican nominee for president that same year. Bush, however, sought to compromise with the Birchers.

Despite never having held public office, Bush ran for the Senate as a Republican in 1964 against the liberal Democratic incumbent, Ralph Yarborough. In doing so, he did not run in the moderate mold of his father. Rather, Bush ran as a conservative Goldwater Republican, supporting prayer in schools, criticizing the United Nations, and opposing the civil rights act. While he lost to Yarborough, he outperformed Goldwater in Texas.

Two years later, Bush made a successful run for the House, becoming the first Republican congressman from the Houston area since Reconstruction. In his four years in Congress, he compiled a relatively moderate voting record. Doing a turnabout on civil rights, he faced criticism for backing LBJ's fair-housing bill in 1968, saying he believed that African American soldiers serving in Vietnam should not face discrimination upon returning home.[4] Back in Houston, Bush defended his decision to a skeptical hometown audience, telling them, "Somehow it seems fundamental that this guy [a minority Vietnam veteran] should have a hope. A hope that if he saves money, and if he wants to break out of a ghetto, and if he is a good character and if he meets every requirement of purchaser—the door will not be slammed solely because he is a Negro or because he speaks with a Mexican accent."[5] Believing he had changed some minds, Bush later said that the speech gave him the best feeling he ever had in public life. A family friend explained the shift by saying, "George understands that you have to do politically prudent things to get in a position to do what you want."[6]

At the urging of President Nixon, Bush ran for the Senate again in 1970, with the promise of another position should he lose. Bush thought he would face off with the liberal Yarborough once more, but the incumbent lost a primary challenge to a more moderate Democrat, Lloyd Bentsen.[7] Unable to run to the right of Bentsen in conservative Texas, Bush lost again. Nixon's people later complained that Bush was unwilling to use the attack ads they suggested, previewing his initial reluctance to do so in 1988.[8]

After losing the Senate race, Nixon appointed Bush ambassador to the United Nations, where he began to develop the foreign policy expertise that would be so key to his term as president. Then Nixon asked Bush to become chair of the Republican National Committee (RNC) in 1973, where he succeeded Dole in the position. Although Dole was unaware, Bush had already accepted the job when Nixon officials asked the Kansas senator to travel to New York to urge him to take the position. When he discovered this later on, Dole was angry because "he felt that Bush had let him beg." The incident led to a long-term enmity between the two. "I always sort of thought John Mitchell [Nixon's attorney general] called Bush. I was just up there for appearance's sake," recalled Dole, who wanted to stay as chair.[9] While leading the RNC, Bush defended the president during Watergate. That position was followed by one-year sojourns as envoy to China and director of the CIA, where he helped rebuild morale in the agency after the scandals and investigations of the post-Watergate era. Following his time with the CIA, Bush resumed private life in Texas in 1977 but yearned for a return to politics.

In 1979, he declared his candidacy for president. Running as an establishment moderate, he supported the Equal Rights Amendment and opposed a constitutional amendment to ban abortion, two positions that were anathema to the grassroots conservatives who were increasingly central to the nominating process. Bush pulled an upset victory over Ronald Reagan in the Iowa caucus and claimed that he had the "Big Mo," but he lost that momentum when Reagan soundly defeated him in New Hampshire. Bush won a few other big state primaries, famously referring to Reagan's tax proposals as "voodoo economics" along the way, but the Gipper became the nominee.

At the Republican convention in Detroit in the summer of 1980, Reagan first contemplated an arrangement where he would name former president Gerald Ford as his vice president, and the two of them would maintain some kind of power-sharing arrangement. As time passed on the third night of the convention, a deal with Ford seemed more and more unlikely, and Reagan asked, "Who else is there?" When foreign policy adviser Richard Allen suggested Bush, Reagan was reluctant to pick his former rival, saying, "I can't take him; that 'voodoo economic policy' charge and his stand on abortion are wrong." Allen asked Reagan whether he would choose Bush if he agreed to "support this platform in every detail." Reagan said he would reconsider. Eventually, negotiations with Ford broke down, and Reagan asked Bush, who accepted his offer.[10] Bush immediately recanted his positions on abortion and other areas of disagreement, which contributed to his image as a weak leader. "People said, 'Wait a minute. Doesn't this guy have any principles of his own?'" observed Pete Teeley, Bush's campaign secretary in 1988.[11] When Reagan and Bush defeated Carter and Mondale in the general election, Bush became vice president.

And a loyal one at that. Bush headed up task forces for regulatory reform as well as to combat terrorism and drugs. When controversy broke out in Western Europe over the placing of Pershing missiles in the region, he traveled across the Atlantic to reassure the NATO allies. But whatever Bush's achievements as Reagan's second-in-command, the role itself seemed to diminish him in the eyes of the public. "He's emasculated by the office of vice president," analyzed Craig Fuller, Bush's chief of staff.[12]

Bush's campaign advisers clearly understood this challenge. In an executive summary to a twenty-nine-page document titled "Leadership Gap" and dated November 24, 1986, they wrote, "*The Vice President must establish himself firmly in the voters' minds as a leader.*" In language likely inspired by Atwater, the advisers noted that there are a few "*Defining Events*" that "shape the public's view of a candidate," and they said the campaign needed to find a way to bring one about for Bush. Noting that three-fifths of Americans believed they were better off than they had been in 1980, the document's authors observed, "*Just 42 percent feel that the policies of President Reagan should be carried on without change. It is in the difference between those two figures where the 1988 Presidential election will be won or lost.*"[13]

Specifying that they did not want the vice president to break from Reagan, Bush's advisers elaborated, "The *goal is to break with the negative stereotypes and expectations* that are the baggage of a Republican label in the 1980s." They thought of potential defining events, arguing that "speaking out more on issues such as *education* and the *environment* would define the Vice President as an independent leader and thinker, as would *constructive criticism of Big Business.*" The first two issues would become central pillars of Bush's campaign, both in the primary as well as the general election. Summarizing their program for their candidate, the consultants wrote, "In the late 1980s, voters would be attracted to a Republican who is willing to *break ranks* with his party and *demonstrate that Republicans do care about social ills and have better approaches for solving them.* Such a departure from the Reagan Era stereotype of all Republicans as totally opposed to expanding the safety net *could well be a Defining Event for the Vice President.*" Long before the first votes were cast, the intellectual groundwork had been laid for the vice president's centrist pledges to be the "environmental president" and "education president," as well as for his repeated calls to do more for those left out of the 1980s boom, and for the support of "a thousand points of light" of community organizations to deal with poverty.[14]

As the 1988 campaign began, Bush was the favorite for the GOP nomination as Reagan's vice president. He put together a strong campaign team with Atwater as campaign manager. Atwater, along with Fuller, Nicholas

Brady, Bob Mosbacher, Bob Teeter, and Ailes formed what became known as the "Group of Six" that ran Bush's presidential bid. According to Fuller, the title derived from a scheduler who repeatedly listed the men as "G-6" for meetings.[15] Each played a different but important role, and rivals consistently praised the strength of the operation.

Of particular importance was the hiring of Ailes, whose services were strongly desired by the other candidates. Three decades before he started Fox News in the 1990s, Ailes had begun his television career working on the *Mike Douglas Show*, a daytime talk show, in the mid-1960s. Eventually he became executive producer of the program, and he met Richard Nixon before an episode airing in 1967. "It's a shame a man has to use gimmicks like this to get elected," Nixon told Ailes, who responded, "Television is not a gimmick."[16] Hired by Nixon following this encounter, he proved instrumental in constructing the former vice president's "New Nixon" image during his successful 1968 presidential campaign. Ailes went on to work in Republican politics in the 1970s and 1980s, advising a number of candidates, ranging from Kentucky's Mitch McConnell during his first Senate campaign in 1984 to Reagan during his reelection effort that same year. In doing so, he quickly earned a reputation for his toughness and willingness to play hardball, which would be on full display during 1988.[17]

Helped by his organizational advantages, Bush won a resounding victory in the invisible primary, scoring 48 percent of the endorsements in the race, with his nearest rivals garnering only 20 percent apiece.[18] Still, the vice president would have to face down significant challenges to win the nomination as conservatives remained suspicious of him, while Iran-Contra now presented another major obstacle.

Poised to take advantage of the opening was Dole, by then the Senate minority leader. Like Bush, Dole was a World War II veteran, and he had suffered major injuries in Italy in April 1945 that permanently limited the use of his right arm. After a long convalescence from his wounds, the senator had earned undergraduate and law degrees from Washburn University in Topeka and entered local politics, serving first in the Kansas House of Representatives and then as county attorney of Russell County. He moved to the national level and was first elected to the House in 1960, entering the Senate in 1968. When conservatives pressured President Ford to remove Vice President Nelson Rockefeller from his ticket in 1976, they deemed Dole ideologically acceptable, and he became Ford's running mate. During that campaign, Dole drew the most attention for his debate with Carter's vice-presidential nominee, Mondale, when he fumed about the damage caused by "Democrat wars." This moment cemented his reputation for having a mean streak. After Ford's loss, Dole returned to the Senate, running unsuccessfully for the presidency in 1980.

Though Dole has been viewed as a conservative in his early years, he gradually lost the party base's faith as he moved toward the center while the Republican Party edged rightward. In the early 1970s, he worked with liberal icon George McGovern to expand the food-stamps program, and in the 1980s he backed the creation of the Martin Luther King Jr. Day holiday, as well as the extension of the Voting Rights Act.[19] More of a fiscal conservative in the tradition of Eisenhower than a tax cutter in the mold of Reagan, Dole focused on reducing the budget deficit during the 1980s. His willingness to support tax increases to close the gap led him to battle with New Right advocates like Newt Gingrich and Jack Kemp. At one point, Gingrich derisively called Dole "the tax collector for the welfare state."[20]

Kemp set out to be the candidate for conservatives, portraying himself as the natural heir to the Reagan Revolution. Elected to the House from Buffalo in 1970 after a professional football career, the former quarterback became a fierce advocate for tax cuts and supply-side economics. In the 1970s, the conservative economist Arthur Laffer, along with the neoconservative intellectual Irving Kristol and the *Wall Street Journal* editorial page, promoted the idea that cutting taxes would increase work, saving, and investment, boosting economic growth to the point that the cuts would pay for themselves, and deficits would not ensue. Though the idea was rejected by mainstream economists and broke with the traditional balanced-budget-first wisdom that had dominated post–World War II Republican thought, it gained credence among conservatives in the 1980s. Kemp became its foremost backer among elected officials.

Though he lacked the institutional backing of Bush and Dole, Kemp was a clearer ideological descendant of Reagan. The Reagan tax cuts of 1981 were officially known as the Kemp-Roth bill, named for the congressman and Senator William Roth (R) of Delaware. "It was always going to be an uphill battle," remembered Charlie Black, Kemp's campaign manager, "so we basically tried to portray him as the true heir of Reagan."[21] Influenced by his experience as an athlete playing during the civil rights era, the loquacious Kemp repeatedly spoke about expanding the GOP tent and bringing more minorities into the party.[22]

Aiming for religious conservatives was the Reverend Pat Robertson. Frustrated by many of the social changes of the previous two decades, the Christian right began to play a key role in the GOP in the 1980s. Some evangelicals had always been attracted to the Republicans because they believed the party was tougher on communism. Supreme Court decisions banning prayer in the schools in the early 1960s, followed by the *Roe v. Wade* decision legalizing abortion in 1973, angered evangelicals, many of whom had grown up as Democrats in the South. The rise of the women's movement, the gay rights movement, and the battle over the Equal Rights Amendment also mobilized many social conservatives. Still, as late as 1976, the parties were not dramatically different on cultural issues, and a majority of white evangelicals supported Jimmy Carter, himself a born-again Christian.[23]

A final straw for some came when the Carter administration tried to revoke the tax-exempt status of private schools that had emerged in the South after the courts supported busing to achieve school integration in the early 1970s. The Reverend Jerry Falwell, who had previously opposed the involvement of minsters in politics, organized the Moral Majority, the leading organization of the religious right, in 1979. Social conservatives then moved to back Reagan in 1980 because he embraced the pro-life cause, opposed the ERA, and supported other aspects of their agenda. Some commentators even credited the ascendant Christian right for his election.

The son of a Democratic senator and a graduate of Yale Law School, Robertson had developed a business empire as a televangelist with his Christian Broadcasting Network, which he had begun in 1960. The religious right's power in the GOP continued to grow during the 1980s, and Robertson, along with Falwell, led the way. Increasingly, Republican politicians had to be concerned with cultural issues, and abortion became more of a litmus test for local and national candidates, though some evangelicals still believed they did not fully deliver on their promises. Televangelists had gained national prominence, but scandals surrounding some of these men threatened the movement's credibility. Finally, Robertson was a polarizing figure with high negative ratings, as many Americans feared his candidacy could potentially breach the separation of church and state.

Former secretary of state Al Haig and former Delaware governor Pierre "Pete" du Pont IV joined the race as well, but they were never major factors. Nevada senator Paul Laxalt, a friend and ally of Reagan's, got in briefly and tried to claim the mantle of conservative favorite. Yet he departed quickly because of his inability to raise money.[24]

As the race got underway, a clear divide formed between the establishment wing of the party and insurgent conservatives. "Dole and Bush represent the pre-Reagan party, the side of the party Reagan had to beat to win. Kemp, Robertson, and du Pont represent the party Reagan has created," declared Gingrich.[25] The early months of the Republican primary fight, however, were not nearly as eventful as the Democratic contest. Highlights included Kemp's official declaration, as well as the Bush campaign shooting down rumors that the vice president had carried on an affair. Having asked his father about the conjecture regarding infidelity, George W. Bush informed *Newsweek*, "The answer to the Big A [adultery] question is N.O."[26]

By Labor Day, there had been no major scandals, and no debates had been held. Though he had not officially declared his candidacy, Bush remained the front-runner. Dole had closed the gap in the national polls to trail the vice president 34 percent to 23 percent by late July, and he was running ahead of Bush in the Midwest, where many early contests were to be held.[27] However, in what would become a chronic issue, Dole's campaign was plagued by organizational challenges.[28] From early on, Kemp's campaign struggled with similar problems. The congressman also failed to consolidate conservative support behind him, as many social conservatives were drawn to Robertson.

Demonstrating organizational prowess, Robertson won the Iowa straw poll in Ames on September 12. The nonbinding event, which functioned as a fundraiser for the Iowa GOP, served as an early test of strength for candidates. It often favored campaigns with small but highly motivated backers, as attendees traveled from around the state to purchase twenty-five-dollar tickets so they could vote for their candidate.[29] Traditionally, the poll featured a very low turnout, though the 3,843 votes cast in 1987 doubled the number from eight years earlier. Robertson garnered 34 percent of the vote, with Dole finishing second with 25 percent. Bush, who had won the event in 1979, placed third with 23 percent support, and Kemp ended in fourth place at 14 percent.[30]

Robertson's showing revealed the dedication of grassroots social conservatives. "What the Robertson people demonstrated tonight is that they will be out there in February, in the snow and the cold," declared the Iowa Republican chairman, "whether the temperature is 20 above or 20 below." Bush's people downplayed the candidate's poor showing while not totally dismissing it. His campaign secretary commented, "Is it devastating to come in third to Dole? No, it's not devastating. Does it mean we have to crack down and do some work? Yes."[31]

Robertson followed the straw-poll victory with another win in Michigan a few days later on September 15. Switching from a primary to a party convention, the Michigan GOP scheduled its delegate-choosing process ahead of Iowa on the calendar to increase its influence. "The procedures emphasized the role of party regulars and thus seemed safely under the control of elected officials sympathetic to Bush," wrote E. J. Dionne in the *New York Times*. "What came to pass instead," he continued, "were 17 months of acrimonious political brawling."[32] The complicated process posed problems for the vice president's campaign from the outset. "I don't think we ever understood Michigan," recalled Fuller. "Michigan was the most confounding state from the very beginning."³³

In the summer of 1986, Robertson's campaign caught Bush and the other contenders off guard in Michigan by running and electing nearly as many precinct representatives as the vice president. Bush was left with a bare plurality at best, though it wasn't entirely clear who was in the early lead due to the bizarre process.³⁴ Robertson's campaign staff "just flooded the state with their field force and some money and they rolled up the score," according to Black. The 9,000 precinct representatives elected would vote to determine who would attend the state convention, and those at the state convention would in turn decide the delegation to the national convention. The Bush camp tried to expand the number of representatives by 1,200 with the hope of adding more of their own people. However, the Michigan Republican State Central Committee, controlled by an alliance of the Robertson and Kemp forces, rejected this proposal in September 1987. The Bush campaign pledged to fight the issue in the courts, but Robertson's national campaign director believed the reverend was poised to win a majority of the Michigan delegates.³⁵

A few days later on September 18, President Reagan announced a major arms-control agreement with the Soviet Union that would result in the elimination of medium- and shorter-range nuclear missiles. While the final details of the intermediate-range nuclear forces (INF) treaty remained for Reagan and Gorbachev to work out at a summit in the fall, Don Oberdorfer and Lou Cannon wrote in the *Washington Post*, "The INF accord agreed to in principle would be the first U.S.-Soviet treaty actually to reduce the number of offensive weapons rather than to cap their burgeoning growth. And for the first time, it would eliminate an entire class of nuclear weapons." The journalists cautioned that the missiles affected by the treaty only composed about 5 percent of the nuclear arsenals of the two superpowers.³⁶

Vice President Bush praised the agreement, while Dole was more measured. Trying to outflank the front-runners on the right, all of the other challengers opposed it. Everyone agreed the treaty boosted Reagan's then-struggling presidency, with the *Washington Post*'s David Broder and Thomas Edsall calling the accord an achievement "that could wipe out much of the lingering odor of the Iran-contra affair." Bush, the candidate whose fate was most directly tied to Reagan's, clearly benefited, and the Reagan administration's recovery from its postscandal malaise would prove essential to the GOP's hopes of holding the White House in 1988.³⁷

Ten days later, Robertson officially declared his candidacy on October 1. He made the announcement in the Bedford-Stuyvesant section of Brooklyn, where he had lived when he felt the call to join the ministry in 1960. Opening with the music from *Rocky* to signal his underdog status, Robertson avoided religious rhetoric for the most part, talking about how he cared for all Americans.[38] "I want to make sure that we give our children and our grandchildren a better place to live," he said over jeers from protesters. Calling for a return to traditional values, he declared, "I believe the time has come when we as a nation go back to the fundamental moral values that have made this nation great."[39] Polls, however, showed that only 28 percent of Republicans had a favorable opinion of Robertson while 62 percent had an unfavorable view of the televangelist, the worst such figures for any candidate.[40]

On the day Bush made his official announcement two weeks later, *Newsweek* appeared on newsstands. The issue's cover story, titled "Fighting the 'Wimp Factor,'" pictured him steering his boat. Written by Margaret Warner, the piece primarily focused on Bush's life and career. While Warner contended that the vice president entered the race with many advantages, she also noted, "[He] suffers from a potentially crippling handicap—a perception that he isn't strong enough or tough enough for the challenges of the Oval Office. That he is, in a single mean word, a wimp."[41] Needless to say, Bush and his campaign were displeased; the vice president told the *Detroit Free Press*, "It was a cheap shot. I kind of liked that cover picture, but I'd like to take the guy who wrote that headline out on the boat." George W. Bush was also furious. He called a *Newsweek* White House reporter to tell him that the campaign wasn't going to speak to the magazine's reporters anymore, though a Bush campaign spokesman denied this.[42]

Calling the *Newsweek* piece "deeply offensive," Fuller believed it was "clearly timed to again be sort of disruptive."[43] Ailes remarked that the original story had a different focus, and that "the wimp thing got blown up dramatically by the editors." Indeed, Evan Thomas, the magazine's Washington bureau chief, confessed that he inserted the wimp language over Warner's objections, later admitting it was a mistake.[44] Fuller said that the Bush campaign had *Newsweek* publisher Kay Graham and the editor (presumably Thomas) over to the residence to complain about the story, recalling, "It left us with a problem that we had to demonstrate you know that contrary to what *Newsweek* might think here's somebody who's quite capable of defending himself and standing up for himself."[45]

On October 12, Bush made his candidacy official in Texas, outlining some of the major themes of his campaign in remarks written by former Reagan speechwriter Peggy Noonan.[46] He talked of the achievements of the Reagan

Newsweek's "Wimp Factor" cover angered the Bush campaign and created an ongoing issue for it. (Photo courtesy of Enveritas Group, Inc.)

administration, saying the country had come so far from the difficulties of 1980. Likely following the guidance of his advisers from their early campaign memo, though, he distanced himself ever so slightly from Reagan, talking about extending prosperity to those who had not shared in the 1980s expansion. "Our triumph is real—but it's incomplete," declared Bush. "There are those who need help. There are those who've been hurt—and as far as I'm concerned, we'll never be a truly prosperous nation until all within it prosper." Criticizing Republicans who thought it was "soft" and "insufficiently tough" to focus on these concerns, he retorted, "I say to my fellow Republicans: We are the party of Lincoln. Our whole history was protecting those who needed our protection and making this a kinder nation."[47] The last phrase seems to preview his (and Noonan's) call in his acceptance speech at the convention for a "kinder, gentler, nation."

Differentiating himself from the president a bit on education, Bush raised the issue of greater spending for schools, asking, "What could be a better investment?" He also called for a new focus regarding the environment, an area where the Reagan administration had come in for considerable criticism: "Sooner or later, we're going to pay the price for distraction—unless we act now and recommit ourselves to protecting the land that we love."⁴⁸ Some noted that Bush did not mention certain key conservative priorities. *Time*'s Laurence Barrett called the address "Reaganism in a minor key," observing that Bush "omitted any reference to Star Wars, Robert Bork, and such hot-button issues as abortion and school prayer."⁴⁹

While he took some steps toward the center, Bush still delivered red meat to the base of the party. Convinced Bush and other establishment candidates had lost to Reagan in 1980 on the tax issue, Atwater had long wanted his candidate to sign the no-tax promise advocated by Grover Norquist's Americans for Tax Reform. Bush didn't want to sign, though, fearing it would limit his options if elected. At the urging of Atwater and Pinkerton, who were concerned about defusing Kemp's tax-cutting appeal, the vice president rejected tax increases in his announcement speech.⁵⁰ Noting the importance of reducing the deficit, he remarked, "There are those who say we must balance the budget on the backs of the workers and raise taxes again. But they are wrong. I am not going to raise your taxes—period."⁵¹ Though Bush hedged in a CNN interview two days later, saying he would only "consider a tax increase" if "all the spending that could be possibly constrained or cut had taken place," this appears to be the rhetorical origin of his "Read my lips. No new taxes" pledge at the Republican convention.⁵²

Like Dukakis, Bush buttressed his front-runner status with strong fundraising, as he was the only Republican with a truly national network.⁵³ When third-quarter numbers were released, the vice president led his competitors, having raised a total of $12.7 million for the year. Robertson placed second with $11.7 million, but he was in debt due to campaign expenses. Dole had the strongest third quarter of both parties' candidates to finish third overall among the GOP contenders, reaching $7.9 million. Kemp's campaign, however, struggled financially, first having to take out a loan for its direct-mail expenses and then taking out yet another one.⁵⁴

As the campaign heated up, it became clear that the leading candidates were trying to portray a softer and more moderate side to the GOP than had been seen during the Reagan years, reflecting the national political turn to the center. Bush emphasized these qualities in his announcement, while Dole talked about how his wartime recovery had made him more sensitive to the struggles of others. The University of Virginia's Larry Sabato analyzed, "Republicans are raising the issue of compassion because the polls are showing it's a problem for them. It's aimed, clearly, at the undecided and persuadable voter who may be lower-income and middle-income."⁵⁵ Kemp also reiterated the compassion theme, continuing his longtime efforts to reach out to people of color by offering conservative solutions to poverty such as enterprise zones.⁵⁶

Around this time, a forty-one-year-old, high-profile New York City real estate developer named Donald J. Trump, who was then a Republican, flew up to New Hampshire to give a speech. Trump embodied the new wealthy class that had emerged during the 1980s boom—the "masters of the universe," as Tom Wolfe called them in his iconic 1980s novel *The Bonfire of the Vanities*.⁵⁷ This group benefited disproportionately from the economic growth of the era, as top earners saw their incomes grow dramatically while they simultaneously benefited from the bull market of the time.⁵⁸

In the midst of his initial rise to national fame, Trump had recently made the cover of *Newsweek*. "Donald John Trump—real estate developer, casino operator, corporate raider and perhaps future politician—is a symbol of an era," read the cover story, titled "Citizen Trump." "He is a man with the Midas fist. For better or for worse, in the 1980s it is OK to be fiercely ambitious, staggeringly rich and utterly at ease in bragging about it." With the hyperbole the nation would eventually become familiar with, Trump declared, "There is no one my age who has accomplished more."⁵⁹

Many of the other characteristics that would mark his presidency were already on full display in 1987. Trump noted that he didn't have many friends and preferred to rely on family members, as he would do while in office. "No achievement can satisfy what he wants. What he still wants is acceptance from his father," observed one friend. "He's playing out his insecurities on a very large canvas." Finally, there were also early signs of Trump's authoritarian tendencies in the 1980s. One lawyer who'd fought with him alleged that Trump was "a dangerous man" and the kind of leader "who'd make the trains run on time."⁶⁰

The trip to New Hampshire had been set in motion in July, when a Republican Party organizer from the Granite State named William Dunbar, who did not know Trump, started a movement to draft him to run for president. According to Dunbar, none of the leading GOP candidates could win a general election. "I decided we better find someone who is capable of being elected," he recalled.⁶¹ Dunbar said the New York businessman had not requested the draft, and Trump responded, "Anyone would be honored to hear this."⁶²

By the late 1980s, it was clear that the Cold War was waning. Even so, many worried that the United States was already losing the economic battle with Europe and Asia that some policymakers believed would be the central fight in the future. The media highlighted stories about Japanese investors buying famous American landmarks such as Rockefeller Center in New York

City and the Pebble Beach golf course in California. Furthermore, Hollywood films such as *Gung Ho* (1986), *Die Hard* (1988), and *Back to the Future Part II* (1989) portrayed a present and future where American workers toiled away for Japanese bosses.[63] Fears of American decline permeated the culture and could be seen in books like Paul Kennedy's *The Rise and Fall of the Great Powers* (1987).[64] In light of these economic challenges, commentators criticized the fact that America was still subsidizing the defense of economic competitors like West Germany and Japan more than four decades after the end of World War II. Politicians in both parties called for greater cost sharing from U.S. allies.

Along these lines, in September, Trump paid $94,801 to place full-page ads in the *New York Times*, the *Washington Post*, and the *Boston Globe* decrying the weakness of American foreign policy. "There's nothing wrong with America's Foreign Defense Policy that a little backbone can't cure," screamed the headline for the ad in the *Times*. The notice was addressed "To The American People" and titled "An open letter from Donald J. Trump on why America should stop paying to defend countries that can afford to defend themselves." Sounding themes similar to those of his 2016 presidential campaign, Trump wrote, "For decades, Japan and other nations have been taking advantage of the United States." Criticizing the Reagan administration's flagging of oil tankers in the Persian Gulf, Trump declared, "The world is laughing at America's politicians as we protect ships we don't own, carrying oil we don't need, destined for allies who won't help." In the vein of his later "America First" slogan, he continued: "Make Japan, Saudi Arabia, and others pay for the protection we extend as allies. Let's help our farmers, our sick, our homeless by taking from some of the greatest profit machines ever created—machines created and nurtured by us."[65]

Accompanied by a large media contingent that included journalists for ABC's newsmagazine *20/20*, Trump espoused much the same philosophy in his speech to the Portsmouth Rotary Club on October 22. Drawing an audience larger than Dole, Kemp, or Robertson had at the same venue, Trump again attacked U.S. allies as free riders and said these countries should pay off the nation's budget deficit. "There is a way you can ask them and they will give it, if you have the right person asking," declared Trump, adding, "I'm tired of nice people already in Washington. I want someone who is tough and knows how to negotiate. If not, our country faces disaster." In another echo of 2016, Trump suggested seizing Iranian oil fields—just as he repeatedly talked about "taking the oil" from Iraqi fields in the twenty-first century. Despite the draft movement, however, Trump rejected a run in 1988: "I'm not here because I'm running for President. I'm here because I'm tired of our country being kicked around and I want to get my ideas across."⁶⁶ His efforts at least drew the attention of the Bush campaign—Fuller recalled, "We were aware of that."⁶⁷ In the end, the trip might have simply been an effort to promote Trump's book *The Art of the Deal*, which was released in November and would further enhance his national profile.⁶⁸

Trump's brief flirtation with a presidential bid was another example of how the 1988 campaign exemplified trends that would influence modern American politics. His views regarding trade and foreign policy were shaped by this era and reflected mainstream thinking at the time. In many ways his ideology barely shifted in the following years, despite changing circumstances like the further decline of manufacturing employment. His short-lived venture into the arena was also an early sign of the appeal of the blue-collar economic and cultural populism that conservative commentator Pat Buchanan would run on in the 1990s, and that Trump himself would employ so effectively when he ran for president. Trump's foreign policy rhetoric in 2016 was virtually identical to his earlier language, as long as you switch the countries around. China—as opposed to Japan—drew his ire when he actually ran for president. While in office, Trump repeatedly pushed for the NATO allies to spend more on their own defense. Reflecting back in 2016, Dunbar commented, "I think the surprising thing about him [Trump] is that he hasn't changed a lot. What I saw in him then was a brashness and a determination of purpose that was lacking in everyone else. He's still the guy I met in 1987."⁶⁹

Meanwhile, the campaign continued, as the Republicans faced off in their first debate in Houston on October 28. As with the initial Democratic debate, the event aired on PBS as a special edition of Buckley's *Firing Line*.⁷⁰ The major candidates promoted the same themes they had throughout the early stages of the campaign. Stressing his fealty to the president, Bush rejected co-moderator Bob Strauss's request to delineate areas where he differed from the administration. Emphasizing his desire to be the "education president," Bush said he hoped that role would be his domestic legacy, and he again promised not to raise taxes. Dole talked of the need for Republicans to change their image, saying, "Our party has a problem with sensitivity. We're perceived as not caring about people. Real people. We're going to correct that . . . and we're going to do a lot of other things in a Dole Administration."⁷¹ Robertson talked about the importance of strengthening moral values and rejected the idea that he was hurting the party's image by focusing on abortion and school prayer, saying he was bringing Democrats into the fold. While touting his trademark economic conservatism, Kemp also emphasized his pro-life views, no doubt as part of an attempt to unite social and economic conservatives under one roof.

Reagan's INF treaty emerged as a key area of contention between the candidates, as du Pont, Haig, Kemp, Robertson, and to some extent Dole again expressed skepticism regarding the arms-control agreement. As usual, Bush wholeheartedly supported the president, saying, "This is the first time in the nuclear age that we are getting rid of a whole class of nuclear weapons and that's good for my grandchildren and the rest of the world."[72]

In his closing, the vice president suggested people were looking for experience, asserting, "I've been co-pilot for seven years and I know how to land a plane in a storm."[73] Thirty-four percent of viewers called the vice president the winner of the debate in an overnight poll, while Dole, Kemp, and Robertson tied for a second-place finish, garnering 14 to 15 percent of respondents' votes. Bush's national polling lead remained the same.[74] Praising the vice president's performance, Broder noted that he had responded sharply when du Pont suggested he offered no vision of his own; Bush had said, "Pierre, let me help you" before criticizing the former Delaware governor. "A better way to bury the 'wimp' image . . . could not have been found," wrote Broder. Throughout the debate, Broder noted, "Bush showed exactly the instincts that he had so conspicuously lacked" in previous national campaigns and Atwater commented that the "wimp" issue never really came up again.[75] Though Dole's top priority going in was "to control his temper, insiders said," some thought the Kansas senator, in an attempt to, in his own words, "bury the hatchet," hadn't been active enough during the debate.[76]

Shortly thereafter on November 9, Dole officially kicked off his candidacy in his hometown of Russell, emphasizing his local roots. Declaring the budget deficit "the single greatest threat to a prosperous and dynamic America," he pledged to fix it "without raising tax rates." Dole did not mention user fees or deductions and credits, differentiating himself from Bush and Kemp, who categorically rejected any tax hike.[77] With regard to implementing the necessary spending cuts, Dole said everything would be on the table except programs for "vulnerable Americans." To prevent deficits in the future, he advocated a balanced-budget amendment to the Constitution and asked Congress to give the president a line-item veto. Like Bush, he also stressed the importance of improving education and reaching out to those who were struggling economically. In foreign policy, Dole called on the European and Asian allies to carry more of the defense burden and again expressed caution regarding the INF treaty.[78]

Without using his name, Dole implicitly criticized Bush, saying, "I offer a record, not a resume," a clear reference to the many appointed positions the vice president had held. Though he fulsomely praised President Reagan, the Kansas senator took another dig at Bush, remarking, "The Reagan record is not something to stand on. It's not something to run on. It's something to build on."[79] Despite his strong fundraising and polling lead over Bush in Iowa of 36 percent to 30 percent, Dole still faced an uphill battle against the vice president, as his organization remained weaker in the South and New England.[80]

Turning the tables on Robertson, Bush avenged his loss in the Iowa straw poll by winning the Florida version by a margin of 57 percent to 37 percent in November. While Bush triumphed, Robertson continued to demonstrate an impressive ability to turn out a core of highly motivated followers. "Everybody I know that is a Robertson supporter is a zealot," declared one of the reverend's Florida backers. "We are committed."[81] This meant the reverend could perform well in the Iowa caucus, where the laborious process required dedication from its participants, and social conservatives were preparing to play a major role. "This is the first time that Right to Life has ever tried to have an impact on the caucuses," commented the president of the Iowa chapter of National Right to Life, adding, "We see Iowa as critical in 1988."[82]

The Republicans clashed for the second time in the joint debate with the Democrats broadcast nationwide on NBC on December 1. The GOP part was a relatively quiet affair without major attacks by the candidates, with the exception of Haig's sharp challenge of Bush on his role in Iran-Contra. Turning the vice president's closing line from the first debate back on him, the general queried, "Were you in the cockpit, or were you on an economy ride in the back of the plane?" Again, all the contenders except the vice president expressed their doubts about the INF treaty. Robertson said no agreements should be made given aggressive Soviet behavior in Afghanistan and elsewhere, while Kemp demanded the regime obey existing treaties first.[83]

Opposition to the INF treaty clearly represented an appeal to the core party base. One poll showed 62 percent of Americans and 63 percent of Republicans supporting the accord, while another showed three-quarters of probable Republican voters in Iowa and New Hampshire backing it as well.[84] Despite strong public support for the agreement, party activists denounced it, with Howard Phillips, chairman of the Conservative Caucus, calling Reagan "a useful idiot for Soviet propaganda." Conservative leader Richard Viguerie suggested the longtime right-wing hero was "now aligned with his former adversaries: the liberals, the Democrats, and the Soviets."[85]

In Michigan, the courts ruled in favor of the Bush campaign's appeal of the central committee's decision to exclude 1,200 party leaders from voting in the January 14 county conventions. As most of these voters were likely to support the vice president, the decision represented a defeat for the Kemp and Robertson forces. Along with the 9,000 delegates already named, these leaders would cast votes to determine who would attend the state convention. These attendees would in turn vote on which candidate's delegates would go to the national convention.[86]

With great fanfare, Gorbachev arrived in Washington for his summit with Reagan, and the two leaders signed the historic INF treaty on December 8. Bush's involvement offered him a good dose of free positive press, and the treaty also helped the vice president by raising Reagan's moribund ratings. The percentage of people approving of the president's performance rose from 45 percent in November to 56 percent following the summit.[87] A week after the meeting, Dole stood with Reagan at the White House to announce his support for the treaty, explaining that while he still had concerns, they could be resolved with some changes and "without requiring renegotiations with the Soviet Union."[88]

As the first year of the GOP campaign concluded, Bush still led his rivals in national polls while Dole maintained a narrow lead in Iowa of 37 percent to 33 percent.[89] Writing that "the script was less dramatic for the Republicans," Toner noted in the *New York Times* that "some believe 1987 clarified their six-candidate field into a two-man race between the Vice President and Senator Bob Dole of Kansas." Toner added that Robertson was "one of the most unpredictable variables on the Republican side," because of his impressive "organizational strength."[90]

As 1988 began, the top two candidates tangled over who was the true "leader." Dole repeatedly said he performed as a "producer" while Senate leader, with Bush serving as a mere "observer" while vice president. "I'm not sure being in Congress all your life is a part of the answer. I think it may be a part of the problem," responded Bush, citing his years in the oil industry in Texas as important private-sector experience valued by Republicans. Dole countered, "The record speaks for itself. I have a solid record of leadership and he doesn't," adding, "I'm on the front line every day making a difference. When President Reagan wants action he calls Bob Dole."[91]

Bush also faced continuing questions about his role in Iran-Contra, as well as populist attacks from Dole. Saying the vice president hadn't been forthcoming, the *New York Times* editorialized, "It's always been hard to accept that George Bush could, at the same time, be the most 'completely involved' Vice President of modern times, as he and President Reagan assert, and still have been disengaged from the Iran-contra affair, as he asserts."

The paper went on to advise Bush to reveal his advice to the president, who had not demanded his silence, asking, "Why keep hiding in President Reagan's skirts?"[92] At the *Des Moines Register* debate on January 8, Bush grew irritable when the moderator suggested he hadn't answered every question regarding the scandal. "I have answered every question put to me save one," responded the vice president, "and the one question is what'd you tell the president of the United States and I shouldn't do that." He said that he supported the arms sales to improve relations with Iran, that he didn't know about the diversion of funds, and that both the Tower Commission and the congressional investigation confirmed his assertions.[93]

Dole again stressed his humble origins in the debate, offering a contrast with Bush and saying he would bring "traditional small town values" and "experience with real people" to the White House. The senator added that he understood that "real people" have problems, asserting, "Maybe they're disabled. Maybe they're black. Maybe they're white. Maybe they're brown. But they have problems and in some cases there is no place else to turn but the federal government." Dole also said he hoped Iowans would think, "He's one of us" when he won the caucus.[94]

Bush continued to trail Dole in Iowa, in part because Reagan was not as popular in the state as he was elsewhere—42 percent of Hawkeye State voters approved of the president, as opposed to 52 percent of voters nationally.[95] Another poll showed that while the two front-runners ran even among those who approved of Reagan, Dole led Bush by more than two to one among the 25 percent of Republicans who disapproved of the president. Though the agricultural economy in Iowa was starting to recover, it had struggled mightily during the Reagan years, losing 9,000 family farms since 1981, with many more at or near bankruptcy.[96] Some Iowans believed the administration hadn't responded aggressively enough. One farmer complained, "They didn't care two hoops about what happened to me." Drawn to Dole's discussion of his hardscrabble past, he added, "Dole's more of an ordinary sort of person. He's come up the hard way." With a majority of Iowa Republicans disapproving of aid to the contras, the president's foreign policy also weakened Bush's standing in the state.[97]

Meanwhile, Robertson remained in third place, but his support was growing as he barnstormed the state to rally his faithful, focusing primarily on fundamentalist and charismatic churches. Still plagued by very high negative ratings, he faced significant resistance. "Because of his background as a pastor, people are afraid of him. They perceive him as wanting to take over the world," remarked one volunteer. Nevertheless, she predicted that the reverend's showing would "come as a great surprise to a lot of people."[98]

The specter of Iran-Contra continued to stalk Bush, who complained in the fourth debate that the media was more interested in the issue than the voters were.[99] At this point, the *CBS Evening News* had conducted profiles of several candidates, and Dan Rather, the program's anchor, wanted to do one about Bush. Saying he was "comfortable" with Rather, the vice president gave his staff the go-ahead. According to *Time*, CBS never said the interview "would focus exclusively on the Iran-Contra affair." Concerned about how the network might edit a taped exchange, Bush's people demanded a live interview, though this didn't completely allay their fears.[100] "We didn't really trust Dan Rather," recalled Fuller. "We didn't really believe it was going to be this kind of thoughtful exchange discussion for 15 minutes of Bush's thinking on a wide range of issues." Saying he'd known Rather for years, Bush thought it would be fine.[101]

The day before the interview, press secretary Pete Teeley learned that Rather was preparing to focus on Iran-Contra. Worried, Teeley called Ailes and told him to get to Washington. A source at CBS told Ailes, "They're running around the CBS newsroom saying they're going to take George Bush out of the race tonight." The day before, the network had advertised that the interview would be about Iran-Contra.[102] Seeing this, Bush dictated in his diary, "I wonder if it is a straight up deal, or what they're doing."[103] On the afternoon of the broadcast, Rather did "three one-hour rehearsals" and "was coached as if he were a candidate preparing for a debate or a pugilist preparing for a fight, rather than a journalist going into an interview," according to *Time*.[104] Bush remained skeptical, but Fuller and Ailes tried to convince him on the car ride from Andrews Air Force Base to his Senate office that the interview would be about Iran-Contra.[105] "Why don't we plan for it just in case," Ailes told the vice president.[106]

With Rather in the studio, the broadcast began with a five-minute preliminary report showing the contradictions between Bush's comments on Iran-Contra and the public record on the subject. The report suggested Bush first learned that the sale of weapons to the Islamic Republic was a direct arms-for-hostages deal in the summer of 1986, as opposed to discovering this fact after the scandal broke in the fall as he had said. Furthermore, the report showed that Donald Gregg, a member of Bush's staff, might have been involved in North's efforts to supply the contras with weapons.[107] Watching on a screen in his office, Bush grew irritated.[108]

Rather then began the interview portion by asking why Gregg was still on the vice president's staff. Bush fired back by saying that Gregg still had his confidence, and that CBS had misled him by telling him this was going to be a political profile. Rather cited polls showing that some voters, including some of his supporters, thought Bush was hiding something. "I am hiding something," responded Bush, offering his usual refrain. "You know what I'm hiding. What I told the president. That's the only thing." The two proceeded to go back and forth concerning the vice president's knowledge and awareness of various aspects of the scandal.[109]

Then, about six and a half minutes in, Bush dropped a bomb on the veteran journalist. Saying he wanted to talk about why he wanted to be president, Bush told Rather, "I don't think it's fair to judge a whole career. . . . It's not fair to judge my whole career by a rehash on Iran. How would you like it if I judged your career by those seven minutes when you walked off the set in New York? Would you like that? I have respect for you but I don't have respect for what you're doing here tonight."[110] The vice president was referring to an incident from the previous September when Rather, upset that his evening-news broadcast was going to be shortened due to coverage of the U.S. Open tennis tournament, had left the set, forcing the network to show a black screen for several minutes.[111] Contemporary accounts credited Ailes for the line, though Fuller said it was his idea in 2017.[112] Rather concluded by asking whether Bush would hold a news conference prior to the Iowa caucus and answer all questions regarding Iran-Contra. When Bush started to say he had already conducted numerous press conferences, Rather interrupted by remarking, "I gather that the answer is no," then abruptly ended the interview. Angered, the vice president vented to CBS staffers off the air: "I'm very upset about it. Tell your godamned network that if they want to talk to me to raise their hands at a press conference. No more Mr. Inside stuff after that."[113]

That night, calls flooded the network, and both CBS and the Bush campaign said that they overwhelmingly sided with the vice president. "I've been in the business for 20 years and I don't remember a reaction as strong as this one," observed the news director of the CBS affiliate in Charleston, South Carolina. The executive producer of the *CBS Evening News* claimed that he had been very clear with Teely a few days earlier about the nature of the interview, though Teely produced a letter suggesting that the interview was to be part of a series of "candidate profiles" the network was doing.[114]

"I need combat pay for last night, I'll tell you," remarked Bush the next day, while Rather apologized for cutting off the discussion on his following evening's broadcast.[115] Perceptions differed sharply by political persuasion. Sixty-six percent of Republicans believed the vice president had done a "good job" in the interview, while only 22 percent of Republicans thought Rather had "treated Bush fairly."[116] Meanwhile, 66 percent of Democrats thought Rather had been fair, while only 36 percent believed Bush had done a "good job."[117] "Our supporters were wildly enthusiastic," remembered Fuller.[118] Conservatives, long suspicious of both Bush and Rather, rallied to the vice president's defense. "All conservatives have to be sitting on the sidelines cheering him," commented Viguerie. "It's an article of faith that the media is biased against conservatives and Dan Rather embodies that bias."[119]

Atwater called the interview with Rather a "defining moment" for his candidate.[120] Yet while his campaign manager saw the benefit to Bush immediately, Fuller's initial reaction was different. "I wasn't so sure. Bush wasn't so sure," he recalled, adding, "It did have an impact on the undecided voters that you know this guy's not a wimp." Standing up to Rather offered a sharp rebuke to the *Newsweek* "Wimp Factor" cover for Bush, thought Fuller: "By the time the night was over we realized that he had in fact you know caused a lot of people to see him differently. . . . It ended up being more important than we thought."[121] Though the Bush campaign saw the incident with Rather as a plus, polls taken a week later showed that the percentage of Republicans who thought the vice president had strong leadership qualities remained unchanged from before the interview.[122]

At this time, the long and byzantine primary process in Michigan finally came to a close. Upset by Bush's legal victories overruling decisions made by the state committee the Robertson and Kemp forces controlled, many of the reverend's backers left the regular county conventions to conduct their own.[123] Fearing a third-place finish, the Kemp campaign, after allying with the Robertson people, joined with the vice president.[124] "We saw an opportunity to hurt Bush and make him look bad in Michigan, for Kemp to get a bunch of delegates so we made a deal with Robertson," said Charlie Black, Kemp's campaign manager. "And then that fell through. You just couldn't work and trust them, so we went and made a deal with Bush instead."[125]

When the state convention met at the end of January, Bush won thirty-seven delegates, Kemp won thirty-two, and Robertson, who had been poised to win a majority just a few months earlier, garnered only eight. Dole chose not to compete. Frustrated, Robertson's people held their own convention and chose a competing slate, preparing for a battle over recognition at the national convention. Nevertheless, the Bush campaign declared victory. "We've come back from the dead in Michigan," exclaimed national political director Rich Bond.[126]

With Michigan over, attention turned to the homestretch in Iowa, as the battle between Bush and Dole remained very personal. Continuing the attempt to undermine Dole's everyman credentials, Bush campaign materials said that the Doles lived in "Washington's posh Watergate complex," noting, "He and his wife are millionaires and had an income of $2.19 million from 1982 to 1986."[127] Though his aides warned against it, Dole "angrily confronted Bush on the floor of the Senate, demanding an apology and waiving the Bush press release," according to *Newsweek*.[128] The battle between the two front-runners crowded out most of the discussion of the other candidates, and some feared the back-and-forth between the two political veterans could imperil the party's chances in November.[129]

One of the major reasons for the personal nature of the attacks between Bush and Dole was their ideological similarity. Both were moderate conservatives running campaigns designed to move the GOP somewhat toward the center after the conservative turn of the Reagan years. Bush repeatedly talked of being the "education president," pledging to implement more aggressive environmental enforcement policies. Dole stressed the need for the party to be more compassionate, and he released his own environmental program that implicitly criticized Reagan's EPA and Department of Interior.[130] With so many similarities with regard to the issues, biography, ethics, and leadership credentials moved to the forefront of the debate.

Among the more conservative candidates, Kemp began to gain some altitude in New Hampshire, while Robertson remained third in the polls in Iowa, far behind Bush and Dole. But the reverend continued to amass support from evangelicals for his "invisible army," some of whom were Democrats who changed their affiliation just to vote for him, and many of whom were politically active for the first time. "Few of those interviewed said they would be taking part in the caucuses if Mr. Robertson was not running," wrote R. W. Apple in the *New York Times*.[131]

Robertson's emergence certainly surprised his campaign rivals. "We [the Kemp campaign] didn't anticipate the Pat Robertson phenomenon," recalled Black. "I'm not sure anybody did before it happened."[132] Bush's campaign was caught off guard as well; as Fuller remembered, "The Robertson appeal was something that was new. We didn't really know how to exactly deal with it. It was very much outside the realm of I guess maybe what all of us were expecting or had experienced in campaigns before."[133]

Dole maintained a 37-percent-to-23-percent advantage over Bush in the final *Des Moines Register* poll, with Robertson ranked third at 13 percent and Kemp fourth with 11 percent. A closer look at the poll, released the day before the voting, revealed storm clouds for Bush as well as sunny skies for Robertson. Among those definitely attending the caucuses, Dole still led with 35 percent of voter support—but Bush fell to 20 percent, and Robertson rose to 19 percent, a statistical tie. And the passion of the Bush voters vis-à-vis the reverend's backers potentially spelled serious trouble for the vice president.

"Robertson's supporters are especially committed," wrote Kenneth Pins in the *Register*. "While four out of 10 supporters of Bush and Dole say they will definitely attend the caucuses, nearly two-thirds of Robertson's supporters say that."[134] Understanding the peril his candidacy faced, Bush dictated in his diary: "Nervous. Gloom and doom amongst the campaign people. There is a feeling that we are going to get beat. The question is how bad."[135]

The vice president's fears were fully realized, as Dole cruised to his expected victory, winning 37 percent of the vote. Pundits credited the win to his organization and his status as a politician from a neighboring state, as well as to the endorsement of hometown senator Charles Grassley. "The people of Iowa decided Bob Dole can make a difference," remarked the victorious Kansan in his characteristic third-person style.[136]

Stunning the political world, Robertson scored 25 percent of the vote to finish an impressive second, with Bush falling to a disappointing third at 19 percent. "It's a victory for those who want Americans to be No. 1 in the world, and want to restore the greatness of America through moral strength," declared a jubilant Robertson.[137] With a base of support among working-class social conservatives, he led among those with a high-school education or less, as well as with union members.[138] Polls showed that 60 percent of Robertson voters were first-time caucus-goers, as he delivered the former Democrats and new voters he promised.[139] The reverend's get-out-the-vote operation impressed observers, including Estrich: "I swear to god every church bus in Iowa was on the highway on that Monday night and you knew something was happening."[140] Indeed, with a mere fourteen paid staffers, Robertson turned out more voters than any Democrat the same evening. To put that in perspective, Senator Simon, who finished second among the Democrats, had over 150 campaign employees.[141]

Robertson's showing deeply concerned the GOP establishment because of the polarizing nature of his politics. "We're going to reap the whirlwind from these right-wing religious nuts," fumed a Republican strategist.[142] In his diary a few weeks later, Bush said the televangelist's supporters reminded him of the Birchers he had known in Houston, and the vice president feared Robertson voters would not be team players in the fall, predicting, "They will destroy this party if they're permitted to take over."[143] On the other hand, religious conservatives were obviously quite pleased, with one activist commenting, "It [the reverend's success] proves that evangelicals are a major base of support in the Republican Party."[144] It remained to be seen, however, whether Robertson could translate his success from a low-turnout caucus to primaries where he would have to win over a much broader electorate.

Televangelist Pat Robertson's surprising second-place finish among Republicans in the Iowa caucus demonstrated the growing power of the Christian right in the GOP. (AP Photo / Peter Southwick)

Finishing third behind Robertson in a state he had won eight years earlier made Bush the biggest loser—he garnered 17,000 fewer votes than he had in 1980. The vice president's effort was hindered by a series of problems, ranging from the weak farm economy, to Reagan's lower popularity in the Hawkeye State, to constant questions concerning Iran-Contra. While the Rather interview gave Bush a temporary boost, in the end, it might have led to more questions about the arms deal.[145] Some also said Bush had departed from the more user-friendly campaign style he had employed as a little-known former congressman in 1980, because the Secret Service and his staff prevented the incumbent vice president from getting close to the voters.[146] Seeing blood in the water, Dole's people went for the jugular, with campaign manager Bill Brock saying, "It must be considered a devastating loss for Vice President Bush."[147] Bush responded, "This is the beginning. I can't say that I'm not disappointed, but I'm not down, I will guarantee you that."[148] In his diary, he dictated, "It's really gloomy."[149]

Kemp finished fourth with 11 percent of the vote, losing the momentum among conservatives to Robertson. After the poor Iowa showing, "they [the media] kind of quit covering him," Black remembered. Du Pont finished with 7 percent support, and Haig came in last with virtually no support.[150]

Robertson's showing represented a key moment in Republican politics, further cementing the importance of working-class social conservatives to

Bush's Triumph · 119

the party. Nationally, the reverend's backers were more likely to have lower incomes, as well as to be more distrustful of key institutions than traditional Republicans. Not thinking the country was in strong shape, only 47 percent of Robertson voters thought things were going well in 1988, compared with 76 percent of the vice president's supporters. Robertson's people were also less likely to feel that their lives had improved as a result of Reaganomics. Sixty-two percent of them made less than $30,000, compared with 44 percent of Bush supporters.[151]

Virtually all Robertson voters said that religion was important, as opposed to four-fifths of Bush backers. Nearly 60 percent of the reverend's supporters prayed several times a day, while three-quarters of them considered themselves born-again. In comparison, 31 percent of the vice president's voters prayed multiple times daily, and 42 percent of them identified as born-again. Unsurprisingly, Robertson backers were significantly less supportive of gay rights, and 36 percent of them thought abortion should not be permitted under any circumstances, while only 12 percent of Bush backers expressed such views.[152]

While the religious right became a major factor in GOP politics during the Reagan years, by the late 1980s the Moral Majority, the leading Christian conservative organization, was struggling financially. The televangelist scandals of the era had damaged the movement. After the end of the Robertson campaign, Ralph Reed, who backed Kemp in 1988, used the reverend's mailing lists to start the Christian Coalition in 1989. "The genesis [of the new organization] was Pat Robertson's 1988 presidential bid," according to Reed. "Robertson's candidacy, like the Goldwater campaign of 1964 and the McGovern campaign of 1972, was a watershed moment that gave the activists and leaders of a previously marginalized community a chance to play in the big leagues."[153] After the Moral Majority closed up shop, Reed and Robertson's new organization supplanted it as the political arm of social conservatives, playing an instrumental role in the Republican takeover of Congress in 1994 and George W. Bush's primary victory over Senator John McCain of Arizona in 2000.

The Robertson campaign also shaped GOP politics in the long run by changing the nature of the Iowa caucus. Eight years earlier, the elder Bush had won by running as a pro-choice, moderate Republican. The voters Robertson activated in 1988 paved the way for future wins by a very different kind of GOP candidate: pro-life Christian conservative favorites such as Arkansas governor Mike Huckabee, Pennsylvania senator Rick Santorum, and Texas senator Ted Cruz, who finished first in Iowa in 2008, 2012, and 2016, respectively.

For Bush, New Hampshire was now do-or-die. "We could see a path to victory without winning New Hampshire," remarked Fuller, "but it was going to be much more difficult without New Hampshire. So it was pretty much seen as a must win situation."[154] According to New Hampshire governor John Sununu, who was backing the vice president, George and Barbara Bush were "both a bit down" after the Iowa loss. But he reassured the couple: "My message was clear: 'Iowa picks corn. New Hampshire picks presidents.'" Sununu remembered, "The campaign was ready to cash in on the fund of goodwill and support it had accumulated over the past year. I was confident that he [Bush] could and would sail to victory, and I told them so: 'New Hampshire will be about a ten-point victory,' I told the Bushes—and I meant it."[155] Barbara Bush, however, recalled Sununu telling her a year later that he actually didn't believe they were going to win.[156]

Bush arrived in the Granite State with important advantages that he didn't have in Iowa. Unlike the Hawkeye State, New Hampshire had a strong economy. Reagan was also very popular there, making Bush's ties to the president a plus. While he had trailed or been even with Dole most of the year in Iowa, the vice president had led him by twenty points in New Hampshire, though the Kansas senator was quickly closing the gap with his momentum from the Iowa win.[157] Yet Dole's rise was somewhat blunted by all the attention on Robertson, who was unlikely to be as much of a force in a higher-turnout primary in a state with relatively few evangelicals.[158]

The vice president had to get to work quickly. When Reagan lost to Bush in Iowa in 1980, he had several weeks to regain his stride—but Bush would only have eight days. "I'm going to work my heart out over the next few days," declared Bush, "because I want to be, and I think I'm going to be, the next president."[159] Andy Card ran the ground operation, and adjustments had to be made to break with the imperial style of Iowa. "We did make changes in New Hampshire in terms of trying to reduce the footprint if you will of the campaign," Fuller said. "They wanted people they could relate to. We did change the way we advanced events and did events. . . . We managed to give it a different look and feel."[160]

By Friday, February 12, Dole had pulled ahead in the polls, though his lead of 32 percent to 29 percent meant the race remained within the margin of error. Like Dole, Robertson also worked to build on his Iowa success. In a state where Kemp's tax-cutting message resonated, the reverend again fought the Buffalo congressman for the title of conservative champion, running a commercial that ended by declaring, "Pat Robertson is fast becoming the conservative choice."[161]

With Dole charging, Bush faced a defining moment. On February 12, his advisers showed him what became known as "the straddle ad." The term "Senator Straddle" came up in the discussion of framing the ad, Fuller said, and "he [Ailes] loved it. It was shorthand. It was easy to remember." Yet selling the commercial would be difficult because, as Fuller recalled, "We all knew that George Bush wouldn't like it."[162] In the ad, the narrator says Dole "straddled" on the INF treaty and oil-import tax, and "STRADDLE" appears in caps with Dole's picture on either side. The narrator goes on to say, "George Bush says he won't raise taxes period. Bob Dole straddled. And he just won't promise not to raise taxes. And you know what that means." With the word "TAXES" in the middle of the screen and Dole's image on both sides, the text below reads, "He can't say no."[163] After watching the spot, Bush responded, "I just think it's negative. I just don't know if it will work."[164]

The next day, Ailes and Atwater again pushed Bush to approve the ad. "George, I don't think it's so bad," commented Barbara Bush, and the vice president said, "Well you guys know more about the state," leaving Sununu confused. Atwater took this response as a go-ahead to put the commercial on the air.[165] By this time, according to Ailes, "the station logs were closed," but Sununu and Atwater were able to get the ad to air on a station in New Hampshire, while Ailes got it shown on a Boston affiliate.[166]

Expecting such an attack, a Dole staffer recommended an antitax ad to preemptively "inoculate" the senator against those charges. A few days before Bush's intracampaign debate, the Dole campaign tried to tape a commercial where the candidate promised not to increase tax rates, but Dole fumbled the line. The campaign then made another ad using antitax comments the Kansas senator made during a speech, airing it once before Richard Wirthlin, Dole's pollster, took it down, declaring, "We do not have a tax problem and we do not need a tax spot on the air." Yet another ad was made on the subject, but the campaign believed—wrongly—that the deadline for ads had passed.[167] On Saturday, February 13, two key things occurred—the straddle ad began to air, and Wirthlin told Dole he was going to win New Hampshire.[168]

The next day the candidates debated in Goffstown. Among a myriad of points, the Bush camp laid out its strategy: "The debate likely will be a one-hour scramble between the candidates to out right wing each other, and to derail you [Bush] by pushing you to the left. You must use the debate to reinforce the conservative values and issue positions that appeal to your supporters in New Hampshire." Urging their man to stay close to his president, who was very popular in the state, staffers added, "For New Hampshire Republicans, the primary is more than anything else a race to see who is the

The remaining GOP candidates before the last debate prior to the New Hampshire primary: Vice President George Bush, televangelist Pat Robertson, Representative Jack Kemp, former Delaware governor Pete du Pont, and Senator Bob Dole. Former secretary of state Al Haig had dropped out two days earlier. (AP Photo / Jim Cole)

legitimate heir to Ronald Reagan. *You must affirmatively show that you are that person by embracing Ronald Reagan at every opportunity. In addition, you should emphasize the attacks on your positions are attacks on the positions of the President.*"[169]

Bush and Dole generally avoided confronting each other throughout the evening. In a key moment, however, du Pont demanded Dole sign a pledge not to raise taxes, and the senator resisted, saying, "Give it to George. I have to read it first." This response was likely a reference to Dole's critique of Bush for supporting the INF treaty without reading it.[170] Bush campaign officials cheered the exchange with Pinkerton, explaining, "It was so great for us, I mean we knew du Pont wasn't going anywhere, but we knew he was taking on Dole right in front of us, and it worked."[171]

On the final day before the primary, a boost arrived for Bush in the form of Senator Goldwater, the godfather of the modern Right, who came to New Hampshire to endorse the vice president. "He was terrific," Fuller remarked, "He could go anywhere and . . . we would draw crowds and we would draw a lot of enthusiasm."[172] Goldwater also taped a five-minute commercial where he declared, "I believe in George Bush. He's the man to continue the conservative revolution we started 24 years ago."[173]

By this point, polls showed Bush beginning to gain ground and the race in a near dead heat. Dole's pollster, however, still believed his candidate would win.[174] And even if the vice president won in New Hampshire, "Mr. Bush has no chance of the sweeping victory here that he once thought he could rely upon—and which he now needs so badly to erase the memories of his debacle in Iowa," wrote Apple on the day of the primary.[175]

Confounding the polls, Bush not only won but defeated Dole by nine points on primary day, winning by a margin of 38 percent to 28 percent. "Reports of my death were greatly exaggerated," declared the vice president.[176] The straddle ad and the Goldwater endorsement might have made the difference, as the vice president garnered an edge among those deciding over the last three days, while Dole won with voters who made their decision in the three days following his Iowa win.[177] As with the Democratic primaries, it seemed as if the polls were extremely volatile and subject to change depending on last-second television ads and maneuvers.

Bush's ties to Reagan helped him considerably, as 82 percent of voters approved of the president's performance, and the vice president led among that group 41 percent to 23 percent. With the state's open primary, independents could participate in either contest. Dole won independent voters by ten points, but this advantage was more than offset by the vice president's identical lead with the Republicans, who made up 60 percent of the primary voters.[178] Sununu's organization also came in for a good deal of credit for the victory. Back in the pack, Kemp finished a distant third with 13 percent, followed by du Pont, who received only 10 percent despite the endorsement of the conservative *Manchester Union Leader*. In a primary in a state where only one voter out of every ten was evangelical, Robertson finished last, at 9 percent.[179]

But the fireworks didn't end with the voting that evening. With Bush in the studio, Tom Brokaw hosted a dual interview with Dole via remote during NBC News's primary coverage. "We didn't know it was going to be a split screen. I'm sure Dole didn't either," recalled Fuller.[180] Brokaw asked Dole whether he had anything to say to the vice president. Angered over the straddle ad and what he saw as other unfair attacks, the Kansas senator replied, "Stop lying about my record," immediately rekindling memories of the 1976 vice-presidential debate and his image as an angry politician. Watching at home, Dole's communications consultant, Larry McCarthy, said, "It's over."[181] Ailes agreed, saying, "It was 'good night, Bob.'"[182]

Having come to bury Bush in the snows of New Hampshire, the media now praised him as the leader once again. "New Hampshire's bottom line: George Bush is again the man to beat for the Republican presidential nomination," wrote Jacob Lamar in *Time*.[183] "Talk of the 'inevitability' of Mr. Dole's nomination, which followed his victory in the Iowa caucuses last week," wrote E. J. Dionne, "was quickly giving way to similar chatter about Mr. Bush."[184] Dole and his campaign realized they had missed a golden opportunity. "We should have had something to offset Goldwater, something to dominate the news," reflected the Kansas senator, while Brock admitted he had erred in not developing a response to the straddle ad.[185]

Recriminations followed in the Dole camp. "When things go wrong, Dole's not the type to blame himself," commented one aide. While the

Kansas senator could look forward to good opportunities in upcoming contests in Minnesota and South Dakota, he was clearly outgunned by Bush in the South. The vice president had a much stronger organization in the region, and he would again benefit from Reagan's overwhelming popularity among Republicans. "We're not ready to fight on several fronts at once," analyzed one Dole supporter, "and we're not ready for Super Tuesday," when there would be seventeen contests on one day.[186]

The following week, Dole did win the South Dakota primary and the Minnesota caucus, with 55 and 43 percent of the vote, respectively.[187] Anticipating additional defeats in the Midwest, the Bush campaign had pulled out of both states, with Atwater claiming the candidate was focusing on the big prize of Super Tuesday.[188] "The vice president just took a walk on both those states," said Bill Lacy of the Dole campaign, "and we therefore really didn't get any real stature out of those wins."[189] Robertson finished second in both states, and turnout in Minnesota increased significantly, with local officials crediting the reverend for bringing in new voters. Kemp, who was hoping to jump-start his campaign by winning conservatives in Minnesota, finished a disappointing third.[190]

Heading to the South Carolina primary on March 5, Bush held similar advantages to those he had enjoyed in New Hampshire—Reagan was extremely popular in the Palmetto State, and the incumbent Republican governor supported him. In fact, at the behest of the Bush campaign, Governor Carroll Campbell had moved up the primary ahead of Super Tuesday to give the vice president momentum going into the regional primary.[191] Dole's staff did not want him to compete in the state, but after Senator Strom Thurmond, the biggest name in South Carolina politics and a longtime colleague, backed him, he felt duty bound to make an effort. At the same time, the Kansas senator's campaign struggled with internal problems. Brock fired two key staffers, telling them to get their luggage and leave as the campaign plane landed in Florida.[192]

With its large population of conservative Christians, South Carolina seemed like a good fit for Robertson, and the Bush people believed he was a greater threat than Dole. To combat the reverend's appeal to evangelicals, Bush went to several religious colleges and privately told a group of ministers, "I believe in Jesus Christ as my personal savior and always will."[193] The reverend, however, hurt himself with missteps, fumbling the expectations game by declaring he would win South Carolina right after New Hampshire. Robertson also made some bizarre statements, claiming that he had known the locations of U.S. hostages in Lebanon and that the Bush campaign had engineered the revelation of a scandal involving Jimmy Swaggart, a prominent televangelist of the time, in the hopes of discrediting his campaign.[194] Meanwhile, Kemp split the support of the right wing of the Republican Party by staying in and hoping for a good showing in one of the nation's most conservative states.

In the end, Bush won a resounding victory, carrying every county in the state while garnering 49 percent of the vote. Dole managed to edge out Robertson for a second-place finish by a margin of 21 percent to 19 percent. Yet Lacy reflected, "Perhaps in retrospect we should have tried to take a walk on South Carolina to see if we couldn't downplay what was inevitably going to be a Bush win there."[195] The reverend underperformed with evangelicals, winning only a third of their vote. Kemp, despite a late burst of television spending, finished fourth, though he likely drained votes from Robertson, potentially costing him a second-place finish.[196] Atwater was pleased, as he had thought beforehand that a big win could give his candidate a "5-to-8-point bump on Super Tuesday," according to *Newsweek*.[197]

As Super Tuesday approached and his campaign experienced financial trouble, Dole's commercials grew tougher.[198] In three major Florida media markets, the Dole camp aired an ad showing a "man walking through a snowy field without leaving a trace ... a metaphor for Mr. Bush's record of public service." As viewers look at this image, the announcer intones, "He never left a single footprint." The ad, which the Dole campaign had chosen not to air in New Hampshire, suggested that the vice president had accomplished little in public life despite his extensive resume.[199] While campaigning in Missouri, Dole attacked Bush's electability: "The polls show that George Bush can't win in November." Meanwhile, another ad demanded that Bush level with the country regarding his role in Iran-Contra.[200]

But it was to no avail, as Bush cruised to an overwhelming victory, winning 16 of 17 states with 55 percent of the total vote, earning 578 of the 707 delegates available.[201] Robertson could only manage a victory in the Washington caucuses, while Dole came up winless. "A clean sweep. A shutout," exclaimed Atwater, while Bush declared, "I'm now convinced I will be the President of the United States."[202] Refusing to drop out, Dole pledged to make a last stand in Illinois the following week, but "barring some unforeseeable catastrophe," wrote Howard Fineman in *Newsweek*, Super Tuesday had "effectively ended the Republican primary campaign."[203]

After another disappointing result, Kemp dropped out while insisting he would run for the White House again someday.[204] Though clearly more of an ideological heir to Reagan than Bush or Dole, Kemp never picked up steam as a candidate, and he had to fight with Robertson for the support of the conservative wing of the party. In the *New York Times*, William Safire expressed befuddlement at the congressman's weak showing, writing, "His time will come. I am puzzling out why he did not get off the ground with Republicans this year and will pass that along."[205] Given Kemp's organizational problems, Republican campaign adviser Ed Rollins thought the effort was doomed from early on. Black later observed, "Jack had good name ID and popularity among the activists and with some primary voters but not nearly as much identity [and] hard name ID as Bush or Dole."[206]

Further cementing his nomination, Bush won a clear victory over Dole in Illinois on March 15, garnering 55 percent of the vote to the senator's 36 percent. Robertson's poll numbers left him way back. The vice president's coalition followed a familiar pattern, as he performed extremely well among the three-quarters of voters who approved of Reagan, while Dole won among the one-fifth that disapproved of the president. Dole's attacks on Bush's electability fell flat, with 70 percent of Republicans believing the vice president would be the strongest candidate for the party in November. "Illinois is probably the most typical of American states," declared Governor Jim Thompson, a Bush supporter. "And when George Bush defeats Bob Dole by this extraordinary margin, I think that's the end of this talk of electability."[207] Another common element in the vice president's success was backing from the party establishment. Thompson, like Sununu in New Hampshire and Campbell in South Carolina, aided Bush's cause significantly. Even though the vice president now had 70 percent of the delegates necessary for the nomination, and many Dole supporters considered Bush's candidacy in the general election a fait accompli, the Kansas senator said he would continue on.[208]

Dole pressed on to Wisconsin, site of the next primary, but by March 25, he seemed to recognize his fate, saying the vice president's nomination was a "foregone conclusion."[209] Then Kemp endorsed Bush on March 28 in Milwaukee, while polls showed the vice president with a two-to-one lead.[210] Facing the inevitable, the Kansas senator dropped out the following day.[211]

What brought about Bush's relatively easy victory? First, the vice president's links to President Reagan—who was enormously popular among the Republican faithful—gave him a tremendous advantage. These ties helped neutralize the ideological concerns that some rank-and-file conservatives might have had about Bush, making it an uphill battle for Dole. "I'm sort of running against the ghost of Ronald Reagan," the senator fretted at one point.[212] Dionne also argued that Dole's stance as a "neutral commentator," as opposed to a "partisan Republican," on Iran-Contra and other issues might have made it "easier for Mr. Bush to run as a true believer in Mr. Reagan."[213] The party establishment was much stronger in 1988 than it was when

Bush's son Jeb ran unsuccessfully for president in 2016, and the backing of governors in key states helped propel the vice president to victory. Bush also put together a strong team, while Dole's campaign was plagued by organizational problems from the outset as the senator's micromanagement hindered his effort.[214] In the end, Bush won an overwhelming victory by historic standards and received 55 percent of the primary vote, the third-highest share of a party's electorate in an open race since 1972.[215]

But despite the final margin, Dole was poised to potentially knock Bush out with a victory in New Hampshire, and it might have been one moment that shifted the entire race. Lacy ascribed Dole's loss to a variety of factors but cited one in particular: "Our failure to react—and this is a very specific situation—to the [straddle] ad in New Hampshire sort of sealed our fate."[216] Regardless of the negative impression left by Dole's "stop lying about my record" outburst afterward, Lacy concluded, "[The] bottom line in our assessment was that if we didn't win New Hampshire, there was really no way we could come out on top."[217] As with Vermont governor Howard Dean's scream following his debilitating loss in the Iowa caucus in 2004, the damage had already been done.

Bush's victorious campaign and Dole's losing effort reflected a significant shift in American politics. Both men sought to soften the edges of Reagan-style conservatism, while Kemp, who was a truer policy heir of the incumbent president, did not get far. Though it would atrophy significantly over the next three decades, suburban Republicanism remained a vital force in the 1980s and still played a moderating role in the party. After the stagflation and malaise of the 1970s, unemployment and inflation were both low again. With prosperity restored, the electorate turned its attention to quality-of-life concerns, like education, environmental protection, and policies to help those who didn't share in the 1980s boom. As his advisers had suggested following the 1986 midterms, simply regurgitating Reaganism was not going to be a winning philosophy for Bush. The more moderate message previewed the vice president's pledge to seek "a kinder, gentler, America" during the general election, as well as the centrist "New Democrat" philosophy promoted by Bill Clinton during his 1992 campaign and throughout his presidency. At least at the presidential level, American politics was moving back toward the center.

Bush officially wrapped up the nomination after the Pennsylvania primary on April 26, as the vice president garnered the necessary delegates earlier than any major-party candidate in two decades.[218] But there were potential downsides to Bush's early lock on the Republican nod. As soon as the vice president won Illinois, a GOP consultant presciently observed, "The good news is that he knows he is the nominee now; the bad news is that he becomes invisible for five months with Democrats beating on Bush."[219]

With Dukakis's victories over Jackson dominating the news, polls showed Bush trailing the Massachusetts governor by 10 points in mid-May. Perhaps more troubling was the fact that a little over a quarter of voters who backed Reagan in 1984 now favored Dukakis. Reagan's approval rating, crucial to Bush's chances in the fall, stood at a solid but unspectacular 48 percent. Fifty-four percent of Americans were dissatisfied with the way things were going in the country, with only 41 percent satisfied.[220] Furthermore, a closer examination of the results suggested Americans might be looking for a more activist federal government in 1988. In March 1980, a survey showed voters preferring less government to more government by a whopping margin of 54 percent to 32 percent. But by May 1988, sentiments had changed significantly, as the public was now split down the middle on the question, 43 percent to 44 percent. Dole's and Bush's more moderate primary campaigns reflected this national mood. "Bigger government has not been this popular since November 1976," wrote Dionne, "the last time the Democrats won a Presidential election."[221]

Meanwhile, Bush took tentative steps to demonstrate his independence from President Reagan. In May, the administration was in negotiations with Panamanian strongman Manuel Noriega, offering to drop federal drug-trafficking charges against him if he stepped down from power. Within the administration, Secretary of State George Schultz was the strongest proponent of this course, while Bush held serious reservations. While speaking in Los Angeles on May 18, Bush commented on the policy without using Noriega's name, declaring, "Drug dealers are domestic terrorists, killing kids and cops, and they should be treated as such. I won't bargain with terrorists, and I won't bargain with drug dealers either, whether they're on U.S. or foreign soil."[222]

Asked by *Washington Post* reporter David Hoffman whether Bush's statement was a sign of disagreement over how to deal with Noriega, Fuller told him yes—on background. Then Hoffman reported this information, and Fuller and others confirmed it on the record when asked. "This is fantastic," remarked Atwater. The news provided Bush a chance to show some of his own identity, and the vice president noted that people interpreted his position as a break with Reagan, writing in his diary, "I hate doing this, and I don't feel comfortable with it! I like the president so much, and yet, he's wrong on this one." Fuller said this was the most helpful development for Bush between clinching the nomination and attending the Republican convention. "It was all very complicated whenever it came to anything related to, you know, stepping anywhere away from Ronald Reagan," observed Fuller. "He [the vice president] didn't want to do it. He didn't feel it was the right thing to do until the convention as he said. But we knew that we had to find ways to begin to differentiate him from the administration."[223]

To develop Bush's strategy for the fall, pollster Bob Teeter organized a series of focus groups in which moderators discussed the candidates and their positions with a selected number of voters. Of the eight conducted by the Bush campaign, the two held in Paramus, New Jersey, shortly before Memorial Day would prove the most significant. The participants were twenty middle-class Catholics who were part of a vital swing constituency of Reagan Democrats—that is, Democrats who had voted for the president in 1984 but were behind Dukakis at this point.[224] All of the Group of Six, as Bush's campaign team was called, attended, with the exception of Mosbacher, and Atwater remarked, "It was almost startling how little they [the focus group participants] knew about either of the candidates." He added, "It was an issueless campaign."[225]

Using Pinkerton's research, the moderator then presented a number of Dukakis's positions, including the furlough program and his veto of the bill mandating public school teachers to lead students in reciting the Pledge of Allegiance. After hearing about these and other issues, 40 percent of the voters in one group switched to Bush, while 60 percent in another did the same.[226] "We had time to sit down over a three-day period and use those results," said Atwater, "along with a lot of other things that were going on, to, in effect, fashion strategy."[227]

Though Teeter's polls showed the vice president falling eighteen points behind Dukakis, Bush's advisers again had to prod their candidate to go on the attack. At his summer home in Kennebunkport, Maine, Bush watched videotapes of the Paramus sessions one evening and was "stunned by what he saw." The film revealed, among other things, that the group believed the Massachusetts governor "was more conservative than Bush and potentially tougher on drugs." After watching, the vice president concluded, "They don't know this guy's record. They don't know enough about him." With Dukakis, just as with Dole, the vice president made the pivotal decision to try to define his opponent—or to go negative on him, depending on the point of view.[228]

From May 29 to June 3, Reagan held another summit with Gorbachev, this time in Moscow, marking the final shift away from the "evil empire" rhetoric of the U.S. president's first term. While the two leaders put the finishing touches on the INF treaty, there were no major breakthroughs—though the meeting continued Reagan's political comeback from the nadir of Iran-Contra. This would aid his vice president and present challenges for Dukakis. As Estrich later analyzed, "We saw the increases in Ronald Reagan's popularity beginning with the summit in Moscow and continuing from then."[229]

The effect, however, had not yet been seen in polls, and as the nominating season ended on June 7 with the California primary, Apple deemed Bush the underdog in the race. As far as vice presidents went, he was in a "much weaker position" than Richard Nixon had occupied at this point in 1960 while trying to succeed Dwight Eisenhower. And Bush was in "almost as much trouble" as Hubert Humphrey had been at this time in 1968 while attempting to succeed Lyndon Johnson. Like the Paramus focus group, however, the polls showed that Bush and Dukakis were not well defined in the minds of most voters, with a quarter of the electorate unsure of their view of Bush, and a fifth uncertain of their view of Dukakis. "Obviously, with opinion still so incompletely formed," Apple wrote, "substantial swings in sentiment are a strong possibility."[230]

Though it lacked the fireworks of its Democratic counterpart, the 1988 Republican primary also revealed some of the roots of the future of American politics. Pat Robertson's campaign was a central moment in the rise of the religious right, helping to pave the wave for social conservatives to play a pivotal role in the politics of the 1990s and beyond. Dole's and Bush's primary campaigns showed that American politics was moving back toward the center at the national level. And most surprisingly, Donald Trump's flirtation with a presidential run—a mere footnote at the time—offered an early window into the themes he would emphasize in his presidential run almost three decades later.

Like his general election opponent Dukakis, George Bush might not have had the most compelling message, but he was able to employ a superior organization to grind out a victory. In the end, he won relatively easily over Dole, though he nearly lost it all in New Hampshire. As the fall campaign got underway, however, Bush was well behind his Democratic challenger, and his attempt to become the first incumbent vice president to move into the White House since 1836 looked like an uphill battle.

5   The Fight Begins

At some point during the summer of 1988, Atwater put a three-by-five note card in his pocket. The card roughly outlined the Bush strategy to define Dukakis: "High tax, high spending... to the left of Carter-Mondale in opposing every defense program... McGovern/Kennedy/Jackson liberal."[1] Trailing significantly as the general election began, the vice president followed Atwater's script by criticizing Dukakis over the issues emerging out of the Paramus focus group. For a few weeks, Bush gained ground in the polls, pounding away at the governor on the Pledge of Allegiance veto and the furlough program. Labeling Dukakis an out-of-the mainstream 1960s liberal, he capitalized on long-standing concerns that Democrats were soft on crime and insufficiently tough and patriotic—stigmas that had plagued the party since the Vietnam era. These issues would eventually prove central to the fall campaign, as Bush's tactics mirrored those Nixon and Reagan had used to defeat Democrats in four of the previous five elections.

As with the primary season, the period from the end of the nominating process to the Democratic convention in Atlanta also revealed more of the roots of the future of American politics. The Dukakis campaign's innovative efforts with regard to fundraising led to the effective end of the post-Watergate campaign-finance reforms. By exploiting the soft-money loophole, the Dukakis camp found a way around the limits on donations that Congress had imposed into the 1970s, paving the way for the campaign-finance scandals of the 1990s.

At the convention, an American political party debated Palestinian self-determination for the first time. Some in the Jackson wing of the Democratic Party raised the issue, revealing growing support for the Palestinians among progressives. While there was no vote on the plank for Palestinian autonomy, the emergence of this subject foreshadowed a divide within the party that would grow over the next three decades.

And Bill Clinton would introduce himself to the nation, giving the nominating speech for his fellow governor and moderate Democrat. In a moment that was supposed to launch his presidential ambitions, however, the Arkansan nearly short-circuited his White House aspirations with a disastrous performance. Thus was the ground laid for his first national political comeback.

In the meantime, the focus moved to Dukakis, as he claimed the center by naming Texas senator Lloyd Bentsen as his running mate while trying to make peace with Jesse Jackson. Following a strong convention cemented by a well-received acceptance speech, the governor regained his momentum, leaving Atlanta with a big polling advantage and the White House seemingly in sight.

The upheaval of the 1960s transformed American politics. Crime rose dramatically, and Nixon ran on a "law and order" platform in 1968, blaming Democrats, cultural permissiveness, and "activist" Supreme Court decisions protecting criminal defendants, like *Miranda v. Arizona (1966)*, for disorder in the streets. Republicans attacked liberal judges and called for tougher sentencing for criminals, including the death penalty. In one 1968 ad with images of cops, crimes, and drugs in the background, Nixon declares, "We owe it to the decent and law-abiding citizens of America to take the offensive against the criminal forces that threaten their peace and their security," concluding, "I pledge to you the wave of crime is not going to be the wave of the future in America."[2] Democrats often countered that poverty and racism were responsible for these urban problems, while liberals sometimes alleged that calls for "law and order" were simply thinly veiled racial appeals. These explanations often proved unsatisfying to much of the Democratic Party's traditional working-class base.

After the violence by protesters at the Democratic National Convention in Chicago that same year, Republicans also attacked Democrats as unpatriotic, drawing on their perceived associations with the more radical elements of the antiwar movement. "Dissent is a necessary ingredient of change," Nixon states in one ad. The commercial shows images of angry antiwar protesters and burning buildings. "But in a system of government that provides for peaceful change there is no cause that justifies resort to violence," he continues. "Let us recognize that the first civil right of every American is to be free from domestic violence. So I pledge to you we shall have order in the United States," Nixon concludes.[3] Four years later, his chief of staff, H. R. Haldeman, alleged that opponents of a 1972 Nixon peace initiative were "consciously aiding and abetting the enemy of the United States."[4]

Along these same lines, going back to Joe McCarthy's attacks on the State Department in the early 1950s, Republicans had railed against the "elites," often questioning their loyalty. George Wallace used similar tactics in his independent and Democratic campaigns in the late 1960s and early

1970s, declaring in 1968 that he would take all the "briefcase-toting bureaucrats" implementing school integration and "throw their briefcases in the Potomac River." Four years later, he alleged, "The Democratic Party [once] reflected true expressions of the rank-and-file citizens. Long ago it became the party of the so-called intelligentsia. . . . It has been transformed into a party controlled by intellectual snobs, who ignore true expressions of rank-and-file citizens across America."[5] Nixon employed a more restrained version of this cultural populism in 1968 and 1972 to defend the silent majority from the depredations of intellectuals, antiwar activists, and bureaucrats. Reagan followed a similar strategy in his 1980 and 1984 campaigns. Such tactics proved quite effective in moving working-class Democrats into the Republican Party, successfully countering the economic populism espoused by New Deal Democrats and their descendants, like Gephardt and Jackson.

After being largely out of the picture since sewing up the nomination in March, Bush took the fight to Dukakis using this same playbook. During his victory celebration on the night of the California primary, the vice president attacked the governor for vetoing a bill requiring teachers to lead students in saying the Pledge of Allegiance. "Our immediate reaction was how preposterous it was that Bush thought such a matter could be made into a major issue in a national campaign," wrote campaign journalists Jack Germond and Jules Witcover. "So much for how we saw it."[6]

The issue dated to Dukakis's first term as governor, when the Massachusetts state legislature passed a law requiring teachers to direct students in reciting the pledge. If they did not comply, teachers would be fined "five dollars for every two weeks they fail to lead the pledge," according to a May 17, 1977, article in the *Boston Globe*. Dukakis asked the state supreme court for an advisory opinion, and the justices ruled five to two that such a bill would be unconstitutional. In doing so, they cited the precedent of *West Virginia State Board of Education v. Barnette*, a 1943 Supreme Court ruling that a Jehovah's Witness student in West Virginia did not have to participate in the pledge.[7] Dukakis then vetoed the bill, recalling, "I'm not a guy that signs unconstitutional bills."[8]

In overwhelming fashion, the state legislature overrode Dukakis's veto, with the House voting 201-27 and members singing "God Bless America" following the vote. The Senate did the same by a margin of 24-7, with one senator advocating the law's passage "in the name of all that's holy and good, apple pie, and motherhood."[9] Once enacted, however, the bill was never enforced.[10] Among those voting to override was Andy Card, and having already told Jim Pinkerton, the Bush campaign's director of research, about the furlough program, he added, "If you think that's bad, let me tell you about the pledge."[11]

According to Atwater, the vice president "jumped on the pledge of allegiance issue before anybody else in the campaign did. He felt very strongly about it. He believed that it was a legitimate difference between himself and Dukakis." The campaign manager added, "He [Bush] was amazed. He just said, 'This guy is just wrong on this.'" The campaign hierarchy also believed that the governor might play into Bush's hands by not understanding the symbolic importance of the issue. "His [Dukakis's] personality profile, which we took a look at, was of a guy who said, 'I'm right, you're wrong, and here are the reasons' with no regard to how or why people responded emotionally to an issue," said Ailes. "In other words, he may be right technically, but the American people react instinctively to issues like the flag, not technically."[12]

Switching the subject to crime, Bush went further at the Texas Republican Convention in Houston two days later, saying, "Michael Dukakis on crime is standard old-style '60s liberalism." Trying to puncture the governor's centrist image, he called him "a man who holds strong convictions and who speaks in moderate tones, but his views and values are too often, in my judgement, out of the mainstream." The vice president also contrasted his experience in the oil business with Dukakis's background, claiming his opponent was "born in Harvard Yard's boutique." Bush elaborated, "When I wanted to learn the ways of the world, I didn't go to the Kennedy School, I came to Texas, in 1948."[13]

Bush kept up the offensive against Dukakis, moving on to the furlough program. On June 18 in Illinois, Bush asked, "What did the Democratic Governor of Massachusetts think he was doing when he let convicted first-degree murderers out on weekend passes[?]" He went on to say, "I think that Governor Dukakis owes the people of the United States of America an explanation as to why he supported this outrageous program." Dukakis's press secretary responded that Reagan had presided over a furlough program as governor of California, that the federal government maintained such a program, and that crime had fallen in Massachusetts.[14] "I know of no responsible correctional program in this country, with very few exceptions, that doesn't involve furloughs," replied Dukakis himself on June 20.[15]

With regard to the furloughs, Dukakis did not initiate the program in question, as Governor Frank Sargent, a Republican, had signed the legislation into law in 1972. Nor was the Bay State unique in allowing furloughs. A 1984 survey showed that thirty-eight states had such programs, with supporters believing they provided incentives for inmates to behave well while preventing overcrowding and helping prisoners prepare for postprison life.[16] Though thirty-three states permitted some kind of release program for those imprisoned for life, Massachusetts was "the only state to permit furloughs for prisoners serving a life sentence without parole," according to Robin Toner in the *New York Times*. The Massachusetts State Supreme Court—not Dukakis—made prisoners serving life without parole eligible for furloughs because the law did not specifically exclude them. But "the Dukakis Administration long supported, and at times, actively defended, the practice of giving furloughs to inmates serving life without parole," wrote Toner. "In 1976 Mr. Dukakis refused to sign legislation that would have barred such prisoners from receiving furloughs and would have required a number of other restrictions." Dukakis claimed this was a "distinction without a difference," and that "premeditated murder is premeditated murder," with many other states allowing convicted murderers to leave on furlough.[17]

It was the story of William Horton, who was soon to be almost as well known as the candidates themselves, that made the furlough program so controversial, first in Massachusetts and then nationally. In 1974, Horton and two other men murdered Joseph Fournier, a seventeen-year-old boy from Lawrence, Massachusetts—though it's not clear whether Horton himself was the killer.[18] The following year, a court convicted Horton for first-degree murder, sentencing him to life in prison without parole. A decade later, in 1985, he became eligible for furloughs, taking nine of them without incident. While on his tenth in June 1986, he failed to return, and his whereabouts remained unknown for ten months until he terrorized a Maryland couple. "On April 3, 1987, Horton armed with a knife and gun, allegedly held up an Oxon Hill, MD. couple in their home for nearly 12 hours," wrote Bonnie Winston in the *Boston Globe*. "Maryland authorities said he tied up the man in the basement of the house, stabbed him and repeatedly raped the man's 24-year-old girlfriend."[19] Shortly thereafter, Horton was caught after a shootout with Maryland police.

This crime, along with investigations by the Lawrence *Eagle-Tribune*, led many to call for an end to furloughs for first-degree murderers, but Dukakis resisted an absolute ban, with the support of the *Boston Globe* editorial page. In October 1987, a Maryland judge sentenced Horton to two consecutive life terms as well as eighty-five years in prison, declaring, "This man should never draw a breath of clean, free air again. With all due respect to the commonwealth of Massachusetts, I'm afraid William Horton will never return there. I am not going to take the chance that he will be furloughed or released there."[20] Under pressure from the legislature and facing the possibility of a referendum on the subject while he ran for president, Dukakis signed a blanket ban on furloughs for lifers in March. The Bush campaign seized the issue. "By the time this election is over, Willie Horton will be a household name," Atwater told a "meeting of party operatives early in the summer."[21]

In a crucial moment, Bush mentioned the Horton story himself for the first time while speaking to the National Sheriffs' Association on June 22. "I'm opposed to these unsupervised weekend furloughs for first-degree murderers. Put me down as against that," remarked the vice president.[22] *NBC Nightly News* ran a story on the event, and as was sometimes the case, while the vice president didn't mention his race, the report showed Horton's picture. Observing the potency of the case with Reagan Democrats, GOP political consultant Roger Stone noted, "It's a perfect issue to demonstrate that Dukakis is a liberal elitist and that he does not share faith with those exact ethnic Americans he claims to be so close to."[23]

In the same speech, Bush also took aim at what would become another frequent target, the American Civil Liberties Union (ACLU). Alleging, "We've been held hostage by well-meaning and misguided politicians and judges who get their legal views from the A.C.L.U.," he added that the police had been hampered by court decisions limiting searches.[24] In this and other speeches, the vice president attempted to pin the liberal label on the governor, attacking Dukakis's opposition to the death penalty, contending that he would raise taxes, and declaring him soft on defense. "Bush started to paint the picture of Dukakis before Dukakis could," remarked one Democratic consultant.[25]

Some in the media believed these charges, especially the one concerning the Pledge of Allegiance, were weak and unpresidential. Noting that the Bush campaign wanted to do an ad on the pledge issue, Duke University law professor Walter Dellinger, citing the case law, wrote, "They should wait, and if they want to avoid embarrassing themselves, they shouldn't do one at all."[26] Speaking of both issues, Tom Wicker asserted, "Vice President Bush must have little to say of real national importance if he can think of nothing better than to picture Michael Dukakis as soft on crime and weak on patriotism." With regard to the furlough program, Wicker said it was similar to other states' programs, which are "generally regarded by penologists as a useful tool in reducing recidivism and helping criminals turn to a straight life."[27]

Opinions regarding the furlough program were not monolithic by any means. The *New York Times* editorial page said furloughs served a purpose for convicts who would be released in the near future and needed to prepare for life after prison. The paper also noted, "There was no such transition in sight for a Massachusetts murderer named Willie Horton. He had been serving a life sentence without parole." While criticizing the vice president's use of the issue, the *Times* did not exonerate his challenger, adding, "But Mr. Dukakis remains accountable: he oversaw, and overlooked, the poor administration of an otherwise sensible policy, until tragedy struck." Defenders of this policy suggested that chief executives sometimes commute the sentences of those serving life without parole.[28]

Reader's Digest published a piece about the Horton case in July, and Pinkerton said it "created a firestorm at the grass roots." Over the Fourth of July weekend, Atwater took a trip to Luray, Virginia, where he overheard a group of motorcyclists who had read the article discussing the controversy. "I kept talking to them about other things. There was zero interest in the presidential race. But the Willie Horton thing kept sustained interest for 45 minutes," Atwater remembered.[29] "I said to myself this issue has a real life, this issue counts to Americans."[30] The Dukakis campaign was also aware of the danger. As Susan Estrich said, "[Polling showed that] the furlough issue had the highest potential to hurt us, much more potential than anything we could find to run against Bush."[31]

As noted earlier, violent crime had been a major issue in American politics since 1968 and a sore spot for Democrats throughout the intervening two decades. The murder rate increased dramatically during this period, rising from 5 per 100,000 people in 1960 to just over 10 per 100,000 by 1980.[32] Republicans proved adept at stigmatizing their opponents as "soft on crime," while Democrats had often exposed themselves to these charges by stressing rehabilitation and addressing the root causes of crime as the solution. The attacks over Willie Horton, the furlough program, the death penalty, and the ACLU exploited that disadvantage, and as we will see, Dukakis did a poor job of responding to the onslaught.

While Bush began his attacks, the Dukakis campaign started to use more aggressive tactics to raise money for the general election. After the Watergate scandal, Congress passed legislation providing for federal financing of presidential campaigns. In 1988, a time when candidates still accepted public funds, both parties received $46 million after their respective conventions. Individuals could also make "hard money" campaign donations capped at $1,000. Over time, however, various laws and regulations opened the door for unlimited and unregulated donations of "soft money" to the national and state parties. There were no limits on soft money, and while such funds could not be used for ads directly promoting a candidate, they could be employed for "party-building" exercises like "producing generic advertisements, organizing voter registration and getting out the vote," according to Charlie Babcock of the *Washington Post*.[33]

Robert Farmer, Dukakis's chief fundraiser, sought to raise an additional $50 million for the national and state parties, mostly in unregulated funds. "Bob Farmer said to me now we got to go out and raise soft money," remembered Dukakis, "[and] I said wait a second I thought the fundraising was over."[34] While soft money had been used in previous races, Farmer was trying to take it to a new level and scale with his "Victory Fund." According to finance expert Herbert Alexander, "It [soft money] was raised and spent in the 1980 and 1984 presidential campaigns, but the money was raised in low-key efforts (not in the high visibility, competitive ways of 1988) and in smaller amounts."[35]

According to Estrich, the governor was uncomfortable with these extremely large donations, even though they were legal.[36] As a result, though some had donated $250,000 to the party in 1984, Dukakis specified a $100,000 limit and no money from corporations, unions, and PACs.[37] Regardless, "This means the expenditure limits are not meaningful," observed Alexander.[38] Campaign fundraising returned to the go-go days of the early 1970s, with one major donor proudly asserting, "I've raised millions upon millions upon millions for the Democratic Party and I've never seen this happen. We're raising money like it's going out of style. It's beyond comprehension. It's gorgeous. It's so exciting."[39]

At first, the Bush campaign took issue with the large contributions. Rich Bond called the practice "illegal on its face" at one point, and some believed it fundamentally altered the campaign.[40] "What Robert Farmer proposed to do in the summer of 1988 was the fund-raising equivalent of exercising the nuclear option," argued Bob Mosbacher, Bush's finance chairman. "It immediately changed the rules of political engagement, and escalated the stakes—particularly for those, like me, whose chief job was to make sure my candidate had the funds needed to be competitive."[41] They would shortly join the battle.

Meanwhile, Dukakis also started the process of selecting his vice president. Earlier in the campaign, Sasso had thought a southern senator would be an asset, with regard to both the general election and governance. Campaign chairman Paul Brountas took charge of the search, giving Dukakis a memo about the potential ticket the morning after the California primary. "Among other things," wrote *Newsweek*, "he mentioned Jack Kennedy's choice of Lyndon Johnson. The bit of history appealed to Dukakis, who was fond of comparing himself to JFK. It also pointed to a Southerner."[42]

Once the primary season ended, Jackson and his supporters began a month-long bid to convince Dukakis to name him vice president or at least seriously consider him to be the governor's running mate. "No one else at this point that's active in politics has shown the breadth of support I have shown at the polls," declared Jackson, making his case.[43] According to Brountas, many people in the Jackson campaign believed he deserved the position, and the Congressional Black Caucus echoed their sentiment.[44] In mid-June, Bob Beckel, who managed Mondale's campaign in 1984, had dinner with Jackson, telling him with regard to the vice presidency, "I'm worried that your people feel so strongly about it that even if you try to turn them off, they're not going to listen." Jackson responded, "We'll have to wait and see. Sometimes you have to stir up the pot."[45]

Dukakis met with Jackson to discuss the position. However, polls conducted immediately after the primary showed the governor beating Bush with either Bill Bradley or John Glenn as his running mate, but losing with Jackson on the ticket.[46] "Mr. Jackson's chances are rated as almost nil," analyzed Dionne, "both because of Mr. Dukakis's basic caution and because the evidence from virtually all polls is that because of racial attitudes and because his politics are seen as too left-leaning, Mr. Jackson would lose the Democratic ticket far more votes than he would pick up."[47] Early signs pointed to Bradley, Glenn, and Senator Lloyd Bentsen of Texas as the front-runners.[48] Dukakis wanted Bradley, but the New Jersey senator and former NBA star did not feel the time was right. Senator Sam Nunn of Georgia, a leading conservative Democrat, also opted out of consideration.[49]

Before the decision, the Dukakis and Jackson camps worked out an agreement over the future of the nomination process. Jackson had been frustrated in both 1984 and 1988 that he had won fewer delegates than his percentage of the popular vote, and he wanted the party to implement a pure proportional representation system. Devine conducted the negotiations with the Jackson people, recalling that Dukakis supported the change. Not wanting to weaken his position, however, Devine asked the governor not to reveal his stance beforehand.[50]

On June 25, the two sides reached a compromise right before the meeting of the Rules Committee. The agreement reduced the number of superdelegates and ended the practice of giving a bonus delegate to a candidate for winning a congressional district. "It reflects a spirit of goodwill and cooperation," declared Devine at the time.[51] And like many things regarding 1988, the change would have long-term implications. "You could only have PR (proportional representation) primaries and caucuses after that," recalled Devine. "And by the way, that system is one of the reasons that Barack

Obama wound up being the nominee for president. . . . It had a huge impact. It didn't help Jesse Jackson but it helped Obama 20 years later."[52]

Indeed, throughout his 2008 primary battle with Hillary Clinton, Obama ran up significant margins in delegates by winning lower-turnout caucuses in a lopsided fashion. Despite Hillary's wins in big-state primaries with higher turnout, she could not catch up to him once he took an early lead because the proportional representation system limited her gains in delegates. "The reality is that if the Democrats had a winner-take all strategy like the Republicans, Clinton would be the inevitable nominee at this point," commented one Democratic strategist. "In fact, we have a different kind of system. We have a proportional representation system."[53]

As the convention approached, Dukakis sought to bring Jackson into the fold, inviting him for a highly publicized dinner at his home in Brookline on the Fourth of July. But there were major missteps along the way, as the campaign sent no car to pick him up at the airport and served a milk-heavy meal to the lactose intolerant Jackson. When the reverend was about to bring up the vice presidency, one of the governor's daughters unintentionally interrupted the conversation.[54] At a Boston news conference, Jackson reiterated his qualifications, saying, "The fact of the matter is I would be an asset who brings to the ticket the moral authority of social justice."[55] Around this time, Atwater discussed Jackson's visit with a group of Republican activists, remarking, "Maybe he will put this Willie Horton on the ticket after all is said and done."[56]

Distracted by Jackson and the state budget, the governor did little campaigning, frustrating his aides. "The news cycle was dominated by the other side," said one. The Bush attacks seemed to have an impact, as Dukakis's lead fell from fourteen points to five points in the two weeks after the end of primary season.[57]

The vice-presidential decision put the spotlight back on Dukakis. In terms of the criteria for the position, Estrich said, "The key issue for our campaign is how are we going to deal with the liberal label that's going to be stamped all over us."[58] The governor considered a number of Washington elected officials, most of whom had middle-of-the-road reputations, including Representative Lee Hamilton of Indiana, Senator Bob Graham of Florida, and Gore, Gephardt, Glenn, and Bentsen. "All reflect Mr. Dukakis's preference for consensus and moderation over boldness and adventure," wrote Dionne.[59]

A week before the decision, most viewed Glenn as the likely choice. "Many Democrats view the former astronaut as a safe choice by a Presidential candidate noted for caution," wrote Toner, adding that Glenn was a nonsoutherner who would not upset the southern wing of the party and could bring Ohio and its twenty-three electoral votes.[60] Indeed, an informal survey of reporters predicted Glenn would be Dukakis's pick.[61] The governor also developed a strong affinity for Hamilton, who had led the congressional Iran-Contra hearings and could bring important foreign policy bona fides. However, the representative delivered little political upside, with solidly Republican Indiana likely out of reach for the Democrats.[62]

Frustrating the Dukakis campaign, Jackson continued to agitate regarding the vice presidency, the platform, and his role in general. Brountas met with Jackson on July 11 to discuss the second position, though most still believed Dukakis would not choose him. "I assume Jackson will pout for a couple of days and that will be that," one Dukakis aide told the *Washington Post*.[63] Estrich recalled that Jackson was never going to the choice.[64] Dukakis said it came down to four candidates—Gore, Gephardt, Glenn, and Bentsen—and he spent time with all four of them.[65] Contemporary accounts mention Gore, Hamilton, Glenn, and Bentsen.[66]

That evening, Dukakis and his wife sat down with Brountas, Corrigan, and Estrich in Brookline to make the final decision. The governor asked his brain trust for their opinion, and they all selected Bentsen. "That's my choice," said the governor.[67] Asked whether he thought the senator would deliver his home state, Dukakis replied, "It [the choice of Bentsen] had less to do with geography than just who he was [and] what he had done. What kind of senator he had been and . . . what kind of role he would play in the administration."[68] The governor might also have been attracted to the idea of reviving the Boston-Austin axis of JFK and LBJ in 1960.[69]

Originally from southern Texas, Bentsen had served as a decorated pilot in World War II and entered politics upon returning home, becoming the youngest member of Congress when first elected to the House in 1948. After serving three terms, he wanted to make more money for his family and left Congress for the private sector, achieving major financial success in the insurance industry during the 1960s. After defeating Bush in the 1970 Senate race to return to public service, Bentsen tried running for president himself in 1976 as a "Harry Truman Democrat," only to earn a mere six delegates along the way as Jimmy Carter captured the Democratic nomination. Subsequently reelected twice, Bentsen became a respected member of the upper house, ascending to chair the influential Senate Finance Committee in 1987.[70]

Corrigan and Estrich backed the Bentsen pick as part of an effort to combat the Bush campaign's liberal charge and appeal to centrist voters. "It was an outreach to the moderates of the Democratic Party. . . . The Sam Nunn part of the Democratic Party was not pleased with the nomination of Dukakis," remembered the campaign manager.[71] Corrigan agreed, saying Bentsen's inclusion "sent a message that he [Dukakis] wasn't a crazy liberal from the Northeast."[72] Devine would manage Bentsen's campaign, and he wrote a memo outlining the strategy for him, recalling, "The heart of it was that we wanted Bentsen to credential Dukakis and we wanted him to talk about things where Dukakis may not have you know the experience that Bentsen had"—namely, on issues like inside-the-Beltway background and gun control.[73]

Immediately after making the decision, the governor called Bentsen, but the Texas senator had taken his phone off the hook because of constant calls from the press. When Dukakis finally reached him at 6:30 the next morning, Bentsen accepted his offer.[74] The campaign moved to inform Jackson, then in Cincinnati, but Brountas had forgotten to give Estrich the reverend's phone number for that location, so she initially tried him on his regular number. By the time the Dukakis camp sorted the situation out, Jackson was already on a plane to D.C., where he found out about Dukakis's decision from a reporter.[75] Upon hearing about the pick, Jackson said he was "too mature to be angry." Estrich told the media, "No one ever intended for Rev. Jackson to be told by a news reporter. We tried every way we could to get the message to him." The oversight only increased the tension between the two camps. "Many people have a sense of indignation, a sense of insult," responded Jackson the following day in Chicago.[76]

"Pundits pronounced the choice of Bentsen brilliant," according to *Newsweek*'s CW.[77] A few leading media voices, however, believed the normally cautious Dukakis had made an uncharacteristic roll of the dice. Both the *Washington Post* and the *New York Times* featured headlines with the word "gamble" in them.[78] Dionne wrote, "[The Bentsen choice] represents a series of gambles that the Massachusetts Governor's admirers see as bold and his detractors see as dangerous." The journalist elaborated that it would be difficult for Bentsen to carry his own state, and that his relative conservatism could alienate Jackson supporters.[79] By contrast, selecting Glenn might have virtually guaranteed Ohio.[80] Echoing Dionne in *Time*, Richard Stengel wrote, "Dukakis took a deeply calculated risk, an atypical gamble. Bentsen is not a shoo-in to win in Texas, George Bush's adopted state." He added that Bentsen could hurt Dukakis with progressives.[81]

Indeed, Bentsen's record was very centrist—even conservative—as he differed with Dukakis on several key issues. The Texan had voted for the Reagan tax cuts of 1981 and supported the president more than any other Democrat during his first year in the White House. Bentsen also broke with

Dukakis on contra aid, the death penalty, and Star Wars. "Not since 1952, when Adlai E. Stevenson ran with John J. Sparkman, a segregationist from Alabama, has a Democratic ticket been so divided on fundamental issues," wrote David Rosenbaum in the *New York Times*.[82] One analysis described Bentsen as the most conservative Democratic vice-presidential nominee between 1976 and 2016.[83]

Unsurprisingly, moderate and conservative Democrats, especially in the South, applauded the Bentsen pick. "It sends the right signal to the South: that we're running a national ticket that includes the South and that includes the business community," declared the chairman of the Tennessee Democratic Party. One Democratic pollster added, "Lloyd Bentsen makes it more difficult for Bush to attack the ticket as too anti-business or too liberal."[84]

Upset by the miscommunication with their candidate as well as the pick of the centrist Bentsen, Jackson supporters gave the governor and his freshly minted running mate a cool reception at previously scheduled meetings with the NAACP and the Congressional Black Caucus the following day. Members seemed to accept Dukakis's explanation about the phone call, though Congressman John Conyers of Michigan said, "It was something he could have been more sensitive about. I mean, nobody cared whether he would have informed Dick Gephardt in advance, but this one thing was something on which he could have gotten into trouble."[85] Others were less charitable. Maxine Waters, then a California assemblywoman and a national cochair for Jackson's campaign, told *Nightline*, "[I] basically decided that the Dukakis campaign is not serious about involving Jesse Jackson and his supporters in a real way. They weren't simply careless."[86] In fact, some Jackson aides firmly believed the snub had been intentional, though Glenn was also unhappy about how Dukakis notified him.[87]

Of course, the Bush campaign also weighed in, with Atwater explaining why Dukakis would not win Texas: "There's not a thing Bentsen can do about Dukakis being a double-dip liberal."[88] Despite the media's praise, Teeter, echoing Dionne and Stengel, called the choice a "gamble" in an internal campaign memo, observing, "Bentsen is a good national choice in that he is clearly perceived to be qualified to be President, is more conservative than Dukakis, and appears to broaden the appeal of the ticket and make Dukakis look bigger by choosing him." But, Teeter elaborated, "unless he can carry Texas, which I don't think he can, he brings no electoral votes to the ticket. Clearly Dukakis could have guaranteed himself at least one key state and a number of electoral votes with either Glenn or Gephardt."[89] In terms of Bush's reaction, he wrote in his diary a week later, "Bentsen is seen as a stroke of genius even though he's way, way apart on the issues, but we've got to get it in focus. We've got to make people understand how far left Dukakis is."⁹⁰

Raising the possibility of a floor fight over Bentsen, Jackson's differences with the governor and the party dominated the news as the convention approached. Echoing the Freedom Rides of 1961, the reverend led a caravan of buses of his supporters from Chicago to the convention site in Atlanta. Upset that the governor did not discuss the vice-presidential choice with him, Jackson pulled no punches, saying, "It is too much to expect that I will go out in the field and be the champion vote picker and bale them up and bring them back to the big house and get a reward of thanks while people who do not pick nearly as much voters, who don't carry the same amount of weight among the people, sit in the big house and make the decisions." He also said, "The progressive wing of the party seeks inclusion. The Boston-Austin connection leaves Chicago out of the equation."⁹¹ There was talk of former president Carter mediating between the two camps. Though his rhetoric became more conciliatory as he approached Atlanta, Jackson still wanted some kind of "partnership" with the ticket, including the integration of his staff into the national effort, and the opportunity to push the Democratic platform in a more progressive direction.⁹²

Seeking to assert control of the party as he headed to the convention, Dukakis said, "Every team has to have a quarterback—that's the nominee. You can't have two quarterbacks. On the other hand, every team has to have terrific players in the backfield and up in the line. That's the way you win."⁹³ On the eve of Atlanta, things remained so shaky that Ron Brown, Jackson's convention chairman, later made a confession: "My honest view is that our convention was hanging by a thread."⁹⁴

It was a perilous situation for the governor. The convention would be Dukakis's introduction to the nation, and a successful gathering could give the candidate the traditional polling "bounce" and boost his narrowing advantage. By the late 1980s, with the nominations decided well beforehand, the three broadcast networks had moved on from gavel-to-gavel coverage and just showed a few hours of the party conventions in prime time. CNN provided greater coverage but it remained a relatively minor player by comparison, while MSNBC and Fox News did not yet exist. "The parties changed their rules," observed Tim Russert, then a vice president at NBC News, "and that changed the nature of the convention." As a result, ABC, NBC, and CBS significantly cut their staff and resources for the events. Still, with cable only in its infancy, the networks held 71 percent of prime-time viewership during the 1987–88 television season, and huge audiences would tune in to watch the two hours airing each night.⁹⁵

The Fight Begins · 145

In a time when the evening news was vital to how voters got information, *ABC World News Tonight* began its broadcast on the first day of the convention with the story of the important agreement between Dukakis, Bentsen, and Jackson. "Until a few hours ago," anchor Peter Jennings said, "it did not look as if the party's presidential nominee was completely in charge. That has changed."[96] Brountas, Estrich, and Brown had worked out a compromise over the weekend, and Dukakis, Bentsen, and Jackson finalized it on Monday morning. "The cornerstone of the agreement between Dukakis and Jackson was a promise to employ Jackson supporters in positions on the nominee's national campaign staff," wrote Lamar in *Time*. He further noted that "Jackson would also receive a plane and the funding to travel around the country, campaigning for Dukakis and registering voters." When announcing this arrangement, Dukakis said there was "no deal and no fine print," adding, "You don't put it in writing. You understand it. You feel it."[97] Republicans sought to use the new harmony to link Dukakis with the polarizing Jackson, with Ed Rollins declaring, "Is Jesse Jackson going to call the shots? If he is, there are a lot of Americans who aren't going to vote for this ticket."[98]

The party hoped to use the convention to portray the governor as a non-ideological manager.[99] When reporters asked him what he wanted to be the theme of the gathering, Dukakis responded, "Strong, united, progressive. Fiscally responsible. A reflection of a party that has its act together." Mondale called the ticket "moderate" and "competent."[100]

Though national polls showed the race virtually in a dead heat as the convention began, Democrats were extremely optimistic. An ABC / *Washington Post* poll showed that while only 53 percent of Democratic delegates had thought Mondale would win in 1984, a whopping 93 percent of Democratic delegates believed Dukakis would emerge victorious in 1988. "If you want to know why there are likely to be very few dustups over credentials, rules, platforms, or the choice of Lloyd Bentsen," ABC's Jeff Greenfield observed, "it's very simple; unlike the delegates in '84 and '80 and '72, these delegates actually think they got a real chance to win."[101]

As the festivities got underway, the then Texas treasurer and future Lone Star State governor Ann Richards delivered a rousing keynote speech on opening night. Skewering the vice president's roots, she told the audience, "After listening to George Bush all these years, I figure you need to know what a real Texas accent sounds like." Outlining traditional Democratic economic priorities and discussing those left out of the Reagan-era economy, she mocked Bush, declaring, "And now that he's after a job that he can't get appointed to, he's like Columbus discovering America—he's found child care, he's found education." Then, in the most memorable line of the speech, she famously added, "Poor George . . . He can't help it. . . . He was born with a silver foot in his mouth."[102] The Bush family never forgot the speech, and George W. Bush defeated Richards when she ran for reelection as governor in 1994.

The discussion on the floor revealed how the changing electoral environment created new challenges for the Dukakis campaign. Noting that Iran-Contra had dominated the headlines a year ago, ABC's Sam Donaldson asked Senator George Mitchell (D) of Maine whether it would be a central part of the general election. "I don't think it'll be a major issue by itself," responded Mitchell, "but as part of a record of mismanagement, lack of respect for law and deep criminal conduct in this administration. A record unparalleled in modern history." A mere six months earlier the Bush campaign had been struggling to handle questions about the scandal, but it had faded to some extent by the summer. When queried about the biggest challenge for Dukakis and Bentsen, Governor Cuomo explained, "The difficulty, if there is a major one, is convincing the American people that the economy is not as good as the Republicans are going to say it is." Indeed, voters were increasingly optimistic about their situation, providing a tail wind for Bush.[103]

On the second day, the Democrats finalized their party platform with minimal dissension as the Jackson campaign withdrew ten of its thirteen minority planks.[104] Of the remaining three, the party rejected a Jackson-sponsored plank to raise taxes, with Denver mayor Frederico Peña insisting, "A tax hike pitch is an easy grand slam for George Bush," as well as one declaring the United States would not be the first country to use nuclear weapons.[105]

Another key trend that began in the 1988 election emerged when, as part of an agreement between the two camps, another Jackson-inspired plank calling for Palestinian "self-determination" was discussed but did not come up for a vote. Writing in the *New York Times*, David Rosenbaum noted that the issue was being debated "for the first time at an American political convention." Traditionally, there had not been a significant partisan difference concerning Israel, though American Jews supported the Democratic Party in overwhelming numbers.[106]

After twenty years of Israeli occupation, Palestinians in the West Bank and Gaza Strip began an uprising in December 1987 that eventually became known as the first intifada. Every night, international television showed youths in the territories throwing rocks and Molotov cocktails at Israeli soldiers. Many in the United States and around the world believed the Israeli

Defense Forces' response, which initially included live bullets, was disproportionate. This led to growing criticism of the Jewish state's behavior, with unease over Israel's conduct extending to segments of the American Jewish community as well.

Under these circumstances and with the reverend's advocacy for Palestinian rights during the primary, there was a slight increase in Democrats' support for the Palestinian cause, with seven state party conventions calling for some kind of Palestinian autonomy. A poll, however, showed that 55 percent of delegates opposed such a plank in the national platform, with 35 percent supporting it. On this issue, there were sharp differences between the Dukakis and Jackson camps, with 73 percent of the former opposing its addition to the party platform and 81 percent of the latter backing it.[107]

Despite the lack of a vote on the minority plank, its advocates took satisfaction that the debate even occurred. James Zogby, executive director of the Arab American Institute and a Jackson adviser, declared in his speech to the hall, "We're making history today. . . . The deadly silence that has for so long submerged the issue of Palestinian rights has been shattered." Continuing, Zogby offered the following explanation: "We don't need a vote today because we're already winning because we have a debate in our party. Our party is debating an issue that was never debated before." Not everyone agreed with his assessment. Congressman Charles Schumer of New York, a strongly pro-Israel Democrat, sharply criticized Zogby's comments: "[He is] clever but duplicitous, when he says that this is a victory for his platform." The representative's rhetoric upset some in the crowd, and they interrupted his speech with a smattering of boos, forcing the convention chairman, Speaker of the House Jim Wright, to ask for quiet at one point.[108]

Nevertheless, the platform discussion can be seen as an early stage in the process by which the parties changed their relative positions on the Israeli-Palestinian conflict. In 1988, both parties' constituents were roughly equally supportive of Israel.[109] Gradually, however, Republican support for the Jewish state strengthened, as evangelicals like Robertson, who took an unambiguously pro-Israel position, continued to gain power within the GOP. Eventually, conservative Israeli leaders like longtime prime minister Benjamin Netanyahu became extremely close to leading Republican politicians, and backing of Israel became almost as much of a litmus test for the party's presidential candidates as opposition to abortion rights.

By contrast, with the destruction of the peace process in the first decade of the twenty-first century, many liberals grew uncomfortable with the continuing occupation and expansion of settlements throughout the West Bank under successive Israeli governments. Over time, Democrats gradually embraced the notion of a Palestinian state, which they formally endorsed in their 2004 platform.[110] By 2018, the Democrats would be far more split regarding the Israeli-Palestinian conflict than the GOP, with some on the left wing increasingly sympathetic to the Palestinian cause. Senator Bernie Sanders of Vermont spoke out strongly on Palestinians' behalf during his two runner-up campaigns for the Democratic nomination in 2016 and 2020. This divide first began to manifest itself in 1988.[111]

Calling the Democratic platform the shortest in a half century, ABC's Barry Serafin reported, "Without all the usual liberal buzzwords [it] is not going to be a burden at least on the Democratic ticket."[112] The Bush campaign agreed, with one staffer writing, "Overall, the platform was designed to unify the party and avoid a fight over various code words."[113] This was no accident, as the Dukakis campaign purposefully designed it that way. Estrich said she worked to "make sure there were no platform fights that got us caught looking liberal," adding, "I wanted no division right. I just wanted a sort of namby-pamby platform that nobody could use as a noose."[114]

"This is going to be Jesse Jackson's night," observed Jennings as night two got underway. But first Ted Kennedy had his say. Following an introduction by his nephew John F. Kennedy Jr., the liberal icon delivered an impassioned speech for his governor, declaring, "For a long time I have believed that what this country needs is another president from Massachusetts. And now it's going to happen." He praised Jackson and compared the Dukakis-Bentsen ticket to the JFK-LBJ slate. Then, talking about Bush's uncertain responses over his role in Iran-Contra, Kennedy rhetorically asked, "Where was George?" He subsequently referenced a series of controversies from the last eight years, repeatedly querying, "Where was George?" while the convention audience joined in and chanted the phrase. "It brought people into the fray," analyzed Donaldson afterward.[115]

As the evening went on, Atwater weighed in on the proceedings for the Bush campaign, expressing surprise at "the very personal and negative nature of the attack." He added that the Democrats wanted to focus on personalities rather than issues, explaining, "They're still the party that wants to tax and spend a lot of taxpayers' dollars. They're soft on crime, soft on national defense." Again placing the focus on Jackson, Atwater suggested that he was "the dominant figure of the convention," alleging that the Democrats had an "extended" ticket composed of Dukakis, Bentsen, and Jackson, and that the governor and Jackson basically had the same positions. Trying to stick the liberal label to the opposition, Atwater said the party was trying to conceal its true views.[116]

With the schedule running late, Jackson himself finally emerged for his moment just before 11:00 P.M. eastern time, as the prime-time window closed.[117] The Dukakis campaign cleared the hall of the nominee's banners, and many delegates gave their credentials to Jackson people so they could see his speech.[118] Directly linking his campaign with the civil rights movement, the reverend brought Rosa Parks, who started the Montgomery Bus Boycott in 1955, onstage, calling her "the mother of the movement." Furthermore, he added that his success was only possible because of the sacrifices of the era's martyrs and heroes, ranging from the Mississippi Freedom Democratic Party (MFDP) to Dr. King.[119]

After reviewing the ruinous Democratic divisions of the past, Jackson stressed the importance of party unity, declaring, "When we divide, we cannot win." Repeatedly discussing the need to find "common ground," he delineated the differences between his background and Dukakis's. "His foreparents came to America on immigrant ships. My foreparents came to America on slave ships. But whatever the original ships, we're in the same boat tonight," the reverend said.[120] He followed up with his traditional populist appeal, criticizing Reaganomics and inveighing against "economic violence." Describing his own challenging upbringing, Jackson declared that when his name went into nomination, so would the names of everyone else who had faced difficulties. He ended by invoking his signature slogan of "Keep hope alive!"[121]

In the immediate aftermath of the speech, NBC's Ken Bode asked Ron Brown on the floor whether the reverend's supporters were upset their candidate had been pushed out of prime time. "Not at all," Brown replied, "and neither do the people in this coliseum seem troubled at all." Though ratings for the convention fell overall, the speech drew a mammoth television audience, with over 55 percent of those watching television that night tuning in to the networks to see Jackson. By contrast, a mere third of viewers had watched the previous week's episode of NBC's *The Cosby Show*, the top-rated program at the time.[122] Anchor Tom Brokaw and veteran newsman John Chancellor ended NBC's coverage by discussing how the speech might have played outside the hall, with Chancellor commenting, "My judgement is that it was great theater and bad politics for the Democratic Party as Dukakis would like to see it."[123]

Whatever the reaction nationally, peace with Jackson had been achieved, at least for the time being. When asked the following night whether Jackson was pleased, Brown responded, "Oh absolutely. I think everybody in this arena is satisfied and happy tonight."[124] But at what cost? "I don't think you can ignore that fact that before the convention, the news coverage was dominated by Jesse Jackson," analyzed Corrigan, adding that Jackson had received twice the media coverage than Dukakis did in the week prior to the convention.[125] Looking back, he stated, "We wanted to shut down the division in the party," but "the Jackson effort was interfering with that pretty much up until the middle of the convention." Ultimately, the "focus on division hurt."[126]

Later, William Safire speculated that the attention on Jackson was a turning point for Dukakis's presidential prospects: "For three days, all the American people saw and heard was Jesse Jackson. What did Jesse want? See Jesse and his family. Watch the troika of Dukakis-Jackson-Bentsen make up. See Mr. Jackson deliver the most ringingly emotional speech in years. Watch the Jackson supporters, who were telecast as if they filled the hall, seem to dominate the convention."[127] When the campaign ended, Broder seemed to concur, stating, "As scores of voter interviews later evidenced, many of those watching decided—despite the denials by both men—that some secret deal had been struck."[128] Whatever the reality, Jackson's prominence in 1988 and the damage it might have done with Reagan Democrats laid the groundwork for Bill Clinton's efforts to distance himself from Jackson in 1992.

Now the spotlight shifted to Dukakis, as his nomination would become official during the roll call on the third day. "Before this night is over the Democratic convention will finally belong to its party's nominee," Peter Jennings said on *ABC World News Tonight*.[129] Later on, George Will suggested that speeches by Jackson and Kennedy, two of the most divisive figures in the party, had hindered Democrats' attempts to regain the support of the all-important Reagan Democrats. "At long last, the convention is turning to the man the convention is about and it's his job to put on a turn signal," Will said, "and turn the convention not only toward him but a little bit to the right."[130]

That evening, a then little-known forty-one-year-old centrist governor from Arkansas named William Jefferson Clinton strode to the podium to give the sole nominating speech for Dukakis. A close ally of the Massachusetts governor, the ambitious politician was making his first major foray onto the national stage.[131] "He wants to run for president when the opportunity presents itself," David Brinkley said while introducing Clinton. "He's a very bright, talented young man . . . much admired in the Democratic Party." Jennings weighed in by observing that Clinton was "said to be a good speaker."[132]

Things went downhill from there for the future president. With the crowd already riled up, Clinton couldn't get their attention from the outset. Speaking of his longtime friendship with Dukakis, he declared, "I'd like to tell you why I believe Michael Dukakis should be the first American president born of immigrant parents since Andrew Jackson." But the crowd kept chanting "We Want Mike," and Clinton tried to quiet audience members by telling them he needed to explain to the rest of Americans why they should want him as well.[133] "They weren't listening to what I was saying, or trying to say. All they were responding to was the governor's name," Clinton explained. He also said that he had thought the lights would be turned down to help draw the audience's attention.[134]

Trying to spell out the governor's accomplishments, Clinton cited Dukakis's balanced budgets as well as his welfare reform, which he called a model for the nation. Sounding themes he would use again in his own 1992 campaign, Clinton critiqued Reaganomics, noting the stagnating wages faced by many middle-class Americans during the 1980s. At this point, ABC switched away from the speech.[135] Seeing how bored the audience was, NBC had already done the same, with Tom Brokaw noting that Clinton was only halfway through his speech. As Clinton went over his allotted fifteen minutes, the Dukakis campaign, concerned his verbosity would push the roll call out of prime time, entered "Please finish" onto his teleprompter screen.[136] But the Arkansas governor was not using it, and more dramatic steps had to be taken. "This was turning into 1972 in my mind," said Devine, the convention's floor manager, recalling McGovern's chaotic nomination. "I was panicking a little bit." After having first come up behind Clinton out of camera range to signal him to stop, Speaker Wright then made a "slicing gesture across his throat." When Clinton finally said, "in closing," the audience cheered, as the speech had reached twice its intended length.[137] It was nothing short of a disastrous national debut.

A promising political career appeared to be stillborn in front of the whole country as the press and comedians came down on him with a vengeance. "With so many lawyers in one room, you'd think that someone would have told Clinton that he had the right to remain silent," went one quip. Johnny Carson told the nation on *The Tonight Show* that "the surgeon general has just approved Bill Clinton as an over-the-counter sleep aid."[138]

It was less than a laughing matter to Clinton, who said, "It was the worst hour of my life—make that the worst hour and a half." The most important newspaper in his state, the *Arkansas Gazette*, called his Democratic convention speech an "unmitigated disaster."[139] *Newsweek*'s CW analyzed his performance with two comments—"Old CW: president in '96," followed by "New CW: he's finished." To salvage his viability for national office in the future, Clinton would have to move quickly to repair his image. In the wee hours of the morning after the speech, television producers Linda and Harry

Thomason, his friends and allies, discussed the way forward. "Look. He's got to go on the Carson show to make this right," said Linda.[140] As we will see, the "Comeback Kid" would make his first comeback on the national stage. In the meantime, the convention continued.

While the primaries rendered the roll call a mere formality, the campaign arranged for California, the state with the most electoral votes, to have the honor of giving Dukakis the necessary 2,082 delegates to become the nominee officially. Jackson's name had been placed in nomination as well, but once the count was concluded, the convention nominated the governor by acclamation in a sign of party unity. With the nomination formally Dukakis's, Dionne wrote, "The Massachusetts Governor will lead into the campaign the most united Democratic Party in a quarter-century."[141]

Yet as Dukakis prepared for the most important speech of his life, some believed he was still largely undefined as a candidate. "The person of Michael Dukakis has not so far dominated this convention," wrote Anthony Lewis, "or its image in the country."[142] As the final night of the convention began, Will spelled out a key part of the governor's mission: "The Republicans are going to be out to pin the traditional old liberalism—that label on Michael Dukakis and tonight begins his attempt to duck, bob, weave and avoid that."[143]

Bentsen went first. Accepting the vice-presidential nomination, the senator made a DLC-style speech, focusing on expanding economic opportunity while discussing those groups left out of the economic expansion, such as Iowa farmers and Texas oil workers. Declaring that the Reagan administration had written "hot checks" to create the illusion of prosperity through budget deficits, Bentsen said it was becoming more and more difficult for middle-class Americans to own homes or to send their kids to college. Spelling out his running mate's philosophy, Bentsen tried to distinguish Dukakis from traditional liberals. "He knows that government can't solve all our problems, but he also understands that government has an obligation to lead."[144]

Before the nominee himself spoke, his cousin, the Oscar-winning actress Olympia Dukakis, introduced him, narrating a biographical video that dealt with some of the wedge issues his campaign hoped to neutralize. With the attacks over Willie Horton well underway, she told of how Dukakis's father had been robbed and beaten at work. Assuring viewers that crime was more than a political issue for her cousin, she added, "Believe me it's personal."[145] Estrich said that she wanted the governor to discuss the story himself in his acceptance speech to "inoculate" himself on the Horton issue, but that he rejected the idea.[146] To illustrate Dukakis's support for welfare reform,

Olympia talked about Ruby Sampson, a woman who used the Dukakis job training program (ET) to move off of welfare and find work as a surgical technician after fourteen years on public benefits. In order to demonstrate that he was no big-spending liberal, Olympia talked of her cousin's personal frugality, showing that he still used the snowblower he had bought twenty-five years ago.

When the video ended, the actress appeared onstage herself again, invoking the Dukakis family's immigrant origins, which were shared by many of the Reagan Democrats. "We all know that many Americans have come to this country with nothing... nothing but hope. Well today one of their sons stands before you with the opportunity to be president of the United States," she declared. As her remarks concluded, singer Neil Diamond's paean to immigration, "Coming to America," blared in the convention hall as the governor made his way onto the stage.[147]

After a few initial comments, Dukakis continued with the immigration narrative, declaring, "We are going to win because we are the party that believes in the American dream." He added, "And I know, because my friends. I'm a product of that dream and I'm proud of it. A dream that brought my father to this country 76 years ago, that brought my mother and her family here one year later—poor, unable to speak English but with a burning desire to succeed in their new land of opportunity." Hoping to make him a more relatable candidate, Dukakis's family and aides urged him to think of his dad. In an uncharacteristic display of emotion, the governor spoke of his late father, saying with a cracking voice, "How I wish he was here tonight, he'd be very proud of his son."[148]

Critiquing the Reagan years, Dukakis said, "If anyone tells you that the American dream belongs to the privileged few and not to all of us, you tell them that the Reagan era is over... and that a new era is about to begin," adding that it was time "to exchange voodoo economics for can-do economics." Dukakis invoked the idealism of Kennedy and Johnson and returned to the themes of the primary campaign, declaring, "It's time to meet the challenge of the next American frontier—the challenge of building an economic future for our country that will create good jobs at good wages for every citizen of this land, no matter who they are or where they come from or what the color of their skin."[149]

Avoiding the liberal label, the Democratic nominee defined the terms of the fall campaign, famously declaring, "This election is not about ideology, it's about competence." Many on both sides would later cite this contrast as a key mistake. "People keep quoting that and they forget the next couple of sentences," reflected a somewhat frustrated Dukakis. "If you read the

The crowd cheers Michael Dukakis at the Democratic convention in Atlanta on July 21, 1988. The four-day gathering propelled the Massachusetts governor to a seventeen-point lead in the polls. (AP Photo / Doug Mills)

full speech, it says it's about values. . . . You gotta keep reading," he continued.[150] Indeed, the governor went on to say, "It's not about meaningless labels," again rejecting the liberal charge. "It's about American values. Old-fashioned values like accountability and responsibility and respect for the truth," he argued.[151]

In the speech, Dukakis discussed traditional progressive priorities such as universal health care and strengthening the EPA, while also criticizing the sale of arms to Iran. But he also focused on centrist themes during the address. Just as Mondale had done four years earlier, Dukakis emphasized his fiscal conservatism, telling the country, "I've balanced nine more budgets than this administration and I've just balanced a tenth." "We're going to give those on welfare the chance to lift themselves out of poverty," he said of welfare reform, "[and] to get the child care and training that they need."[152] He ended by reciting the Athenian oath, just as he had done in his speech declaring his candidacy the previous year.[153] Perhaps sensing the success of the speech, Dukakis said to his staff afterward, "It doesn't get any better than this."[154]

On the floor, the delegates cheered vociferously for the usually uncharismatic candidate. "People around me were just completely riveted," reported CBS's Lesley Stahl. "He had emotion, he had heart, and this crowd totally loved him."[155] Calling the speech "by far the best hour of his political career," longtime *Boston Globe* reporter Tom Oliphant wrote, "Michael S. Dukakis rose above the occasion last night, casting off a public lifetime of reserve to reach toward people's hearts and hopes, and demonstrating a capacity to lead a nation as well as run a government."[156] *Newsweek*'s CW gushed over the Democratic nominee's convention showing: "Dullness vanquished! Speech snow-blows away skeptics."[157]

Looking back, though, some on both sides believed Dukakis needed to accomplish more with the speech. While Corrigan thought that it did a fine job of establishing the candidate's biography, he argued that the address "did not do enough to set out a platform for the general election."[158] Certain Bush attacks went unanswered, with Estrich recalling, "I wanted him [Dukakis] to lead the Pledge of Allegiance . . . in an effort to inoculate and neutralize the charge that he was somehow unpatriotic."[159] James Baker, who was soon to assume control of the Bush campaign, wrote as follows: "The Dukakis pitch was that he was 'competent,' not ideological. The problem with that approach, however, is that the American people weren't looking—and they have never looked—for a technocrat-in-chief."[160]

Indeed, Baker is likely correct in this regard, as voters usually base their decision on the ideology and performance of the candidate in office. Whatever Bush's strengths or weaknesses as a potential chief executive, he was a longtime public servant with a wide range of experience in both foreign and domestic policy. He was not likely to be seen as less competent than Dukakis. The governor's campaign made an understandable attempt to deflect the liberal label, and the effort was consistent with Dukakis's history of technocratic governance. Even so, by failing to lay out his own ideology and agenda more clearly, Dukakis left the field open for the GOP to define his image for the American public.

In the short term, however, the convention appeared to be nothing short of a tremendous success. Dukakis said he and his camp were going into the fall "with the winds at our backs," while his son, John, remembered, "We left that evening absolutely elated, excited about what lay ahead of us."[161] During the event, Bush went on a camping trip with Baker to Wyoming but clearly understood the challenge he faced, writing in his diary, "I still feel confident that I can win, but the polls are tough."[162] A few sounded cautionary notes, with Edward Walsh observing in the *Washington Post*, "For Dukakis, who remains relatively unknown, with a political agenda that is broad but vague, the toughest tasks still lie ahead."[163] Baker also saw a downside. "They ridiculed him [Bush], both as a public figure and as a human being. If that's how they wanted to play their hand, more power to 'em," he said, adding, "For what it's worth, I think the sharp anti-Bush rhetoric at their convention hurt the Democrats with undecided voters."[164] Many Republicans would defend their later attacks on Dukakis by claiming the Democrats established the harsh tenor of the campaign in Atlanta.

The only remaining question was whether Dukakis would get the traditional convention "bounce" and move up in the polls. A few days later, the answer came back an emphatic "yes"—a Gallup poll showed Dukakis with a lead of 55 percent to 38 percent over the vice president. This was a dramatic shift from the mere six-point advantage (47 percent to 41 percent) he'd held in the last preconvention poll.[165]

The dramatic fluctuations in the polls revealed just how different late twentieth-century politics was from its early twenty-first-century counterpart. In an era when voters' partisan loyalties were looser, a significant portion of the electorate moved back and forth between the parties over time and during one particular race. In 1964, 61 percent of the country voted for Democrat Lyndon Johnson in his landslide win over Barry Goldwater, only to be followed by the same percentage backing Republican Richard Nixon over George McGovern eight years later.[166] Certain voters routinely cast a ballot for a conservative southern Democratic congressman and a Republican president, while others did the same for a moderate northern Republican congressman and a Democratic president. In the era of network-news dominance that stretched from the early 1960s to the mid-1990s, voters largely received similar information, as ideological media outlets did not yet reinforce partisan loyalties. Thus, with larger numbers of persuadable voters available, Bush and Dukakis tried to move to the middle and focused their attention on swing voters, while twenty-first-century politicians have primarily devoted their energies to turning out their base voters.

Similarly, more states were in play, as polling swung back and forth, leaving many more electoral votes up for grabs. On the third night of the convention, Will noted that the Dukakis-Bentsen ticket's burgeoning fortunes were making it competitive in a wide range of states, including GOP bastions such as Oklahoma and Indiana. He added, "We now have a hard time excluding states from the category of battleground."[167] As a result, both candidates ran nationwide campaigns, competing in far more regions than their successors would in the presidential elections between 2004 and 2020, when the red-blue divide had taken hold. Ignoring the talk of the GOP's "lock" on the Electoral College, the Dukakis campaign left Atlanta pledging to run a fifty-state strategy. This approach provided a striking contrast with early twenty-first-century elections, when stronger partisan identification meant both parties routinely conceded large swaths of the country to the other side, and a small number of swing states decided the outcome.[168]

As the general election campaign got underway, Bush worked to define Dukakis as an out-of-the-mainstream 1960s liberal, hammering away at the furlough program, Willie Horton, and the Pledge of Allegiance. Though he achieved some success in this regard, the spotlight shifted back to the governor and his efforts to deal with Jackson while selecting his vice president.

After choosing Bentsen, making amends with Jackson, and conducting a well-organized and successful convention, Dukakis tried to seize the center and got a boost in the polls, emerging with a seventeen-point margin. Things couldn't have looked brighter for the Democratic nominee. "If you asked me in August of 1988 I would have said Dukakis is on his way to being elected president," recalled the *Boston Globe*'s Curtis Wilkie. "Then everything went kind of haywire."[169]

6   Coming Out of Reagan's Shadow

Again behind in the polls, George Bush prepared for his convention and the moment he would officially emerge as the nominee. But first he had to choose his vice president. In an attempt to maximize interest, he held off making the announcement until New Orleans and largely made the selection on his own. "Why did George make the decision alone, then hold the choice close to the vest?" asked his close friend and campaign chairman James Baker. Baker explained, "Well, he had been vice president for eight long years. . . . I think he wanted to use the selection of his running mate to step out of the shadows and assert his authority as leader of the party."[1] In picking Indiana senator Dan Quayle, a relative unknown, Bush surprised virtually everyone, including his own staff, creating serious problems for his campaign as he simultaneously tried to introduce himself to the nation.

Quayle became the first baby boomer on a national ticket, and his nomination signaled the political arrival of that generation. His emergence also brought a central decision faced by his age cohort—whether to serve in the Vietnam War—to the center of American political debate for the first time. Questions surrounding his admission into the National Guard and the discussion over whether he had avoided combat in Southeast Asia weakened Quayle's candidacy from the outset. And from 1988 onward, debates over Vietnam-era behavior became a perennial question for baby-boomer politicians.

The difficulties with Quayle's nomination also led to enduring changes in how candidates chose their vice presidents. Largely unknown to the country and national press beforehand, the Indiana senator hadn't been fully vetted before his ill-fated debut on the national stage. After the difficulties with Quayle, politicians increasingly turned to well-known and well-established figures over the next two decades to prevent a similar distraction.

In addition, another ambitious boomer, Bill Clinton, recovered from his poor convention speech and salvaged his national aspirations, beginning what would be a series of political comebacks that became the hallmark of his career. Rather than going on a conventional news show in response, he sought out an entertainment program. In doing so, he demonstrated that the influence of the traditional media gatekeepers was beginning to decline, as he turned an appearance on *The Tonight Show* into political gold and a launching pad for his 1992 campaign.

Meanwhile, Dukakis lost his postconvention lead, as he was distracted by rumors concerning his health and his focus on gubernatorial work. The Republicans resumed their traditional attacks on Dukakis and the Democrats as soft on crime, weak on defense, and poor economic managers. As had been the case in June and early July, as well as in almost every national race since 1968, these critiques proved effective. But Bush also softened his message by reaching for swing voters in the middle on education and the environment. And despite the distraction over Quayle, Bush delivered a strong acceptance speech, got a solid bounce, and took control of the race.

After a successful convention and with a large lead in hand, Susan Estrich went home to California for the first time since Christmas, only to receive a phone call in the middle of the night. With ten events planned the following day, Dukakis had ordered the campaign plane back to Boston because he wanted to deal with gubernatorial business. When she asked to speak to him, Estrich was told "He doesn't want to talk to you," and nine of the events were canceled. "To this day I cannot tell you [why]," commented Estrich, saying that the candidates needed to be campaigning because she knew their lead was "soft and squishy as jello." Once back in Massachusetts, Dukakis would only see her after 5:00 P.M. in Boston because he was going to concentrate on state business during regular working hours.[2] "He went back to Massachusetts to being governor and treated the campaign as a sideline," recalled Estrich.[3] Indeed, Dukakis spent "all or part of sixteen of the twenty-five days" between the two conventions in Massachusetts, according to Germond and Witcover.[4] Even after the GOP convention, he still tended to home business, going on a two-day tour of nine cities in western Massachusetts.[5] "The summer went horribly," remembered Estrich.[6]

Meanwhile, Clinton plotted a recovery from his disastrous national debut. Having decided the Arkansas governor should appear on *The Tonight Show Starring Johnny Carson*, his friend Harry Thomason contacted Hollywood publicist David Horowitz the day after the nominating speech. Horowitz in turn spoke to Fred de Cordova, Carson's longtime producer. De Cordova told Horowitz that Carson had never had a politician on the show, insisting, "He's not going to now." This is a sharp contrast with twenty-first-century politics, where such appearances are routine. Later that day, Thomason had another idea, calling de Cordova himself and asking, "O.K., you've never had a politician on, but what if he comes on and plays the saxophone?" Clinton would then be a musician. De Cordova laughed and spoke to the comedic legend, who agreed to have Clinton on the show.[7]

At this time, Carson reigned as the unrivaled king of late-night television, having easily pushed aside multiple competitors over almost three decades on top. Carson's first successful challenger, *The Arsenio Hall Show*, would not premiere until six months later, and Jon Stewart and Stephen Colbert were more than a decade away from their debuts. With little counterprogramming except for Ted Koppel's ABC news program *Nightline*, a massive audience watched *The Tonight Show* every night, providing Clinton a golden opportunity to repair the damage.

Satirizing Clinton's convention speech, Carson started with a seemingly interminable introduction while some audience members chanted "We Want Bill," mocking the "We Want Mike" refrain from the Democratic convention. At various points, Carson seemed ready to end the intro and bring Clinton onstage—only to continue speaking. He then said, "In conclusion," and the audience cheered Carson just as they had Clinton when he had uttered the same words a week earlier.[8]

Clinton came onstage, and Carson asked, "How are you?" while humorously putting an hourglass on the table to time his response. Asked what had happened at the convention, Clinton responded, "It just didn't work I mean what can I tell you." Joking, he said, "My sole goal was achieved, however. I wanted so badly to make Michael Dukakis look great and I succeeded beyond my wildest expectations," one of many self-deprecating remarks during the interview. Crediting the governor for his sense of humor, Carson praised him for coming on the show despite the zingers he'd aimed at him in the interim. Asked whether he would run for president in the future, Clinton said, "I'd like to do it some time," but explained that he hadn't run in 1988 because he felt he hadn't "fulfilled [his] commitment to [his] state," and because his daughter was too young at age seven. Clinton concluded by playing the saxophone with Doc Severinsen and the show's band.[9]

In a remarkable turnaround, the reviews for Clinton's performance on *The Tonight Show* were as rapturous as they had been negative for his convention speech. "Arkansas Gov. Bill Clinton has gone from the media doghouse to media darling in one short week," read an AP story published the next day, "and all it took was a smile, a few self-deprecating jokes and a song."[10] Giving him an up arrow, *Newsweek*'s CW did a 180: "Old CW: Finished! New CW: Famous! Plays sax on Carson! Al Gore, eat your heart out."[11]

Clinton's successful performance on *The Tonight Show* accelerated the growing importance of nontraditional media, as the power of the network

After a disastrous nominating speech for Dukakis at the Democratic convention, Arkansas governor Bill Clinton went on *The Tonight Show Starring Johnny Carson* to revive his national political career. The appearance drew high praise, helping pave the way for his own nomination four years later. The gambit also showed the growing importance of nontraditional media in American politics. (AP Photo / Bob Galbraith)

evening news and the major mainstream newspapers began its long fade. Though these institutions had acted as gatekeepers for most of the post–World War II period, no longer would they monopolize the news environment. Politicians found that they could reach voters—especially those less inclined to turn out—through syndicated morning and afternoon talk shows. Late-night talk shows on the broadcast networks, like *The Tonight Show* and the *Late Show with David Letterman*, increasingly featured politicians on a regular basis, and they were also effective means of reaching voters.[12] As cable expanded, more venues emerged, and in the spring of 1992, Texas billionaire Ross Perot announced his third-party candidacy on CNN's *Larry King Live*. And when Clinton trailed Perot and Bush in the polls during the 1992 campaign, he used the same playbook, going on *The Arsenio Hall Show* to play the saxophone again. Whereas Carson rarely had politicians as guests, by the 2000s appearances on late-night talk shows like *The Daily Show* and *The Colbert Report* would become as commonplace as an interview on *Nightline* or *60 Minutes*.

Moreover, Clinton had rescued his national political career from potential oblivion for the first time, demonstrating the resiliency he would show throughout the 1992 campaign and his entire presidency. The bounce back from the Atlanta speech started Clinton's pattern of overcoming significant obstacles, sometimes of his own making. He survived what Hart could not when Gennifer Flowers alleged before the New Hampshire primary in 1992 that she and the Arkansas governor had engaged in a prolonged extramarital affair. After this revelation, Clinton finished a strong second in the Granite State to become the "Comeback Kid." Forced to declare his own relevance after Republicans seized control of Congress for the first time in forty years halfway through his first term as president in 1994, he came back to easily win reelection two years later. And when the Monica Lewinsky scandal and impeachment threatened his presidency in 1998–99, Clinton yet again endured, showing an ability to recover from setbacks greater than most in public life.

And the future president played a major role in Dukakis's campaign as one of his national campaign chairmen. "Clinton was going to school" in 1988, recalled Estrich, who said she spoke to the Arkansas governor every night, adding, "He was more on top of the numbers than Dukakis was."[13]

Meanwhile, the campaign continued. Starting at the Atlanta convention, the acolytes of fringe political candidate and conspiracy theorist Lyndon Larouche spread the story that Dukakis had received psychiatric treatment after the death of his brother in 1973 and following his electoral defeat in 1978.[14] Such speculation posed a serious threat, as George McGovern's 1972 effort had been permanently damaged when it was revealed that his running mate, Senator Thomas Eagleton of Missouri, had previously undergone electroshock treatment. Citing privacy, Dukakis had not released his full medical records, relying instead on a letter from his personal physician attesting to his good health.[15]

While the mainstream outlets avoided the story, according to *Time*, "Bush operatives called news organizations . . . to suggest follow-up stories about Dukakis' medical records or his brother's death."[16] Atwater, who had once described an opponent in South Carolina who'd undergone electroshock treatment as "someone who was hooked up to jumper cables," might have promoted the narrative.[17] "He tried to get me to write about Governor Dukakis having psychiatric problems," remembered conservative columnist Bob Novak. "It really was a slander."[18] As the rumors swirled, the conservative *Washington Times* ran a story on them on August 2, and the Bush campaign released a statement declaring the vice president in "excellent and vigorous" health. The vice president's camp claimed the statement had nothing to do with the innuendo circulating around the governor.[19]

The issue then gained national attention at a presidential press conference on August 3. A reporter from the *Executive Intelligence Review*, a Larouche publication, asked Reagan whether Dukakis should release his medical records, and the president replied, "Look, I'm not going to pick on an invalid." Noises followed from the press corps. Reagan quickly apologized, saying he "attempted to make a joke in response to a question," adding, "I think I was kidding, but I don't think I should have said what I said. I do believe that the medical history of a President is something that people have a right to know, and I speak from personal experience."[20]

Reagan's quip "just kind of came out of the blue," according to the governor.[21] The same day, Dukakis asked his doctor to release additional medical information and declared he had never sought psychiatric counseling. All three network newscasts reported the kerfuffle. CBS led its nightly broadcast with the story, with Bruce Morton explaining, "This is a story about a rumor and how the news media was forced to report it." He added later, "So Dukakis has denied a rumor. There was never any evidence supporting the Larouche charge. But the publicity it received may say something about how this campaign will go."[22] Calling the president's apology unnecessary, Dukakis gave him the benefit of the doubt, saying, "We all occasionally misspeak, Governors and Presidents as well."[23]

Thirty years later, the governor was far less charitable. "This was not an inadvertent slip," he said, noting that the remark disrupted the campaign. "We spent a whole week trying to convince people that I was really quite healthy."[24] Dukakis fell eight points in the polls overnight.[25] "'Dukakis not crazy. More at 11.' That hurt," analyzed Estrich, and Corrigan recalled an astonishing thirty-five-point fall with white men under age thirty.[26] The CW gave Dukakis a down arrow, writing, "Played good defense on 'shrink' issue but it was still defense."[27]

The day after Reagan's comment, Dukakis traveled to campaign at the Neshoba County Fair in Philadelphia, Mississippi. His trip reflected the broader range of competitive states available before the hardening of the partisan divide in the twenty-first century made the Magnolia State unmistakably red. While speaking at the event, which is a traditional gathering point for politicians in the state, Dukakis made no direct reference to the infamous murders of civil rights workers Michael Schwerner, Andrew Goodman, and James Chaney nearby, even though it was the twenty-fourth anniversary of the discovery of their bodies. White supremacists killed the three men in 1964 during the voter-registration campaign known as Freedom Summer. Their deaths would gain renewed attention a few months later in December 1988 with the release of the film *Mississippi Burning*, and its controversial depiction of the FBI's investigation into the crime.[28]

Defending himself, the governor noted that he had said it was a "special day" and believed people understood what he was discussing. President Reagan had drawn controversy when he made a similar trip to the fair immediately after the Republican convention eight years earlier, invoking his support for states' rights while not mentioning the killings.[29] Both the

New York Times and Jackson criticized Dukakis for not making greater mention of the three slain men.[30]

As the Dukakis campaign continued to combat the mental health story, Baker resigned as Treasury secretary on August 5 to become campaign chairman for Bush. Though Baker was happy at the Treasury, he wanted to help out his friend's campaign.[31] With Bush trailing by double-digits, Baker took over at a perilous time. He fully understood the challenge, having told some people he expected the vice president to lose because of the natural fatigue after eight years of Republican control.[32] Understanding that the vice president had to demonstrate his own identity, Baker reflected that Bush could not ride to victory solely on the administration's record. Instead, the candidate needed to "say how he would change things for the better."[33] Seeking to double down on the message the campaign had used to close the gap before the Democratic convention, Baker said, "We wanted it to be about lower taxes. We wanted it to be about strong defense," adding, "And we wanted to brand him [Dukakis] as a liberal, which we successfully did, and someone who had absolutely no idea about foreign and security policy."[34]

Bush had already begun his search for a vice president. Early on, Trump expressed his interest in the number two spot to Lee Atwater. Clearly perplexed by the offer, Bush referred to it as "strange and unbelievable."[35]

Unlike Dukakis, the vice president would not campaign with his prospective partners, and as he already knew most of the players, he believed one-on-one interviews were unnecessary as well. Playing it close to the vest, Bush hired Robert Kimmitt, a Washington attorney, to check the background of those under consideration. To protect their privacy, only he and Kimmitt would see the findings. "By keeping the information away from his political advisers, however," Baker commented, "George might have missed an opportunity to head off the trouble that lay ahead."[36]

While Dukakis had named Bentsen prior to his convention, Bush planned to make his selection on the third night in New Orleans. There was a lot of discussion by the networks then about the value of covering conventions, Fuller remembered, and "the announcement of the vice president created a news story and created excitement."[37]

At some point, Bush began meeting with a group of his staff each week—sometimes more than once a week—and had them offer up their top three choices. "The interesting thing about that technique is that, in a way that I didn't really fully appreciate until later," recalled Fuller, "it favored somebody like Dan Quayle, who wasn't often on the top of somebody's list, but after you'd name two—and you wanted to have a different approach to the third—he was frequently third on people's lists. Even some people who forgot that they had him on their list, I might add."[38]

Nicholas Brady, who replaced Baker at Treasury and had known Quayle during his short stint as a New Jersey senator, appears to have been the first to suggest his Indiana colleague.[39] Ailes had worked on Quayle's 1986 Senate reelection, while Teeter had done polling for him since his first House run in 1976, and both were positive about him, as was Fuller.[40] In a July memo, Ailes made the case for the young senator, writing, "We may need several bold strokes between now and the election. One would be a choice of someone unexpected as vice president who symbolizes youth and the future of the party."[41] Baker said he only offered his advice once, when he and Bush went on their camping trip in Wyoming during the Democratic convention: "I don't recall the details, but I remember that I thought Bob Dole and Dan Quayle were the most logical choices."[42] In late July, Bush wrote in his diary of Quayle, "He wouldn't get instant credibility, but it would make a generational difference."[43]

"When George Bush called me, to talk about the Vice Presidency, I knew that it was serious because he didn't really owe me anything," recalled Quayle, saying that he hadn't endorsed the vice president in the primary, though he did not support his colleague Dole, either.[44] After discussing it with his wife, he agreed to be considered.[45] He warned Kimmitt: "'One of the things that really needs to be done if it's going to be me is you need to work on an introduction.' I said, 'You've got to figure out how you're going to introduce me to the American people. I'm still the junior Senator from Indiana. Yes, I have a track record and it's good, and I've risen high very quickly. People in Washington clearly know who I am but the American people don't.' And he said, 'We recognize this.'"[46]

Many names appeared in the initial media speculation, especially Dole and Kemp, but Quayle was not one of them. With hindsight, Quayle wrote that it would been better if his name had been in the spotlight earlier. "If I had had some really serious scrutiny from the press, if I had taken off the snorkle and emerged above the water line," Quayle wrote, "I might have avoided some of what followed."[47] Reaching the same conclusion, Baker made a suggestion: "The way to handle a proposed vice presidential nominee who has not been tested in national or big-state politics or high appointive office . . . is to float the name a few weeks before the convention and let the games begin."[48]

Quayle's stock rose in the Bush camp for a number of reasons, including the fact that it did not appear that any of the potential nominees could deliver a swing state with precious Electoral College votes. One aide commented,

"The only question that had to be answered was whether we thought he had the stature to handle the job. Once we decided he did, he became the leading candidate."[49]

On Friday, August 12, three days before the start of the convention, Bush met with his advisers regarding the vice-presidential selection. According to an article by Gerald Boyd in the *New York Times*, the list had been narrowed to six people: Dole, Kemp, Quayle, Senator Pete Domenici of New Mexico, Senator Alan Simpson of Wyoming, and Dole's wife, Elizabeth Dole, who had been Reagan's transportation secretary. The article discussed the pros and cons of all the finalists, including the fear that Dole might be a "loose cannon" and did not excite conservatives.[50]

Near the beginning of the piece, Boyd wrote, "Aides to the Vice President said surprisingly strong support had emerged for Senator Dan Quayle of Indiana." Saying advisers still saw him as a "dark horse," the article made it clear that he would energize the conservative wing of the party. But given the more prominent names on the list, "people didn't dwell on it. . . . It wasn't that it wasn't put out there. . . . It just wasn't something that people really focused on," remembered Fuller.[51]

Some speculated that Baker leaked Quayle's name to the press to kill his chances. Baker rejected this idea, calling it "Baloney!" He added, "That's the kind of stuff that happens and then once it's reported you can't get a retraction and it gets locked into the lore."[52] Quayle, who was unsparing in his later criticism of Baker, agreed, saying that if he had wanted to take his name out of consideration, Baker "could have gone directly to his friend George Bush and insisted."[53] Some insiders, however, did begin to warn about the dangers of a Quayle selection.[54]

Each staff member listed his top three choices at the meeting. Given that the better-known candidates all had liabilities of some kind, every member of the G-6 except Mosbacher included Quayle in his top three. With each candidate receiving three points for being a first choice, two points for being a second, and one point for being third, Quayle came out on top.[55]

Quayle spoke with Kimmitt for the third time on the weekend prior to the convention. The questions asked were more detailed this time, and they included an inquiry into his National Guard service during the Vietnam War. Given the military draft of the era, everybody of the baby-boomer generation had to make a choice regarding serving in the war. The government carried out the draft in such a way that it placed the burden of fighting disproportionately on poor and working-class Americans, as more affluent people could receive educational deferments. And because many other middle-class citizens served in the reserves, President Lyndon Johnson repeatedly refused to call them up during the conflict to avoid greater debate over his policy. Given these dynamics, many young men of the era sought to join the guard—where spots were limited—to avoid combat service, thereby furthering class tensions. Kimmitt, a Vietnam veteran himself, asked Quayle, who came from a wealthy Indiana publishing family, "Did you pull strings?" Quayle responded, "No."[56]

As the convention approached, Kemp and Dole remained the subject of media speculation, but they had largely been ruled out by Bush. Though they made the cut to the final six, Bush didn't have great personal chemistry with either of them, and they both threatened to take some of the spotlight away from the top of the ticket.[57] "Dole would be more instantly perceived as President," wrote Bush in his diary on Saturday, August 13, "and Quayle is more exciting and new, and though people wouldn't know much about him, they would get to know him pretty quick."[58]

Dole, Kemp, and Quayle all went on ABC's *This Week with David Brinkley* on the day before the convention and "engaged in a kind of 'nationally televised audition,'" according to Taylor and Broder in the *Washington Post*.[59] On NBC's *Meet the Press* the same morning, Simpson effectively removed himself because he believed some of his stances would hurt Bush, notably his pro-choice view on abortion, declaring, "Once you flunk that litmus test, you're doomed."[60] As reflected by the success of the Robertson campaign, religious conservatives were increasingly assertive in the process, and Bush himself had had to change his abortion stance in 1980 when he joined the ticket. In June, J. C. Willkie, the head of National Right to Life, wrote to Bush explaining his organization's position in that regard. The letter read, "We are convinced that a pro-abortion person would convince those yet-to-be convinced Democrat crossovers that their 'suspicions' are correct and would doom the ticket. Just as certainly, a pro-life person could lay all those concerns aside and provide the confidence and enthusiasm needed to bring those several million voters aboard again." Willkie then included a list titled "Possible Vice Presidential Candidates Who Support Roe v. Wade and Would Lose Millions of Pro-Life Votes for Bush," which included Simpson and Governor Tom Kean of New Jersey, who was delivering the keynote address at the Republican convention.[61]

"We're here for the changing of the guard from Ronald Reagan to George Bush," declared Jennings as ABC's coverage of the Republican convention began. "Four days for Republicans to convince Americans to stay the course."[62] The Bush people were very focused on the transition.[63] The keynote address was moved to day two so that the first night would be all about the incumbent president's valedictory.[64] Jeff Greenfield commented that

Reagan would be an anomaly for an outgoing president—a figure popular enough to be an asset on the trail for his potential successor.[65]

Every day, the Republicans provided their surrogates with a "line of the day" to focus their message for the convention. For day one, it was "Ronald Reagan and George Bush inherited an economy in decline, a weak nation, losing its stature in the world. They took bold action to make America great again." This statement was followed by a list of the improvements in various economic statistics since the Carter era. GOP speakers would remain faithful to this script throughout the convention.[66]

The main event of the first night arrived when Reagan came onstage, receiving a long ovation from the enthusiastic delegates. Setting the template for other speakers over the four nights, he spelled out how conditions had improved since he came into office in 1981, declaring, "Eight years ago, we met at a time when America was in economic chaos, and today we meet in a time of economic progress. We met then in international distress and today with global hope." He talked of the gains made domestically as well as in foreign policy, saying, "Not one inch of ground has fallen to communists," and "American and Soviet relations are the best they've ever been since World War II." Emphasizing that these policies had been enacted despite the strong opposition of "liberal elites," he alleged, "They [liberals] resisted our defense buildup, they resisted our tax cuts, they resisted cutting the fat out of government, and they resisted our appointments of judges committed to the law and the Constitution." While he acknowledged the budget deficit, the president deflected the blame onto congressional Democrats. "Yes it's [the deficit is] much too high," Reagan said, "but the president doesn't vote for a budget and the president can't spend a dime. Only the Congress can do that."[67]

Discussing his vice president's role in reducing government regulations, Reagan declared, "And George was there," offering a clear rebuke to Ted Kennedy's "Where was George?" speech from the Democratic convention. The crowd chanted, "George was there! George was there!" "George played a major role in everything that we have accomplished in these eight years," Reagan asserted. "Without George Bush to build on those policies," he continued, "everything we've achieved will be at risk. All the work, sacrifice, and effort of the American people could end in the very same disaster that we inherited in 1981." The president added that Bush's experience was necessary to deal with Gorbachev: "This is no time to gamble with on the job training." He continued, telling his vice president, "Go out there and win one for the Gipper." This speech marked the end of Reagan's role at the convention, as the attention shifted to Bush.

Bush was moving toward his decision, which he'd said he would make by the time he reached New Orleans. Dole put the final nail in the coffin of his chances on Monday night when he agreed when a reporter asked him whether the selection process was "demeaning."[68] At the same time, Quayle was becoming more certain he would be the nominee.[69]

On the morning of Tuesday, August 16, the Bush campaign prepared to go to the convention, and the vice president was concerned about "leaving these other guys dangling for 36 hours."[70] After an intelligence briefing, Fuller told Bush that he did not need to reveal his selection. However, Fuller still wanted to know whether Bush had made his final decision. As the group flew to Andrews Air Force Base, Fuller told Baker that he thought the vice president had not made up his mind, and this could be a problem if the press asked him about his choice when they got to New Orleans. "He's not good at faking something, I thought," Fuller recalled.[71] Baker spoke to Bush, and the vice president assured him that he'd made his decision, though he didn't tell his campaign manager yet. In the hopes of surprising the media, Baker told Fuller they should make the announcement when they got to New Orleans, even though it would disrupt the existing convention schedule. "I'm pretty sure Baker thought it was Kemp," remembered Fuller, adding, "None of us thought it was Quayle, by the way," even those supportive of the Indiana senator. "The campaign staff knew it was either going to be Dole or myself. That was a given. They just assumed that it was going to be Dole," concurred Quayle.[72]

When they arrived in Louisiana for the ceremonial passing-of-the-torch meeting with Reagan at Belle Chase Naval Air Station, Bush told the president of his pick. Then, Fuller related, "Bush and Baker go into a bathroom and Bush tells him it's Quayle. [Then] they come out, and I could see Jim was a little surprised."[73] According to *Newsweek*, when Bush informed the rest of the staff, "the sound of silence filled the room, a stillness born more of surprise than disapproval. . . . Bob Teeter would tell friends later that he had nearly fallen out of his chair" upon hearing the news.[74]

The campaign then had to notify those who hadn't been chosen and find Quayle. Reaching the Indiana senator, Bush told him, "You are my choice, my first choice, my only choice."[75] Discussing the logistics of the announcement, Quayle told Baker that he thought it would be difficult for him to get through the crowds to the site, then asked whether a driver would be sent to him. Baker said no, as the campaign was trying to maintain the element of surprise, and he informed Quayle that his initial task as running mate was to find a way to get there. The campaign chairman then told him, "This

Indiana senator Dan Quayle's overly excited reaction to his nomination as vice president in New Orleans on August 16, 1988, began what would be a rocky ride as the number two person on George H. W. Bush's ticket. (AP Photo / Dennis Cook)

decision is revocable." "We both laughed," Quayle recalled, adding, "It was the last laugh I would have for a long, long time."[76]

Bush was riding in a riverboat along the Mississippi, and he and his staff were going to make the announcement when they docked. When the ship first passed by the dock, Quayle could not be found. Then the ship made a second pass—and at this point the campaign had found him.[77] "I've always felt we did him [Quayle] a terrible disservice by the way this announcement rolled out," Fuller remarked, adding, "We just denied ourselves the ability to really prepare for it." Emerging as the selection, Quayle seemed overly exuberant as he accepted the position, with some comparing his behavior to a game-show contestant.[78] Vice President Bush introduced Quayle, the first baby boomer on a national ticket, as "a young man born in the middle of this century in the middle of this country."[79]

"I was surprised by, but only mildly concerned about, Dan's excess exuberance," thought Baker. "Part of the craziness of the announcement was Quayle was trying to work his way on a warm day through the crowd. Bush was excited. Quayle was excited," Fuller observed, "[but] neither had really prepared for this moment and you know we got what we got."[80] Staffers were clearly caught off guard, as Pinkerton sent an intern to buy the *Almanac of American Politics* so he could have some background material about his candidate's choice.[81]

Shortly after the announcement, Mosbacher came by Bush's hotel room to convince him of the need to match the Dukakis campaign's soft-money operation. He recalled Bush's concern that "some people [would] get the perception that they [could] buy influence," but Mosbacher insisted, "We have to do this. We cannot disarm unilaterally." The vice president eventually agreed. "Now, we had a chance of pulling to the starting line of the fall campaign in a competitive financial position," Mosbacher remembered, declaring the following day, "We intend to match the Democrats plus $1."[82]

The battle for soft money had now been joined, much to the chagrin of good-government reformers like Fred Wertheimer of Common Cause, who lamented, "The campaign this year is going to be the most we've ever seen from the standpoint of illegal money being raised and spent."[83] Senator Mitch McConnell (R) of Kentucky, who would become Wertheimer's nemesis with his career-long opposition to campaign-finance reform, recommended the end of public funding, explaining, "What's happening here is we're reverting to massive contributions. It smacks of the way we used to operate in the early 1970s."[84] Thus, a process had begun by which the post-Watergate public funding system would be essentially rendered null and void by the early twenty-first century.

The party also settled on its platform, which was significantly longer than the Democratic one. While the Democrats tried to avoid a platform that made them look too liberal, the Republicans took the opposite approach. "[The] document reiterates the staunchly conservative principles of the Reagan era but seeks to leave Bush's imprint on such emerging issues as AIDS and child care for working parents," wrote Toner.[85] Sununu, who chaired the platform committee, claimed, "It was probably the most conservative Republican platform ever, even more conservative than the platforms of 1980 and 1984."[86]

Jennings and Brinkley interviewed Baker, who would officially become campaign chairman the following day, during ABC's convention coverage. Stressing Quayle's government experience, Baker said, "This is a bold reach across generations if you will," and "He's an ideological choice to some extent, but he is a generational choice if you will." A lot of floor discussion revolved around Quayle's potential appeal to the baby-boomer generation. Presciently, Jennings asked, "I assume you have done all of the background checks. There are no skeletons?" Baker replied thus: "We have done . . . an extensive job of background checks. We don't think that there is anything in there that will represent a problem." Despite Baker's confidence, he was quite mistaken—the real controversy was yet to come.[87]

Former Reagan UN ambassador Jeanne Kirkpatrick—a neoconservative who had become disenchanted with the Democrats in the 1970s because she believed they had become too dovish on foreign policy—gave the first of two keynote speeches that evening. She sharply criticized Dukakis's approach to foreign policy in an attempt to make him look weak on defense. "If you look at their record it is clear that the basic approach hasn't changed since George McGovern was nominated in 1972 and since Jimmy Carter was elected in 1976." She added, "Michael Dukakis doesn't say he will leave us defenseless against Soviet missiles. But that is the inevitable consequence of abandoning SDI [The Strategic Defense Initiative].[88] Michael Dukakis does not advocate the spread of communism in Central America or Africa. But he opposes American aid to the contras and to UNITA [The National Union for the Total Independence of Angola], the only forces blocking the spread of communism."

Vietnam had damaged Democratic credibility on foreign policy, and the GOP had relentlessly attacked the opposing party as soft on defense since then. Employing many of the same arguments Republicans had used against Democrats since the 1960s, Kirkpatrick echoed her attacks from the 1984 convention on the "San Francisco Democrats" who "blame America first." "Michael Dukakis simply doesn't take the need for defense seriously," she alleged, "but Michael Dukakis is more worried about an American president's misuse of power than about an adversary's use of power against us."[89]

New Jersey governor Tom Kean delivered the other keynote. As more of an old-school, northeastern Rockefeller Republican, he represented somewhat of an outlier in an increasingly conservative party. Kean's appearance in such a prominent slot revealed that the GOP, like the Democratic Party, was more heterogenous in the 1980s than it would be in the twenty-first century. At one point, centrists were full partners—or even in control of the Republican Party—nominating brethren like Wendell Willkie, Thomas Dewey, Dwight Eisenhower, and Gerald Ford for president. By this time conservatives largely dominated the GOP, but there was still a reasonably prominent moderate wing.[90] Kean's speech outlined the Bush campaign's major themes of the convention and the campaign, attacking Dukakis as weak on defense and on his supposed willingness to raise taxes. Meanwhile, they softened the edges of the Reagan message by talking about the need to assist the poor and do more about education and the environment. The latter focus showed that Republican conservatism was slightly moderating by the late 1980s.

Kean, like some others, suggested the Democrats were trying to hide their true ideology, explaining, "Those liberal Democrats are trying to hide more than the colors of our flag—you see they're trying to hide their true colors." Continuing Kirkpatrick's attacks on foreign policy, he told the audience to watch out for the "Dukakis Democrats," asserting, "They may try to talk like Dirty Harry but they will still act like Pee Wee Herman."[91]

Using another traditional post-1960s Republican line of attack, Kean suggested Democrats would raise taxes, alleging, "They call for an end to economic violence. What it really means is taking from those who work and simply giving to those who don't. And what does it add up to? More taxes." Mocking Ted Kennedy's convention rhetoric, he continued, "And where is Ted Kennedy? Ted Kennedy is off promoting mandated health insurance and that idea seems so eerily similar to a colossal program for socialized medicine right out of the platform of George McGovern. And what does that mean? More taxes!" Kean kept the refrain going: "And what does the name of Dukakis sound to you like. More taxes!"[92]

But like Bush had during the primary, Kean shifted to the need to do more about those left out of the 1980s expansion. "We also care about those who are not so fortunate," he declared, adding, "The simple truth is there are no spare Americans any longer. To those who are ill-schooled, ill-trained, or ill-housed, we must reach out and lift the artificial weights that Lincoln promised. As Republicans we will do it not only because economically it is the only thing to do [but] because morally it's the right thing to do." Kean elaborated that big government programs weren't the solution, stating, "The Democrats gave us the War on Poverty and poverty won." He further explained, "We offer poor Americans not the junk food of more big government but the full meal of good private-sector jobs. We offer them Jack Kemp's urban enterprise zones and the job training partnership act of Dan Quayle."[93]

Robertson gave a speech that evening as well, praising Quayle effusively and reflecting conservative satisfaction with the selection. "The conservatives in the Republican Party are so happy they don't quite know what to do. They are delighted with Dan Quayle," observed Brinkley. Hume added, "There is a sense that this was a bold move by a politician who is not always known for making bold moves."[94]

The following day, print accounts outlined Quayle's career and the relatively positive initial reactions to Bush's decision. "In choosing Dan Quayle as his running mate, George Bush has selected a man in his own image: pleasant, affable, conservative—as well as rich and good-looking," wrote Susan Rasky in the *New York Times*. First elected to the House in 1976, Quayle then rode the Reagan landslide to a Senate victory over liberal lion Birch Bayh in 1980. Quayle had been taken lightly in the House, but Rasky pointed out, "In the Senate he has established himself as a diligent legislator, willing to tackle complex military issues and faithfully pulling his weight for conservative causes dear to the heart of the Reagan administration."[95] Helen Dewar and David Broder echoed this assessment in the *Washington Post*: "Colleagues say Quayle is bright but no intellectual. He has demonstrated an ability to master complex issues and muster arguments in debate, which he approaches with vigor and passion that has sometimes led to heated and biting exchanges in the Senate."[96] Though he had a conservative voting record, he had worked across party lines at times, passing the Job Training Partnership Act of 1982 with Ted Kennedy. Some, however, did question Quayle's qualifications for a national ticket. An anonymous Democratic Senate colleague assessed his suitability thus: "He is not in the same league with Bob Dole or Pete Domenici or Dick Lugar [Indiana Republican colleague Sen. Richard G. Lugar] in terms of being a heavyweight."[97]

Conservatives continued to praise the decision, with Dick Cheney, then a Wyoming congressman and chair of the House Republican Conference, saying, "He's [Quayle is] an excellent choice. . . . There are a lot of us in our 40s who are happy to see a colleague, a peer, become part of the leadership team."[98] Disapproving, the *New York Times* editorialized, "By choosing Dan Quayle, an amiable, little-known ideologue, Mr. Bush has turned to youth, energy—and the right."[99]

Much was made of Quayle's resemblance to movie star Robert Redford, and some even suggested this might help him close the ticket's gender gap with female voters. Quayle did not think this was useful, saying, "The assertion by a couple of Republican strategists that my supposed 'good looks' played well with female voters was dumb and condescending and didn't help matters." It was also noted that his grandfather owned several newspapers and that his family was quite wealthy, though Quayle complained that his own net worth was vastly exaggerated. He claimed, "My net worth in 1988, including my house was $854,000, a tiny fraction of Lloyd Bentsen's."[100]

Dukakis's public response to Quayle's selection was very muted; he called the senator "not very well known," then said, "But I assume and expect the vice president will make the reasons known for his picking him."[101] Estrich remembered, "Our first reaction when we heard Dan Quayle was chosen was pleasant surprise."[102] She believed it must have been Bush's decision, contending, "I knew he couldn't be the choice of the rest of the guys."[103] The Dukakis campaign's first talking point criticized Bush for caving to the right wing, asking, "If Bush can't stand up to the extremists in his party, how is he going to fare across a table from Gorbachev?"[104] Later, Dukakis said, "I thought it [Bush's choice of Quayle] was a lousy one. He certainly wasn't picked because somebody thought he'd make a great president if something happened to the president."[105]

Bush and Quayle held a joint press conference that morning. The vice president began by calling his running mate "one of the rising stars in the Republican Party." He added that he chose the Indiana senator for three reasons: First, he was "qualified." Second, their opinions were aligned—as Bush said, "We agree on the fundamental challenges that face this country."

Coming Out of Reagan's Shadow · 175

Finally, Bush said of Quayle, "I believe he will help our cause in every part of the country."[106]

Regarding his Vietnam-era service in the National Guard, Quayle faced two questions. "You're tough on defense. Do you think it's going to be a handicap in the campaign because you didn't fight in Vietnam?" asked a reporter. "No, I do not," the Indianan responded. Later in the press conference, another journalist queried, "Senator Quayle, there's been so much made of the fact you're a baby boomer. . . . Graduating in 1969, the Vietnam era, you chose to go in the National Guard rather than to service in Vietnam. Can you give us a little bit of what you were thinking during that time?" Quayle gave a meandering answer about growing up in Huntington, Indiana, eventually ending with the admission "I did not know in 1969 that I would be in this room today, I'll confess."[107]

"Uh-oh. Our candidate had just provided a new definition of 'selective service,'" thought Baker.[108] Later, Quayle explained, "What I meant was that I hadn't been especially reflective about that decision back then—I just pursued an option that was available to me. I didn't view the decision in the larger historical context, as the media seemed to think I should have." He elaborated further: "Unfortunately my answer seemed to imply that, if I'd been more politically calculating at the time, I would have made a different decision. I sounded vaguely apologetic about my service with the Guard, and that is absolutely the last thing I felt then or feel today. I also sounded as if I had joined the Guard to escape the war."[109]

Appearing on all the networks during convention coverage that evening, Quayle told Jennings and Brinkley that he was a generational choice and offered a look toward the future. When asked why he joined the National Guard instead of going to Vietnam, Quayle said the force offered him the chance to go to law school.[110] Given that he'd made the decision twenty years earlier, he told Brokaw on NBC that he couldn't recall whom he'd told that he wanted to get into the guard. In addition, he claimed he didn't know "if phone calls were made."[111] "I was talking about phone calls made in search of information about openings," Quayle explained later, "not phone calls made to use 'influence,' which is how the remark was interpreted."[112] As the evening progressed, the campaign organized to discover the exact circumstances surrounding his entry into the National Guard. "[Birch] Bayh tried to make it an issue in my campaign in 1980, so I should have been a little bit more alert," recalled Quayle.[113]

While Quayle made the rounds on television that evening, so did Donald Trump, as part of a media campaign orchestrated by longtime adviser Roger Stone.[114] Interviewed by Larry King on CNN, he said he "probably" wouldn't have accepted the vice-presidential slot and praised Quayle's performance at the press conference. When King described Trump as either an "Eastern Republican" or a "Rockefeller, Chase Manhattan Republican," he then asked the businessman whether he was a "Bush Republican." Previewing his blue-collar populism of 2016, Trump responded, "The people that I do best with are the people that drive the taxis. You know wealthy people don't like me 'cause I'm competing against them all the time and they don't like me and I like to win. The fact is I go down the streets of New York and the people that really like me are the taxi drivers and the workers." Ironically, given his harsh attacks on the Bushes three decades later, Trump said that he was at the convention as a guest of Bush and Mosbacher, and that he was supporting George H. W. Bush—who was going to make a great president.[115]

Questioned about why he was involved in politics, Trump replied, "I enjoy it. I enjoy the system. I doubt I'll ever be involved in politics beyond what I do right now. But I do enjoy the system. I find it a really a really beautiful thing to watch. A beautiful machine." This comment was a far cry from the "drain the swamp" rhetoric of 2016. Asked about the boomlet regarding him running in the fall, Trump declared, "I never had any intention and I won't be running for president."[116]

Trump was not the only twenty-first-century Republican president on the floor that night. Serving as a Texas delegate, George W. Bush demonstrated the same folksy persona he would display as president when interviewed by Donaldson. Asked whether there was anything at all wrong with his father, his eldest son simply replied, "The only thing wrong with him is that he won't brag about himself enough." When the exchange concluded, Donaldson called him "a chip off the old block." It would be the Texas delegation that gave the elder Bush the necessary delegates to achieve the nomination during the roll call, with W. calling him "the best father in America."[117]

Twelve years before his own successful run, the son played an important role in the campaign, serving as his father's "eyes and ears," according to Baker. "The president knew he could rely on W. to report truthfully on what was going on," Baker added. Despite the traditional apprehension regarding a close family member's involvement in a campaign, most Bush staffers praised the son's performance, though it seems he was motivated more by loyalty to his dad than by any ideology. Notably, W. became close to Atwater and often defended him to others, though he didn't wholeheartedly embrace the latter's approach to politics. "He [George W. Bush] wasn't afraid to attack," commented one campaign worker, "but I never saw him show any glee in taking people down."[118]

Coming Out of Reagan's Shadow · 177

After three days of speeches and with a nominee in hand, the GOP message was now clear to the nation. "The Republicans plan to paint the Massachusetts Governor as inexperienced and therefore risky and as too liberal on a broad range of issues," wrote Dionne, "especially crime, the death penalty, military strength, and taxes—in an effort to reach pro-Reagan Democrats and independents."[119] It was the same strategy the party had used to defeat the Democrats for a generation.

The same evening as the nomination, Baker organized a group of staffers to discern the exact circumstances surrounding Quayle's entrance into the National Guard. "Make damn sure your recollections are accurate. If you cannot remember something, say you can't," he told the Indiana senator earlier. Baker also reminded Quayle, "The one thing you *cannot* do is go out there and say something that turns out to be untrue. That would put the vice president—and yourself—in a terribly compromising position."[120] The staff got to work. "We stayed up all night trying to figure out what happened and how to handle it," Black recalled, "and I even woke up [future Indiana Governor] Mitch Daniels at 2 o'clock in the morning and asked him to come over to Baker's suite 'cause he would know people around Indianapolis he could call to try to figure this out."[121]

Most importantly, Bush adviser Richard Darman and Robert Kimmitt went to Quayle's hotel to talk to him and his father to get all the information they could regarding the situation. While he and his father did not remember everything, according to *Newsweek*, "Quayle recalled having phoned home about his decision, and his father in turn had rung up one or two past or present employees who had been senior guard officers—for information, he insisted, not influence."[122] Indeed, a retired National Guard official who was working for Quayle's father admitted to trying to assist the younger Quayle.[123] Though he still had much to check, Darman reported back to a nervous campaign that "Quayle was not hiding some unexploded bombshell."[124]

But this was not before there was limited talk of dropping him from the ticket. "It was a very brief discussion. Somebody raised it; somebody said that's nuts. And we went on," said Ailes.[125] Black's recollections are similar; he asserted that such comments came "only from second or third-string people. Not from the nominee or inner circle."[126] Nobody wanted a repeat of 1972, when McGovern never recovered from dropping Eagleton from the ticket.

While Quayle would remain on the ticket, the morning papers reflected and reinforced the Indiana senator's declining fortunes. A *Washington Post* headline read, "Bush Wins; Victory Shadowed by Questions about Running

Mate's Past."[127] In the *New York Times*, Steven Roberts wrote, "Vice President Bush's selection of Senator Dan Quayle of Indiana on Tuesday as his running mate initially drew high marks for political boldness, but a more measured debate has since begun over the 41-year-old Senator's qualifications and standing in Congress."[128]

Who was to blame for this controversy? Kimmitt, who had spearheaded the vetting process, wrote the following to Baker on August 18: "I did discuss the Guard issue, both in my first interview of Quayle and in my report to the Vice President. It would therefore be inaccurate for either of them to indicate the matter was not discussed before the selection or that the issue of favoritism (my term, as opposed to 'preferential treatment') was not raised in these discussions. Your comment—that it is your understanding that these matters were considered during the selection process—is the accurate position."[129] Blaming a lack of readiness for the kerfuffle, Quayle added, "There was just a total lack of preparation to deal with my candidacy. You have to deal with me entirely differently than you deal with Bob Dole."[130]

Of course, Bush would deliver his acceptance speech that evening and—as with Dukakis—it would serve as his introduction to the country in many ways. Despite his many years of public service and two terms as vice president, Bush still remained undefined in the minds of many voters, and with the Quayle controversy dominating the convention, his address took on even greater importance.[131]

Peggy Noonan was charged with writing the speech. Having worked for Reagan from 1984 to 1986, she had provided the prose for several of his most famous speeches, notably the "Boys of Pointe du Hoc" address in Normandy on the fortieth anniversary of D-Day in 1984, and his Oval Office address to the country after the *Challenger* disaster in 1986. A former Democrat from an Irish Catholic family, Noonan empathized with the working-class Reagan Democrats who were so crucial to the outcome of the election.[132]

In terms of the content of the speech, a key debate emerged over the language surrounding taxes. Though Bush had ruled out a tax increase in his announcement speech in October, he equivocated at other times during the campaign. From the beginning, advisers like Atwater and Pinkerton pushed hard for a strong antitax stance, and Noonan put declarative language in the draft ruling out a tax increase, with the vice president saying, "Read my lips. No new taxes."[133] "Jack Kemp told me, 'Hit hard on taxes,'" wrote Noonan. "Bush will be pressured to raise them as soon as he's elected, and he has to make clear he won't budge."[134]

Republicans had criticized Democrats since the 1960s and LBJ's Great Society for their "tax and spend policies." To combat this charge, Carter ran as a fiscal conservative in 1976. Then Reagan's tax cuts and military buildup, along with his failure to significantly cut domestic spending, had led to large budget deficits during the 1980s. These shortfalls became the dominant fiscal issue of the time. As we saw earlier, Mondale called for tax increases during his run in 1984 to establish his fiscally conservative credentials, but this simply revived the old nostrum that Democrats will raise taxes.

Knowing their candidate would inherit a large budget deficit if elected, several Bush advisers, including Darman, Teeter, and Fuller, opposed an absolute statement, believing a tax increase might prove necessary. Seeing a first draft, Darman told Ailes and Noonan that the language was "stupid and irresponsible."[135] He recalled, "I was told that the no-new-taxes commitment had been made before. I noted that it had not been etched in the public mind via prime-time television."[136] For a week, Bush's advisers battled over the final language for the speech. Regarding "read my lips," Noonan told Darman and Teeter, "Whatever you guys do don't screw with these lines." Ailes liked the "Clint Eastwood" factor in the lines, perhaps hoping it would make the president seem like the actor's "Dirty Harry" character. Still, Darman excised the language from later drafts, only to have Noonan put it back in the text. According to Bob Woodward, "Darman wondered why a speechwriter was, in effect, setting policy."[137]

Darman couldn't appeal directly to Bush on the subject because the vice president believed he had leaked information about him to the press during the Reagan years. Baker, who had given Darman his role in the process, likely could have gotten the language vetoed, but he did not advocate for its removal. Given his desire to be budget director if Bush won, "Darman raised his objections only mildly" in the last meeting about the speech with the vice president present. The all-important phrase remained in the final draft and would a have major impact on the election—as well as on Bush's term in office. "He was 17 points down (after the Democratic convention). The people were looking for the home run, they were looking for the life raft," commented one Bush official in 1992. "Things were not good at the time he made that speech. So it had to be a different type of speech. It had to be definitive, draw the line."[138]

Of course, Quayle had to give his acceptance speech as well. Early on, he expressed his pride in serving in the National Guard, and the crowd cheered in response. Interjecting, Jennings commented, "There is in this hall almost a feeling that they want to help him overcome this problem." Like other speakers, Quayle referenced the difficulties of the Carter years and the accomplishments of the Reagan administration. Trying to link Dukakis with past unsuccessful Democrats, the Indianan declared, "We do not need the future the Democratic Party sees. The party of George McGovern, Jimmy Carter, (Booing from audience) Walter Mondale . . . just wait it gets better . . . Ted Kennedy . . . and now his buddy Michael Dukakis." He continued, "That future has America in retreat. That future has higher taxes and a guaranteed loss of job opportunities and that future has more government intervention in the lives of all of us." Previewing Bush's speech, Quayle added, "George Bush will not raise your taxes period! And let me tell you something else, Michael Dukakis will."[139]

Referencing his status as the first baby boomer to reach these heights, the Indiana senator said, "I am privileged to be the first person of my generation to be on a national ticket. I don't presume to talk for everyone of my generation, but I know that a great many will agree with me when I express my thanks to the generation of George Bush for bringing us to an era of peace and freedom and opportunity." Concluding, Quayle added, "My generation has a profound debt to them, and we will pay it by making sure that our children and the generations that follow will have the same freedom, the same family values and a future bright with opportunity."[140]

Before Bush's speech came the standard bio video, narrated by conservative actor Charlton Heston. With the idea of the World War II generation as the "Greatest Generation" emerging, the film reviewed the candidate's enlistment as a pilot during the war. Fortuitously for Bush, Sid Rogich, the campaign's director of advertising, had obtained dramatic footage of the young airman's submarine rescue in 1944, which aired as part of the program.[141] The video also described the rest of Bush's career and showed Reagan offering his backing, declaring, "I trust George Bush. America can trust him too."[142]

Beginning his speech, Bush claimed underdog status and said he was proud to have Quayle as his running mate. Discussing how he had helped Reagan for the past eight years, Bush declared, "Now you must see me for what I am. The Republican candidate for president of the United States. And now I turn to the American people to share my hopes and intentions and why and where I wish to lead." Joking, he added, "But I'll try to be fair to the other side. I'll try to hold my charisma in check." He talked about seeing his life in terms of missions, concluding, "The most important mission of my life is to complete the mission we started in 1980. And how. And how do we complete it. We build on it."[143]

Laying out his disagreements with Dukakis, Bush claimed, "The differences between the two candidates are as deep and wide as they have ever been in our long history." Rejecting Dukakis's contention that the election was about competence—not ideology—he insisted, "This election isn't only about competence, for competence is a narrow ideal. . . . Competence is the creed of the technocrat." Seeking to draw a clear ideological contrast with his opponent, Bush said, "The truth is this election is about the beliefs we share, the values that we honor and the principles that we hold dear."[144]

Sticking with the central theme of the convention and recalling Reagan's "Morning in America" rhetoric, Bush stressed the difference between the economic record of the Carter years and the 1980s, especially lower unemployment and inflation. He made a promise to the young people who barely remembered the days of gas lines and high inflation: "You have the opportunity you deserve and I'm not going to let them take it away from you." With regard to inflation, he stated, "We arrested it. And we're not going to let it out on furlough."

Harking back to his speech declaring his candidacy, Bush acknowledged there were those who had not shared in the growth of the era. "Things aren't perfect in this country," he admitted. "There are people who haven't tasted the fruits of the expansion." He added, "Economic growth is the key to our endeavors. I want growth that stays, that broadens and that touches, finally, all Americans." Praising the cooling of global tensions, he credited the Reagan administration's policies for these advances, cautioning, however, that "a prudent skepticism" was warranted regarding the Soviet Union.[145]

Understanding that some voters wanted something fresh after eight years of Republican control, Bush said, "We will surely have change this year, but will it be change that moves us forward, or change that risks retreat?" Noting that FDR had said "we shouldn't change horses in midstream" in 1940, Bush asked, "Doesn't it make sense to switch to the one who's going the same way [if change becomes necessary]?"[146]

Stressing the importance of community, he also talked about the vital importance of civic institutions in the United States. "For we are a nation of communities, of tens of thousands of ethnic, religious, social, business, labor union, neighborhood, regional and other organizations, all of them varied, voluntary, and unique," Bush explained. Citing a list of such organizations, he said they made up a "brilliant diversity spread like stars," famously adding the memorable Noonan phrase "like a thousand points of light in a broad and peaceful sky."[147]

Explaining the concept, Noonan wrote, "It was my favorite phrase in the speech because its power is born of the fact that it sounds like what it is describing: an expanse of separate yet connected entities sprinkled across a broad and peaceful sky, which is America, the stretched continent." She elaborated, "Why stars for communities? I don't know, it was right. Separate, bright and shining, each part of a whole and discrete. Why a thousand?

I don't know. A thousand clowns, a thousand days—a hundred wasn't enough and a million is too many."[148]

Outlining key differences with Dukakis that would dominate the fall campaign, Bush first asked, "Should public school teachers be required to lead our children in the Pledge of Allegiance? My opponent says no and I say yes." Bush continued, "Should society be allowed to impose the death penalty on those who commit crimes of extraordinary cruelty and violence? My opponent says no but I say yes." He added that children should be able to say a voluntary prayer in schools. Then Bush asked and answered yet another question: "Should free men and women have a right to own a gun to protect their home? My opponent says no but I say yes."[149] Stressing his pro-life views, he stated, "We must change from abortion to adoption." Returning to criminal justice, he declared, "I'm the one who believes it is a scandal to give a weekend furlough to a hardened first-degree killer who hasn't even served enough time to be eligible for parole."[150] According to Bush focus groups, the remarks regarding the death penalty and furloughs received very high responses from the audience.[151]

Then, very crucially, he added, "And I'm the one who won't raise taxes." Bush elaborated the point as follows: "My opponent won't rule out raising taxes. But I will and the Congress will push me to raise taxes, and I'll say no, and they'll push and I'll say no, and they'll push again and I'll say to them. Read my lips. No new taxes."[152] The hall cheered and the television audience shared the thrill, as the campaign's focus groups gave the line the highest ratings in the speech.[153]

Turning to some of the more centrist themes he discussed during the primary, Bush spoke of the need to improve education and to include the disabled, as well as to focus on protecting the environment. Speaking of racism, he remarked, "We're on a journey into a new century. And we've got to leave that tired old baggage of bigotry behind." Then, in another enduring phrase, Bush expressed his desire for "a kinder and gentler nation."[154] Not everyone was pleased, however. Nancy Reagan saw the words as an implicit critique of her husband's presidency, and she supposedly responded to them by asking, "Kinder than who?"[155] This line from Bush's speech again reflected the slight moderation of conservatism in the late 1980s.

Talking about having seen the difficult decisions a president must make, the vice president said that it all comes down "to the man at the desk." Asking who should sit there, he emphatically declared, "I am that man." Pledging to always move the country forward, he declared, "This is my mission and I will complete it."[156] He then ended by leading the audience in reciting the Pledge of Allegiance.[157]

George H. W. Bush delivers his acceptance speech at the Republican convention in New Orleans. (George H. W. Bush Presidential Library and Museum)

Like Dukakis, Bush had risen to the occasion and met the moment in his acceptance speech. "That's a good speech," commented Jennings, and Brinkley agreed, observing, "It was good. It's a George Bush I haven't seen before." Hume said the address introduced the delegates and the country to the George Bush his friends always talked about.[158] While sharply criticizing the Quayle pick, longtime *New York Times* reporter James Reston asserted, "The Vice President made the best speech of his long and distinguished career." "Never before had he [Bush] looked or sounded so Presidential," the journalist added.[159]

Bush was pleased as well, writing the following in his diary: "The press was building it [the acceptance speech] up and up and up—had to do this, had to do that—and it was the biggest moment of my life, which it was; and almost setting expectations so high, that they couldn't be matched and, yet, they were." He also admitted, "Immediately after the speech, I knew it was good. . . . At conventions you can't tell because of the mandatory 'spontaneous' demonstration; but there was something different, and there was something special about it all, and I felt that it had worked."[160]

Though he was happy with his speech and stood behind Quayle publicly, Bush might have had second thoughts regarding his choice. According to historian Herbert Parmet, he wrote in his diary on August 21, "It was my decision, and I blew it, but I'm not about to say that I blew it."[161] When Parmet's book was released in 1997, a Bush spokesman suggested the entry had been taken out of context.[162] Interpreting his old friend's words, Baker said, "The way it was done, we did blow it. We did blow it. And I bet that's what President Bush meant. I think that's what he meant."[163] In parts of a diary entry from the same day that he included in a volume published in 1999, Bush wrote, "Of course, we're plagued by the Quayle/National Guard Service and they've been pounding the poor guy. . . . I think the press understands that there has been a feeding frenzy over Quayle, but they haven't proved he did anything wrong. A few demonstrators are cropping up yelling about Quayle being a draft dodger, but there is going to be an awful lot of people out there that understand that the Guard is honorable; that he played by the rules; and that's the point."[164]

Regardless, it wasn't immediately clear whether the controversy hurt Quayle and the ticket in the minds of the voters. Indeed, "three-fourths of voters interviewed Thursday night [the last night of the convention] (74%) said they did not have a less favorable opinion of Quayle 'because he chose to serve in the National Guard during the Vietnam War,'" according to George and Alec Gallup. Only 13 percent of respondents had a less favorable opinion of the Indiana senator. Furthermore, 36 percent said the choice made them more likely to support the ticket, as opposed to 33 percent saying it made them less likely to do so. Bentsen's numbers, however, were much stronger, with 48 percent responding that he made them more likely to vote for Dukakis, as opposed to only 28 percent saying he made them less likely to support the governor. Another poll offered perhaps the most troubling statistic for Bush and Quayle as the fall campaign began, stating, "67% rated Bentsen as qualified to serve as president while only 43% currently offer this assessment of Quayle."[165]

Whether it hurt the ticket or not, the Quayle selection represented a seminal moment in American politics, as every baby-boomer presidential candidate for the next thirty years would face the fateful question of "What did you do in the war?" Clinton's avoidance of the draft dogged him throughout his first campaign and never completely disappeared as an issue for some voters. Though George W. Bush's National Guard service never became as serious a problem for him as it did for Quayle, he, too, faced media scrutiny about how he gained admission to the guard and whether he completed his tour of service. On the other hand, John McCain's and John Kerry's military service in Vietnam became central parts of their political biography. As late as the 2016 presidential election, forty-three years after the end of American military involvement in the Vietnam War, Donald Trump's medical deferment for bone spurs remained a subject of discussion. "Looking back, Vietnam was an obvious question. All in my generation have answered the question: Clinton, Gore, and George W.," Quayle observed, adding, "Vietnam was a defining moment for my generation."[166]

The controversy surrounding Quayle also meant the end of presidential candidates naming their vice president during the convention. "Nobody should ever do that again," reflected Baker, "where you spring it on the press at the convention because then that's all they've got to write about is anything they can find. And that wasn't Dan's fault. It was really our fault, but we couldn't do it any other way."[167] Since then, nominees have picked their running mates before the convention and carried momentum from their selection into the event.

In another likely reaction to the Quayle experience, for the next two decades, candidates also took a cautious "first do no harm" approach and avoided picking unknowns for their running mates. Politicians of both parties only chose vice presidents who had been vetted through their own presidential campaigns (Al Gore, Jack Kemp, John Edwards, Joe Biden) or were well-established Washington figures (Dick Cheney, Joe Lieberman). Baker seemed to have reached this conclusion himself, writing, "The best way to avoid this sort of thing, however, is not through background checks; it is to select nominees who have already had a run at national politics, high-profile senate or gubernatorial races in states such as New York, California, Florida, Texas, or federal appointments requiring Senate confirmation." He continued, "You can be sure that the background of these kind of candidates have been vetted by the toughest possible investigators—their opponents and the press."[168] McCain's pick of then-unknown Alaska governor Sarah Palin in 2008 marked an end to this practice and might have reflected the fading memory of the Quayle selection.

Despite the Sturm und Drang regarding Quayle, Bush received a solid bounce from his convention, moving from trailing Dukakis 49 percent to 42 percent to leading him 48 percent to 44 percent, a 6-point shift.[169] This was similar to Dukakis's 7-point bounce and in line with the 6.2-point average for convention bounces between 1964 and 1992.[170] More impressive was how the convention changed the vice president's image in the minds of the electorate. Previously, 59 percent of voters had seen him as "sincere," while 74 percent viewed him that way after he formally accepted the nomination. Forty-nine percent had seen him as "warm and friendly" prior to New Orleans, while 65 percent thought so subsequently. And, in a strong counter to the "wimp factor," the percentage of voters who saw Bush as "strong" grew from 42 to 57. Finally, Bush's favorable/unfavorable rating, which had been a nagging problem throughout the campaign, also improved, rising from 51 percent / 42 percent to 60 percent / 33 percent. Multiple convention speakers' attacks on Dukakis might have taken their toll on the governor's image, as his favorable/unfavorable rating fell from 61 percent / 30 percent to 55 percent / 32 percent.[171]

Facing a seventeen-point deficit after the Democratic convention, Bush returned to the themes that had worked so successfully to narrow his opponent's similar advantage in June and July. Using the post-1968 GOP playbook, he and his allies attacked Dukakis and the Democrats as soft on crime, weak on defense, and prone to raising taxes. To strengthen their rhetorical hand, the Bush campaign also invoked the memory of the stagnation of the Carter years, trying to deflect calls for change after eight years of Reagan by reminding the country of the gas lines and malaise that preceded them. But in an era when there were significant numbers of swing voters, Bush—like Dukakis—tried to seize the center, especially on education and the environment. This message, however, was almost derailed by the poor handling of Dan Quayle's selection as vice president. The controversy over the pick distracted attention at the convention, but the ticket survived it—though it led to long-term changes in how candidates chose their running mates. In the end, the Bush-Quayle team left New Orleans with a nice bounce and a lead in hand. And they would never relinquish it.[172]

7   The Debates Take Center Stage

Michael Dukakis wasn't feeling well as he faced the most important moment of his race for president. He knew he had to show that, despite his opposition to the death penalty and the controversy over the Massachusetts furlough program, he was concerned about violent crime and understood its impact on its victims. He had practiced the answer to this debate query several times. He would talk about how crime had affected his own family.

CNN's Bernard Shaw was ready to ask the question that would become the signature moment of his long journalistic career. Infuriating him, his fellow panelists tried to talk him out of his decision. He would go ahead anyway.

John Sasso, Susan Estrich, and the rest of the Dukakis campaign brain trust waited nervously. They knew the second debate was probably their last chance to change the trajectory of the race. Trailing in the polls since the Republican National Convention, their candidate had a little momentum coming out of the first presidential debate and the vice-presidential debate.

And then the fateful moment came in the first question, which Shaw posed. "Governor, if Kitty Dukakis were raped and murdered, would you favor an irrevocable death penalty for the killer?" the journalist asked. Dukakis's response would go down in history and virtually seal the election for Bush.

Coming out of New Orleans with the lead, Bush stayed on the attack on the Pledge of Allegiance and Willie Horton, cementing his postconvention advantage over Dukakis. Attention to Quayle subsided for a bit, and using similar tactics to those employed by GOP nominees since 1968, Bush and his allies continued to paint the governor as out of the mainstream, calling him soft on crime, weak on defense, and insufficiently patriotic. Though politics has always been a contact sport, some believed the Bush attacks went beyond the norms, breaking traditional rules of fairness and accuracy. Then came the debates. Dukakis's narrow win in the first debate, along with Bentsen's trouncing of Quayle in the vice-presidential debate, gave the campaign faint hope. The polls remained relatively close despite the governor's infamous ride in a tank. But then came the second presidential debate, when Dukakis's performance—especially his response to the first question—appeared to seal the win for Bush.

Meanwhile, more of the roots of modern American politics came into view, as *Saturday Night Live* truly began its influential use of election-year political sketches. As Clinton's appearance on *The Tonight Show* demonstrated, these skits and other nontraditional programming that would emerge in later years, like *The Daily Show* and *The Colbert Report*, would play a major role in defining the images of candidates. Though it was only in its infancy, the early stages of this phenomenon were visible in 1988.

Climate change, a subject that would be much discussed in twenty-first-century politics, gained unprecedented attention in 1988, truly becoming a national issue for the first time. Reflecting this, the subject surfaced in a presidential or vice-presidential debate for the first time.

And both Bush and Dukakis sought to claim the middle, aiming for swing voters. On the one hand, the vice president aimed to show that he was more centrist by declaring he would be the "environmental president." On the other hand, Dukakis continued to promote his record on welfare reform and fiscal discipline. Their dual efforts helped pave the way for the centrist "New Democrat" presidential politics that would dominate the 1990s.

Punching back at the attacks over the Pledge of Allegiance, Dukakis delivered one of his fiercest responses to Bush on August 23, declaring, "If the vice president is saying he'd sign an unconstitutional bill, then in my judgement he's not fit to hold the office." The governor added, "The highest form of patriotism is dedication and a commitment to the Constitution of the United States and the rule of law."[1] The following day, Bush responded sharply, asking, "What is it about the Pledge of Allegiance that upsets him so much? It is very hard for me to imagine that the Founding Fathers—Samuel Adams and John Hancock and John Adams—would have objected to teachers leading students in the Pledge of Allegiance to the flag of the United States." As was often the case during the campaign, the pledge was recited by the crowd—led by none other than Charlton Heston.[2] The next day, Bush continued speaking about the pledge and also went after the ACLU: "He [Dukakis] says—here's an exact quote—he says 'I am a card-carrying member of the ACLU.'" Continuing with a McCarthy-era flourish, Bush declared, "Well I am not and never will be."[3] Cheering the return to a focus on the Pledge of Allegiance at the August 26 campaign-management meeting, Atwater offered this analysis: "[The] Quayle story turned Wednesday, crowds have been warm and he is perceived as being harangued by the press. Yesterday the campaign story came back in perspective with the VP being the story on the offensive with the Pledge issue and defense."[4]

Dukakis talked about how every first-year law student knew the cases about mandating the pledge, and internal documents reflected the campaign's often legalistic approach to the controversy.[5] This strategy was no doubt born of the predominance of lawyers in the upper echelons of the campaign. Memos on the subject, many written by future Supreme Court justice Elena Kagan, defended the governor's veto by focusing on *West Virginia State Board of Education v. Barnette* and on the advisory opinion from Massachusetts's supreme court saying the bill requiring teachers to lead students in reciting the Pledge of Allegiance was unconstitutional. Perhaps sensing this approach was not working, Harvard law professor Laurence Tribe, who had played a central role in the fight to defeat Robert Bork's nomination to the Supreme Court the previous year, wrote Kagan, Dukakis, and other members of the campaign to offer some sound bites to handle the subject. The professor explained, "[I am] partly inspired by my sense that the issue needs to be dealt with less legalistically and more simply."[6]

Indeed, the pledge debate was taking a toll on Dukakis's numbers because the controversy went beyond simple legality, emerging as a key cultural dispute that resonated with many Reagan Democrats who viewed the governor's veto as unpatriotic. On *Meet the Press*, Broder commented, "[Bush] has picked out three or four issues that he's hammering hard and the common thread of all of it is that he is really trying to build a wedge between Governor Dukakis and those Reagan Democrats using the social issues, like the 'Pledge of Allegiance' and the veto of that bill."[7] Unsurprisingly, Ailes agreed, alleging the governor's view was "defendable only by left-wingers, lunatics, and liberal lawyers."[8]

"Maybe my lawyer's hat was on too tight," conceded Dukakis, who didn't think the Pledge of Allegiance veto would be an issue. "Maybe I was being a little too legalistic," he mused.[9] When an adviser suggested having John Glenn make an ad responding to the attacks, the governor opposed such a commercial, even though the former astronaut and American hero was on board.[10] "The Pledge was mishandled," according to Corrigan, though he elaborated, "[It] certainly wasn't a big issue facing the country in the summer of 1988.... It was just brought up as a negative attack. It was just brought up to say you know to question his patriotism.... The net effect was to keep Dukakis on the defensive and to keep him from getting his message out."[11]

Agreeing, the *New York Times* editorial page wrote, "As a political ploy, it [the attack on the pledge veto] demeans Mr. Bush, insults his opponent and threatens to turn the Pledge—an honorable and decent ritual—into a political football." The editorial board elaborated, "The Pledge expresses noble sentiments and celebrates shared values. But the Pledge is not the issue. The issue is whether the Pledge can be required. It does nothing to elevate the level of political discourse to turn a complex constitutional question into a litmus test of patriotism—or of how to vote in November."[12] Taking the opposite view, the *Wall Street Journal* editorial page suggested, "Symbolically it [the debate over requiring the Pledge of Allegiance] is a truly revealing issue." The paper linked the matter to the legacy of the 1960s, explaining, "It says much about unresolved questions of the nature of our republic, including the wounds this country still suffers from the Vietnam War's self-doubt." In addition, the editorial board contended that Dukakis privileging the advice of an advisory opinion from his state supreme court over his legislature revealed his belief in judicial activism.[13] The Bush campaign welcomed the opposition of certain mainstream media outlets, with Pinkerton commenting at a meeting, "*Washington Post* and *NY Times* ran editorials today denouncing our use of the Pledge issue. This is sure sign that it is a good effective issue for us."[14]

Around this time, Senator Steve Symms (R) of Idaho falsely alleged, "There are pictures around . . . of Mrs. Dukakis burning an American flag while she was an antiwar demonstrator during the '60s." Though the campaign vigorously denied the accusation, Dukakis said nothing himself, with Estrich unable to explain why.[15] While Symms offered no proof for his assertion, "his [the governor's] advisers worried that the damage was already done," according to Larry Martz in *Newsweek*.[16]

Infuriated by what he saw as outright falsehoods on the part of the Bush campaign, Corrigan complained, "There were lies told about Michael Dukakis. There were lies that he was seeing a shrink. There were lies being spread about his wife burning the flag."[17] Regarding Symms, Corrigan alleged, "That stuff's all commissioned by the campaign."[18] In terms of Bush staffers' knowledge of the flag-burning story, the transcript of the August 26 campaign meeting shows Andy Card saying, "On Steve Symms, Kitty Dukakis story, we are not the source and don't know of any pictures of her burning a flag." It's not clear from campaign records whether Card was saying that was the truth, or whether he was saying that should be the campaign's message.[19]

If coordinated, Symms's attack was part of a continuing effort to link Dukakis to 1960s radicalism. A small number of antiwar protesters burned American flags during the Vietnam War, garnering significant media attention. Such behavior alienated blue-collar voters—many of whom were opposed to the conflict—often pushing them away from antiwar candidates they might have supported otherwise. This memory became an albatross around the neck of Democratic politicians in subsequent years, and the GOP was invoking the Pledge of Allegiance and everything else possible to remind voters of it in 1988.

While using the pledge to define Dukakis as an out-of-the-mainstream liberal, the vice president simultaneously sought to get to his left on the environment. With the emergence of the environmental movement in the 1970s, many Americans, especially in the suburbs, became increasingly concerned about the issue. The Reagan administration faced a significant backlash over the choice, and then over the behavior of James Watt as secretary of the interior and Anne Gorsuch Buford as administrator of the Environmental Protection Agency (EPA). Watt and Buford were perceived as trying to undermine the very mission of the agencies they led. Many moderate suburban Republicans—still an important constituency at this time—supported a more progressive approach to the issue.

Proudly calling himself a "Teddy Roosevelt Republican"—alluding to Roosevelt's historic support for conservation—Bush journeyed to Massachusetts to call attention to the pollution in his opponent's home state, specifically in Boston Harbor. As governor, Dukakis twice asked the EPA for waivers to delay cleaning up the harbor, though such an effort was underway by 1988. The campaign's internal talking points emphasized that the problem lay with delays in approving the waivers, as well as with a lack of support from the federal government.[20] Independent voices placed blame on both sides.[21]

Taking a boat through the harbor on September 1, Bush declared that the governor's strategy had been to "delay, fight, anything but clean up," adding, "Two hundred years ago, tea was spilled into this harbor in the name of liberty. Now it's something else. We've got to do better."[22] While there were a few counterprotesters in the water, Dukakis regretted not doing more. Reflecting, "I think that was one where we just kind of muffed the kind of response," he said he should have been there to greet Bush, promote his own efforts to clean up the harbor, and emphasize the need for more federal assistance.[23] Instead, Dukakis and his campaign stayed with their plan to meet with students at a science museum in Los Angeles and "[we] were blown off the local evening news in Los Angeles with us here and Bush in Boston," analyzed California campaign director Tony Podesta.[24]

In 1988, events like the harbor tour were essential to dominating the coverage on the evening news—the way most Americans received information about the race.[25] According to Dukakis advance man Matt Bennett, "In the late '80s, when network news was still incredibly important, there would be an event every day that was designated as the kind of event of the day" to be the main story on the evening broadcast.[26] At this time, the most important media battle was winning the story line at the start of the evening newscast, and the Bush campaign's success in this regard was vital to their candidate's victory in the fall.[27]

Some, however, viewed the network reporting as quite superficial. While all three networks covered the harbor event, Germond and Witcover wrote that "only ABC made any serious attempt to sort out the complex story of who was responsible for not cleaning up Boston Harbor."[28] NBC's and CBS's reporting focused more on campaign strategy and imagery. CBS's Bob Schieffer called Bush's Boston Harbor trip "floating political theater," noting that the candidate's strategy was to "convince voters that the Massachusetts Miracle is just a mirage." James Baker seemed undisturbed by this critique, explaining, "All three networks gave the tour extensive airtime. [CBS] described the event as 'floating political theater.' Exactly."[29] Indeed, there was growing criticism of the horse-race nature of the electronic media's coverage, with Jonathan Alter of *Newsweek* writing, "The networks make some effort to go beyond the mud wrestling but their analytical pieces may be lost in the scuffling."[30]

In fact, 1988 represented the last hurrah for these institutions as dominant forces, as cable and nontraditional programming grew in importance.[31] CNN earned plaudits for its coverage of the 1990–91 Persian Gulf War, and by 1992 the situation had already begun to change. Perot launched his third-party bid on CNN's *Larry King Live*, while Bill Clinton pursued younger voters on MTV. After 1988, a more diverse media environment would emerge where cable networks, the internet, and other sources gained equal or greater prominence.[32]

Part of this greater diffusion was talk radio, as the Bush-Dukakis battle was also the last presidential election where the medium didn't play a major role. In 1987, the Federal Communications Commission (FCC) repealed the Fairness Doctrine, which had long limited opinion-driven shows on radio. Shortly thereafter, on August 1, 1988, Rush Limbaugh's show went into national syndication, paving the way for conservative radio hosts to play a central role in elections in the 1990s and beyond.[33]

Two weeks later, the Bush campaign ran a negative ad following up on the Boston Harbor tour.[34] Showing pictures of polluted water, the piece delineates the problems with the harbor, saying Dukakis had the chance to do something about them but "chose not to." Referring to "the dirtiest harbor in America" while the commercial shows a sign reading "Danger / Radiation Hazard / No Swimming," the narrator ominously concludes, "And Michael

Dukakis promises to do for America what he's done for Massachusetts."³⁵ In what would become a pattern as the fall progressed, some would later critique the commercial's accuracy. Analysts noted that the governor had in fact begun a cleanup effort, and that the radiation-hazard sign was not from Boston Harbor. Instead, the notice was posted in an area where navy subs were once repaired, thus giving a distorted impression of the situation.³⁶ Malcolm McDougal, a Republican ad person who had worked for Gerald Ford but was friends with Dukakis, called the spot "a disgraceful piece of innuendo."³⁷

Though he defined Dukakis as a liberal, Bush's strong critique of the governor's environmental record showed that the GOP in 1988 departed not only from the Reagan era but also from the party's direction in subsequent years. While the elder Bush claimed the mantle of Teddy Roosevelt, future GOP nominees would not seek the title of "environmental president," even to the point of questioning the validity of the science regarding climate change. Though the party had moved sharply to the right by 1988, it was still more centrist than its twenty-first-century iteration.³⁸

With the seventeen-point lead gone and his campaign falling in the polls, Dukakis turned to his old friend Sasso for help. Though his right-hand man had moved on to work at an ad agency after the Biden tape incident, he had remained in touch with Dukakis and others in the campaign's high command. Kitty Dukakis proved instrumental in facilitating Sasso's return, telling her husband he would lose if he didn't bring him back. Though initially reluctant, Sasso agreed to return, taking the title of vice chairman. However, given his close relationship with the candidate, he would likely be in charge of the campaign.³⁹ At a campaign meeting shortly thereafter, Atwater observed, "Sasso's return will be a net plus for Dukakis. He is good and voters don't care about campaign staff enough for his return to be a negative."⁴⁰

Now Sasso had to develop a plan for the homestretch of the campaign. Everyone involved understood that the race and the White House were rapidly getting away from them. Referring to Dukakis aides, Barney Frank commented, "They said they have two weeks to turn the campaign around." The new plan was to focus on the "middle-class squeeze," as many Americans were struggling to pay for college and housing despite the low unemployment and low inflation of the late Reagan years.⁴¹ Borrowing from Gephardt's primary message, the Dukakis camp also looked to focus on America's declining position vis-à-vis Japan and some of its other trading partners. "If the issues on voters' minds are America's place in the world and the family squeeze we win," concluded Sasso. "If it's peace and prosperity, we lose."⁴²

But it wasn't clear that that was the case as many voters interviewed in a St. Louis suburb seemed willing to stay the course with the GOP regardless of the "squeeze." A couple of twentysomething middle-class voters worried about their child care and health insurance costs remained supportive of Bush because they feared a Dukakis presidency would return the country to the malaise of the late 1970s. "I am working class, but I like the way the economy goes when the Republicans are in," one explained, adding, "In my lifetime since I was old enough to understand, the economy hasn't done well when the Democrats are in. We've had a good living for the last eight years." The other voter also recalled the Carter years, saying, "[He] is the only other president I've known," and "I think about how and everything was when Carter was in. Reagan seemed to do so much good for the economy."[43]

Some Bush supporters seemed to be more focused on crime and cultural issues. Dissatisfied with both candidates, one conflicted constituent, who declared he was "pretty hard core on capital punishment," concluded he would probably vote for Bush because of Dukakis's positions on gun control and the death penalty. While the Pledge of Allegiance did not come up much among this group, one voter stressed its importance, observing, "Little kids in school have to be taught things. One of them is that there were a lot of good people who died for this country."[44]

There remained a few faint signs of hope for Dukakis among this constituency, which revealed that an old-style economic populist message might prove effective for him. One union member who had voted for Reagan in 1984 expressed frustration that the incumbent wasn't helping workers and wanted a tougher trade policy toward Japan. Furthermore, some of the vice president's backers fretted that Bush was "too upper, upper class, too much for big business."[45]

With his culturally populist attacks, however, Bush had shed the elitist label and placed it tightly around Dukakis's neck. Some Democrats pushed hard to fight back: "They're running a class war against us, saying we're a bunch of Cambridge-Brookline eccentric literature professors. We've got to fight that back and say that they're the party of privilege, the party of the rich folks," declared one person involved in discussions on how to revive the governor's campaign.[46] Indeed, Shrum, who authored many of Gephardt's populist speeches, had given Dukakis a similar text to deliver on Labor Day. While it "didn't lean as far into a Gephardt-like message as what he did at the end," Shrum said, the address "was an attempt to argue that the real question here was who was going to fight for the middle class, who was going to fight for working families." Dukakis didn't give the speech, telling Shrum that he couldn't deliver it because it wasn't him.[47]

Indeed, Dukakis resisted a populist message for most of the general election. Estrich wanted Dukakis to run ads showing a helicopter flying over Bush's vacation home in Kennebunkport to depict the vice president as a wealthy elitist. "Dukakis absolutely vetoed it," according to Estrich. He also resisted attacking Bush as a country-club Republican, saying, "I'm not going to play that kind of politics."[48] This reluctance might have been shaped by his experience with McCarthyism, as the Wisconsin senator's success caused many liberal intellectuals to fear that populism could easily descend into demagoguery. "He feared the downside, the dark side of populism," reflected Corrigan, suggesting that the governor's attitude came from reaching political consciousness during the early 1950s.[49]

On September 6, an independent group called the National Security Political Action Committee—also referred to as Americans for Bush—started showing an ad featuring two different pictures of Willie Horton.[50] Echoing Atwater, Floyd Brown, a political consultant for the group, announced, "When we're through, people are going to think that Willie Horton is Michael Dukakis' nephew."[51] Larry McCarthy, who had worked for Dole in the primaries, put the ad together, later saying, "This is every suburban mother's greatest fear." McCarthy admitted, "[I] debated whether I could get this by the cable television network officials and on the air," and he added, "The guy looked like an animal. . . . And frankly because he was black I thought longer and harder about putting him in there." Horton claims the menacing photo was taken after he had been held in solitary confinement for several weeks, elaborating, "I would have been scared of me too."[52] McCarthy first sent the networks an ad without Horton's picture—then followed it with the one with his image.[53]

The Horton commercial, along with the other spot about the furlough program, was to air on "CNN, the Nashville Network and other cable networks," according to the *Washington Post*. The "Weekend Passes" ad, which ran for twenty-eight days, notes Bush's support for the death penalty for first-degree murderers and alleges the following about Dukakis: "[He] not only opposes the death penalty, he allowed first-degree murderers to have weekend passes from prison. One was Willie Horton who murdered a boy in a robbery, stabbing him nineteen times. Despite a life sentence, Horton received 10 weekend passes from prison. Horton fled, kidnapped a young couple, stabbing the man, and repeatedly raping his girlfriend. [Kidnapping Raping Stabbing appear in large letters.] Weekend prison passes. Dukakis on crime."[54]

"Weekend Passes" became notorious in the annals of political advertising, with many believing the commercial played a central role in Bush's victory. It also became the prototypical example of an effective negative ad. A quarter century later, the *New Yorker*'s Jane Mayer called the spot "the political equivalent of an improvised explosive device, demolishing the electoral hopes of Dukakis."[55] Others have cast doubt on such claims, noting that the advertisement only appeared on cable stations at a time when relatively few people watched cable. Yet this assertion does not capture the ad's full reach, as it likely gained a greater audience when McCarthy gave a copy to the *McLaughlin Group*, a popular syndicated political talk show, which aired it.[56] Then there were three partial or full showings on the national evening-news broadcasts between October 21 and 24—long after the commercial stopped running.[57] Such replaying of political ads like the Horton ad and others represented another change from previous campaigns, as the network news showed 125 excerpts of commercials in 1988 as opposed to a mere two in 1968.[58] Despite this additional airplay, there are other reasons to question the importance of "Weekend Passes"—regardless of the ad's legendary status. The governor already trailed in the polls by the time it began to air, and the race was all but over when it was replayed on the nightly news.[59]

Though the group showing the commercial was supposed to be independent and not connected to the Bush campaign, much evidence suggests potential linkage—which would have been illegal. The National Security Political Action Committee gave Baker a letter offering not to run the ad, but the campaign chairman only asked the group to desist three days prior to the end of the commercial's run. "If they were really interested in stopping this," observed Brown, "do you think they would have waited that long to send us a letter?"[60]

McCarthy was also a former employee of Ailes and a later investigation by the Federal Election Commission (FEC) revealed that the two men spoke on a number of occasions during the campaign. "Each denied coordinating the commercial to help Bush," wrote Charlie Babcock in the *Washington Post*, though the FEC general counsel thought their statements regarding the subject were inconsistent. Another former Ailes employee worked on the Horton ad while also working for the Bush campaign, though it was disputed whether he was a strategist or a technician.[61] For his part, Ailes later testified that his relations with McCarthy were "strained." He also stated, "In the case of the Willie Horton ad it was very clear to me that that ad would generate a backlash from the liberal media—which is an oxymoron, as you know—and I felt it was unnecessary."[62] Despite both parties' denials of coordination, the general counsel's report concluded that "there were deliberate contacts between agents of the two committees," and that "information obtained through discovery calls into question those denials."[63] The

Democrats on the FEC claimed the investigation did not go far enough, as one of the Republican commissioners declared that there was no collusion, but that Ailes and McCarthy had "demonstrated some bad judgement that risked the appearance of or provided an opportunity for collusion."[64]

The campaign's leadership rejected any suggestion of coordination, with Baker commenting that he "found the commercial offensive and said publicly that the Bush campaign deplored it and wanted it off the air." The chairman further asserted, "The Bush-Quayle campaign did not produce this commercial, the National Security Political Action Committee did, and it was wholly independent of our organization." With regard to allegations of having it both ways, Baker said, "I have three responses. First, as far as I know—and I was the campaign chairman—we had nothing to do with the ad. Second, given the uproar that followed, I'm fairly sure it did us more harm than good. Third, I truly deplored the Horton ad. I condemned it then and I condemn it now."[65] Concurring, Fuller reflected, "We could say till we were blue in the face that this was an independent expenditure committee that we had nothing to do with. Which I always thought was true and I still think is true." But he added, "Still the damage was done."[66] Estrich sharply disagreed, declaring, "The idea that they had no control over the dissemination of some of the ugliest stuff that was being disseminated struck me as absurd."[67]

Though Reagan's friendly relations with Gorbachev showed the Cold War was thawing, national security continued to be an important issue for voters. Dukakis remained at a disadvantage with Bush vis-à-vis foreign policy, as Democrats had generally been since 1968. Nixon had very effectively attacked McGovern on the issue in 1972, with one ad showing various programs and military personnel supposedly disappearing due to the South Dakota senator's defense cuts.[68] Carter had sought to inoculate himself on the issue by running as more of a hawk four years later. But his administration's mishandling of the Iranian hostage crisis and relations with the USSR had only deepened his party's problem, and Reagan was able to campaign as being tougher on the Soviets in 1980 and 1984, respectively. And as we saw in chapter 1, during the latter campaign against Mondale, a Reagan ad famously showed the Republican candidate seemingly taming "the bear" of the USSR.

Seeking to allay this weakness, the Dukakis campaign planned "Defense Week" beginning Monday, September 12. "The key issue for the week is defense, which MSD [Michael Dukakis] will be pushing in the first half of the week," read a campaign memo. "LMB [Lloyd Bentsen] will be echoing some of this." Dukakis's talking points show he was trying to demonstrate the need to strengthen the military's conventional arsenal. The following point appeared among a series of issues for the candidate to address: "MSD wants to reverse the administration's neglect of conventional defense. He wants weapons that we need and weapons that work."[69]

On the first day of "Defense Week," Dukakis spoke in Philadelphia and then made a trip with John Glenn to a GE aircraft-engine plant in Evendale, Ohio, where some in the crowd booed the governor.[70] The next day Dukakis traveled on to Chicago to give a speech on foreign relations. He subsequently went to the General Dynamics plant in Sterling Heights in Macomb County, Michigan—the heart of Reagan Democrat country—and to an appointment with some unfortunate presidential campaign history.

Matt Bennett, then a twenty-three-year-old advance person, scoped out the trip to Michigan where Dukakis was going to ride in a tank and then make a speech about national security. In his journal, he wrote, "The reasoning behind the tank event was simple.... Dukakis had been under attack by the Baker-Ailes brigade for being too dovish."[71] Arriving five days beforehand as the site director to inspect the situation, Bennett discovered that Dukakis would have to don a hat for safety purposes. Putting your candidate in headwear violated an unwritten rule of American politics dating back to Calvin Coolidge in the 1920s, and the campaign had been particularly careful to avoid putting the governor in a hat.[72] Bennett informed the higher-ups that they had a potential problem. "This is going to be a freaking disaster," he told the director of advance.[73] "We raised such a fuss that they did something I've never seen done before or since." The campaign leadership sent trip director Jack Weeks, off his usual role on the candidate's plane, to come to Sterling Heights to investigate.[74]

On the day of the visit, Weeks arrived. After seeing Paul Holtzman, the lead advance person for the trip, in the helmet, he declared, "You look like a goofy fuck. No helmet." Bennett said that a compromise was developed where Dukakis would make a run with the helmet on and then another where he took it off as he made a slow pass by the cameras.[75] In his journal, Bennett wrote, "I told him [Weeks] the brutal facts: Dukakis would look like a goof if he wore the helmet, but he wouldn't be able to hear, and he would feel genuinely unsafe without it." Bennett added, "Jack ruled that he would wear the helmet for the fast passes, and doff his headgear for a slow, picture taking pass."[76] Recalling no compromise plan, Weeks believes there was supposed to be no helmet, period.[77]

When he arrived at the plant, Dukakis was accompanied by future secretary of state Madeline Albright, who was serving as a foreign policy adviser to the campaign. "The people at [General Dynamics] gave him the helmet,

Dukakis's ride in a tank in Sterling Heights, Michigan, on September 13, 1988, became a Bush campaign commercial and an infamous moment in American political history. (AP Photo / Michael E. Samojeden, File)

and they told him—and he hesitated—'You have to wear this because this is where the audio equipment is so you can hear what the instructions are,'" according to Albright. To avoid the image of the five-foot-eight Dukakis getting into the eight-foot M1A1 tank, the governor entered the vehicle behind closed doors.[78]

Initially, the tank emerged from the garage with Dukakis not wearing the helmet.[79] As the tank rolled out for its practice run at great distance from the reporters, it stopped for a moment. Weeks thought it was out of fuel; describing his thoughts at the time, he said, "The headline running through my head is 'Dukakis campaign runs out of gas.'" The tank began to move back toward the assembled reporters, and the governor, to Weeks's surprise, was wearing the helmet with his name on it. Accounts of these events differ. Gordon England, then a vice president at General Dynamics and future secretary of the navy, rode in the tank with Dukakis, and he remembered the decision for the candidate to wear the helmet being made much earlier.[80] "His [Weeks's] story is that somehow you know his orders were countermanded and that there was a screw up and Dukakis put the helmet on when he shouldn't have," said Bennett, who thought that explanation unlikely given the deference General Dynamics would have given Weeks as a representative of the potential next president.[81]

Many of the reporters laughed uproariously as Dukakis headed toward them, smiling and pointing. "Everyone around me in the press corps was doing the same thing. Either laughing or pointing or looking at each other. . . . What's this? How can he do this to himself?" remembered Sam Donaldson.[82] As the governor got out of the tank after the end of the photo op, Bennett observed, "[He] didn't yet know of the humiliations to come when he arrived back to the shop to dismount, and he was bubbling with the same kind of enthusiasm that Neal and I ended our rides with. As he was climbing out of the tank, we all told him he looked great (we had really thought that), and he was pumped up for his speech when he hit the rope line."[83]

It's not clear whether all of Dukakis's people were immediately aware of how poorly the event had gone. "I wasn't sure it was the best thing we ever did," commented future Clinton press secretary Joe Lockhart, "[and] I wasn't sure it was the worst thing. I just knew we had another event in an hour."[84] Bennett, who played such an instrumental role in organizing the photo op, wrote, "By the time they were preparing to leave, the staff was getting wind of the very unflattering angle that the press was adopting." He added that one aide told him, "Nice event, Matt. It may have cost us the election. But besides that, it was great."[85]

Given the stigma that emerged surrounding the event, it's noteworthy that initial news accounts weren't especially critical. NBC's Chris Wallace began his report that evening by saying, "Don't call Mike Dukakis soft on defense. Today he rode across the plains of Michigan like George Patton on his way to Berlin." Of Dukakis's speech afterward, Wallace observed, "He said little that hasn't been said by Ronald Reagan. But for a candidate who is trying to show that he's in the mainstream on foreign policy that may not be so bad." On CBS, Bruce Morton declared, "Biff. Bang. Powy. It's not a bird. It's not a plane. It's presidential candidate Mike Dukakis in a M1 tank." Noting that campaigning is all about the visuals, he further said, "If your candidate is seen in the polls as weak on defense, put him in a tank." There were signs of clouds on the horizon, however, as Democratic pollster Harrison Hickman commented, "When you see Mike Dukakis on a tank, I think the first thing you wonder is: why is Mike Dukakis on a tank?" In another ominous bit of foreshadowing, Dukakis asked the crowd during this speech, "So what did you think. Did I look like I belonged there up in that tank?"[86] Watching the news that evening, the campaign became concerned, with Mindy Lubber, the scheduling director, saying, "Regardless of anything that came out of the governor's mouth, we saw the picture, which was Mike Dukakis with his head sticking up in that goofy hat."[87]

Unsurprisingly, the video had the opposite effect on the Bush campaign, putting staffers in a celebratory mood. Black recalls seeing the tank ride and Atwater responding, "This is a gd disaster. What the hell is this guy doing?" Euphoric campaign staffers high-fived one another. They called Ailes, who arrived shortly thereafter, declaring it "unbelievable." Baker also considered the tank image damning, observing, "There's no kind or gentle way to say this: Dukakis looked goofy. The photo of that event has to be one of the most damaging in political history."[88] At the Bush campaign-management meeting on the sixteenth, Atwater said, "[The tank ride] served to prove one of the first rules Strom Thurmond taught me—A political candidate should never be photographed in a funny hat."[89]

On an episode of the *McLaughlin Group* taped a few days later, conservative panelists Bob Novak and Pat Buchanan made their feelings clear about the tank photo op. "Is Dukakis effectively neutralizing George Bush's perceived defense superiority?" host John McLaughlin asked Buchanan. The former Nixon and Reagan staffer responded with what would become the conventional take on the event: "Dukakis looked like he was riding around in the sidecar of a motorcycle at 12 years old in that tank, John. I do not think he is. I think this is one issue where Bush really has done well, I think." McLaughlin turned to Novak, who agreed: "That is something that everybody in the world saw, and they are laughing about it. That is the first time that Dukakis has really been a laughingstock, and it is no coincidence that the tracking polls that night and the next night showed a downside for Dukakis."[90]

With the first debate approaching on September 25, the campaign was still struggling, despite Sasso's changes.[91] In a memo to the campaign cochairs, congressional Democrats, and surrogates, Estrich wrote the following: "For several months George Bush has been doing to Mike Dukakis what he did to Bob Dole in the primaries: he and his campaign organization have systematically distorted Dukakis' record." She added, "At the same time Bush has been embellishing his own. Finally, Bush has made a bold face attempt to walk away from the Reagan/Bush legacy on family issues, the environment, and education." Listing some of the distortions, Estrich urged backers to make them clear on the stump.[92] Campaign officials confessed the Pledge of Allegiance had turned out to be a more effective issue than expected.[93]

Meanwhile, the Bush strategy remained clear. In a memo about press availability, Baker outlined the campaign's plan "to keep Dukakis on the defensive with the following themes":

1. His positions on the issues are outside the mainstream.
2. He is deceiving the American people about them, and
3. He has raised and will continue to raise several false issues simply to cloud the campaign and distract the American people from focusing on the important issues.

Baker asserted that Bush needed to continue to puncture Dukakis's economic record in Massachusetts as well.[94]

Some voters explained why they had made the shift from one candidate to another, and a few of their responses suggested the Bush campaign's efforts to define Dukakis had been successful. "When you called me on the poll, I was strongly for Dukakis, based on his convention speech," reflected a sixty-year-old independent who had voted for Reagan in 1984. "But I've reneged on my support for him," the voter stated. "I don't go along with his stands on the pledge of allegiance, abortion, drugs and prison release. I've completely changed my mind." A fifty-five-year-old Democrat who had also backed Reagan in 1984 commented, "He doesn't have the experience. I would hate to have another Jimmy Carter in office." Such switches were typical, as Bush's support among those approving of the president had risen from 56 percent in August to 75 percent by mid-September. On the other hand, Dukakis's support among this crucial bloc had fallen from 25 percent to 14 percent. In light of these shifts, Bush maintained an eight-point lead overall, and Republicans began to turn the key of the Electoral College "lock," which had seemed loose after the Democratic convention, back into place.[95]

But before the debate Bush made another foray into Dukakis's backyard, returning to the crime issue that had proved so effective in his campaign. After months of lobbying from his campaign, the Boston Police Patrolmen's Association, the largest union in the Boston Police Department, voted fifty-one to zero to endorse the vice president. Unidentified officials cited the furlough program and Dukakis's opposition to the death penalty as their rationales for backing Bush. The union had supported Reagan in 1984, and though the governor and his allies, including Boston mayor Ray Flynn, made last-ditch efforts to stop the endorsement, Dukakis used this history to diminish its importance. "This is a union that has a history of endorsing Republicans. It doesn't come as a surprise," responded Dukakis. The governor still had the backing of many other law enforcement groups, including the Massachusetts Police Association and the Massachusetts Police Chiefs Association.[96]

Arriving to receive the endorsement in person, Bush held an event at a restaurant in East Boston. "As police officers in the capital city of Massachusetts, we know Governor Dukakis well and we can state publicly that he is no friend of police," remarked the union's president. In line with his campaign's overall strategy, Bush referred to the governor as "out of the American mainstream" on crime and called attention to his own support for the death penalty, declaring, "Some crimes are so heinous, so outrageous, so brutal that the death penalty is warranted."[97]

Scrambling, Dukakis organized a counter event the same day with national police groups in Boston, including one from Texas. "We're here to give George Bush what Joe Friday used to ask for. The facts, ma'am, just the facts," the governor announced."[98] A campaign press release from the day screamed, "Saying that George Bush was trying to recover from the humiliation of losing the endorsement of 8,000 Texas lawmen to Gov. Michael Dukakis and his inability to secure a single national police endorsement, scores of crime fighters from all over the country joined the Democratic nominee to show their support for the Dukakis record on crime."[99] Throughout the campaign, internal documents showed the governor's people trying to promote the decline in crime in Massachusetts to offset Bush's attacks on the furlough program and the death penalty.[100]

The Dukakis response impressed some in the Bush campaign. Paul Manafort, who would later run the Trump campaign in 2016, observed, "We should take note of the fact that Dukakis's campaign organization has become more efficient as evidenced by the Police rally he put together, with 18 hours notice of our trip to Boston."[101] On *NBC Nightly News*, Chris Wallace agreed, noting that "by moving fast . . . Dukakis was able to take some of the steam out of the vice president's embarrassing surprise." The newsman elaborated, however, that "even here on the governor's own turf, Bush was playing offense and Dukakis [was] scrambling to catch up."[102]

Attention now turned to the upcoming television debates between the candidates. While the history of presidential debates began with the famous Kennedy-Nixon debates of 1960, no more were held until 1976, when Ford and Carter debated three times. The ritual of the vice-presidential debate began that year with a confrontation between Bob Dole and Walter Mondale. Reagan and Carter only debated once in 1980, though that face-off close to the general election was seen as pivotal to the outcome. Reagan then squared off with Mondale twice in 1984. The Dukakis campaign wanted four debates in 1988, but Bush's people demanded fewer—seemingly threatening to hold none at one point—and the two camps eventually agreed to hold two.[103]

Bush did extensive debate prep with Darman, who played Dukakis, and came in wearing a tank hat at one point.[104] Pinkerton prepared the questions.[105] Putting together a thorough briefing book with points regarding 101 issues, campaign staff specified what they saw as the seven major Dukakis lines of attack, ranging from Iran-Contra to Quayle to the regulatory task force. The briefing materials also outlined eight key attack issues, including the Pledge of Allegiance, the furlough program, doubts about the "Massachusetts Miracle," and the ACLU.[106]

In a memorandum written five days before the face-off with Dukakis, Bush's "debate team" laid out their goals for their boss. "Your most important objective for the debate must be to show that you are clearly as big as the job," they wrote, "[and] someone voters can feel comfortable with as leader of the free world. You must project an image that is relaxed, confident, unflappable, in control." Urging him to fight back against the governor, Bush's staffers told him, "The theme of your counterpunches should be that Dukakis's views are out of the mainstream and that he is trying to deceive the American people." Telling the vice president to focus on international issues, they argued, "The more the debate focuses on national security and foreign affairs, the better." Interestingly, while the debate team suggested that the economic recovery was one of Bush's strengths, they instructed him not to sound excessively positive regarding the economy so as not to open up a line of attack for the governor.[107]

The Dukakis campaign viewed the debates as a crucial moment. According to an internal memorandum, the camp's first talking point was as follows: "The debate with Bush is an opportunity for Governor Dukakis to be seen and heard on the same stage as the incumbent Vice President. Like the convention acceptance speech, it is one of the few moments in a campaign when the voters can see and hear the candidate unedited and not chopped into 30-second sound bites." However, the document noted that merely being on the same stage was important: "This is not expected to show up immediately in the polls, but it will have a profound, if not subtle, effect on the race."[108]

Dukakis's debate prep seemed more haphazard than the vice president's. When Tom Donilon took over two and a half weeks before the showdown, the campaign did not have a workable briefing book. "It's worthless. I don't know what to do," said Donilon, and the campaign had to put together a new one.[109] Given the overall state of things, Estrich recalled being with Clinton and Albright prior to the first debate and fearing Dukakis was going to perform quite badly.[110]

Though Bush led by six points going into the debate, the race was still reasonably open, as over a third of voters remained either undecided or willing to switch their preference, reflecting the weaker party attachments of late twentieth-century politics. With regard to the governor's expectations, Schneider said, "Dukakis needs to reassure people that he's safe, pragmatic, and doesn't have a bunch of wild ideas."[111]

With PBS's Jim Lehrer moderating and a panel of three journalists questioning the candidates, Wake Forest University hosted the debate on September 25 on its campus in Winston-Salem, North Carolina. Dukakis again emphasized his centrist themes, talking about the ten budgets he balanced in Massachusetts and his efforts to move people from welfare to work, while also stressing his support for universal health care. Asked about his perceived lack of passion by Peter Jennings, Dukakis said, "I care deeply about people, all people, working people, working families, people all over this country who in some cases are living from paycheck to paycheck," adding that he was deeply concerned about those who couldn't pay for health insurance and college.[112]

Citing Dukakis's comments from the summer of 1987 that he was a "strong liberal Democrat" and a "card-carrying member of the ACLU," Bush said he didn't question the governor's passion. He instead clarified, "My argument with the governor is do we want this country to go that far left." Jennings noted that Bush repeatedly used the phrase "card-carrying" and that some had suggested he was questioning the governor's patriotism. The ABC anchor then asked, "What is so wrong with the governor being a member of an organization which has come to the defense of, among other people, Colonel Oliver North?"[113]

"Nothing's wrong with it," responded the vice president, "but just take a look at the positions of the ACLU." He continued, "But, Peter, please understand, the liberals do not like me talking about liberal. They don't like it when I say that he says he's a card-carrying member."[114] Bush used the word "liberal" seven times in the debate.[115] Spelling out a number of ACLU positions he rejected, the vice president conceded, "He [Dukakis] has every right to exercise his passion." Yet Bush added, "As what he said, a strong, progressive liberal. I don't agree with that. I come from a very different point of view. And I think I'm more in touch with the mainstream of America." He then noted that he would have found a way to sign the pledge bill.[116] The Bush campaign's focus groups showed very high approval for this portion of the discussion.[117]

Responding sharply by his low-key standards, Dukakis declared, "Well, I hope this is the first and last time I have to say this. Of course, the vice president is questioning my patriotism. I don't think there's any question about that, and I resent it. I resent it." Again discussing his heritage, Dukakis elaborated, "My parents came to this country as immigrants. They taught me that this was the greatest country in the world. I'm in public service because I love this country. I believe in it. And nobody's going to question my patriotism as the vice president has now repeatedly." He added that Bush had presided over the Senate for years and never demanded the Pledge of Allegiance be recited.[118] In retrospect, the governor regretted not going further, saying, "I should have said to Bush in one of the debates 'so you would sign a bill the court said was unconstitutional.'" Dukakis pondered another rejoinder: "Maybe I should have turned to him and said: well I'd rather be a member of the ACLU than the National Rifle Association. I didn't say that."[119]

Another interesting exchange emerged when Dukakis was queried about his opposition to the death penalty as well as his pro-choice position on abortion. Saying he was tough on crime, Dukakis cited the decline in crime in Massachusetts and raised the fact that the federal furlough program had given leaves to many drug traffickers. "Well, the Massachusetts furlough program was unique. It was the only one in the nation that furloughed murderers who had not served enough time to be eligible for parole," responded the vice president. "The federal program doesn't do that," Bush pointed out. "No other state programs do that." He then reiterated his backing for capital punishment, declaring, "And so I am not going to furlough men like Willie Horton, and I would meet with their, the victims of his last escapade, the rape and the brutalization of the family down there in Maryland. Maryland would not extradite Willie Horton, the man who was furloughed, the murderer, because they didn't want him to be furloughed again. And so we have a fundamental difference on this one."[120]

When asked about his vice-presidential selection, Bush defended Quayle, declaring he'd been unfairly treated. "I see a young man that was elected to the Senate twice, to the House of Representatives twice," explained the vice president. Referring to the baby boomers, he asserted, "I see a man who is young and I am putting my confidence in a whole generation of people that are in their 30s and in their 40s." Favorably contrasting his pick with his opponent's, Dukakis declared, "I think the American people have a right to judge us on this question, on how we picked a running mate, a person who is a heartbeat away from the presidency. I picked Lloyd Bentsen, distinguished, strong, mature, a leader in the Senate, somebody whose qualifications nobody has questioned. Mr. Bush picked Dan Quayle." The governor added, "I doubt very much that Dan Quayle was the best qualified person for that job. And as a matter of fact, I think for most people the notion of President Quayle is a very, very troubling notion tonight."[121]

Overall, the debate was fairly contentious, with Bush noting this toward the end. "I had hoped this had been a little friendlier an evening," he joked, "[because] I wanted to hitchhike a ride home in his tank with him [Dukakis]." In his closing, the vice president said he represented change and didn't want the country to return to the malaise of the Carter years. "We've had a chance to spell out our differences on the Pledge of Allegiance here tonight and on tough sentencing of drug kingpins and this kind of thing. I do favor the death penalty. And we've got a wide array of differences on those [issues]," he remarked. Continuing, he added, "But in the final analysis—in the final analysis, the person goes into that voting booth, they're going to say, who has the values I believe in? Who has the experience that we trust?

Who has the integrity and the stability to get the job done?" Echoing his convention speech, Bush concluded, "My fellow Americans, I am that man and I ask for your support."[122]

Also summarizing his philosophy in his closing, Dukakis mentioned his immigrant heritage and the obligation he felt to give back to the country that had given his family so much. "I believe in the American dream," explained the governor. "I'm a product of it and I want to help that dream come true for every single citizen in this land, with a good job at good wages, with good schools in every part of this country and every community in this country." He talked about providing health care to all, and about his desire "to build the best America," elaborating, "The best America doesn't leave some of its citizens behind. We live—we bring everybody along. And the best America is not behind us. The best America is yet to come."[123]

Postdebate commentary suggested that Dukakis had earned a narrow victory, but that the race remained largely unchanged. "I think both candidates did extremely well. They both defended their positions. But Governor Dukakis perhaps had more to gain tonight than George Bush and perhaps he gained it tonight," analyzed Donaldson on ABC afterward.[124] Both Tom Brokaw on NBC and Bob Schieffer on CBS asserted there was no "knockout."[125] In the *Washington Post* the next day, Broder wrote, "Michael Dukakis kept the presidential race alive and in doubt tonight by showing a nationally televised debate audience that he could deflect George Bush's efforts to place him outside the mainstream of American politics."[126] Concurring, Dionne observed in the *Time*s that rather than giving either candidate the upper hand, "the contest was left more muddled than before and as open as it had been at any point since last spring." Dionne added, "As the lesser-known contender, Governor Dukakis of Massachusetts clearly achieved one of his major objectives, which was to present himself as a plausible President of the United States."[127] Reflecting this argument, the preferences of a group of Reagan Democrats in Macomb County seemed unmoved by the exchange.[128] A few days later, a Gallup poll showed that while 38 percent of those surveyed thought Dukakis had won the debate, and 29 percent thought the vice president had won, Bush still lead the race overall 47 percent to 42 percent.[129]

Ironically, the ACLU may have been a short-term winner from the debate, as interest in the organization surged. "We've been getting hundreds of calls from people who want to be members," said Norman Dorsen, the group's president, a day after the tête-à-tête. "A lot of them [are] asking for membership cards so they can also be card-carrying members of the A.C.L.U.," he explained.[130] Bush kept up the attack, trying to link Dukakis to the group by suggesting it would play a major role in his Supreme Court appointments if elected.¹³¹ "The A.C.L.U. has replaced the flag and the Pledge of Allegiance as George Bush's hot-button 'values' issue," wrote Margaret Carlson in *Time*.¹³²

To address these attacks, Dukakis's internal talking points show the campaign trying to highlight areas where he disagreed with the organization.¹³³ Looking back, the governor reflected, "I wasn't under any illusions that my ACLU membership would be uncontroversial," adding, "Frankly I was proud of it." Dukakis said the organization does important work. "I think card-carrying was a mistake on his part," analyzed Corrigan. "For him it was sending a message. A sort of a lighthearted message to liberals, free-speechers, but it probably resonated negatively with a lot of people."¹³⁴

Meanwhile, preparation began for the vice-presidential debate between Bentsen and Quayle, and as with the presidential debate, expectations would play a central role in how the media and the country interpreted the outcome. The Dukakis campaign understood this, with one staffer writing to Devine two weeks beforehand, "Because Senator Quayle's qualifications for office have been questioned in the campaign, the public expectation, or at least the press expectation, is that Senator Bentsen will outperform Quayle. We need to minimize this expectation." Other goals for the debate included reiterating the governor's proposals, emphasizing Bentsen's qualifications, "raising doubts" about the Indiana senator, and making clear in "these attacks not only that Senator Quayle [was] not qualified but that his selection [reflected] the Vice President's poor judgement when faced with big decisions."¹³⁵

Given the Indiana senator's rough introduction to the country, the Bush people were worried about the kind of impression he would make. As Black recalled, "We [the Bush campaign] were concerned."¹³⁶ Since the convention, Quayle had chafed at the controls placed on him by his handlers, Stuart Spencer and Joe Canzeri. "They just turned it over to them," observed Quayle, saying that no one thought about how to run a campaign designed for him. He also noted that the advisers were devoid of ideological commitment and made it seem like they carried a heavy burden simply by managing him.¹³⁷ In addition, the campaign largely kept Quayle away from key areas, as Andrew Kohut of Gallup called concerns about the VP nominee the campaign's "Achilles heel." Many who had praised the Indiana senator before his selection recanted their support; Fuller recalled that "some people who were supportive later distanced themselves."¹³⁸

Beginning three weeks before the face-off, former secretary of state Henry Kissinger worked to get Quayle up to speed on foreign policy. Ailes also worked with the senator, and the staff came up with 200 possible questions for him. Quayle engaged in two mock debates with Oregon senator Bob Packwood, but in retrospect, the Indiana senator felt he came in too prepared—almost overrehearsed.[139]

Though the pundits had cheered his nomination at the convention, Bentsen hadn't made much of an impression since, and the ticket trailed in Texas, just as some of the doubters regarding his selection had predicted.[140] And the debate seemed an unlikely place to turn things around. Having come of age prior to the era of television, Bentsen was not eager for the face-off and even wanted to find a way to get out of it. But he did prep with Congressman Dennis Eckhart of Ohio, who played Quayle in mock debates. Though Bentsen was not especially good at the outset, he improved dramatically, with Devine commenting, "He worked really, really hard to make himself an accomplished debater in a short period of time."[141]

Media attention focused squarely on Quayle. "The Vice-Presidential debate Wednesday is Senator Dan Quayle's moment in political history, when he can overcome, or confirm, the public's unease about him as a candidate, a possible Vice President and a potential President, analysts in both parties agree," wrote Dionne.[142] "In Vice Presidential Debate, the Main Question May Be Quayle," read a *Washington Post* headline, as Robert Barnes and R. H. Melton argued in the accompanying article, "A strong performance by Quayle could begin to erase what a number of polls suggest is a continuing problem for George Bush's presidential candidacy."[143]

Regarding Bentsen, who was said to be "edgy and nervous," Democrats feared he had little chance to win because of the low bar set for his opponent. "All Quayle has to do is show up and it'll be a draw and a draw is a win for Quayle," claimed an aide for the Texas senator.[144] In response, the Dukakis campaign sought to raise expectations for the Indiana senator. As one internal talking point read, "The challenge for Dan Quayle is not whether he can stick to a 90 minute script of soundbites and one liners prepared by Roger Ailes. The challenge is to convince the American people that Dan Quayle is qualified to be a heartbeat away from the Oval Office and a heartbeat away from being the commander in chief of the free world."[145]

The debate took place in Omaha, Nebraska, on October 5, and Judy Woodruff of PBS moderated. She began by asking Quayle why so many people in his own party questioned his selection, and the Indiana senator replied that he had more experience on key issues than Dukakis. "This debate tonight is not about the qualifications for the vice presidency," responded Bentsen, echoing the first campaign talking point. "The debate is whether or not Dan Quayle and Lloyd Bentsen are qualified to be president of the United States," the Texan contended.[146]

Largely aiming his fire at the governor, Quayle returned to the dominant theme Bush and his campaign had been pushing since June—that Dukakis was a liberal and outside the mainstream. In one answer, he referred to the governor as liberal on three occasions, including calling him "one of the most liberal governors in the United States of America." At the same time, though, Quayle attacked Dukakis's environmental record and suggested Bush would be better in that area. On foreign policy in Latin America, Quayle alleged, "The governor of Massachusetts is simply out of step with mainstream America." Toward the end, he declared, "Michael Dukakis is the most liberal national Democrat to seek the office of presidency since George McGovern," citing his opposition to a number of defense programs. "Leave Bentsen alone.... I just went after Dukakis," Quayle recalled, saying he tried to use the "L" word promiscuously. "I must have used that I don't how many times. A lot."[147]

Though it is hardly remembered for it, the debate witnessed the first question in a presidential or vice-presidential debate about global warming, which was just emerging as a national and international concern. Though the scientific evidence had been building for years, 1988 was a crucial turning point in the rising awareness of the phenomenon. In June, NASA scientist James Hansen testified before Congress concerning the reality of man-made climate change.[148] Explaining the importance of Hansen's appearance, Philip Shabecoff wrote in the *New York Times*, "Until now, scientists have been cautious about attributing rising global temperatures of recent years to the predicted global warming caused by pollutants in the atmosphere, known as the 'greenhouse effect.'" Telling the lawmakers that four of the hottest years on record had been in the 1980s and that 1988 would be the warmest of all, Hansen declared, "Global warming has reached a level such that we can ascribe with a high degree of confidence a cause and effect relationship between the greenhouse effect and observed warning."[149]

Addressing Bentsen first, John Margolis of the *Chicago Tribune* prefaced his question thus: "Senator we've all just finished—most [of] America has just finished one of the hottest summers it can remember, and apparently this year will be the fifth of the last nine that are among the hottest on record." The journalist added that many scientists thought man could be a cause of the rising temperatures, and he asked what should be done and whether Bentsen would support a "substantial reduction in the use of fossil fuels." The oil-state senator replied that America should make it easier to use natural gas, and he then stated, "The greenhouse effect is one that has to be a threat to all of us, and we have to look for alternative sources of fuel." Quayle weighed in as well: "Now the greenhouse effect is an important environmental issue. It is important for us to get the data in, to see what alternatives we might have to the fossil fuels and make sure that we know what we're doing."[150]

Twice in the debate, Brit Hume asked Quayle what he would do if a tragedy struck and he became president. First, Quayle said he would say a prayer "for [himself] and for the country I'm about to lead. And then [he] would assemble his [Bush's] people and talk." He then turned to a discussion of his experience in Congress. When Hume's turn to question came up again, he asked, "What would you do next?" The Indiana senator replied that he wouldn't get into hypotheticals and again talked of his congressional experience, including his time on the Armed Services Committee and meetings he'd had with foreign leaders.[151]

Brokaw returned to the question for a third time, and Quayle responded again with a description of his Washington experience. This time he added, "I have far more experience than many others that sought the office of Vice President of this country. I have as much experience in the Congress as Jack Kennedy did when he sought the Presidency. I will be prepared to deal with the people in the Bush administration if that unfortunate event would ever occur."[152] Quayle had made the comparison before on the stump, and his advisers cautioned him against making it during the debate. "I was told not to make any reference to Kennedy, was warned that it could backfire," wrote Quayle.[153] Cameras showed Bentsen viscerally reacting when he heard the comparison.

Then, in a moment that would go down in history, the Texas senator responded to his opponent: "Senator, I served with Jack Kennedy. I knew Jack Kennedy. Jack Kennedy was a friend of mine. Senator, you're no Jack Kennedy." The audience roared with approval. "That was really uncalled for, Senator," retorted Quayle. Bentsen replied, "You're the one who was making the comparison, Senator. And I'm one who knew him well. And frankly I think you're so far apart in the objectives you choose for your country that I did not think the comparison was well taken." Quayle said he didn't realize what a bad moment it was at the time.[154]

Given the line's iconic status, it is not surprising that there is some dispute over its origin. It did not appear in a memo of potential one-liners the Dukakis campaign had prepared by September 30.[155] In a collection of "LMB [Lloyd Bentsen] Prepared Answers" for the debate faxed two days before the face-off, Bentsen's scripted response for "JFK" was, "Just a minute, Dan. You've quoted / compared yourself to JFK several times now. But I served with John Kennedy, spent time with him in Texas, he was my friend. And he did more than move people with his words; he helped them by his actions." Following this answer, Bentsen was to discuss some policy

Texas senator Lloyd Bentsen, Dukakis's vice-presidential nominee, stole the show in his debate with Indiana senator Dan Quayle. Bentsen remarked that his opponent was "no Jack Kennedy" after Quayle compared his own governmental experience to that of the late president. (AP Photo / Ron Edmonds, File)

differences between the late president and Quayle, then end by saying, "So Dan, you and other Republicans should stop invoking JFK's name when you vote against everything he stood for." In another one-liner, the Texas senator referred to Watt and Gorsuch as the "Bonnie and Clyde of environmental protection." As he did with many of his responses, Bentsen delivered this remark almost verbatim from his prepared answers—"Bonnie and Clyde of environmental policy."[156]

Initial accounts suggested that while Bentsen claimed his response was spontaneous, the idea likely emerged during a mock debate. Eckhart repeated a line Quayle had used frequently on the stump—that he had as much experience as John Kennedy had when he ran for president. As relayed by press spokesman Mike McCurry at the time, Bentsen retorted, "You're no more like Jack Kennedy than George Bush is like Ronald Reagan."[157]

In 2007, Bob Shrum wrote that he knew of Quayle's penchant for making the JFK comparison and believed the Indiana senator would revert back to it under pressure. Shrum recalled an exchange with the Texas senator while at the debate prep: "Had Bentsen known JFK? Yes, he had served with him. Did he feel comfortable, if the chance came, telling him he was no John Kennedy? Sure. The moment was worded, practiced, and polished in the mock debates."[158] When Shrum had lunch with Bentsen after the campaign, the senator thanked him for not going to the press and telling him about his role.[159]

On the other hand, Estrich remembered Bentsen hearing Eckhart make the comparison during prep, being surprised, and asking permission to challenge Quayle. Bentsen told her that he and JFK had been friends, and that he was going to say the Indiana senator was no Jack Kennedy.

Fact-checking, she asked for some background, and the Texas senator said he and his wife had attended Kennedy's wedding. Going into the debate, Estrich anticipated the moment. Elaborating that Clinton was going to be their "chief spinner," she remembered him asking her what to look for in the debate. "Just pray for John Kennedy," replied Estrich.[160]

Interestingly, NBC's postdebate commentary did not see it as a Bentsen rout. Brokaw returned from his role as questioner to opine, "No one tonight scored a decisive victory," while Chancellor suggested Quayle actually did himself some good by not appearing to be the lightweight depicted by the Democrats. Anticipating the historical narrative surrounding the face-off, Andrea Mitchell presciently observed that the JFK line was "by far the most dramatic moment of the debate," adding that the Indiana senator appeared rehearsed at times.[161]

Unlike the close contest between the top of the ticket, the undercard showed a clear victory for the Texan. A CBS poll declared Bentsen the winner by a margin of 50 percent to 27 percent, while an ABC poll gave him a winning margin of 51 percent to 27 percent.[162] "The debate coverage focused on the Kennedy line," recalled Quayle.[163] With regard to the pundits, conservatives were among Quayle's strongest critics, with Charles Krauthammer writing, "Quayle was simply incapable of going beyond his script," and "The debate was about Quayle and he lost it."[164] Concurring, George Will observed, "Did he prove himself presidential? No. He stayed in step with the top of the ticket."[165]

Bush's internal numbers were even worse, showing that a group of voters in the Cleveland suburbs thought Bentsen won 65 percent to 18 percent. Prior to the debate, the group was split 29 percent to 27 percent for Bush, with 45 percent undecided. Afterward, the group shifted to a margin of 39 percent for Bush and 33 percent for Dukakis, with 29 percent undecided. "Although the long-term effects of the debate remain to be seen, in the short term the Democratic ticket got a larger boost than the Republican ticket," wrote Julie Weeks of Market Opinion Research to the Bush campaign on October 7.[166] At a campaign meeting, Atwater was more positive, declaring, "Dan Quayle was the big winner in the debate. We now have this debate behind us and we can focus again on the issues and the top of the ticket." Atwater added that the Bush camp needed to back Quayle, and that comments critical of him were "disloyal" and "totally unacceptable."[167] In a less-than-ringing defense of the bottom half of his ticket, Baker appeared unenthusiastic while speaking to CNN: "When you think about what might have happened, we have to be pretty happy."[168]

For a moment, the Dukakis campaign seemed to again have life. "The two debates so far in the 1988 campaign appear to have done exactly what the Republicans feared," wrote Dionne. "They have helped revive a badly wounded Democratic ticket."[169] The national polls closed by a few points.[170] Sasso brought in new ad people who had created a highly successful campaign for John Hancock Insurance but had never made political commercials.[171] Their new advertisements focused on Quayle's lack of qualifications and took aim at the marketing of George Bush's campaign.

Around the time these ads aired, the Bush campaign started showing its most famous commercial, "Revolving Door." Filmed in Utah in black and white for "dramatic effect," according to Rogich, the ad shows guards manning a prison and shots of prisoners going through a revolving door.[172] The narrator intones, "As governor, Michael Dukakis vetoed mandatory sentences for drug dealers. He vetoed the death penalty, his revolving door prison policy gave weekend furloughs to first-degree murderers not eligible for parole." The screen then displays the text "268 escaped." "While out many committed other crimes like kidnapping and rape. And many are still at large ["Many are still at large" appears on screen]. Now Michael Dukakis says he wants to do for America what he's done for Massachusetts. America can't afford that risk."[173]

Unlike "Weekend Passes," the ad does not use Willie Horton's name or picture, and the prisoners marching through the door are mostly white. "We were very sensitive to the commercial itself because of the disproportionate amount of minorities in prisons," said Rogich. He further stated, "You'll see that it is really disproportionate the other way, without minorities," noting that white students from Brigham Young University portrayed the prisoners.[174] Reinforcing this idea, Atwater said, "Frankly, we were worried there were too many blacks in the prison scene, so we made sure that on the retake there were but one or two."[175] Some have noted, though, that the Black prisoner is the only one to look up at the camera.[176] "I didn't have a problem with the Bush campaign ad per se. I thought it was a legitimate ad," reflected Estrich. "Crime is a legitimate issue," she added, "[but] I took issue with, you know, Lee Atwater standing up and saying I'm going [to] make Willie Horton, you know, Mike Dukakis's running mate."[177]

Others sharply criticized the commercial's inaccuracies. "The Bush ads contained mistruths and lies," Brountas alleged. He continued, "For example, the Horton ad said there were 268 escaped Massachusetts convicts who fled after parole, giving the impression they were all first-degree murderers. The Horton ad had to be the lowest kind of campaign ad that we have ever seen in presidential politics."[178] Some independent experts agreed. "The ad invites the inference—false—that 268 first-degree murderers were furloughed by Dukakis to rape and kidnap. In fact only one first-degree murderer, William Horton, escaped furlough in Massachusetts and committed a violent crime," wrote Kathleen Hall Jamieson, a professor at the University of Texas, "although others have done so under other furlough programs, including those run by the federal government and by California under the stewardship of Ronald Reagan."[179] Indeed, two felons committed murder while on furlough during Reagan's tenure as governor of the Golden State and he did not end the program. Others noted that furlough programs were used across the state and federal prison systems, with almost 10 percent of prisoners receiving a temporary release with few crimes as a result. "Use of furloughs for prisoners in the U.S. is widespread, successful, and relatively problem free," analyzed the editor of *Corrections Compendium*.[180]

On the lighter side, *Saturday Night Live* aired its fourteenth season premiere on October 8, hosted by Tom Hanks. As would become commonplace over the next three decades, the show aired a mock presidential debate skit. Cast member Dana Carvey played Bush, and John Lovitz portrayed Dukakis, while Hanks led the faux debate broadcast as Peter Jennings. To question the candidates, Kevin Nealon impersonated Sam Donaldson, and Jan Hooks played Diane Sawyer.

Riffing on Jennings's question regarding Dukakis's passion from the first debate, Nealon/Donaldson mocks the governor, saying his advisers think of him as "distant and aloof, a bit of a cold fish." He eventually asks the candidate, "Do you have the necessary passion to lead this country?" Completely devoid of any emotion, Lovitz/Dukakis responds as follows: "Sam, that kind of aspersion on my character, quite frankly, makes me—well, there's no other word for it—enraged . . . enraged. Maybe I shouldn't say that in the heat of the moment, but I can't control myself and . . . well I apologize for flying off the handle. I'm just sorry my kids had to see me like this."[181]

Later, mirroring another question from the first debate, Carvey/Bush is asked by Nealon/Donaldson what he would do about the homeless problem. Carvey/Bush repeatedly responds by saying a version of "stay the course, a thousand points of light," and by telling Hooks/Sawyer that he needs to stop because his time is up. She keeps assuring him that he has plenty of time remaining to answer. "Let me just sum up," he concludes, repeating, "On track. Stay the course. Thousand points of light. Stay the course." Hooks/Sawyer then asks the governor for his rebuttal, and in one of the most memorable moments in the history of *SNL* political satire, a frustrated Lovitz/Dukakis blurts out, "I can't believe I'm losing to this guy!" The audience cheers in response.[182] Then an *SNL* writer, future Minnesota senator Al Franken wrote the line.[183]

In another example of the emergence of nontraditional media in politics, *SNL* election sketches got their start—or at least a restart—in 1988. They have continued on ever since, often influencing our perceptions of the candidates. While Chevy Chase's impression did so much to shape Gerald Ford's image back in *SNL*'s debut season in 1975-76, the show moved away from politics a bit when original producer Lorne Michaels exited in 1980. Dick Ebersol then took over the reins, and he "was not as enamored of political humor as Lorne was," according to television critic Tom Shales, who cowrote a book about the history of the program.[184] When Michaels returned in 1985, politics returned as well. Longtime *SNL* writer Jim Downey declared, "So it was really back in '88 when we . . . sort of what you think of as *Saturday Night Live* political sketches started happening."[185]

In the years to come, *SNL* satire—like the late-night talk shows—would have a profound impact on the image of multiple candidates. In 2000, at the urging of President Clinton, Al Gore's advisers had him watch Darrell Hammond's impersonation of him constantly repeating his idea of a "lockbox" to protect Social Security, as well as constantly sighing.[186] Some liberals blamed Will Ferrell for presenting a humanized version of George W. Bush that made him more palatable to the electorate. Tina Fey's Sarah Palin proved so uncanny that many came to believe that Palin actually said that she "could see Russia" from her "house," even though it was Fey who made the remark. And Alec Baldwin's Trump so infuriated the president that he couldn't stop tweeting about it.

Meanwhile, the real-life Dukakis remained frustrated about GOP tactics, calling them "just disgraceful." Defending his membership in the ACLU in an interview with the *New York Times*, he said, "I don't agree with them on everything. They've been critical of me on some things. But I think it's important that we have an organization in this country that protects the rights of people," including Oliver North and "Republican students who demonstrate in front of the Nicaraguan and Soviet embassies." Saying he would "get the truth out" over the last month of the campaign, Dukakis declared, "We're going to make sure that the Bush record on crime and drugs and the environment is very well known before the 8th of November."[187]

While tactics were increasingly becoming a central issue, the fundamentals of the race continued to move in Bush's favor as the all-important second presidential debate approached. While the vice president only led the polls 47 percent to 42 percent, Dionne wrote, "Voters are increasingly optimistic about the state of the nation and satisfied with President Reagan's performance, and they continue to be wary of government programs." According to the *NYT*/CBS poll, 60 percent of Americans now approved of Reagan's job performance, his highest number since Iran-Contra had broken in the fall of 1986. The president's political revival posed a serious challenge for the Dukakis campaign, with Corrigan going as far as to say that "Reagan made the prospect of a Democrat winning very difficult."[188]

On the other hand, Quayle seemed to be a drag on the ticket, as Bush did four points better when voters were only asked questions with the presidential nominee's name. Coming out of the vice-presidential debate, Bentsen had become the most popular of the four candidates. Interestingly, polls showed Dukakis and Bush even outside the South, with the vice president holding a commanding 51-percent-to-36-percent lead below the Mason-Dixon Line. The attacks over the death penalty, furloughs, and Willie Horton seemed to be having a major impact, as pro–capital punishment voters, who had been split evenly between the candidates in July, had shifted significantly toward Bush. At this time, 78 percent of voters supported the death penalty, and by October they backed the vice president by a margin of 52 percent to 38 percent.[189]

The second debate in Los Angeles appeared to be the last chance for Dukakis to change the trajectory of the race, and given their ticket's success in the first two debates, the staff believed victory was still possible.[190] Unbeknownst to the candidates, even before the debate started there was an extraordinarily important discussion between the moderator and the three panelists that could have changed the course of the election. As moderator, CNN's Bernard Shaw would ask the first question. When he met with *Newsweek*'s Margaret Warner, NBC's Andrea Mitchell, and ABC's Ann Compton at Compton's hotel room to discuss their questions beforehand, Shaw told them what he was going to ask Dukakis. Upon hearing the subject, the three women immediately tried to talk him out of it.[191]

Why? Shaw informed them he would start the debate by asking the governor whether he would favor the death penalty if Kitty Dukakis were raped and murdered. "I was stunned—and I recoiled," remembered Warner. Compton was upset as well, and Mitchell commented, "It was the women against Bernie. The use of the words 'rape' and 'murder' . . . it all came together and affected the women differently than it did the one man." Angered, Shaw said, "I was outraged at the time that a journalist would try to talk a fellow journalist out of asking a question."[192]

Ignoring the counsel of his colleagues, Shaw went forward, memorably beginning the debate at UCLA's Pauley Pavilion by asking, "Governor, if Kitty Dukakis were raped and murdered, would you favor an irrevocable death penalty for the killer?" With little emotion, the governor responded,

Bush and Dukakis face off in the second of their two debates. The encounter in Los Angeles would be forever remembered for Dukakis's unemotional response to CNN anchor Bernard Shaw's question about whether he would favor the death penalty if his wife was raped and murdered. (George H. W. Bush Presidential Library and Museum)

"No, I don't Bernard and I think you know that I've opposed the death penalty during all of my life. I don't see any evidence that it's a deterrent and I think there are better and more effective ways to deal with violent crime." Dukakis went on to cite the decline in crime in Massachusetts, as well as the need to fight a more effective war on drugs.[193]

Immediately, both sides realized this was a crucial moment. In the back room, Fox chairman Barry Diller asked Estrich, "It's over, isn't it?" "Yes," Estrich responded simply.[194] Corrigan thought everybody knew Dukakis's answer was a problem right then, and according to Bennett, "all the air went out of the room."[195] Black, who was with Ken Khachigian monitoring what the two candidates were saying, remembered, "We looked at each other and we folded up our notebooks and said we don't have to track this debate anymore this election's over."[196] Baker was more circumspect: "It's too much to say that I knew right then that the race was over, but it would be hard to lose to someone who couldn't manage to get visibly angry about the rape and murder of his wife." Bush's campaign chairman elaborated, "The American public identifies with crime victims. In a way that is difficult to explain but easy to understand, his [Dukakis's] lack of passion and his overintellectualizing a simple, human question essentially proved everything we had said about his being soft on crime."[197]

The campaign had prepared an answer in advance for such a question regarding Willie Horton and the victims of crime. "I know what it's like to be the victim of crime," Dukakis was supposed to say. He was then to refer to his family's history with crime, which included his father being robbed and tied up at his office, as well as his brother being killed by a hit-and-run driver.[198] "The answer had been practiced," remembered Corrigan. "What had been practiced was at least identifying with crime victims and then talking about the reasons for his approach to criminal justice policy," and according to one account, this response had been rehearsed no fewer than thirteen times.[199] Indeed, Dukakis had discussed the two incidents while campaigning in Lewiston, Maine, only a few days earlier, declaring, "So I don't need any lectures from Mr. Bush on crime-fighting or on the sensitivity or compassion we must extend to the victims of crime."[200]

"I think what happened was if you're an opponent of the death penalty you're asked that question in many forms and I basically answered it as I've always answered it," reflected Dukakis, who granted that it was not the appropriate response for a nationally televised debate. Looking back, though, he still didn't think the answer was as bad as perceived then. While some questioned the appropriateness of Shaw's query, the governor said, "I thought it was a perfectly legitimate question," adding, "There was nothing unfair about it." Dukakis noted that he had pushed for Shaw to be on the panel so there would be a person of color as a questioner in one of the debates.[201] From the other side, Bush thought that his opponent gave a "politically correct" answer instead of saying, "I'd kill him [my wife's hypothetical rapist and murder] if I get my hands on him."[202]

Though the debate is remembered for that one moment, it was only the beginning, as the candidates returned to some of the central themes of the campaign. Asked about the growing criticism of his tactics and negative campaigning, Bush replied, "And what I've had to do is to define not just my position, but to define his. And I hope I've done it fairly. And the reason I've had to do that is that he ran on the left in the Democratic primary, ran firmly and ran with conviction and ran on his record." Again returning to the governor's comments about being a liberal during the primary and being a member of the ACLU, the vice president added, "But what I don't like is this left-wing political agenda. And therefore I have to help define that. And if he's unwilling to do it, if he says ideology doesn't matter, I don't agree with him." Dukakis responded by saying he rejected labels and wanted the country to move ahead, while the vice president thought the status quo was fine.[203]

Continuing to promote himself as a nonideological manager, Dukakis again emphasized his fiscal conservatism and talked about moving people from welfare to work. "And the Ruby Sampsons and Don Lawsons, hundreds of thousands of welfare mothers in this country and in my state and across the country who today are working and earning," declared the governor, "are examples of what can happen when you provide training for those welfare mothers, some day care for their children so that those mothers can go into a training program."[204]

Throughout the debate, Bush continued to use the "L" word in a pejorative fashion. With regard to Social Security, he declared, "We have made the Social Security trust fund sound and it is going to be operating at surpluses, and I don't want the liberal Democratic Congress to spend out of that Social Security trust fund or go and take the money out for some other purpose." When asked whether he had any ideological tests for Supreme Court appointments, the vice president responded, "I don't have any litmus test. But what I would do is appoint people to the Federal bench that will not legislate from the bench, who will interpret the constitution. I do not want to see us go to again—and I'm using this word advisedly—a liberal majority that is going to legislate from the bench."

Toward the end of the debate, Mitchell quoted criticism from former presidents Carter and Nixon regarding the desultory nature of the campaign and asked the vice president whether he would agree to another debate. Bush rejected another debate and alleged that the Democrats had begun the attacks at their convention, especially with the speeches by Ted Kennedy and Ann Richards. He also blamed the media for focusing on the horse race as opposed to policies and issues. "I'm not keeping count, but I think Mr. Bush has used the label 'liberal' at least 10 times," replied Dukakis, "If I had a dollar, George, for every time you used that label, I'd qualify for one of those tax breaks for the rich that you want to give away."[205]

When the debate ended, Estrich came on the stage and spoke to Dukakis, who simply told her, "I'm sorry," adding, "I blew it." Reflecting, she said, "Exactly what we were worried about [happening in the first debate] happened in the second debate."[206] With the polls still relatively close, the governor had missed his opportunity. "He need[ed] to jar something lose tonight," commented Morton on CBS, "and that certainly didn't happen." Donaldson concurred on ABC: "He needed a big one. . . . Whatever it was I don't think he got it."[207]

The Debates Take Center Stage · 221

With Dukakis needing a strong performance to shake up the race, the debate appeared to be a major victory for Bush. Teeter called his candidate "a clear winner," while Darman said, "It was a clear win." Estrich did not challenge their assessment, offering this analysis: "We do not expect to see a change [in the poll numbers] overnight, but we do expect to close the gap in the next few weeks."[208] Polls confirmed the two camps' interpretations, as a CBS poll gave the vice president an advantage of 48 percent to 25 percent in the debate, with an ABC survey showing a lead of 49 percent to 33 percent, and the *Los Angeles Times* an edge of 47 percent to 26 percent.[209]

Accounts did not all immediately focus on the Shaw question. In fact, it was not discussed in either ABC's or CBS's postdebate coverage, and Dionne did not mention it in his piece on the debate.[210] Broder, however, wrote, "The tip-off that this was not to be the night Dukakis supporters hoped for came with the first question, a deliberately shocking query from Cable News Network's Bernard Shaw." The dean of Beltway reporters suggested that Dukakis answered "as if it were the most routine matter in the world" and showed no empathy for the victims of crime.[211]

By the day after the debate, the Shaw question and the governor's response had clearly taken center stage. "Much attention today was focused on Dukakis' answer to the first question posed by moderator Bernard Shaw of Cable News Network," wrote Walsh in the *Washington Post*.[212] "Over and over, Democrats cited Mr. Dukakis's failure to give a more personal response when he was asked if he would still oppose the death penalty if his wife, Kitty, were raped and murdered," wrote Dionne, "even as many Democrats, and some Republicans, sympathized with Mr. Dukakis for having to answer such a question."[213] One congressional Democrat called Dukakis's response "an ice man answer." The governor's aides expressed their frustration that he hadn't discussed his family experience with crime, though Kitty Dukakis declared, "It was an outrageous question; it really was."[214]

The two camps were now in completely different mind-sets. Fearing overconfidence, Bond relayed Baker's worries at the campaign meeting the next morning. "JAB III [Baker] reminds everyone that this race is not yet over," declared Bond, "and we must all work twice as hard in the crucial final days of the campaign."[215] The Dukakis camp didn't have to worry about overconfidence, as it looked like the campaign was all but over. "What the polls that night showed was something that looked an awful lot like 1980," said Estrich, recalling Carter's landslide loss to Reagan—"that the bottom was falling out on us."[216]

Indeed, the first major postdebate poll by NBC News and the *Wall Street Journal*, released a few days later on October 17, showed the gap growing dramatically, with Bush enjoying an overwhelming 55-percent-to-38-percent lead. His efforts to portray his opponent as outside the mainstream had clearly been successful. "[Seventy-one] percent of likely voters believe that Mr. Bush 'represents traditional American values,'" wrote Rich Jaroslovsky in the *Journal*, "while only 48% believe that Mr. Dukakis does." [217]

The campaign had come full circle, from Dukakis having a seventeen-point lead after the Democratic convention to Bush holding the same advantage three weeks from Election Day. These developments again reflected the wider range of swing voters and weaker party attachments during this time period as compared to the 1990s and beyond. The vice president looked to be in complete control—but it turned out the race wasn't quite over yet.

8   One Final Charge

After the second debate, the election result appeared to be a foregone conclusion, with Vice President Bush seemingly on an easy path to the White House. Beyond Dukakis's poor performance on the stump, it appeared that the same problems that had bedeviled national Democrats over the previous two decades were sinking his campaign. As they had since Nixon's election in 1968, the GOP successfully attacked perceived Democratic weaknesses on a familiar range of cultural issues. Race also continued to be a problem for the governor, as he tried to mobilize Black voters while simultaneously avoiding alienating working-class Reagan Democrats.

Staring a landslide loss in the face, Dukakis rejuvenated his campaign by switching to a Gephardt-style populist message, belatedly responding to his opponent's attacks and embracing the liberal label he'd assiduously avoided for most of the year. As the campaign drew to a close, though, Bush's campaign tactics become the central issue in a way rare in American politics. Some claimed his attacks were not merely negative but blatantly dishonest, becoming a drag on him in the stretch run. While the vice president still achieved an overwhelming victory, he had to survive a late scare from the charging governor. In the election's aftermath, both sides debated whether the outcome had been preordained by peace, prosperity, and Reagan's popularity, or whether the governor and his advisers had blown a winnable race.

More of the roots of the future of American politics came into view as the election drew to a close. Though he lost by a significant margin in the popular vote, Dukakis's closing kick allowed him to show his party an Electoral College path to reclaim the White House and keep it for most of the foreseeable future. With his strength in the Northeast, Midwest, and West Coast, the Massachusetts governor laid the groundwork for the "Blue Wall" of states that would enable the Democratic Party to hold the presidency for twenty of the thirty-two years between 1992 and 2024, while only losing the popular vote once.

The second debate reaffirmed a central problem of the governor's campaign—his inability to woo back Reagan Democrats. In Houston, a group of union members watched Dukakis's performance. "Not once in the 90-minute debate did he draw a cheer from the 30-odd blue-collar voters," wrote journalist R. W. Apple. "He didn't talk about our issues," explained the business manager of the union local; Dukakis's positions on social issues also turned off many members.[1]

One subject that bothered some of the blue-collar Texans was gun control, which played an important role in the election, even though it never reached the overt prominence of the Pledge of Allegiance, Willie Horton, and the ACLU. Back on August 26, Bush had sharply attacked the governor on gun rights in Longview, Texas, alleging, "[Dukakis] wants to disarm the people in this state except the military and the police."[2] This assertion was based on a comment the governor supposedly made to an NRA director in 1986 and appeared in *Gun Week* magazine—though Dukakis vehemently denied making the remark.[3] After Bush's comments, Kirk O'Donnell of the Dukakis campaign fired back a press release stating, "In what is becoming a habit for Vice President Bush, he has once again misrepresented Governor Dukakis's position on an important issue." Calling Bush's comments a "complete fabrication," O'Donnell's statement further declared, "The fact is that Mike Dukakis supports the right of hunters and sportsmen to own guns for recreational purposes, and for other law-abiding citizens to own guns for the protection of their homes, consistent with the laws of their states."[4] Campaign talking points produced that same day echoed O'Donnell.[5] Nevertheless, radio ads and campaign billboards repeated Bush's and the NRA's message throughout Texas. "We can't carry this area for him if we can't get past gun control," analyzed the executive secretary of the AFL-CIO in Harris County.[6] "Well, obviously, I wasn't taking people's guns away in Texas," recalled Dukakis, saying, "[George W. Bush] ran around Texas telling them that that's what I was doing."[7]

The efforts to attack Dukakis on guns went beyond Texas. One NRA ad or direct mailing read in giant letters, "DUKAKIS WANTS TO BAN GUNS IN AMERICA." This message seemed to resonate, as a CBS report showed an Arkansas man telling his son, "He's going to take our guns away from us," then asking rhetorically, "We can't vote for him, can we?" Noting that the Razorback State was a southern state the Dukakis campaign believed it could win because its residents hadn't benefited as much from Reaganomics, Lesley Stahl narrated, "Bush's assault on Dukakis's liberalism pushed economic issues into the background." She added, "The issue that has hurt Dukakis more than any other in Arkansas is gun control."[8]

Indeed, it was gun control, along with a whole range of cultural issues like the pledge, crime, the ACLU, and defense, that weakened Dukakis's appeal to rural whites in Texas, Arkansas, and across the South. These concerns had had the same effect on other national Democrats since the 1960s. Walter Dean Burnham, a government professor at the University of Texas, suggested, "[Dukakis] doesn't stand a lot of chance with yellow-dog Democrats who like to put their guns on the pickup roof and go quail hunting." Former LBJ aide George Christian concurred, observing, "These are the kind of issues that've been selling down here for 20 years, going right back to George Wallace."[9]

Though Dukakis tried to seize the center with his talk of fiscal responsibility, this kind of technocratic message simply didn't resonate with rural southern whites. Molly Ivins, a more progressive Texas Democrat, suggested that the campaign made a mistake in trying to pursue the Reagan Democrats and should have tried to mobilize new voters instead. "Dukakis can't win because he can't get Bubba. Bubba's gone," said Ivins. She contended, "He'll come back and vote for a populist Democrat, but he's not going to vote for a stiff from Cambridge."[10] As a result, Texas—a state no Democrat had won the presidency without carrying at the time—seemed to be out of reach for Dukakis despite Bentsen's presence on the ticket.

Corrigan hypothesized that the Dukakis campaign erred in thinking it could spend money for the presidential race through Bentsen's Senate campaign as well. "What happened instead was that voters were given the choice of you could vote for both guys you liked," Corrigan reflected. "You could vote for Bentsen and Bush." Indeed, some of the Bentsen for Senate literature—probably from local party officials—suggested people could vote for both Bush and Bentsen. "It's possible that Glenn would have been better [as a running mate]," reflected Corrigan.[11]

Race also continued to be a confounding issue for Dukakis, as he struggled to generate excitement among African Americans, partly due to his poor relationship with Jesse Jackson. In late September, the campaign started a major ad blitz aimed at the Black community. "[The advertisements] feature two things that have so far not been much in evidence in Mr. Dukakis's campaign," wrote Michael Oreskes of the *New York Times*—"music and the Rev. Jesse Jackson."[12] Former congresswoman Barbara Jordan (D) of Texas, the first African American woman elected to Congress from the South, called out Jackson for his anemic support for Dukakis.[13] Relations between the Democratic nominee and Jackson had been strained. The Dukakis camp had asked him not to campaign in certain states, though Sasso had taken steps to settle matters, speaking with the reverend on a daily basis. Jackson did campaign for the ticket, and Maureen Dowd wrote on October 18 that in order to avoid blame for a poor Dukakis performance among African

Americans, "Mr. Jackson has launched a blazing defense of the Democratic Presidential nominee, of liberalism, and of himself."[14]

But feelings remained raw among some Jackson backers. One aide commented, "If they [Dukakis and Bentsen] lose, they'll only be getting what they richly deserve," while a Jackson supporter from Oakland declared she wouldn't vote for the governor because "they didn't recognize Jesse after all the work he did for them."[15] In the end, though, Estrich seemed to praise Jackson's role. "Jackson came around" and spent time campaigning and doing voter registration, she recalled, adding, "Jackson was not the problem."[16]

The same racial and cultural divisions that weakened Dukakis in the South also played a crucial role in the governor's struggles in key midwestern states he needed for an Electoral College victory. "He's got the worst of both possible worlds," observed Cleveland's Republican county chairman. "He's had to keep his distance from Jesse Jackson because he's afraid of the reaction, so he's got the blacks mad at him. And he's getting killed on the social issues in the ethnic community." Indeed, Dukakis's support among Catholics had fallen from 55 percent after the convention in July to 40 percent prior to the second debate.[17]

Crime also seriously weakened Dukakis with this constituency. Citing the governor's response to the Shaw question, a candidate in Chicago who had already switched from the Democrats to the Republicans declared, "He's not a real guy. Most guys would say, 'Hey, I'd kill him myself.'" Meanwhile, the NRA in Michigan geared up for a full-court press to back the vice president, with one official commenting, "I've seen more N.R.A. 'Defeat Dukakis' bumper stickers than I have our own Bush stickers."[18]

Increasingly, commentators traced the Bush campaign's successes and the Dukakis campaign's difficulties to race and other divisions in American society emerging from the turbulent 1960s. "In the 1988 presidential campaign," wrote Anthony Lewis, "race is the dirty little secret: a highly significant factor that no one mentions out loud." Citing the Horton ads, Lewis noted, "Willie Horton happens to be black. There he was in the Bush television ads, night after night. The message did not have to be more explicit: Dukakis stands for softness toward threatening black criminals." Looking at the Bush attacks more broadly, Bill Schneider analyzed: "Crime, gun control, law and order: the whole agenda originated in the racial polarization of the late 1960s—black power, violence, the perceived failure of the Great Society. And Bush uses the social issues to define Dukakis as a 1960's liberal. The fear of crime originated in racial fear. In some places—Chicago, notably—fear of crime is associated with fear of domination by blacks. The more white ethnics see the Democratic Party dominated by blacks, the more they are afraid." Schneider concluded, "I don't argue that Bush is running strongly because he is a racist. He is not a racist. But there is a racial component [to his campaign]."[19]

At this time, the Dukakis campaign retooled its message for one final push, shifting to the more class-based, populist theme first proposed in August. "We switched to that because the bottom fell out [after the second debate]," remembered Estrich. With a deficit so large, the Dukakis camp feared major losses in Congress as well. Estrich added, "We had to get the base. We had to get back to 46–47%. Even if in doing so that was going to be our ceiling."[20]

Shrum wrote a series of five-minute television spots for Dukakis, echoing the "On Our Side" message that his client Senator Howard Metzenbaum was employing very successfully in his reelection campaign in Ohio. After rejecting such a theme both in late August and around Labor Day, Dukakis now embraced it with gusto.[21] "You could argue whether it was the right message or not but it was a message," reflected Shrum.[22]

Campaigning on October 18 in Michigan, Dukakis sounded less like a reserved technocrat and more like a fiery populist. "We're going to stand up and fight for American companies and American products and American jobs," declared the governor in Kalamazoo. In Saginaw, he said of his opponent, "[He] wants to help those who already have it made. I want to help every American family make it." In what became a common refrain over the race's final weeks, Dukakis then added, "He's on their side, Lloyd Bentsen and I are on your side."[23] But just as he adjusted his message, a familiar tank drove back onto the screen.

As he watched the governor riding in the tank back in September, Sid Rogich thought, "*Why would they ever let him put a helmet on?*"[24] The next day he started to put together a commercial, though the networks wouldn't sell him their video of the event. Eventually, the Bush campaign obtained independent footage and put together an ad.[25] Ailes likely played a role in the spot's creation as well.[26] But with a significant lead in hand, Rogich didn't want to put the piece on the air. "It was pretty certain that we were going to win this race, according to trackings, and I didn't want to run the commercial." Calling James Baker at the campaign headquarters, he urged against it, but the campaign chairman responded, "Well, we're taking a vote around the table and you lost." "The vote was six-to-one, you lose," Baker added.[27]

Debuting during game three of the World Series on October 18, the commercial shows Dukakis riding in the tank, with some added sound effects of shifting gears and engine noise.[28] The narrator repeats the text rolling down the screen, which starts with "Michael Dukakis has opposed virtually every defense system we developed," then lists a number of programs the governor allegedly opposed, and ends with an image of Dukakis wearing the helmet and approaching the camera in the tank. "Now he wants to be our commander in chief," the narrator declares as Dukakis's image freezes. Then the screen reads and the narrator declares, "America can't afford that risk."[29]

Bennett recalled his reaction when he heard about the ad: "I felt horrible. I felt guilty and I felt dread. I felt like it was going to be very effective."[30] Without the commercial, the tank ride might have faded away in the pre-YouTube era, but the spot ensured it would never be forgotten.

With hindsight, the governor made an admission: "Now, should I have been in the tank? Probably not, in retrospect. But these days when people ask me, 'Did you get here in a tank?' I always respond by saying, 'No, and I've never thrown up all over the Japanese prime minister [which Bush did as president].' But, you know, things happen."[31] Diminishing the incident's importance, he added, "I didn't lose an election because of the helmet and the tank and that stuff."[32] Bennett agreed, saying, "It was one more brick in the wall," one more event sowing Republicans' long-standing distrust of Democrats on national security. He added that he would have thought he cost the governor the election if it had been a closer result.[33]

Belatedly responding to the tank ad and the Bush attacks in general, the campaign prepared a commercial called "Counterpunch," which briefly shows the tank ad rumbling on a television screen until Dukakis turns off the set. "I'm fed up with it," the governor declares. "[I] haven't seen anything like it in 25 years of public life; George Bush's negative tv ads: distorting my record, full of lies, and he knows it." Elaborating, "I'm on the record for the very weapons systems his ads say I'm against," Dukakis says both he and Bush want a strong defense, and that the ad isn't about defense, but rather "about dragging the truth into the gutter." Switching to the new populist message, Dukakis argues, "The real question is will we have a president who fights for the privileged few or will we have a president who fights for you." He criticizes the vice president for supporting tax breaks for the wealthy, declaring, "I'm fighting for you and your family," and promising to push for jobs, better health care, and education.[34]

On *Meet the Press* that weekend, host Chris Wallace challenged Black regarding the accuracy of the tank ad. "We overlaid facts that are absolutely documented," responded Black. "He [Dukakis] has opposed every one of those weapon systems. And we had to call his hand on the fact that he is not strong on national defense." Despite assertions by both DNC chairman Kirk and Wallace that the governor supported the weapon systems mentioned,

Black claimed that Dukakis had "flip-flopped," stating, "We don't buy it."[35] Also rejecting the governor's critique, Baker wrote, "We were charged with distorting Dukakis's position," adding, "My answer is that we did nothing more than take an image his campaign had created and put it on the air with factual commentary about how he had opposed or criticized most of the new weapons systems and defense initiatives of the Reagan administration."[36]

The Dukakis campaign also produced an ad going after Bush regarding the federal furlough program. "George Bush talks a lot about prison furloughs. But he won't tell you that the Massachusetts program was started by a Republican and stopped by Mike Dukakis," the narrator says. "And Bush won't talk about the thousands of drug kingpins furloughed from federal prisons while he led the war on drugs," the speaker continues. The ad shows a picture of a furloughed heroin dealer, who happens to be Hispanic, who has raped and murdered a pregnant mother of two. Her picture is displayed as well. The ad concludes by saying, "[The] real story about furloughs is that George Bush has taken a furlough from the truth."[37] Estrich explained the change in strategy: "After 10 weeks of the furlough ad we felt—some say the time was long overdue—it was time for us to call George Bush on his hypocrisy in attacking a program and an isolated incident in Massachusetts when there were exactly comparable isolated incidents at the federal level, as there were also in California."[38]

The newly aggressive posture begged the question: Why wait so long to respond? To answer such a query, campaign talking points explained, "MSD [Michael Dukakis] had hoped that George Bush would stop his campaign of distortion and deception so that the real issues in this campaign would have a chance to be heard. But it's clear that George Bush can't afford a debate on the real economic challenges facing working families. Mike Dukakis is determined to have this campaign focus on the real challenges and so are the voters."[39]

Upon reflection, the governor admitted, "First I made a very serious mistake and this was my decision. Nobody else's. That we would not respond to the Bush attack campaign." Elaborating on his "huge mistake," Dukakis explained that he thought the country was tired of the polarization of the Reagan years: "I thought people would respond a lot more to a kind of positive thing which is what I am anyway."[40] Though many in the Democratic Party urged him to fight back earlier, the candidate was not alone in this view. As Corrigan attested, "He was getting advice from people like Mario Cuomo who said don't engage on this. If you ignore it will go away. If you engage . . . it's like changing the channel to their message. There were people who were counseling him to not amplify the charges by repeating them."[41] Dukakis recalled the New York governor telling him, "Don't pay any attention to this Bush stuff. You know you're a positive guy. Don't worry about it." Dukakis continued, "Four days before the election we were campaigning together in Queens and he said that was the lousiest advice I ever gave you." Even so, the governor made it clear that the responsibility for the decision was solely his.[42]

As the race moved toward its conclusion, the Bush campaign's strategy became the dominant subject of discussion, with Anthony Lewis writing, "From the Republican convention on, the aim has been to portray Mr. Dukakis as unpatriotic, soft on crime, somehow alien and strange." Concerning this approach, Lewis concluded, "There is an element of nativism in it."[43] Clinton noted how successful Bush's camp had been in defining Dukakis, suggesting, "I'm not sure that his record is too liberal for the people of Arkansas. It's the way people perceive his value system. People won't vote for an alien. It'd be like asking them to vote for somebody from another country for president."[44]

Saturday Night Live commented on this aspect of the campaign, as well as what some saw as its superficiality, running three commercials satirizing the Bush tactics during the October 22 episode. With patriotic music in the background, the fake ads first show pictures of Presidents Kennedy, Lincoln, and FDR, as well as Vice President Bush. The narrator notes the men's height, as they all stand over six feet tall, then says, "But Michael Duk-akis is 5'5½"," even though the governor actually stood 5'8". The ad then concludes, "Bush. He's Taller."[45] Another lists the background of several famous presidents, saying they are all of "white, northern European heritage," like Bush. Each president's picture is placed on a map of Europe on the country his family comes from. The narrator again says, "But Michael Duk-akis," as Dukakis's picture is placed on Greece. "Bush. He's Whiter," the narrator concludes.[46] A third advertisement begins by stating, "John F. Kennedy's parents were born in America" and featuring a picture of JFK surrounded by an American flag. The ad continues by specifying that several other presidents' parents were also born in America, including Bush's. "But Michael Dukakis's parents," says the narrator while a Greek flag is seen in the background of the governor's image. The commercial ends with the narrator stating, "Bush. His parents were born in America."[47]

In the aftermath of "Revolving Door" and the tank ad, the critiques of the Bush campaign grew more serious than those of the *SNL* variety. "This is the first year that I can remember in presidential history in which we've seen nationally aired ads and ads aired in regional markets that are actively distorting the other person's record," declared Jamieson on *Meet the Press*.

She further explained, "[These ads are] not just prompting false inferences, but stating as true something that's false. In the past, when we saw that, it was narrow cast into tiny little areas of the country, in the places the press wouldn't ever hear or see." Laying down the gauntlet, Jamieson concluded, "Overall, in terms of fairness and accuracy, Bush is running the dirtiest campaign that I've seen since 1964."[48]

On the same program, Black rejected these accusations, saying, "[The campaign has] presented assertions and facts that are all documented and true." Unsurprisingly, Bush himself had little patience for the charges, revealing as much in his diary a few days earlier, on October 18: "Now you keep reading that it's the worst campaign in history—the ugliest, the meanest. The media was not about to define Michael Dukakis, and a lot of them are liberals; and not only are they not about to define him, they come to his defense."[49] Baker agreed, pointing out, "There's also a place in politics for going after the other guy." He also elaborated, "I make no apologies for going after Dukakis on prison furloughs, the Pledge, or anything else. He led with his chin on a lot of these issues, and we used them to take it out."[50]

Criticism of the Bush campaign grew more intense when both Bentsen and Jackson suggested the continuous attacks on the Massachusetts furlough program featured a racial dimension.[51] "When you add it up, I think there is [a racial element], and that's unfortunate," commented the Texas senator. After a meeting with Dukakis in Boston, Jackson observed, "There have been a number of rather ugly race-conscious signals sent from that [Bush] campaign." The reverend continued, "The use of the Willie Horton example is designed to create the most horrible psycho-sexual fears, the furlough ad with black and brown faces rotating in and out of jail, the use of the Jackson-Dukakis ticket symbolism, which is distortion, referring to me as a Chicago hustler." While Dukakis did not comment on the matter himself, Sasso told the media that the governor agreed with his vice-presidential nominee.[52]

Needless to say, the Bush campaign sharply disagreed, with a spokesman saying, "The whole idea is childish to say there is some sort of racial overtone in the Horton case. The issue isn't Willie Horton, the issue is why did he get out and why didn't Michael Dukakis stop it."[53] Bush himself called the allegation "some desperation kind of move," adding, "[The governor is] weak on crime and defense and that's the inescapable truth."[54] At the October 24 campaign meeting, Atwater warned his colleagues, "Everyone should be prepared for a tough final two weeks," adding, "Dukakis is flat out of issues, so his campaign is trying to shift the focus of the race to things like 'dirty-pool' tactics and charges of racism."[55]

The media weighed in on the charges as well. Defending the "Revolving Door" ad, conservative columnist Charles Krauthammer challenged Jackson's assertion that it showed images of people of color, noting, "The inmates going through that door are disproportionately white. The whole feel of the commercial is of a Cool Hand Luke southern prison gang, where the good guys and bad guys are white."[56] Bush also found an unlikely ally in the *Washington Post* editorial page, which wrote, "We think it's a phony, no more credible than those vicious and baseless charges that the Bush campaign had been making about Gov. Dukakis' patriotism."[57] Not everyone agreed, with Merle Black, a political scientist at the University of North Carolina, describing an ad he saw showing Horton's picture as "updated 1988 George Wallace-style politics."[58]

Denying there was any racial motivation in using the Horton case when both campaigns debated the subject at the postelection forum at Harvard, Atwater contended, "When I first heard about this issue, I didn't know who Willie Horton was. I didn't know what race he was." He added, "Finally, obviously, when it came to our attention that Willie Horton was black, we made a conscious decision—Roger was there at the meeting when I took the lead—not to use him in any of our paid advertising, on television or in brochures." Ignoring his own connections with the independent group that produced the commercial, Ailes said, "I want to point out that the Bush campaign never used Willie Horton's picture in any paid advertising." Furthermore, Ailes noted that the Dukakis campaign showed the picture of an Hispanic convict in their furlough ad.[59]

Estrich countered, "My point is that although you may not have mentioned Willie Horton by name in your furlough ad, George Bush mentioned his name regularly in his speeches." She added, "Each time he did—or at least often when he did—it would lead to network stories. We would have a little network recap that would show a picture of Willie Horton and newspaper stories that would show a picture of Willie Horton."[60] Perhaps even more than the National Security PAC ad, this was the way the Horton story and image spread across the nation, as television pieces airing "Revolving Door" sometimes mentioned Horton as well, perhaps linking them together in the public mind.[61] Though newspapers didn't often show Horton's picture, his visage appeared on fifteen different evening-news programs from December 1987 onward. Thirteen of these newscasts aired after Bush cited Horton for the first time on June 22—and at least four of these images were shown on days when the vice president mentioned Horton's name. Sometimes, multiple images of Horton appeared in the same story.[62] Unpersuaded, Atwater replied to Estrich, "The American people do not think that it's racist to mention someone's name. That's why the charge never went anywhere. That is why the *Washington Post* and many other publications in most states wrote editorials saying it wasn't a racist campaign."[63]

Asked why he had not used a more egregious case where the governor pardoned a white convict who had then gone on to murder someone, Atwater responded that he didn't know of that case until after the election. "Had I known about it," he said, "we would have been smart to go with that and never mentioned Willie Horton. In other words, if the guy was white, there would have been zero questions about our intent."[64] Looking back, Dukakis himself had no doubt that the use of Horton was racist, declaring, "Sure it was.... You kidding me. The black guy who assaults a white woman. I mean come on. Pretty obvious what was going on here."[65]

While the Bush campaign did not directly use Horton's picture in its materials, some state and local parties did. Infamously, the Maryland GOP distributed a flier showing Dukakis's and Horton's picture at the top with the caption "Is This Your Pro-Family Team for 1988?" in between. The flier went on to ask, "By now you've heard of the Dukakis-Bentsen team? But have you heard of the Dukakis–Willie Horton team?" Telling a rough version of how Dukakis handled the furlough situation, it concluded, "You, your spouse, your children, your parents, and your friends can have the opportunity to receive a visit from someone like Willie Horton if Mike Dukakis becomes President. Do you want that to happen?"[66] "That is totally out of bounds, totally unauthorized," critiqued Baker when asked about it by Lesley Stahl on *Face the Nation* on October 30. Baker further stated, "It was not authorized by the campaign.... You cannot control every party organization throughout the country. The Democrats cannot control every party organization that they have in the country."[67] Atwater later reiterated that the Bush campaign instructed local parties not to use Horton's image, and Ailes explained, "I have been in this business for 20 years. You've got guys out there printing it. You can't control it."[68]

The criticism of the campaign and the Bush tactics in particular continued, as the *New York Times* endorsed Dukakis while editorializing, "The 1988 campaign has been unusually superficial."[69] According to one survey, while Bush received more newspaper endorsements than Dukakis by a margin of 241 to 103, he garnered the fewest ever for a Republican nominee. Indeed, the number of papers deciding not to endorse at all was the highest since the poll was first taken in 1932. Among those following this path was the *Washington Post*, which declared, "This has been a terrible campaign, a national disappointment." Though the *Post* had endorsed the Democratic candidate in every election since 1976, it sharply criticized Dukakis on national defense. However, it also added, "[Bush] was really the major source and cause of the tawdriness of this campaign and much of what he said was divisive, unworthy, and unfair."[70] Not everyone agreed, with the *Wall Street Journal* editorial page heaping praise on the Bush team for bringing important issues into the arena: "We've heard, of course, that George Bush and Roger Ailes have run an unprecedentedly 'negative campaign.' The Beltway media are singing this chorus because this election is not turning on what they regard as the issues—the deficit, how much to raise taxes, how much to cut the defense budget." Lauding Ailes and Bush, the paper continued, "With the pledge, the furlough program and the ACLU, they pumped some genuine voter concerns into the election."[71]

Though the major newspapers still played an important role, as the primary season first indicated, television was the main game in town in 1988 and television ads proved pivotal to the election's outcome. "The next president will have been chosen in a campaign dominated as never before by television," wrote Oreskes in the *New York Times*, while polling eminence Louis Harris declared, "The simple story of this election is that the Bush commercials have worked and the Dukakis commercials have not."[72] There was talk of disarray and a lack of direction on the part of the governor's team.[73] Looking back, however, some questioned the centrality of the Bush attack ads, noting that the vice president had seized the lead in the polls even before the famous thirty-second spots regarding Boston Harbor, Willie Horton, and furloughs began to air.[74]

While television was key to how voters received information, the medium offered candidates less time to explain their message than it had even two decades earlier. The average period a candidate received to speak fell from forty-two seconds in 1968 to a mere ten seconds by 1988. Whereas candidates often received as much as a minute of time to speak uninterrupted in 1968, neither Bush nor Dukakis ever received that much time on the evening news in 1988.[75] Overall, the two candidates had 56 percent less speaking time on the network news than Nixon and Humphrey had had in 1968.[76] Noting that he had said the election was not about ideology but about competence, Dukakis later lamented, "I was wrong. It was about phraseology. It was about 10-second sound bites. And made-for-tv backdrops. And going negative."[77]

Echoing the charge that the 1988 campaign was harsher and more negative than previous contests, a *Washington Post* headline labeled it the "TV Era's Nastiest Presidential Race."[78] Oreskes agreed in the *New York Times*, writing, "Experts on Presidential campaigns say this is the first time in a Presidential race that candidates have used advertising at least as much to bash the other side as to promote themselves." Oreskes went on to say, "The old wisdom that more was expected of Presidential candidates seems dead."[79] Asserting that Reagan's 1980 and 1984 ads were largely positive, Devine concurred, concluding, "I think that's really the big political legacy of that [1988] campaign. That that kind of tactic of destroying your opponent going after them very aggressively is the way to win. You know I think that carried over into the 90s and I think it continues through today."[80]

While Jamieson and others argued the campaign was unprecedentedly negative and dishonest, others who examined the election rejected the notion. "The advertising in 1988, despite all the claims, did not usher in a new era of American politics," writes political scientist John Geer. "It was the news media's coverage that brought about a new era," he contends, arguing that the media's growing emphasis on the horse race and greater focus on negative ads contributed to the belief that the campaign commercials in the 1988 presidential election were harsher than those from the 1988 presidential race.[81] LBJ's infamous "Daisy" ad of 1964, which implied a Goldwater victory might precipitate a nuclear war, immediately drew widespread condemnation and was quickly pulled. It never garnered much attention from contemporary news sources. By contrast, in 1988 the media treated "Revolving Door" as just another attack in the campaign, and the commercial continued to run.[82]

Whatever its true level of negativity, voters seemed turned off by the 1988 presidential campaign, with some predicting the lowest turnout in forty years.[83] *Newsweek*'s October 31 cover read, "Mud in Your Eye: A Nasty Race Trips Up Pundits and Turns Off Voters." Dionne wrote in the *New York Times* that "a majority rated the campaign as dull," adding, "After the 1984 landslide nearly three-fifths of voters called that contest 'interesting.'" According to Dionne, the electorate seemed to blame both sides for false charges. And regardless of the critiques of the Bush campaign, it had proved highly effective with the electorate. Dionne stated, "49 percent of all registered voters said Mr. Dukakis would not be tough enough in dealing with criminals; 36 percent said he would. By contrast, 61 percent saw Mr. Bush as sufficiently tough with criminals and only 25 percent said he was not." The attacks had been even more successful on national security issues, as "forty-one percent of the probable electorate said Mr. Dukakis would weaken the nation's defenses; [while] only 3 percent said this of Mr. Bush." Voters also saw Dukakis as significantly more likely to raise taxes.[84]

Regardless of the harshness or accuracy of their tactics, Bush and his Republican surrogates adroitly used the Pledge of Allegiance, Willie Horton, and furloughs to cast Dukakis as a left-wing radical with values outside the national mainstream. They also used these issues to argue that Dukakis

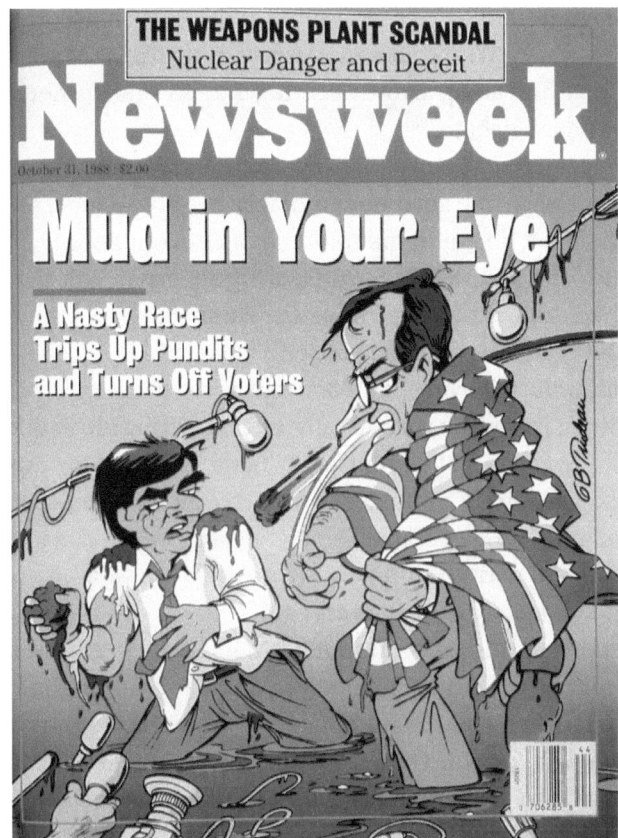

This *Newsweek* cover illustrates the frustration many felt with regard to the campaign tactics in the 1988 election. (Photo courtesy of Enveritas Group, Inc.)

was somehow vaguely anti-American—a tactic that had worked well for the GOP since it had attacked McGovern as the candidate of "acid, amnesty, and abortion" during the 1972 campaign. Republicans would attempt to do the same thing—albeit with less success—to Bill Clinton and Barack Obama in later years. Some of the roots of the birther campaign against Obama can be seen in some of the attempts by more extreme elements of the party to cast the Massachusetts governor as an un-American Eastern European ethnic. Still, Dukakis and his brain trust were not without blame, as they failed to see the symbolic power of these issues to voters, especially Reagan Democrats. The Dukakis campaign's legalistic and analytical responses to these emotional topics exacerbated the challenge it faced, making an already difficult race for the candidate even more of an uphill battle.

After Bush took a huge lead in the aftermath of the second debate, the polls tightened a bit in the next week to ten days as Dukakis promoted populist themes. However, the NBC poll showing a seventeen-point margin might simply have been an outlier.[85] *Newsweek*'s CW gave Bush a down arrow: "Old CW: It's over. New CW: Did someone say it's over? Not *us*." Praising the governor, CW gave him an up arrow: "Peering into his soul, he finds the fire he should have had in debate."[86]

A day after the vice president attacked Dukakis for dividing the nation with the new populist message, the governor embraced the liberal label on October 30, declaring, "I'm a liberal in the tradition of Franklin Roosevelt and Harry Truman and John Kennedy."[87] Surprised, Shrum explained, "He went beyond what I had drafted or what I think the campaign had anticipated when he went out and started calling himself a liberal."[88]

Responding mockingly the following day, Bush told a crowd in Kentucky, "Headlines. Read all about it. My opponent finally, after knocking me in the debate, called himself the big 'L,' called himself a liberal." Meanwhile, the vice president's campaign quickly produced a new commercial showing pictures of a less popular group of national Democrats: McGovern, Carter, and Mondale. In the ad, the narrator intones, "Why would we want to go back to the tax-and-spend policies of eight years ago?"[89]

Toward the end of the race, the governor ran ads reinforcing the Shrum message, with all of them saying, "As President, Michael Dukakis will be on your side."[90] In Ohio and Texas, some commercials emphasized economic nationalism while attacking Japan. One Texas ad shows Bentsen, who had become a star surrogate since his bravura performance in the vice-presidential debate, addressing his hometown audience and declaring, "In Japan they pay higher wages than in Texas. In the White House Mike Dukakis and I will change that. I know him. You know me. We're going to put America first."[91] The DNC got into the act as well, with an ad suggesting that the GOP was selling the country to foreigners. The spot displays an image of the Bank of Tokyo, and the narrator later says, "The Democratic Party believes it's time to stand up for American workers and American products. If you agree, vote Democratic. Vote to Put America First."[92]

Dukakis did an interview with Shaw and switched from the first subject the CNN anchor asked about to return to his question from the second debate. Calling the query fair, the governor confessed, "It took me aback a little bit." He added, "Kitty is probably the most—is the most—precious thing, she and my family, that I have in this world. And, obviously, if what happened to her was the kind of thing you described, I would have the same feelings as any loving husband and father." Asked whether he might feel like killing the perpetrator, Dukakis responded, "I think I would have that emotion. On the other hand, this is not a country where we glorify vengeance. We're a country that believes in the law and I believe very strongly in the law." As he was supposed to do in the debate, Dukakis invoked the toll crime had taken on his family, concluding, "And I guess had I had to do it again, that's the kind of answer I would have given."[93]

As both camps geared up for the final week, Dukakis's poll numbers had closed a bit from his postdebate low, but Bush still maintained a significant lead. On November 2, Atwater privately told his colleagues, "All of the public polls look good in the 10–13 point range. I believe that the race is actually closer than that and we can not let up in the home stretch." Atwater also said he expected the contest to get closer before Election Day, warning, "We could slide badly if we take our eye off the ball and let up."[94] Indeed, ABC showed the vice president up 55 percent to 42 percent, while CBS had him ahead 53 percent to 41 percent.[95]

On the other side, the Dukakis campaign had abandoned its national approach, shifting to an eighteen-state strategy in the hopes of winning the Electoral College while losing the popular vote.[96] Though unaware of it, the governor's staffers were laying out the winning path for future Democratic presidential candidates, focusing their energies on New England, the industrial Midwest, and the West Coast, along with a few southern states. Most affiliated with the campaign thought it was a long shot, and Estrich believed Dukakis had no chance after the second debate and began giving money to state parties—with the candidate's permission—to help down-ticket Democrats. "I wanted Dukakis to come out of this not being a pariah in the party," said his campaign manager.[97]

At this point, Reagan had taken to the hustings to campaign for Bush and other Republicans. "He committed to do anything we asked him to," remembered Black, "and we didn't ask him to go out and travel and do a lot of stuff but he did some at the end." Black added, "But he mainly wanted to stay out of the way."[98] In Nevada on November 1, the president assailed Dukakis's new theme, declaring, "Of course the liberals now are saying that they're on your side. I guess they think that that will make it easier for them to reach their hand around and put it in your pocket." Rejecting the governor's attempt to link himself to popular Democrats of the past, Reagan continued, "Don't be fooled, folks. George Bush's opponent is not Harry Truman and he's no F.D.R." Truman and Roosevelt were Democrats the president had voted for when he was one of them. It was clear that Reagan's popularity, which had grown significantly in the previous three months, was proving to be a huge asset for his vice president. "It's Reagan who's winning the election for Bush and Quayle. He's providing the strong record," analyzed Bill Schneider. "Bush's part principally has been to portray Dukakis as a risk."[99]

This view even impacted satire on the final weekend before the election. *SNL* aired more political skits, including one titled "Dukakis after Dark," in which the governor, believing the election essentially over, uses his thirty minutes of paid airtime to hold a party rather than make a final attempt to persuade voters. Exchanging his conservative suit for a Hugh Hefner–style jacket, Lovitz/Dukakis explains to host Matthew Modine, playing Bentsen, that they are going to lose, saying, "We represent unpopular and discredited views." A fictional Willie Horton attends with Victoria Jackson/Donna Rice as his date, and Lovitz/Dukakis apologizes that he won't be able to give him a presidential pardon. As the skit concludes, Lovitz/Dukakis humorously presents the emerging explanation for his defeat, telling the audience in an unemotional monotone, "The one thing that really hurt us is the fact that Reaganomics works. It really does. I mean aren't you better off than you were eight years ago? I know I am. How about the rest of you? I wish you weren't but you are. You are better off. And there's no denying it."[100]

While *SNL*'s Dukakis was resigned to defeat, his real-life counterpart still believed a 1948 Truman-style comeback victory possible, as he was spurred on by large crowds in Philadelphia, Chicago, and Milwaukee. In Lexington, Kentucky, he declared, "I smell victory, don't you?" as he continued to espouse his "On Your Side" message. "We're going to take back our government from the influence peddlers and the sleaze merchants," the governor said in Queens. "We're going to take back America from dishonest contractors and polluters."[101]

Polls offered a small degree of hope for the governor, as the *NYT*/CBS poll showed Dukakis only down by eight compared with thirteen two weeks earlier. Toward the end, he seemed to be gaining among union members, some of whom had been attracted to Bush on cultural issues but might have been swayed by the economic populist message during the last few weeks. Later deciders were also going to the governor, partly because they blamed Bush for the negative nature of the campaign.[102] "I think there were many who thought that those Bush attacks would go to Bush's character," commented Estrich. "In the last few weeks of the campaign he may have paid some price for running a negative campaign," she continued, "but he paid a much smaller price than Michael Dukakis did."[103]

As had been the case in recent weeks, tactics came to the forefront on the last Sunday talk shows prior to the election, with some suggesting that a victorious Bush would have no mandate because of the campaign he'd conducted. On *Face the Nation*, a Democrat was quoted as saying, "If Bush wins, it's because Willie Horton is better known to the American people than Dan Quayle." Stahl asked Bentsen about some Democrats saying they wouldn't give Bush a honeymoon because of the harsh tenor of the campaign. Slightly later, Bentsen replied, "I don't think he gets any brownie points for the kind of campaign he's run. It's been an extremely negative one. So that doesn't give you any mandate."[104]

On *Meet the Press*, it was noted that an NBC poll showed Bush leading by only five points, though Teeter suggested the campaign's polling had that figure more like nine. Bentsen also appeared on the program, and Broder asked whether he'd advised Dukakis to respond to the Bush attacks. "Well that's correct," replied Bentsen. "But he's a very positive man and really hates negative advertising. I could understand his objections to it. But I'm from Texas where we look on politics almost as a contact sport and so when someone comes after you you return it."[105]

"You know a lot of people are saying that this has been the worst presidential campaign in memory," commented Wallace, adding, "The most negative. The worst choice of candidates." While Broder responded that the 1972 Nixon-McGovern contest had been worse, Apple disagreed: "I think it has been the worst in the sense that it's been the most disappointing. These guys were capable of better. I don't think McGovern and Nixon were."[106]

During the program, Broder asked Teeter about Quayle's whereabouts on the campaign trail, a question many were posing as the election rapidly moved toward its conclusion. The senator had declared independence from his handlers a week after the disastrous debate with Bentsen. Even so, the day before the election, Richard Berke wrote in the *New York Times*, "Mr. Quayle has been one of the most exposed, yet invisible Vice-Presidential nominees in modern times." Berke noted that Bush's running mate had been sent to small markets and had done little campaigning with the vice president and no network interviews.[107]

Nevertheless, the Dukakis campaign continued to run ads against Quayle, with Richard Viguerie noting, "He's under house arrest," and "The Democrats wanted to make Quayle the major issue but they can't find him."[108] Later, the Indiana senator suggested that the governor's focus on him might actually have helped Bush, commenting, "If they wanted to go after the Vice-Presidential candidate and put all the energy into going after the Vice President, fine, because then they'd be giving more of a free ride to the President, and people really don't vote for the Vice Presidential candidate."[109]

In the face of Dukakis's charge, the Bush campaign sought to shore up its support in the midwestern battleground states, going to Michigan, Ohio, and Missouri. One Bush campaign official observed, "What we're seeing is a halt in a decline in some of the key states. We've looked at it. Our base is strong. We feel good with the electoral strength we have in both our strong states and those that are leaning toward us." A more senior aide summarized the situation: "If we win Ohio and New Jersey and you don't see us lose anything surprising in the South and the West, then I don't see how he can really do anything."[110]

While on the stump, the vice president mocked the allegations of negative campaigning coming from the other side. "He [Dukakis] seems to forget the personal attacks, night after night on me, on my character at that idiotic Democratic convention," charged Bush, reiterating his campaign's standard defense. "And so now all that is left is this daily whining about a negative campaign."[111] Keeping up a frenetic pace, Dukakis campaigned in "9 states, [and] 11 cities . . . in a 48-hour scramble to defy the pundits and the polls predicting victory for Vice President Bush," wrote Toner.[112]

As Election Day arrived on November 8, the only chance for a Dukakis triumph was to win a narrow Electoral College victory while losing the popular vote. One Bush aide thought this feat possible, even though no such split had occurred since 1888. Yet that outcome was not out of the question. Polls showed that Bush's popular vote advantage was buttressed by an overwhelming lead in the South of 57 percent to 35 percent, while he and the governor essentially split the electorate in the rest of the country.[113]

As part of a last-ditch effort to win, Dukakis did fourteen interviews for key states as the voting occurred.[114] "We saw a path to potential victory if we could win some of these close states," remembered Devine, adding, "We thought the thing was in play right until the very end."[115] The candidate himself remained optimistic, recalling, "I was doing television feeds at seven o'clock at night on election night. Did I think we had a shot? Yeah I thought we had a shot. I wasn't kidding myself."[116]

At the start of NBC's election coverage, Tom Brokaw told his audience that they would know much more about the election's result "in the next hour or so."[117] "There wasn't too much doubt about the outcome," recalled Quayle, "but the forty-state victory was not the landslide people remember. Pennsylvania and Illinois turned out to be very close, and Ohio reasonably so; there were just enough toss-ups to give the beginning of the evening just a little bit of suspense."[118]

"Michigan was a real crusher," according to Corrigan, because it was the eighteenth state in the campaign's eighteen-state strategy, and when the Wolverine State fell, Dukakis knew it was over.[119] CBS first called the election for Bush at 9:17 P.M. eastern time, with ABC following two minutes later.[120] A little over an hour later, at approximately 10:30 P.M., NBC made the declaration of Bush's victory unanimous.[121]

When the dust finally settled, Bush had won forty states to Dukakis's ten for an Electoral College landslide of 426 to 111 (with one faithless elector),

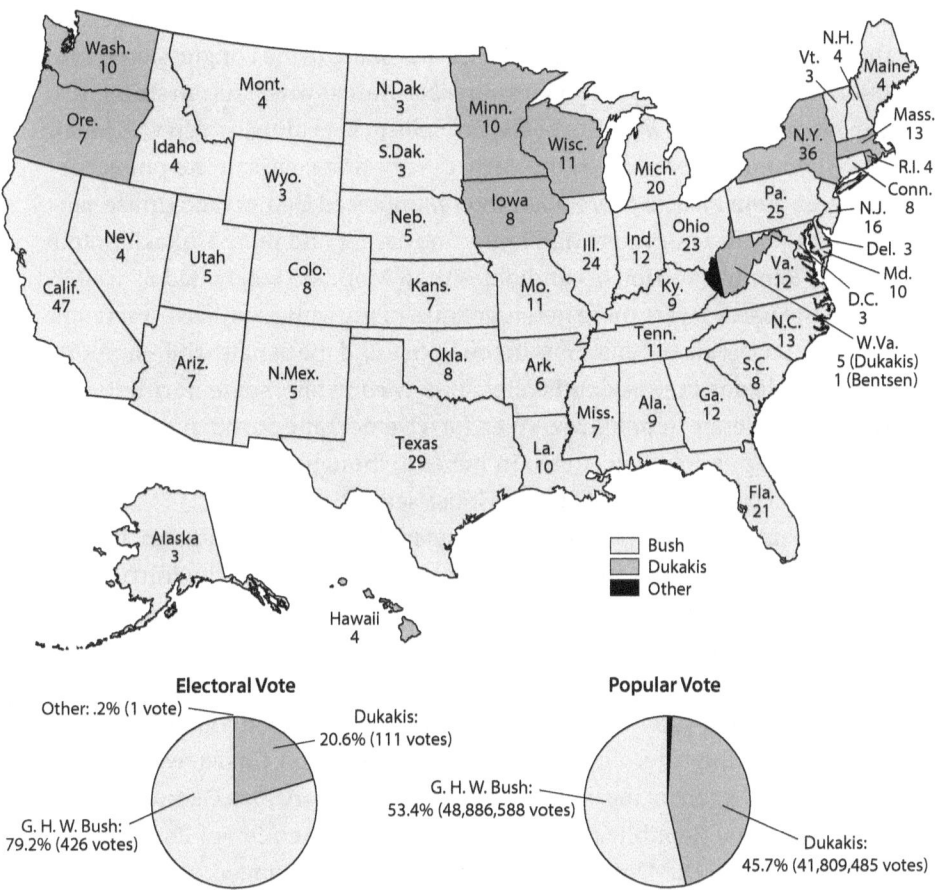

1988 Electoral College votes by state. Bush won forty states in the kind of Electoral College landslide unheard of in twenty-first-century politics.

giving the GOP its fifth win in six presidential elections.[122] As of 2020, no one else has achieved such an overwhelming margin, as Bush's victory preceded the red-blue divide that left most states consistently falling into one party column or another. In the popular vote, the vice president earned 53.4 percent—a share of the popular vote larger than anyone has managed as of 2020—to the governor's 45.7 percent, for a 7-million-vote margin.[123] But the election was actually closer than those figures show. "A perfectly executed shift of about 590,000 votes in 11 states," wrote Dionne, "less than one vote for every hundred cast—would have given Mr. Dukakis a narrow electoral college majority."[124] Bush became the first vice president to succeed his president since Martin Van Buren in 1836, and the Republican Party won three straight terms in the White House for the first time since 1928. On the other side, Dukakis's showing was the best performance by a Democrat since Jimmy Carter in 1976.

Despite his convincing win, Bush lacked coattails. Democrats increased their margin in the House, winning a greater share of the congressional vote than the vice president and picking up seats in areas where he ran strongly.[125] The 1970s and 1980s were the heyday of split-ticket voting, which was much more common then than in the early twenty-first century. The phenomenon grew from 1984, as more Bush voters supported Democratic House candidates than Reagan voters had four years earlier and more Dukakis voters backed Republican House candidates than Mondale voters had as well.[126] When the parties were more heterogenous, many white southern voters still backed conservative Democrats in the House and the Senate while supporting Republicans in presidential elections. Meanwhile, some northern and western moderate Republicans voted for a Democratic president and for the GOP in congressional elections. In the end, though, no twentieth-century president's party would hold fewer House seats than Bush's.[127]

The Democrats also picked up one seat in the Senate. In addition, further illustrating the divided allegiances of the era, seventeen of the thirty-three senators elected won their seats while the opposite party won the presidency in their state. For example, while Bush carried Tennessee easily with 58 percent of the vote, Democratic senator Jim Sasser cruised to reelection with 65 percent of the vote. On the other hand, Dukakis took Rhode Island with 56 percent of the vote, while Republican senator John Chafee won reelection with 55 percent of the vote.[128] By 2016, after conservative Democrats had largely become Republicans and most liberal and moderate Republicans had switched to the Democrats, this dynamic had changed considerably. Split-ticket voting declined to the point that no senator was elected from a state won by the presidential candidate of the other party. In 2020, only one senator accomplished this feat.[129]

Just as Reagan had for the last two years of his term, Bush would face a Congress controlled by the opposition party. "The American voters gave George Bush and the Republican Party a pattern-breaking presidential victory," wrote Broder, "but blurred the import of their decision by cautiously opting once again for divided government in Washington."[130] The same contentment that propelled Bush to victory likely did the same for congressional Democrats. As political scientists Alan Abramowitz and Jeffrey Segal observe, "For many citizens, voting for a Democratic candidate for Congress—like voting for George Bush—constituted an endorsement of the status quo."[131] As a result, many questioned whether Bush had a "mandate" to implement his agenda.[132]

First and foremost, Reagan's popularity provided the underpinnings of Bush's victory. According to the *New York Times*, Reagan's approval rating was 56 percent, "roughly the same proportion that voted for Mr. Bush," analyzed Dionne. In addition, "roughly 84 percent of Mr. Bush's ballots came from Americans who approved of Ronald Reagan." ABC News exit polls showed that Bush won 93 percent of voters who "wanted to keep the Reagan course," while Dukakis won 90 percent of those who wanted a change.[133] "Ronald Reagan's extraordinary popularity had much more to do with George Bush's victory over Michael Dukakis," write Abramowitz and Segal, "than did 'the L word,' the Pledge of Allegiance, and Willie Horton combined."[134]

Prosperity was also central to Bush's success. Among the 40 percent of voters citing the "national economy" as the "issue the candidate addressed best," Bush's margin of victory was 53 percent to 46 percent, very similar to the popular vote. "When an out-of-power party must contend for the presidency in a period of peace and relative prosperity, it is likely to lose," writes political scientist Everett Carll Ladd. He concludes, "That was the Democrats' problem in 1988."[135]

While the economy was important, the vice president won votes from nearly 90 percent of those who cited "military spending" or "foreign affairs" as the matter the candidate approached best. Bush also earned votes from 70 percent of those who cited "crime" as the candidate's strongest position. In addition, he won by a margin of three to one among those who said the death penalty was an important issue. Roughly one in ten voters cited either the furlough program or the Pledge of Allegiance as important in their calculus, with the vice president carrying those voters by a margin of roughly five to one. Gallup surveys showed the pledge issue resonated much more strongly in the South than in the rest of the country.[136]

Dukakis did best among those citing health care, the poor, or job creation as the "issue the candidate addressed best." He also performed strongly with voters who decided over the last week, likely helped by the late-campaign populist message and some Americans' frustration at Bush's campaign tactics.[137]

With regard to demographics, Bush won among all age groups except those aged eighteen to twenty and sixty and above. His strongest group was twenty-five- to twenty-nine-year-olds, a group that had come of age under Reagan and embraced his optimistic, entrepreneurial brand of conservatism. This demographic was embodied in popular culture by Alex P. Keaton, the beloved character played by Michael J. Fox on the hit NBC sitcom *Family Ties*. Bush also won among baby boomers, many of whom might have responded to his attempts to frame Dukakis as an extreme 1960s liberal.[138]

Dukakis eked out a narrow victory among those between the ages of eighteen and twenty-four, causing some to speculate that the trend of young people going to the GOP might have come to a halt. The governor's strongest backing, however, came from those over sixty years old, many of whom leaned to the Democrats because they had come of age during the New Deal / Fair Deal era of the 1930s and 1940s. This group might have responded enthusiastically to Dukakis's closing populism and invocations of FDR and Truman.[139]

Bush led among whites 55 percent to 44 percent, continuing a trend—no Democrat had won that group since 1964. ABC / *Washington Post* polls showed the governor winning 90 percent of the Black vote, in line with the post-1964 voting behavior of the community, while CBS / *New York Times* polls had that number a bit lower at 86 percent. The *Times* poll also showed Dukakis winning 69 percent to 30 percent among Hispanics.[140]

First observed in 1980, the gender gap—where Democrats performed more strongly among women and Republicans performed more strongly among men—remained firmly in place. Bush won men 54 percent to 44 percent, while Dukakis won women 52 percent to 47 percent—though the *New York Times* gave Bush an advantage of 50 percent to 49 percent. This dichotomy would continue to be a central divide in American politics into the 1990s and well into the twenty-first century. In terms of class, Bush won voters making over $20,000 a year, and Dukakis won among those earning less than $20,000. While Bush did not perform as strongly with Democrats as Reagan had in 1984, he did win 16 percent of Democrats, while Dukakis only won 8 percent of Republicans.[141]

As predicted, voter turnout reached historic lows, dropping to 50.2 percent. This was the lowest level since 1924, as the negativity of the campaign no doubt turned off many voters. "We had abysmal, vacuous elections and the people responded accordingly," analyzed Committee for the Study of the American Electorate director Curtis Gans, who broke down the data.[142] Notably, though Dukakis's margins among Blacks were similar to those of Democratic presidential candidates since the civil rights era, African American turnout trailed 1984 levels and fell more than white turnout. Some attributed this decline to the persistent tension between the Dukakis and Jackson camps.[143]

With regard to differences by region, the lack of dramatic disparities in state voting patterns reflected the fact that the 1988 election preceded the more fixed red-blue divide of later years. Only two states exhibited "polarized" voting patterns—defined as the winning candidate performing ten points above or below his/her national percentage of the popular vote. The number of polarized states grew dramatically over the next three decades, reaching 22 in 2016 and 21 in 2020, respectively.[144] At the local level, 42 percent of voters lived in "landslide counties" in 1988—defined as those in which elections are decided by twenty points or more. After falling in 1992, their numbers gradually grew to a whopping 62 percent of voters by 2016, before falling slightly to 58 percent in 2020. This data all reflected the sorting of people's living patterns by partisan affiliation in the interim.[145] Indeed, Bush was the last Republican to win the majority of the nation's 100 most populous counties, taking 57 of them to edge out his rival by a margin of 49.7 percent to 49.2 percent. As of 2020, only one Republican has even won 40 percent of the vote in those regions (George W. Bush in 2004), and between 2008 and 2020, these areas became the heart of the modern Democratic Party. Democratic standard-bearers have routinely carried 85 or more of those counties, reaching 91 out of 100 by 2020.[146]

While Bush won a landslide in the Electoral College, the electoral map would turn out to be one of the most important legacies of the 1988 election. Unsurprisingly, Bush swept the South and the Rocky Mountain West, taking all of those states and mostly by significant margins. He won the popular vote in the South by a margin of three to two, and these regions would remain the base of the Republican Party throughout the 1990s and into the first decades of the twenty-first century.

The Northeast proved to be Dukakis's strongest region, where he won his home state along with Rhode Island and New York. He also performed strongly on the opposite coast, winning Washington and Oregon—becoming the first Democrat to win a West Coast state since 1968—and coming only 350,000 votes short in California. "If we'd had a chance of winning, we'd have carried California," reflected Estrich. "That just went with the East Coast falling," she pointed out. The governor won traditional progressive strongholds in Minnesota and Wisconsin, along with Iowa, where the weak farm economy cost Bush in the caucus and likely did so again in the general election. West Virginia and Hawaii rounded out Dukakis's states. "The [closing] strategy worked so that it closed enough so that you know we carried 10 states," remarked Estrich. "We should have carried a few more."[147]

In fact, while Bush won the states stretching east across the industrial Midwest from New Jersey to Wisconsin, Dukakis made very strong showings in Illinois and Pennsylvania, where he rallied only to lose by respective margins of 51 percent to 49 percent and 51 percent to 48 percent.[148] Recognizing this, Dionne wrote, "The 1988 Presidential election marked a decided shift in the strength of the Democratic Party to the Midwest and the West." He added that this development confirmed the South's move into the GOP as well. "The result is that the Democrats might now be in a position to put together electoral majorities without the South," Dionne contended. He continued, "Some Democrats say these gains in the midst of defeat portend future victories, much as Alfred E. Smith's gains in the big cities in 1928 foreshadowed the New Deal coalition created in 1932 or as Barry Goldwater's southern strength in 1964 foreshadowed the Republicans' future in the South."[149]

This proved to be prescient analysis. The 1988 election laid the groundwork for what would eventually be called the "Blue Wall," as the Democrats' dominance of the West Coast, New England, and the industrial Midwest would frequently carry them into the White House over the next three decades. Those regions would become the centerpiece of Bill Clinton's, Barack Obama's, and Joe Biden's victories, as well as the oh-so-close losses of Al Gore and John Kerry.[150] Bush would be the last Republican to carry a number of vote-heavy states until 2016; the most notable of these were Michigan and Pennsylvania. Prior to Trump's election in 2016, some pundits talked of an insurmountable Democratic advantage in the Electoral College just as they had spoken of a Republican one in 1988.[151]

Although Trump punctured the "Blue Wall" in Wisconsin, Pennsylvania, and Michigan in 2016, Biden reclaimed those states four years later. Through the 2020 election, the GOP has not won any of the West Coast states since Bush, and the same holds true for Illinois. Though Clinton, Obama, and Biden won key southern states in their victorious campaigns, they did not need them to ensure victory. After their devastating defeat in 1988, Democrats would only lose the popular vote once between 1992 and 2020.

In terms of other principals in the race, *Newsweek*'s CW offered its final take in the magazine's postelection issue. Among the disparate figures receiving an up arrow were Reagan—"'87 CW: another failed president. '88 CW: so great he even elected Bush"—and Trump—"Good N.Y.-D.C. Trump Shuttle service could sway Eastern media elite." Though Gore's campaign ended rather poorly, CW said, "Old CW: miserable campaign. New CW: valuable campaign experience."[152] Indeed, Gore's run likely laid the foundation for his selection as vice president four years later.

Those receiving down arrows included the Democratic convention—"Old CW: brilliantly bland love fest. New CW: disastrous Jesse show"—and Arthur Schlesinger Jr.—"So much for historian's long-predicted cyclical swing back to liberalism." With regard to Dole, CW stated, "Forget White House. Trapped as Senate water carrier for man he hates."[153]

Finally, postcampaign analysis revealed what many had said during the race—that 1988 had fundamentally altered the way presidential candidates raised money. Reports revealed that Dukakis had raised $68 million in soft money, while Bush had raised $54 million. The overall impact was clear.

"The net impact of the influx of soft money was to undermine the public finance system imposed in 1974 after the Watergate scandal," concluded Larry Eichel of the *Philadelphia Inquirer*.[154]

A debate quickly emerged over whether structural factors or campaign tactics were more responsible for the race's outcome. "Scholars of presidential elections said they were sure that in-depth analysis of the unprecedented mass of polling data this election generated will demonstrate that peace and prosperity were the fundamental forces behind Bush's victory," wrote Broder. Using the economic growth numbers for the six months prior to the election as well as the inflation rate over the previous two years, Yale economist Ray Fair, designer of the most respected economic election model, had predicted a "narrow Republican victory" in August.[155] Given the overall situation, another academic observed, "Any GOP presidential nominee in 1988 would have had to work awfully hard to lose."[156]

On the other side, some believed it was a winnable race, criticizing Dukakis and his Massachusetts-based team for being too insular and for being outmaneuvered by the more experienced Bush squad. The Dukakis campaign also came under fire for its failure to respond to the Bush attacks until it was too late. Many said the governor should have strengthened his team and brought veteran Democrats into the fold after he won the nomination. Estrich said that she pushed Dukakis to do so, but that he believed it was unnecessary.[157] "We run our presidential campaigns with amateurs. The Republicans run theirs with professionals," declared Democratic veteran Bob Squier. Agreeing, the chairman of the Tennessee Democratic Party alleged, "We had an arrogant candidate, an amateur campaign, and an aggressive opposition."[158]

Some went further, arguing that it was not just the quality of the campaign staff, but the party's message and the legacy of the 1960s that remained the central problem. "Bush ran on the same script as Nixon did in 1968—coddling criminals, soft on defense," noted Carter adviser Stuart Eizenstat, adding that the party kept nominating candidates vulnerable to the same attacks. Shapiro echoed this sentiment in *Time*: "The meanness of George Bush's attacks coupled with the ineptitude of Michael Dukakis' campaign tends to obscure an important truth for the Democrats: the party is still doing penance for the 1960s. The code words like Willie Horton, the Pledge of Allegiance and the A.C.L.U., which the Republicans used to fuel the politics of resentment, all come out of Richard Nixon's playbook."[159]

Previewing the key themes of his 1992 campaign, Clinton explained why the Democratic Party must seize the center: "You must be considered in the mainstream on the shared values of the American people, the ability to defend the nation and the strength to enforce its laws. We have yet to learn that lesson."[160] From the opposite end of the party's ideological spectrum, Ted Kennedy asserted, "This election was eminently winnable" and described how the governor should have embraced the liberal label earlier.[161]

At the Harvard postelection session, both camps debated this question extensively. "A consensus emerged that Dukakis never had much of a chance to win," according to Dionne and David Gergen, "and blew what small opportunity he had."[162] Corrigan claimed that given everything going against Dukakis, his campaign couldn't afford any mistakes, while Estrich cited Reagan's growing popularity and peace and prosperity as difficult obstacles to overcome. On the other side, Ailes believed the governor could have won if he'd done better in the second debate.[163]

In later years, the principals embraced sharply differing views on the subject, with many of the political professionals rejecting the structural explanations offered by the academics. On the Bush side, Baker wrote as follows: "The fact of the matter is that when the Democrats nominated Michael Dukakis, they all but elected George Bush. No matter how many reporters and editorial boards referred to him as a moderate—and no matter that he presented himself as a nonideological centrist—he was in fact a classic Democratic liberal in the mold of George McGovern and Walter Mondale." Baker further noted, "Eight years of Republican peace and prosperity made it even harder to pitch the liberal agenda." Crediting his candidate and friend as well, he added, "George won because he offered the three most important things American voters look for in a president—someone who shares their vision of America, someone with whom they are comfortable, and someone who can lead."[164]

Unlike the head of his campaign, Black believed Dukakis could have won "if he [had] ran a better campaign," explaining, "He had to finesse off those liberal positions. Not necessarily repudiate them but then get on offense on some things where swing voters thought we were on the wrong side. But he stayed on defense most of the time." And the veteran GOP consultant concluded, "You just can't let your campaign team put you in a tank."[165]

Some in the Democratic camp believe the governor could have won if he had dramatically changed his approach. Saying the race was winnable by "somebody," Estrich posited that a "different Dukakis" could have defeated Bush. Yet this would have been difficult because, as she noted, the governor was very much who he was as a person.[166] Shrum agreed, stating, "He would've had to become almost a different person," one who could "talk about things that . . . he didn't usually talk about. But it turned out at the end when he did he was very comfortable with them." In this analysis, Shrum referenced the class-conscious message of the campaign's last three weeks.[167] Given Dukakis's lead at the convention, Bennett thinks that the election was winnable, but by a challenger who made change the message as opposed to competence.[168]

Another school believes that a different candidate could have defeated Bush, reaching back to the Hart scandal as the source of the Democratic Party's demise. "Hart had been as close to a lock for the nomination—and likely the presidency," wrote Matt Bai in 2014 in his book on the Rice scandal, "as any challenger of the modern era."[169] Rejecting this idea, Pinkerton argued that the Colorado senator would not have won either, explaining that "Bush was on the right side of peace and prosperity, I think we would have won against almost anybody. Bush won pretty big, fifty-four percent of the vote and if he hadn't had Quayle it would have been fifty-six. I mean it would have been a big victory I think."[170] "The fact that Reagan was pretty popular was going to make it tough for anybody," analyzed Bennett, who also said, "You could argue that Hart absent the scandal might have been a stronger candidate." For his part, Shrum believed Hart, Gephardt, or Biden would have had a very good chance to beat Bush.[171]

And what of Dukakis himself? What did he believe thirty years after his defeat? "I think it was a winnable race," the governor declared in 2017. Asked about his campaign's legacy, he remarked, "One legacy is you better not sit there doing nothing while the other guy's pounding you."[172]

In the end, though, Bush likely would have won even if Dukakis had responded more swiftly and adroitly to the Bush-Atwater attacks. Though the recovery hadn't benefited everyone, the economy had improved dramatically from where it had stood when Reagan was inaugurated on January 20, 1981, and memories of the stagnation of the Carter years remained fresh. Bush also reaped the good feeling from the receding of Cold War tensions during Reagan's second term, while Democrats were still struggling to overcome the stigmas of the 1960s. Though Iran-Contra seemed to give the Democrats an opening two years earlier, the scandal had faded from the headlines by Election Day, and Reagan's approval ratings had rebounded. Dukakis could certainly have run a much better campaign, but the fundamentals likely represented too much of a head wind for any candidate in any case.

Epilogue The Legacy of 1988

In the years between the 1988 and the 1992 elections, the legacy of the Bush-Dukakis race loomed over American politics, and the dominant lesson of 1988—that one must always fight back against attacks—took hold. This lesson deeply influenced Bill Clinton's run for the White House, as the Arkansas governor and his staff made sure to quickly respond to the Bush campaign's broadsides. At the same time, the Willie Horton ad developed the stigma it still retains today, becoming synonymous with negative campaigning, as Democrats turned the spot on its head and used it as a weapon to neutralize new GOP attacks. Meanwhile, various aspects of American politics with roots in the 1960s, 1970s, and 1980s that reached fruition in 1988 came into greater focus. Notable among these were the strength of certain groups within both parties and a more general move toward the center, along with a more confrontational press and the continued growth of nontraditional media. A newer trend arose as politicians of both parties embraced draconian anticrime policies to make sure a future Horton could never be employed against them. The post-1988 desire to look "tough on crime" accelerated the rise of mass incarceration, impacting criminal-justice policy well into the next century.

Despite the importance of the 1988 election, fate would not be kind to the race's combatants. George Bush ascended to levels of popularity rarely experienced by a modern American president after the nation's victory in the Persian Gulf War in 1991, only to suffer an ignominious election defeat a mere eighteen months later. Though Dukakis chose not to run again, his political career ended on a similar note, with his state hammered by a recession and his popularity in free fall.

On January 20, 1989, George H. W. Bush took the oath of office, becoming the forty-first president of the United States. In an era that would be remembered as far less contentious than the period that followed in the 1990s and early twenty-first century, the new president called for bipartisan cooperation. "There has grown a certain divisiveness," Bush remarked. "We have seen the hard looks and heard the statements in which not each other's ideas are challenged but each other's motives. And our great parties

Bush takes the oath of office as the forty-first president of the United States on January 20, 1989. (George H. W. Bush Presidential Library and Museum)

have too often been far apart and untrusting of each other. It's been this way since Vietnam," he observed, again reflecting some of the 1960s divisions that shaped his battle with Dukakis. Declaring that "the old bipartisanship must be made new again," he reached out to the "loyal opposition" for cooperation. "Let us negotiate soon and hard. But in the end, let us produce. The American people await action. They didn't send us here to bicker. They ask us to rise above the merely partisan."[1]

Though certainly not remembered in history like FDR's inaugural in 1933 or JFK's address in 1961, the speech received a largely positive response. In the *New York Times*, R. W. Apple called it "moderate, non-ideological, and modest," noting that Bush was calling for "subtle yet significant corrections in the nation's course." He elaborated that the new president "assured the Democrats that he counted them as friends and as loyal Americans—an implicit effort to make peace with his Democratic rival for the Presidency, Michael S. Dukakis, and with others who felt that in the heat of battle last year he had purposely impugned their patriotism."[2]

One Democrat who watched the speech and complimented it was none other than Dukakis himself. "I am sure that other members of my party were touched as I was by the sense of optimism," the governor observed, "the call to duty and the generosity of spirit by which you called on all of us in your Inaugural Address to work together to eradicate homelessness, wipe out the scourge of drugs that poisons our children and build a stronger, more secure America." Of course, the Democratic nominee—who was invited to the proceedings but did not attend because of work obligations—did not hide his disappointment: "I'd be less than candid if I didn't say I'd like to be the guy raising his hand and taking the oath today."[3]

Bush's first year in office went well, as the economy continued to grow. At the same time, a reverse domino theory seemed to take hold, as communist governments fell one by one across Eastern Europe. Gorbachev did not intervene to stop reform as Soviet leaders had done in the past, leading to the epochal fall of the Berlin Wall in November 1989.[4] As his first year in office concluded, Bush's approval ratings surpassed 70 percent.[5]

Alas, the year did not go as well for Dukakis. After he ruled out a run for a fourth term as governor in January, everything went downhill. The prosperity of the "Massachusetts Miracle" started to fade along with the rest of New England's economy, a precursor to the national recession of 1990-91. To combat these new fiscal problems, Dukakis proposed a series of tax increases and spending cuts. The governor's approval rating fell from 79 percent at the time of his victory in the New Hampshire primary in February 1988 to 41 percent by April 1989.[6] "Very few times in recent political history have politicians untouched by personal scandal plummeted as quickly as Dukakis has in the past year," noted a July UPI story.[7] Problems also emerged on the personal front, as Kitty Dukakis entered rehabilitation for alcohol abuse in February, a condition brought about in part by the stress of the presidential campaign. In his final State of the State speech in January 1990, Dukakis noted that the state "took an unfair beating" in the campaign, declaring, "I feel terrible about it." "Trying to do two jobs at the same time was more difficult and more grueling that I expected," he elaborated, adding, "I underestimated the toll it would take on my family, too."[8]

Other candidates from the race moved into different roles. Having relinquished his House seat to run for the presidency, Jack Kemp became Bush's secretary of housing and urban development, giving him the opportunity to put in practice some of his conservative antipoverty ideas. Dick Gephardt moved within one spot of being Speaker of the House when he ascended to the rank of House majority leader after scandals brought down both Speaker Jim Wright and Majority Leader Tony Coehlo.

The legacy of Dukakis's loss hovered over the Democrats as planning began for 1992. Many in the party advocated a stronger move to the center, a course charted by Bob Dole and Bush in the 1988 Republican primaries and by both candidates in the general election. Shortly after the race ended, John Sasso, Dukakis's campaign manager, urged Democrats to be tougher in handling Jesse Jackson in the future. Ron Brown, the new chairman of the Democratic National Committee, emphasized what Democrats needed to say: "There is no one tougher than Democrats when it comes to protecting our children from drugs, when it comes to protecting our cities against crime, and when it comes to protecting our nation against aggression and terrorism." Clinton, now chairman of the Democratic Leadership Council, observed in 1990, "While we favor tax fairness and think the middle class is overtaxed, we don't think the Democratic Party should lead with class warfare."[9]

In June 1990, in a crucial moment for his presidency and the Republican Party, Bush took a dramatic step to solve the deficit problem, retracting his no-new-taxes pledge during budget negotiations with Congress. "It is clear to me that both the size of the deficit problem and the need for a package that can be enacted require all of the following," wrote the president: "entitlement and mandatory growth reform; tax revenue increases; growth incentives; [and] discretionary spending reductions." Conservatives howled in protest.[10]

As the budget fight continued, the trajectory of Bush's presidency changed dramatically when Iraq invaded Kuwait on August 2, 1990. The United States and its allies quickly began a military buildup in Saudi Arabia as part of Operation Desert Shield to contain Saddam Hussein and prevent him from advancing farther in the region. "This will not stand. This will not stand, this aggression against Kuwait," the president famously declared.[11]

But fiscal challenges remained at home. Bush and the congressional leadership worked out a plan to raise gas, alcohol, and cigarette taxes while cutting some domestic spending. Income taxes would not be hiked. Addressing the country, Bush explained to a national television audience on October 2, "I cannot claim it's the best deficit-reduction plan possible; it's not. Any one of us alone might have written a better plan. But it is the best agreement that can be legislated now."[12]

In a key moment in the continuing emergence of the right wing of the GOP, Gingrich, now the House Republican whip, broke with his president to lead a rebellion against the agreement. Both sides were unable to get sufficient backing for the plan, and it failed by a margin of 254 to 179. Journalist E. J. Dionne reflected on events a quarter century later: "It was the ritual political punishment of George H. W. Bush on the tax cut issue by conservatives that established there could be no heresy of any kind on the question. The line was drawn on October 5, 1990, in a House vote that might be seen as the first Tea Party roll call. For more than three decades, it would define the GOP." In the following years, moderate Republicans, already on the decline by 1990, would see their numbers dwindle to virtually nil. The more heterogenous parties of the 1970s and 1980s would give way to the more homogenous and ideologically consistent parties of the 1990s and early twenty-first century, making compromise more and more challenging.[13]

Forced back to the drawing board, Bush negotiated another agreement, relying more heavily on Democratic support this time. The second compromise bill, supported by a coalition of Democrats and northern moderate Republicans, raised income taxes, increasing the top marginal rate to 31 percent. "The train is leaving the station," declared Representative John Kasich (R) of Ohio, a conservative opponent of the bill, "and it's got the taxpayers' wallets right on it."[14]

Meanwhile, Dukakis's long career in public office was about to conclude. Despite the travails of the Massachusetts economy, he used his farewell address to emphasize the progress the state had made since he first came to office fifteen years earlier. "I refuse to let the difficulties of the past two years blot out how much we've done and how far we've come from the dark and dismal days of 1975," declared the governor.[15]

As Dukakis stumbled toward the exit, Bush reached unparalleled heights midway through his term. Following months of debate, with some predicting a Vietnam-style quagmire, Operation Desert Shield became Operation Desert Storm and turned into a rousing success. Thirty-eight days of air bombing and 100 hours of ground combat expelled the Iraqi Army from Kuwait in the clearest triumph for the U.S. military since World War II. Declaring the Vietnam syndrome defeated, Bush ascended to levels of popular approval unheard of for an American president, reaching as high as 91 percent in one poll.[16] Only Harry Truman had seen these levels of popularity right after he entered the White House and Germany surrendered.[17]

The war made Gen. Colin Powell, who had led the military to victory as the first African American chairman of the Joint Chiefs of Staff, a national hero. Discussion of the general replacing Dan Quayle as vice president began, with many going so far as to tout him as a future president. Following on the brief Jackson boomlet three years earlier, a Black president was becoming more and more a part of the mainstream national conversation.[18] Powell would later flirt with entering the presidential race in 1995, only to decline to enter in the end.

In March 1991, Lee Atwater, who had become chairman of the RNC after the campaign, died after a yearlong battle with brain cancer at the age of forty. Two years earlier, he had briefly joined the board of trustees of Howard University, the nation's most prestigious historically Black university, but he was forced to step down following protests by a student body angered by the Bush campaign's use of Willie Horton. In his final months, he apologized for some of the tactics he employed, telling *Life*: "In 1988, fighting Dukakis, I said that I 'would strip the bark off the little bastard' and 'make Willie Horton his running mate,'" saying now he was "sorry for both statements: the first for its naked cruelty, the second because it makes me sound racist, which I am not."[19]

As the next presidential campaign slowly got underway, the Willie Horton ad began to take on a greater stigma as Democrats tried to prevent the emergence of new wedge issues. In October 1990, Bush vetoed a bipartisan civil rights bill on the grounds that it would force employers to create quotas to hire minorities. In December, Gephardt claimed, "Republicans were seeking a successor to the Willie Horton issue."[20] Dukakis had no doubt this was going to be a central issue in the 1992 campaign, alleging, "Willie Horton has been replaced by Willie Quota."[21] Such efforts were likely forestalled, however, when Bush signed a different version of the bill in the fall of 1991.[22]

Though the most prominent Democrats stayed out of the contest because of Bush's postwar popularity, Clinton became the fifth candidate to enter the race when he declared in October 1991. Calling for a change after three Republican terms, he outlined the major themes of his "New Democrat" philosophy, declaring, "Together I believe we can provide leadership that will restore the American dream—that will fight for the forgotten middle class—that will provide more opportunity, insist on more responsibility and create a greater sense of community for this great country." Sounding much like Gary Hart had in his announcement four years earlier, Clinton rejected ideological labels, saying, "The change we must make isn't liberal or conservative. It's both, and it's different." Like Dukakis, he stressed welfare reform and balanced budgets.[23]

With high poll numbers, Bush seemed to be in an extremely formidable position to win reelection. However, with the economy weakening, the first major sign of trouble appeared in November in Pennsylvania, where a little-known senator named Harris Wofford routed Bush's former attorney general, Dick Thornburgh, in a special election. Democratic governor Bob Casey had appointed Wofford, a former JFK adviser on civil rights, to the upper house after moderate Republican John Heinz had died in a plane crash earlier in the year. Given Thornburgh's close ties to the Bush White

House, where he also chaired the Domestic Policy Council, many portrayed the defeat as a repudiation of the administration. Republicans disputed this, of course, but one pollster prophetically concluded, "[The result] sends a very dramatic message, first to the White House that Bush is not invincible and that health care is one of the cutting edge issues of the 1992 elections."[24]

Yet another bad omen for Bush arrived when conservative columnist Pat Buchanan began a primary challenge against him a month later. Buchanan launched a series of attacks on the incumbent in his announcement speech. "Why am I running?" he asked. "Because we Republicans can no longer say it is all the liberals' fault," Buchanan then said. "It was not some liberal Democrat who declared, 'Read my lips! No new taxes!,' then broke his word to cut a back room budget deal with the big spenders."[25]

Echoing Gephardt's protectionism, Buchanan broke with GOP free trade orthodoxy, declaring, "As for the predatory traders of Europe and Asia, who have targeted this or that American industry for dumping or destruction, if I am elected, they will find themselves on a collision course with the President of the United States." Mirroring some of Trump's 1987 rhetoric and anticipating many of the Donald's 2016 themes, he called for a "new patriotism, where Americans begin to put the needs of Americans first, for a new nationalism where in every negotiation, be it in arms control or trade, the American side seeks advantage and victory for the United States."[26]

As the battle for New Hampshire got underway on both sides, many of the other issues that emerged in 1988 surfaced again in Clinton's campaign. As they had with Hart, members of the press corps concerned with personal foibles placed the Arkansas governor under fire over alleged adultery when Gennifer Flowers claimed to have engaged in a long-term affair with him. Like Quayle, Clinton found himself subjected to questions regarding his efforts to avoid the Vietnam-era draft. Thus his candidacy was very much on the razor's edge on the eve of the primary in February 1992.

Just as he did after the disastrous 1988 convention speech, Clinton recovered from these revelations, campaigning tirelessly to the last minute to finish a surprisingly strong second to former Massachusetts senator Paul Tsongas, earning himself the moniker of "Comeback Kid." On the GOP side, Buchanan repeatedly hit Bush for breaking the "read my lips" pledge to achieve a stronger-than-expected runner-up finish, delivering a major blow to the president.[27]

A nationally unknown long shot when he declared in April 1991, no candidate dealt with more comparisons to Dukakis than Tsongas, a fellow Greek American from Massachusetts. "All of 1991, that was question No. 1. Do you think the country's ready for another Greek from Massachusetts?" mused

Tsongas. He went on to declare at one point, "I'm a Greek from Massachusetts who fights back."[28] This combativeness included referring to Clinton as "pander bear" on the stump, alluding to what some saw as the Arkansas governor's attempts to please all constituencies.

When Tsongas dropped out after Clinton handily defeated him in the South and Midwest, Susan Estrich criticized his unwillingness to get tough on the trail. "Paul Tsongas's campaign didn't just run out of money yesterday; he didn't have the stomach for the fight," she wrote. Estrich added, "Mr. Tsongas wasn't the right man to take on the president—not because his ideas were wrong, but because you can't beat George Bush by throwing beanbags." She said that despite calling him "pander bear" on occasion, Tsongas had been unwilling to attack Clinton's character, which was his best chance for victory. In her mind, this reluctance showed that the former senator lacked the mettle to prevail in a tough general election campaign. "Paul Tsongas claimed that he'd learned from the Dukakis example, but he hadn't really," Estrich continued. She explained, "The real lesson is that you need to fight first. The best defense is a good offense. Bill Clinton certainly knows that. I expect him to be on the attack against George Bush every day, starting today."[29]

But before he went after Bush, Clinton first sought to further position himself as a moderate "New Democrat" by distancing himself from Jesse Jackson. Though the reverend hadn't run this time, he retained a power base within the party, and Clinton took a very different approach to him than Dukakis had. At a meeting of Jackson's Rainbow Coalition in June, Clinton criticized the African American rapper and activist Sister Souljah, who had been a panelist at the conference. A couple of weeks after the Los Angeles riots in 1992, she told a *Washington Post* reporter, "If black people kill black people every day, why not have a week and kill white people." In his speech to the coalition, Clinton repudiated her remarks, which some saw as a blatant effort to court white voters who disliked Jackson. "In that context Clinton's speech was arrogant, and it was cheap," commented Roger Wilkins, a longtime civil rights leader. "He came there to show suburban whites that he can stand up to blacks. It was contrived."[30]

A month later, perhaps learning from the Quayle experience, Clinton chose Gore—a fully vetted national figure—as his running mate, receiving a largely positive response. Stanley Greenberg, a Clinton pollster who had criticized Gore's 1988 campaign, observed: "The whole response to his candidacy today has been free of skepticism in large part because he ran before, he's tested and experienced."[31]

As the convention approached, Dukakis praised his friend Clinton, calling him "the Republicans' worst nightmare: a tough, smart, progressive

Southerner." Showing little sympathy for his former rival, then struggling in the polls because of the weak economy, the former Massachusetts governor observed, "Poor old Bush, he can't seem to come to grip with things." Offering advice on how to deal with attacks, Dukakis argued, "The most effective way to deal with a negative campaign is to turn it into a character issue on the guy who is doing it." He also explained why he was reluctant to offer counsel to Clinton, saying, "If I knew anything about this business I'd be talking to you from the Oval Office."[32]

It was clear that Jackson, who had played such a central role in Atlanta four years earlier, would not have nearly the same prominence in New York City in 1992. There would be no bus trip to the convention, no high-profile negotiations with the party standard-bearer over the platform. After Jackson unenthusiastically endorsed Clinton in his convention speech, R. Drummond Ayres noted in the *New York Times*, "The political reality is that Jesse Jackson, for now, is not the commanding force he once was, and he is political pro enough to know it."[33]

In his acceptance speech, Clinton joked about the interminable 1988 address, declaring, "Well I ran for president this year for one reason and one reason only. I wanted to come back to this convention and finish that speech I started four years ago." Discussing the economic struggles of Americans during the recession, the governor discounted Bush's glass-half-full explanations: "The incumbent president says unemployment always goes up a little before a recovery begins. But unemployment only has to go up by one person before a real recovery can begin." Clinton then turned a key phrase from Bush's acceptance speech from four years earlier around on him, concluding, "And Mr. President, you are that man."[34]

Applying another lesson of 1988, Clinton did not take any break after a successful convention that saw him get a considerable bounce, in part due to the fact that third-party candidate Ross Perot dropped out of the race at the same time. "Four years ago, Michael Dukakis left the Democratic convention with a 17-point lead in the polls. He went home to Massachusetts, where for the better part of a month he frittered away his advantage," wrote Steve Daley in the *Chicago Tribune*. Daley added, "There will be no days of rest for Arkansas Gov. Bill Clinton and his running mate."[35] Instead Clinton and Gore went on the offensive, taking a bus tour through the swing states to capitalize on their momentum.[36]

Taking a page out of Bush's playbook, Clinton went to his opponent's home state and appeared with police officers in Houston. He pushed back on the Horton issue, though not explicitly, declaring, "Four years ago this crime issue was used to divide America. I want to use it to unite America."

A longtime supporter of the death penalty who had returned to Arkansas to preside over an execution during the primaries, Clinton was determined not to be outflanked on the issue.[37]

As Bush headed into the Republican Convention, the religious right extended the power it had gained through the Robertson campaign in 1988 to cement even greater control of the party message and platform. "We are here to celebrate a victory," exclaimed a euphoric Ralph Reed. "Within the past hour, the Republican Party passed a pro-life, pro-family platform! The feminists threw everything they had at us! We won and they lost!" "Family values" would be the central message of the convention, and many in the fading moderate wing were not given a role, causing some to stay home. "This image of a far-right party, this is not the party I belong to," reflected retiring senator Warren Rudman (R) of New Hampshire, who didn't make the trip in part due to his displeasure with the platform.[38]

Buchanan launched the culturally conservative assault in Houston with his famous "culture war" speech on the opening night. "There is a religious war going on in this country. It is a cultural war, as critical to the kind of nation we shall be as was the Cold War itself, for this war is for the soul of America," he declared, laying down the stakes. "And in that struggle for the soul of America, Clinton & Clinton are on the other side, and George Bush is on our side."[39] Alleging that the Republican Party had been taken over by the religious right, Clinton responded as follows: "You look at who has been featured. It's the Pat Robertson, Pat Buchanan, Jerry Falwell, Phyllis Schlafly wing of the party. They control it now. They've got George Bush right where they want him."

As the Democrats would do in response to many of the negative attacks in 1992, Clinton invoked Horton as a defense against some of the GOP critiques of feminists and others on the cultural left. "What they're [Republicans are] trying to do is kind of make it a Willie Horton thing against all independent working women, trying to run against them in a way that I think is really lamentable," the Arkansas governor said. One *New York Times* headline even read, "In 1992, Willie Horton Is Democrats' Secret Weapon."[40]

As the general election campaign got underway, Clinton presented a very different image than Dukakis had four years earlier, but many of the men's policies were similar. "Thirty-nine of the 40 specific proposals in his [Clinton's] national economic strategy," wrote Christopher Georges of *Washington Monthly*, "were virtually identical to policies proposed in 1988 by Michael S. Dukakis." In September, Clinton would propose a significant welfare reform proposal—another one of the Massachusetts governor's central planks—though the Arkansas governor's more straightforward call to put an "end to welfare as we know it" might have had more appeal to Reagan Democrats.[41] Once in office, Robert Reich and Larry Summers, policy advisers to the Dukakis campaign, would serve in Clinton's cabinet as key architects of his economic policy.

Just as it had for Quayle, Vietnam-era service proved a vexing issue for Clinton. Though it hadn't tripped up his journey to the nomination, the Bush campaign kept raising the subject during the fall. "Among some voters, the draft could set off the same kind of resonant contrast that the Pledge of Allegiance issue did four years ago," wrote Toner in September, "in which the Republicans made claim to the symbols and traditions of nationhood." Bush's people had to convince the skeptical incumbent to use the nontraditional media to get his message out. "By the time we were running in '92 you had cable and the sitting president of the United States had to go on Larry King [*Larry King Live* on CNN]," recalled Black, exclaiming, "Hell, you should have seen us persuade him of that!"[42]

On King's program, the president questioned why Clinton had traveled to the Soviet Union as a student in 1969. "I don't want to tell you what I really think, because I don't have the facts. But to go to Moscow one year after Russia crushed Czechoslovakia, not remember what you saw?" Bush told King, "I really think the answer is, level with the American people."[43] Unlike Dukakis, Clinton responded strongly to these accusations, invoking his opponent's family history in their first debate: "But when Joe McCarthy went around this country attacking people's patriotism he was wrong. He was wrong. And a senator from Connecticut stood up to him named Prescott Bush. Your father was right to stand up to Joe McCarthy, you were wrong to attack my patriotism."[44]

And that proved to be a key difference between the Dukakis and Clinton campaigns. The latter set up a "War Room" to respond to the charges coming from the Bush camp, whereas the former fought back too late. Clinton's deputy campaign manager George Stephanopoulos, who had also worked for Dukakis, noted that the lesson of the 1988 election was "first of all, respond."[45] Dukakis understood this, saying, "When Bill Clinton ran in '92, people forget this, the Bush campaign came at him every bit as hard if not harder then they came at me. So what was the difference? He created this small unit in his campaign, a lot them had worked for me. And their exclusive job was to anticipate and respond to attacks."[46]

On the other side, Louis Harris called the Bush reelection effort the most incompetent campaign he'd seen, and some on the GOP side believed that without the late Atwater and the departed Ailes, the Bush people were simply not as tough the second time around.[47] "All were good people, but none had the political focus and aggressiveness we had in the 1988 campaign," wrote Sununu, who had resigned as White House chief of staff after a scandal. "The hard-edged old trio—Lee Atwater, Roger Ailes and I—were no longer part of the campaign effort. Lee had passed away, Roger was on his way to changing the face of cable news, and I had stepped aside hoping the lightning would follow me."[48]

Indeed, Ailes had returned to television, producing a program for Limbaugh, who made his first major impact in a presidential election in 1992, when he was courted by Bush because of his program's conservative audience.[49] Ailes would go on to work at CNBC and then to create Fox News in 1996. He employed many of the same slash-and-burn tactics he had used so effectively in 1988 to build Fox into a powerhouse that would shape the conservative movement for the next two decades.

Regardless of the absence of Ailes and Atwater, it also appeared that some of the post-1968 wedge issues such as crime and national defense might not have the same punch they once did. The end of the Cold War deprived the GOP of what had been its biggest issue advantage since the Vietnam War, as foreign policy was no longer as salient to voters, despite Bush's efforts to tout his handling of the fall of communism and the Gulf War. Clinton also expressed more openness to the use of military force abroad than previous Democrats had.

The Arkansas governor also co-opted the crime issue, which had so devastated Dukakis, with his support for the death penalty and the police. Mocking his tough-on-crime narrative as part of the show's reinvigorated political satire, *SNL*'s Bernard Shaw, played by Tim Meadows, poses the same question to Clinton that the real-life Shaw did to the 1988 Democratic presidential nominee, asking, "If Kitty Dukakis were raped and murdered, would you favor the death penalty for her assailant?" After the moderator reproaches Shaw/Meadows and tells Clinton, played by Phil Hartman, that he doesn't have to answer the question, Clinton/Hartman says that he is happy to reply, declaring, "Obviously, none of us wants to see Kitty Dukakis raped and murdered. But if she had to be murdered I would hope it would be in Arkansas. Because no state is tougher on crime."[50]

In the end, though, it was in the inimitable words of Clinton campaign manager James Carville—"the economy, stupid"—that carried Clinton to victory over Bush. With the recession technically over but unemployment still high, "economic worries easily overcame the social concerns that had dominated most of the last six Presidential elections, all but one of them won by the Republicans," wrote Apple in his postelection analysis, "Concern about jobs—and about the closely allied subjects of health care and education—trumped racial tensions, fears about crime and even fervent appeals to patriotism."[51]

In winning, Clinton built on the Electoral College path Dukakis had begun to lay out four years earlier to pick the GOP's Electoral College "lock." While he and his fellow southerner Gore made important inroads below the Mason-Dixon Line, they also carried key midwestern swing states like Illinois and Pennsylvania that Dukakis had come so close to winning in his late surge in 1988. The pair consolidated the Massachusetts governor's gains on the West Coast as well, taking Washington and Oregon while adding California to the Democratic column. Thus did the "Blue Wall" that had started to come into view four years earlier consolidate into the map that would allow Democrats to control the White House for most of the next three decades.

While the legacy of the 1988 race could be felt most strongly in the 1992 election, it would continue to echo in American politics for years to come, especially with regard to Willie Horton. Fear of being seen as "soft on crime" pushed many Democratic politicians to back "three strikes and you're out laws" like Clinton's 1994 crime bill, thereby contributing to the rise of mass incarceration, which especially affected minority communities. "The worst impact of the '88 campaign was that it raised a generation of politicians who were afraid to be honest about crime," Estrich analyzed. "And because they were afraid to be honest about crime," she continued, "they voted for bills that they knew made no sense that would result in overincarceration of nonviolent criminals at the expense of violent criminals. The legacy of Willie Horton is prison construction, overincarceration, turning crime from a policy issue to a values issue."[52]

In 1993, Gephardt continued to battle globalization, taking on Clinton in an unsuccessful drive to prevent the passage of the North American Free Trade Agreement (NAFTA). He was joined in the fight by a strange-bedfellows alliance that included Buchanan and Perot, who both effectively used a similar protectionist, antiestablishment message in their 1992 and 1996 presidential campaigns to appeal to blue-collar workers. Many other candidates employed the same approach well into the twenty-first century, as both parties were often divided between grassroots opposition to trade agreements and establishment support for such accords. For example, when Congress voted to back China's entry into the World Trade Organization (WTO) in 2000, one-quarter of Republicans and two-thirds of Democrats opposed the measure, while it was strongly backed by President Clinton and the presumptive GOP nominee, Texas governor George W. Bush.[53]

In 1996, Clinton ran successfully for reelection—defeating a ticket with two Republican contestants from 1988, Dole and Kemp—by pledging to balance the budget while at the same time preserving "Medicare, Medicaid, education, and the environment." The latter two were important pillars of Bush's 1988 campaign, showing that his effort to soften the edges of Reaganism was indeed a precursor to a more moderate politics, at least at the presidential level, in the 1990s. Congress, of course, did move to the right after the Republican takeover of the House and Senate in 1994.

Taking the soft-money project pioneered by Farmer and the Dukakis campaign to a new level, the Clinton campaign broke fundraising records in 1996, raising huge sums of unlimited contributions through the DNC, leading to congressional investigations and major critiques of the campaign-finance system. Eventually, the McCain-Feingold bill of 2002 banned these unlimited donations to the political parties, although new kinds of loopholes emerged. Thus 1988 began a process by which the post-Watergate public financing system totally broke down, continuing with the Clinton scandals, followed by George W. Bush forgoing public funds for the GOP primary in 2000, and Barack Obama doing the same in the general election in 2008. By 2016, virtually no candidates were applying for such support.[54]

In addition to spurring a harsher criminal-justice policy, the stigma surrounding the Horton ad only grew in the following years, as it was often cited when some perceived a candidate appealing to racial or religious bias. When supporters of George W. Bush spread vicious rumors about Senator John McCain of Arizona during the South Carolina primary in 2000, Anthony Lewis compared the younger Bush to his father, writing in a column headlined "Willie Horton Redux," "Of course Governor Bush cannot be blamed for the tactics of 1988. But the parallel cannot be missed. Here again an honorable man's campaign stooped to conquer—and surrogates did the dirty work." That same year, Bill Bradley tried to use the issue against Gore in the Democratic primary, blaming him for inflaming racial tensions by introducing Horton in the 1988 primaries—though Gore only raised the furlough program and not Horton himself.[55]

Though Jackson's progressive multiracial coalition could only go so far because the center of the party held in 1988 and into the 1990s, one supporter from that campaign picked up the mantle. Nearly three decades later, Bernie Sanders, like Jackson, employed a class-based message to advocate national health insurance and a series of other major economic reforms in hopes of uniting working-class voters of all backgrounds. Citing Roosevelt's 1936 and Jackson's 1988 campaigns as his inspirations, Sanders defied expectations to finish second in the Democratic primaries in both 2016 and 2020. Steve Cobble, who served as a national delegate coordinator for Jackson in 1988, declared, "He took from what Jackson did in '87 and '88. That you could put issues that had been ignored directly into the center of the public process by running for president and stating your message correctly." Nina Turner, one of Sanders's campaign cochairs in 2020 and among his most prominent African American surrogates, observed, "It really is the same template."[56]

As late as 2018, in the final days of a toughly fought midterm campaign, Republicans produced an ad showing a video of a convicted cop killer who was Hispanic and had entered the country illegally. The accompanying text begins, "Democrats Let Him into Our Country," and ends with "Who Else Would They Let In?"[57] President Trump embraced the ad, posting it on his Twitter feed, and comparisons to the Horton ad immediately began, with Aaron Blake of the *Washington Post* declaring that the 1988 commercial "remains the most infamous political ad in modern American history."[58] Floyd Brown, who, unlike Atwater, never disowned the use of Horton, praised the new ad, saying it would help Republicans in the midterms.[59] The Dukakis camp weighed in as well, with Estrich asserting, "There's a lesson from the Horton ad episode that Democrats should take to heart. Don't let him get away with it." She added, "Call it what it is. The president's new ad is racism."[60]

As violent crime fell from the mid-1990s onward, people on both sides of the aisle reconsidered the more draconian policies passed in part because of Horton, particularly their impact on nonviolent offenders caught up in the war on drugs. Despite bipartisan support for reforming the system, a major obstacle still remained. "The most vivid reason is the lingering specter of Willie Horton," wrote Carl Hulse in the *New York Times* in 2016, as Senate minority whip Dick Durbin (D) of Illinois remarked that the furloughed felon "is still part of the legend and lore of American politics."[61] Overcoming the doubts of Senate majority leader Mitch McConnell (R) of Kentucky, who was particularly concerned about the Horton issue, Congress did pass such a bill in 2018, a rare moment of across-the-aisle cooperation in a polarized time.[62]

On November 30, 2018, George H. W. Bush died at the age of ninety-four. At the time, he was the most popular living president, and his passing brought encomiums from across the political spectrum. He was recalled as a true gentleman and a sharp contrast with the current occupant of the office, Donald Trump—who had first achieved political prominence in the 1988 cycle.[63] As he lay in state in the Capitol, his former primary rival Dole—then age ninety-five—had himself lifted out of his wheelchair to salute his political competitor and fellow member of the "Greatest Generation." Dukakis praised his former opponent's foreign policy: "When it came to the international side of things, he was a very wise and thoughtful man." The governor, who had gone on to teach at Northeastern University and UCLA in the years since leaving the statehouse, added, "Obviously we disagreed pretty strongly on domestic policy and I wasn't thrilled with the kind of campaign he ran, but I think his great contribution was negotiating the end of the Cold War with [Soviet leader] Mikhail Gorbachev."[64]

And the discussion of the campaign would be one of the few discordant notes during the week the nation celebrated the life of the forty-first president. "The tributes to former President George Bush in recent days have focused on his essential decency and civility and his embrace of others, including even his onetime opponents," wrote Peter Baker in the *New York Times*. "But the 'last gentleman,' as he has been called, was not always so gentle," Baker continued, referring to 1988.[65] Headlines concerning the presidential race included "How George H. W. Bush Exploited Racism to Win the Oval Office" and "How the Willie Horton Ad Factors Into George H. W. Bush's Legacy."[66]

Indeed, this is the frame through which the election has been viewed in the three decades plus since its conclusion. But it was about so much more. As we've seen, it provided the roots for so many of the trends that have shaped our politics since then, and we continue to feel its echoes today.

Notes

INTRODUCTION

1. "Election Night 1988 NBC News Coverage," YouTube Video, November 8, 1988, 3:45:17, www.youtube.com/watch?v=j6DuWpHmN-c&t=6222s; "The 1988 Elections; Bush Victory Talk: 'I Mean to Be a President of All the People,'" *New York Times* (hereafter *NYT*), November 9, 1988.

2. Quoted in Runkel, *Campaign for President*, 197.

3. Key, "Theory of Critical Elections"; Schattschneider, *Semisovereign People*; Sundquist, *Dynamics of the Party System*; Burnham, *Critical Elections and the Mainsprings*.

4. Germond and Witcover, *Whose Broad Stripes and Bright Stars?*; Black and Oliphant, *All by Myself*; Blumenthal, *Pledging Allegiance*; Simon, *Road Show*; Cramer, *What It Takes*.

5. Germond and Witcover, *Whose Broad Stripes and Bright Stars?*, 413.

6. Foner, *Give Me Liberty!*, 841.

7. Dan Balz, "George H. W. Bush Was the Accidental Catalyst That Built the New Republican Party," *Washington Post* (hereafter *WP*), December 2, 2018.

8. Pitney, *After Reagan*. In 2019, the University Press of Kansas published *After Reagan* by John Pitney Jr., a political scientist at Claremont McKenna College. Pitney's work is the first academic book on the election. My manuscript was basically completed prior to my awareness of his study, and any similarities are purely coincidental. Pitney does view the election as an important turning point in American politics, seeing some of the demographic trends and partisan shifts that were afoot in 1988, as well as a few of the new features of American politics, like the impact of video technology, major sex scandals, and changes in campaign finance. However, he doesn't capture the full extent of the new elements that emerged in 1988. I lay them out below and then throughout the book. Rabbe, *Above the Fray*; Bartlett, *Race for the White House*, "Bush vs. Dukakis"; *16 for '16: The Contenders*, episode 3, "The Technocrats."

9. *16 for '16: The Contenders*, episode 3, "The Technocrats."

10. Among others, see Fraser and Gerstle, *Rise and Fall of the New Deal Order*; Edsall and Edsall, *Chain Reaction*; Perlstein, *Before the Storm*; Perlstein, *Nixonland*; Perlstein, *Invisible Bridge*; and Perlstein, *Reaganland*.

11. Among others, Perlstein, *Nixonland*, and Isserman and Kazin, *America Divided*.

12. George Wallace, "Speech at Madison Square Garden," Teaching American History, October 24, 1968, https://teachingamericanhistory.org/document/speech-at-madison-square-garden/.

13. "Transcript of Acceptance Speeches by Nixon and Agnew," *NYT*, August 9, 1968.

14. Edsall and Edsall, *Chain Reaction*; Carter, *Politics of Rage*; and Rieder, *Canarsie*, among others, stress the importance of race-based appeals to the rise of the GOP after the 1960s. Lassiter, *Silent Majority*, and Kruse, *White Flight*, emphasize a color-blind suburban-rights ideology that employed more race-neutral language. Crespino, *In Search of Another Country*, focuses on the cultural issues that emerged in the 1970s and 1980s and energized the religious right as a primary reason for voters switching to the GOP. More recently, Rolph, *Resisting Equality*, has reemphasized the importance of race while Maxwell and Shields, *Long Southern Strategy*, link race-based and culturally based appeals together to explain the rise and continued strength of the Republican Party and conservatism. Meanwhile, Miller, *Nut Country*, traces the roots of a race-based "Southern Strategy" to Dallas in the 1950s, and McGirr, *Suburban Warriors*, looks at the emergence of

suburban conservatism in the West in the 1960s. Finally, Phillips-Fein, *Invisible Hands*, and Waterhouse, *Lobbying America* examine the importance of conservative think tanks and business lobbies to the emergence of the Right.

15. E. J. Dionne Jr., "Candidates Wage Battle to Dawn of Election Day," *NYT*, November 8, 1988.

CHAPTER 1

1. "How Groups Voted in 1984."
2. Walter Shapiro, "America: Reagan Country," *Newsweek*, Election Extra, November 1984 / December 1984.
3. "Presidential Job Approval."
4. "Labor Force Statistics."
5. Hedrick Smith, "Economy the Key Issue," *New York Times* (hereafter *NYT*), November 7, 1984.
6. For more on Mondale's career and 1984 campaign, see Gillon, *Democrats' Dilemma*.
7. Tom Morganthau, "Help Wanted," *Newsweek*, Election Extra, November 1984 / December 1984.
8. "Representative Geraldine Ferraro 1984 Acceptance Speech," C-SPAN Video, July 18, 1984, www.c-span.org/video/?3444-1/representative-geraldine-ferraro-1984-acceptance-speech.
9. "Mario Cuomo 1984 Democratic National Convention Speech," C-SPAN Video, July 16, 1984, www.c-span.org/video/?323534-1/mario-cuomo-1984-democratic-national-convention-keynote-speech.
10. "Transcript of Mondale Address Accepting Party Nomination," *NYT*, July 20, 1984.
11. "Transcript of Mondale Address Accepting Party Nomination."
12. Germond and Witcover, *Wake Us When It's Over*, 409, 413.
13. Germond and Witcover, *Wake Us When It's Over*, 416–18.
14. "1984 Reagan vs. Mondale," The Living Room Candidate, accessed July 25, 2022, http://www.livingroomcandidate.org/commercials/1984.
15. "1984 Reagan vs. Mondale."
16. "1984 Reagan vs. Mondale."
17. "1984 Reagan vs. Mondale."
18. "October 21, 1984 Debate Transcript."
19. Lehrer, *Tension City*, 28.
20. Tom Morganthau with Howard Fineman and Nancy Cooper, "Republican America?," *Newsweek*, November 5, 1984.
21. Evan Thomas, "Election '84: Every Region, Every Age Group, Almost Every Voting Bloc," *Time*, November 19, 1984.
22. Kurt Andersen, "Election '84: Way Down but Not Quite Out, the Democrats Regroup," *Time*, November 19, 1984.
23. Shapiro, "America: Reagan Country."
24. Andersen, "Election '84."
25. Greenberg, *Middle Class Dreams*, 32–42.
26. Andersen, "Election '84."
27. Dudley Clendinen, "The Medium and Mondale," *NYT*, November 9, 1984.
28. Tom Wicker, "In the Nation; The New Reality," *NYT*, November 9, 1984.
29. Andersen, "Election '84."
30. Charles Peters, "A Neo-Liberal's Manifesto," *Washington Post* (hereafter *WP*), September 5, 1982.
31. For more, see Geismer, "Atari Democrats."

32. David Broder, "Big Majority of Big Spenders," *WP*, November 3, 1974. For more on the class of 1974, see Lawrence, *Class of '74*, and Perlstein, *Invisible Bridge*, 317–39.

33. John Herbers, "Party Looks Inward for Ways to Regain Majority," *NYT*, November 8, 1984.

34. Jonathan Alter with Vern E. Smith, Gloria Borger, Eleanor Clift, and Thomas M. DeFrank, "Can George Do It?," *Newsweek*, Election Extra, November 1984 / December 1984.

35. Alter with Vern E. Smith, Gloria Borger, Eleanor Clift, and Thomas M. DeFrank, "Can George Do It?"

36. E. J. Dionne Jr., "Bush vs. Dole: Behind the Turnaround," *NYT*, March 17, 1988; Brady, *Bad Boy*, 39.

37. Thomas B. Edsall, "GOP Battler Lee Atwater Dies at 40," *WP*, March 30, 1991; Brady, *Bad Boy*. See also Forbes, *Boogie Man*.

38. For overviews of Reagan's life and presidency, see Cannon, *President Reagan*; Reeves, *President Reagan*; Wilentz, *Age of Reagan*; and Brands, *Reagan: The Life*.

39. Phil Gailey, "Dissidents Defy Top Democrats; Council Formed," *NYT*, March 1, 1985.

40. Gailey, "Dissidents Defy Top Democrats."

41. Phil Gailey, "Democratic Group Seeks Mainstream," *NYT*, May 19, 1985.

42. Norrander, *Super Tuesday*, 25; James R. Dickenson, "South Moving to '88 'Super Tuesday,'" *WP*, December 24, 1985.

43. James E. Dickenson, "Southern Democrats See 'Super Tuesday' in '88," *WP*, February 8, 1986.

44. From, *New Democrats and the Return to Power*, 89. "The DLC didn't create Super Tuesday, but because most of the Super Tuesday advocates were active in the DLC," wrote From, the organization's founder, "most of the press thought it was our idea."

45. John Margolis, "A Super-Dumb Idea from the South," *Chicago Tribune*, March 3, 1986; R. W. Apple, "Delivering the South," *NYT*, November 30, 1986.

46. Dickenson, "South Moving to '88 'Super Tuesday'"; Dickenson, "Southern Democrats See 'Super Tuesday' in '88."

47. Norrander, *Super Tuesday*, 28.

48. Martin Tolchin, "Baker and Conservatives Viewed as New Leaders," *NYT*, November 6, 1980.

49. E. J. Dionne Jr., "Parties Heighten Efforts to Bring Voters to Polls," *NYT*, November 2, 1986.

50. Steven V. Roberts, "The Elections: Measuring the President's Coattails; Democratic Senate May Impede Reagan," *NYT*, November 5, 1986.

51. "Presidential Job Approval."

52. Jacob Lamar, "The Teflon President's Teflon Coattails," *Time*, November 17, 1986. Reagan travel number from E. J. Dionne Jr., "Democrats Rejoice at 55–45 Senate Margin But Still Seek Agenda to Counter Reagan; Big Political Shift," *NYT*, November 6, 1986.

53. "Reagan Assails Democrats in Speech," *NYT*, November 3, 1986.

54. Dionne, "Democrats Rejoice at 55–45 Senate Margin."

55. Dionne, "Democrats Rejoice at 55–45 Senate Margin."

56. Bernard Weinraub, "The Elections: Fate of the Reagan Agenda; Reagan Vows to Finish His 'Revolution,'" *NYT*, November 6, 1986.

57. E. J. Dionne Jr., "Elections; Democrats Gain Control of Senate, Drawing Votes of Reagan's Backers; Cuomo and D'Amato Are Easy Victors; What Awaits Congress; Broad G.O.P. Losses," *NYT*, November 5, 1986.

58. Lamar, "Teflon President's Teflon Coattails."

59. Dionne, "Democrats Rejoice at 55–45 Senate Margin."

60. Weinraub, "Elections: Fate of the Reagan Agenda."
61. Lamar, "Teflon President's Teflon Coattails."
62. Dionne, "Elections; Democrats Gain Control of Senate."
63. Lamar, "Teflon President's Teflon Coattails."
64. "Majority Now Says There Is a 'Great Deal' of Difference."
65. Englehardt, "Trumped by Race."
66. "Abortion Trends by Party Identification," Gallup.com, accessed July 27, 2022, https://news.gallup.com/poll/246278/abortion-trends-party.aspx.
67. "A new system of ideologically defined parties had not yet emerged by the 1980s." Rosenfeld, *Polarizers*, 267.
68. David S. Broder, "Democrats Can't Afford to Be Smug," *WP*, November 12, 1986; William Schneider, "Insider's View of the Election," *Atlantic*, July 1988.
69. Phil Gailey, "The Elections: Dealing with the Issues: Hopefuls in '88 Race See New Political Contours," *NYT*, November 6, 1986.
70. "Morning Line: How 1986 Might Affect 1988," *Time*, November 17, 1986.
71. Gailey, "Elections: Dealing with the Issues." Dukakis is not listed in the article, and it's not clear whether he was one of the candidates polling at 2 percent.
72. "Morning Line: How 1986 Might Affect 1988."
73. Gailey, "Elections: Dealing with the Issues."
74. "EXECUTIVE SUMMARY: The Leadership Gap," November 24, 1986, Box 7, "The Leadership Gap—November 25, 1986 [Analysis of George Bush for 1988 campaign]," Robert Teeter Collection; emphasis in original.
75. Bernard Weinraub, "President Defends Iranian Contacts; Arms Not 'Ransom,'" *NYT*, November 14, 1986.
76. Bernard Weinraub, "President Orders Sales of Weapons to Iran Stopped," *NYT*, November 20, 1986.
77. Brands, *Reagan: The Life*, 633.
78. Joel Brinkley, "Contra Supplies: Mystery Unravels," *NYT*, November 20, 1986.
79. Bernard Weinraub, "Reagan Names 3 to Examine National Security Council; Other Iran Inquiries Widen," *NYT*, November 27, 1986.
80. For an overall look at the Iran-Contra scandal, see Draper, *A Very Thin Line*.
81. Fuller interview.
82. "Presidential Job Approval."
83. Howard Fineman, "Politics: Running Away from Reagan," *Newsweek*, December 15, 1986.
84. Dukakis interview.
85. David Broder and Maralene Schwartz, "Dukakis Strategy Plays to Strengths," *WP*, April 24, 1988.
86. Dukakis interview.
87. Dionne, "Bush vs. Dole: Behind the Turnaround."
88. Bernard Weinraub, "Dole Tests Iowa Political Waters, Preparing '88 State Organization," *NYT*, January 22, 1987.
89. E. J. Dionne Jr., "Poll Gives Hart and Bush Clear Leads for Nominations," *NYT*, January 25, 1987.
90. E. J. Dionne Jr., "Decision Said to Reshape Contest in '88," *NYT*, February 20, 1987; E. J. Dionne Jr., "New Democratic Breed Fills Cuomo Void," *NYT*, February 21, 1987.
91. Dionne, "New Democratic Breed Fills Cuomo Void."
92. Dionne, "Poll Gives Hart and Bush Clear Leads."
93. Schlesinger, *Cycles of American History*.
94. Schlesinger, *Cycles of American History*, 47.

95. Fuller interview.
96. *Tower Commission Report*, xviii.
97. Steven V. Roberts, "The White House Crisis: The Tower Report Inquiry Finds Reagan and Chief Advisers Responsible for 'Chaos' in Iran Arms Deals; Reagan Also Blamed," *NYT*, February 27, 1987.
98. E. J. Dionne Jr., "The White House Crisis: The Politics; Report Seen as Strengthening Democrats for '88 Race," *NYT*, February 27, 1987.
99. Dionne, "White House Crisis: The Politics."
100. E. J. Dionne Jr., "The White House Crisis; Bush Says Iran Deals 'Failed the American People,'" *NYT*, February 28, 1987.
101. For a full examination of Bush's role in the Iran-Contra affair, see Meacham, *Destiny and Power*, 299–306.
102. Fuller interview.
103. E. J. Dionne Jr., "Poll Shows Reagan Approval Rating at 4-Year Low," *NYT*, March 3, 1987.
104. "The Reagan White House: Transcript of Reagan's Speech: 'I Take Full Responsibility for My Actions,'" *NYT*, March 5, 1987.
105. E. J. Dionne, Jr. "The Reagan White House Republicans Praise Reagan Speech; Democrats Wary About the Future," *NYT*, March 5, 1987.
106. E. J. Dionne Jr., "Democrats Urged Not to Pin Hopes on Iran Arms Cases," *NYT*, March 8, 1987.
107. Dionne, "Democrats Urged Not to Pin Hopes on Iran Arms Cases."
108. "Looking for Mr. Right," *Newsweek*, November 21, 1988, 36.

CHAPTER 2

1. Fox Butterfield, "Dukakis," *New York Times* (hereafter *NYT*), May 8, 1988.
2. Dukakis interview.
3. Butterfield, "Dukakis"; James R. Dorsey, UPI, November 11, 1974.
4. Geismer, *Don't Blame Us*, 254–55.
5. Judis and Teixeira, *Emerging Democratic Majority*, 38.
6. Alan Ehrenhalt, "Last Hurrahs for the New Deal," *Washington Monthly*, January 1976, 57.
7. Ehrenhalt, "Last Hurrahs for the New Deal," 58.
8. Shrum, *No Excuses*, 60.
9. Dukakis interview.
10. Dukakis interview.
11. Thomas Edsall, "A Troubled First Term: Reformer's Refusal to Bargain Led to Exile," *WP*, July 10, 1988.
12. Dukakis interview; Edsall, "Troubled First Term."
13. Edsall, "Troubled First Term."
14. Frank, *Frank*, 74.
15. For more on Dukakis's ideology and governorship, see Geismer, *Don't Blame Us*, 251–79.
16. Joe Klein, "Ready for the Duke," *New York Magazine*, August 17, 1987, 28.
17. Don Holt with Phyllis Malamud, "The Duke's Downfall," *Newsweek*, October 2, 1978; Dukakis interview.
18. "Cleared for Takeoff," *Newsweek*, November 21, 1988, 43.
19. "Long Bio," Dan Payne Communications, 10-13-1982, OID 35527, Julian P. Kanter Commercial Archive.
20. "Cleared for Takeoff," 43; Michael Reese with Phyllis Malamud and James Doyle, "Getting a Second Chance," *Newsweek*, September 27, 1982.

21. Dudley Clendinen, "Dukakis Winner in Primary for Massachusetts Governor," *NYT*, September 15, 1982.

22. Dukakis interview.

23. The office manager of the Massachusetts Community Development Finance Corporation Association remarked, "It's a kind of '80s' liberalism, not an antibusiness '60s' liberalism." Thomas Edsall, "Engineering a Comeback; New Persona, Policies Buoy Second Term," *Washington Post* (hereafter *WP*), July 11, 1988.

24. See Osborne, *Laboratories of Democracy*, 175–210.

25. Dukakis interview.

26. E. J. Dionne Jr., "Agreeing to Agree; Dukakis Leads a Party Fed Up with Discord," *NYT*, June 12, 1988. "Accepting the complaints of their working-class supporters that they did not want to pay for 'free lunches for the poor,'" wrote Dionne, "the new Democrats approach welfare through job training, as in Mr. Dukakis's own program in Massachusetts."

27. "Massachusetts Election Statistics." Unemployment ranged from 3.9 percent to 4.1 percent during 1986. "Labor Force and Unemployment Data."

28. "How the Governors See It: A Newsweek Poll," *Newsweek*, March 24, 1986, 32.

29. Dukakis interview.

30. "Cleared for Takeoff," 44.

31. Dukakis interview.

32. Corrigan interview.

33. "Cleared for Takeoff," 43.

34. "Cleared for Takeoff," 44.

35. E. J. Dionne Jr., "Dukakis Says He Will Run for President," *NYT*, March 17, 1987; "Statement of Governor Michael S. Dukakis on the Occasion of the Announcement of His Candidacy for President of the United States of America, Boston Common—April 1987," Box 24, Folder 1269, Michael S. Dukakis Presidential Campaign Records; "Dukakis Announcement," C-SPAN Video, April 29, 1987, www.c-span.org/video/?3308-1/dukakis-announcement.

36. Matthew L. Wald, "Dukakis Opens Presidential Quest Stressing His Record as Governor," *NYT*, April 30, 1987.

37. "The MacNeil/Lehrer NewsHour, 4/29/87 (Dukakis Interview)," Box 50, MacNeil/Lehrer Show (VHS), 4/29/1987, Michael S. Dukakis Presidential Campaign Records.

38. Dukakis interview.

39. "MacNeil/Lehrer NewsHour."

40. *NBC Nightly News*, Box 50, Massachusetts Economy Story, Tom Brokaw, NBC (VHS), 1987, Michael S. Dukakis Presidential Campaign Records.

41. Dionne, "Dukakis Says He Will Run for President."

42. Dionne, "Dukakis Says He Will Run for President."

43. Wald, "Dukakis Opens Presidential Quest."

44. Dukakis interview.

45. Walter Shapiro, "The Loneliest Long-Distance Runner," *Time*, April 27, 1987.

46. Cohen et al., *Party Decides*, 203–4, 5, 10–11; Paul Taylor, "Politicians Refuse Rides on Hart's Bandwagon," *WP*, March 13, 1987.

47. Shapiro, "The Loneliest Long-Distance Runner."

48. Runkel, *Campaign for President*, 18.

49. "Public Trust in Government, 1958–2021."

50. Pakula, *All the President's Men*.

51. "CBS Reports: Teddy (11-4-1979)," YouTube Video, November 4, 1979, 46:13, www.youtube.com/watch?v=sfza38euZSY.

52. Bai, *All the Truth Is Out*, is the most comprehensive look at the Hart scandal.
53. E. J. Dionne Jr., "Courting Danger: The Fall of Gary Hart," *NYT*, May 9, 1987.
54. Howard Fineman, "Gary Hart: A Candidate in Search of Himself," *Newsweek*, April 13, 1987; Bai, *All the Truth Is Out*, 84.
55. Robin Toner, "Hart, Stressing Ideals, Formally Enters the 1988 Race," *NYT*, April 14, 1987.
56. Jim McGee, Tom Fiedler, and James Savage, "The Gary Hart Story: How It Happened," *Miami Herald*, May 10, 1987.
57. Bai, *All the Truth Is Out*, 88–90.
58. McGee, Fiedler, and Savage, "Gary Hart Story."
59. E. J. Dionne Jr., "Gary Hart: The Elusive Front-Runner," *NYT*, May 3, 1987.
60. Bai, *All the Truth Is Out*, 107.
61. McGee, Fiedler, and Savage, "Gary Hart Story."
62. McGee, Fiedler, and Savage, "Gary Hart Story."
63. Jim McGee and Tom Fiedler, "Miami Woman Is Linked to Hart Candidate Denies Any Impropriety," *Miami Herald*, May 3, 1987.
64. E. J. Dionne Jr., "Paper and Hart in Dispute over Article," *NYT*, May 4, 1987.
65. McGee, Fiedler, and Savage, "Gary Hart Story."
66. Anthony Lewis, "Abroad at Home; Degrading the Press," *NYT*, May 5, 1987.
67. Tom Wicker, "In the Nation; Much to Regret," *NYT*, May 9, 1987.
68. "Gary Hart's Judgment," *NYT*, May 5, 1987.
69. Alex S. Jones, "Stakeout of Hart Seen as Fair Game," *NYT*, May 5, 1987.
70. Peter J. Boyer, "Networks Differ on Coverage of Hart," *NYT*, May 5, 1987.
71. McGee, Fiedler, and Savage, "Gary Hart Story."
72. Dionne, "Paper and Hart in Dispute over Article."
73. Jon Nordheimer, "Woman in the News; An Actress in Turmoil; Donna Earle Rice," *NYT*, May 5, 1987.
74. "Transcript of Hart's Remarks to Newspaper Publishing Group," *NYT*, May 6, 1987.
75. Dionne, "Courting Danger."
76. "Gary Hart Press Conference," C-SPAN Video, May 6, 1987, www.c-span.org/video/?3680-1/gary-hart-news-conference.
77. "Gary Hart Press Conference."
78. Dionne, "Courting Danger."
79. Dukakis interview.
80. Meacham, *Destiny and Power*, 309.
81. Paul Taylor, "Hart to Withdraw from Presidential Campaign: Post Query on Liaison 'Accelerated Inevitable,' Aide Says," *WP*, May 8, 1987.
82. "Transcript of Hart Statement Withdrawing His Candidacy," *NYT*, May 9, 1987.
83. "Gary Hart Press Conference."
84. "Transcript of Hart Statement Withdrawing His Candidacy."
85. "Transcript of Hart Statement Withdrawing His Candidacy."
86. "Gary Hart Presidential Withdrawal Announcement," Vanderbilt Television Archive, accessed March 6, 2019, https://tvnews.vanderbilt.edu/broadcasts/659901. (Records at Vanderbilt Television Archive in Nashville, Tennessee, suggest all three major networks broke in.)
87. "Hart Withdraws from Race, 5-8-87," Box 55, News, (14 Tapes) (VHS) (1986–1988), Michael S. Dukakis Presidential Campaign Records.
88. Alex Jones, "Hart Photo: Asking Price Set at $25,000," *NYT*, May 31, 1987.
89. R. W. Apple Jr., "Changing Morality: Press and Politics," *NYT*, May 6, 1987.

90. Bruce Schulman, "What 'The Front Runner' Gets Wrong about American Politics," *WP*, November 20, 2018, www.washingtonpost.com/outlook/2018/11/20/what-front-runner-gets-wrong-about-american-politics/.

91. Corrigan interview.

92. Glenn Garvin, "New Film Says the Miami Herald's Gary Hart Story Transformed Journalism. Did It Really?," *Miami Herald*, November 13, 2018. "When people say that the Hart episode was pivotal," commented David Greenberg of Rutgers University, "I don't really see that. It wasn't a turn, it was a link in a chain."

93. *16 for '16: The Contenders*, episode 4, "The Visionaries."

94. Estrich interview. According to "Teacher at Harvard Chosen by Dukakis to Head Campaign," *NYT*, October 9, 1987, Estrich became "deputy campaign manager" in March 1987.

95. Cohen, *Party Decides*, 205-7. The "Seven Dwarfs" moniker seems to have originated with a *Des Moines Register* editorial cartoon from May 12, 1987. Edward Walsh, "In Iowa, Political World Turns Topsy-Turvy," *WP*, May 16, 1987.

96. E. J. Dionne Jr., "Gephardt Aided Most in Iowa by Hart Absence, Poll Finds," *NYT*, May 19, 1987.

97. Mickey Kaus and Eleanor Clift, "The Many Faces of Dick Gephardt," *Newsweek*, March 7, 1988.

98. From, *New Democrats and the Return to Power*, 60.

99. Susan Rasky, "Washington Talk: Congress; Debate on Rebel Aid Has Ring of Campaign Trail," *NYT*, February 4, 1988; "Gephardt Announcement," C-SPAN Video, February 23, 1987, www.c-span.org/video/?3305-1/gephardt-announcement.

100. E. J. Dionne Jr., "Gephardt Opens Campaign for Democratic Nomination," *NYT*, February 24, 1987.

101. Stuart Auerbach, "Democratic Candidates Part on Free Trade," *WP*, May 16, 1983.

102. "Gephardt Announcement."

103. Shrum interview.

104. "Mr. Gephardt's Bleak Promises," *NYT*, May 17, 1987.

105. R. W. Apple, "Hotly Contested Primaries Likely in Both Parties in New Hampshire," *NYT*, May 10, 1987.

106. Howard Fineman, "The Democrats Prep for an '88 Free-for-All," *Newsweek*, May 18, 1987.

107. Maureen Dowd, "Dukakis Taking a Cool and Pragmatic Approach to Democratic Nomination," *NYT*, June 14, 1987.

108. E. J. Dionne Jr., "Key Hart Supporters Shift to Dukakis," *NYT*, June 3, 1987.

109. Richard Berke, "Democratic Cash Flows to Dukakis," *NYT*, June 21, 1987.

110. E. J. Dionne Jr., "Democrats Hold Presidential Debate," *NYT*, July 2, 1988.

111. "A Firing Line Special: The Democratic Presidential Candidate," YouTube Video, July 1, 1987, 1:58:22, www.youtube.com/watch?v=WjSXHY39P-0.

112. "MSD Campaign / Firing Line: All Candidates, 7.1.87," Box 55, Firing Line Democratic Candidates (VHS), 1987, Michael S. Dukakis Presidential Campaign Records.

113. Andrew Rosenthal, "85 Iowans See Debate and Pick Victor," *NYT*, July 3, 1987.

114. Walter Shapiro, "On the Firing Line, Mostly Blanks," *Time*, July 13, 1987.

115. Dionne, "Gephardt Opens Campaign for Democratic Nomination"; "Gephardt Intensifies His Criticism of Dukakis," *NYT*, July 5, 1987.

116. E. J. Dionne Jr., "Gephardt Trades Barbs with Kemp," *NYT*, July 21, 1987.

117. Joe Klein, "Ready for the Duke," *New York Magazine*, August 17, 1987, 30.

118. Corrigan interview.

119. James P. Pinkerton interview, Presidential Oral Histories.

120. Mickey Kaus with Mark Starr and Eleanor Clift, "Yes, We Have a Front Runner," *Newsweek*, July 20, 1987; R. W. Apple, "The Nation: In Democratic Field No One Is Nearing the Winner's Circle," *NYT*, August 23, 1987.

121. Cohen et al., *Party Decides*, 206.

122. Apple, "Nation: In Democratic Field."

123. David Maraniss, "On Brink of Running, Clinton Called It Off," *WP*, February 7, 1995. See also Maraniss, *First in His Class*, 438-43.

124. Warren Weaver Jr., "Democrats, in Iowa Debate, Make Reagan Their Target," *NYT*, August 24, 1987.

125. "1987 Democratic Presidential Debate at the Iowa State Fair," YouTube video, August 23, 1987, 1:49:53, www.youtube.com/watch?v=Yj6ecd_pVP4&t=1520s.

126. Kenneth Noble, "Hart Moves to Mend Faces with Labor Leaders," *NYT*, February 14, 1987.

127. E. J. Dionne Jr., "Biden Joins Campaign for the Presidency," *NYT*, June 10, 1987.

128. Corrigan interview; Robin Toner, "Biden, Once the Field's Hot Democrat, Is Being Overtaken by Cooler Rivals," *NYT*, August 31, 1987.

129. Stuart Taylor Jr., "Powell Leaves High Court: Took Key Role on Abortion and on Affirmative Action," *NYT*, June 27, 1987; Gerald M. Boyd, "Bork Picked for High Court; Reagan Cites His 'Restraint'; Confirmation Fight Looms," *NYT*, July 2, 1987.

130. "Little Big Men," *Newsweek*, November 21, 1988, 54.

131. Runkel, *Campaign for President*, 20.

132. Toner, "Biden, Once the Field's Hot Democrat."

133. Maureen Dowd, "Biden's Debate Finale: An Echo from Abroad," *NYT*, September 12, 1987.

134. Dowd, "Biden's Debate Finale."

135. David Yepsen, "Candidate Biden Rapped for Borrowing Anecdote," *Des Moines Register*, September 12, 1987.

136. Yepsen, "Candidate Biden Rapped for Borrowing Anecdote."

137. *NBC Nightly News*, September 12, 1987, Vanderbilt Television Archive, Vanderbilt University, Nashville, Tenn.

138. Biden, *Promises to Keep*, 184.

139. Runkel, *Campaign for President*, 70; Dowd, "Biden's Debate Finale."

140. Biden, *Promises to Keep*, 185-86; Andrew Rosenthal, "Washington Talk: Presidential Politics; From Biden's Case, Lessons on Damage Control," *NYT*, September 28, 1987.

141. Runkel, *Campaign for President*, 71.

142. Maureen Dowd, "Biden Is Facing Growing Debate on His Speeches," *NYT*, September 16, 1987.

143. E. J. Dionne Jr., "Biden Was Accused of Plagiarism in Law School," *NYT*, September 17, 1987.

144. Runkel, *Campaign for President*, 73.

145. Robin Toner, "Biden Assails New Report of Dishonesty," *NYT*, September 21, 1987.

146. Mickey Kaus with Eleanor Clift, Howard Fineman, and John McCormick, "Biden's Belly Flop," *Newsweek*, September 28, 1987.

147. Toner, "Biden Assails New Report of Dishonesty."

148. E. J. Dionne Jr., "Biden Withdraws Bid for President in Wake of Furor," *NYT*, September 24, 1987. Many of Biden's advisers from the 1988 campaign worked for his successful 2020 campaign. Alex Thompson and Tyler Pager, "They Failed Spectacularly in '88. Now, These Biden Aides Are Getting Sweet Redemption," Politico, January 19, 2021, www.politico.com/news/2021/01/19/joe-biden-1988-campaign-redemption-460332.

149. David S. Broder, "Biden Ends Presidential Campaign," *WP*, September 24, 1987.

150. Ponce de Leon, *That's the Way It Is*, 45.

151. Andrew Rosenthal, "Washington Talk; From Biden's Case, Lessons on Damage Control," *NYT*, September 28, 1987.

152. Paul Taylor, "Winnowing of Candidates Is Off to an Early Start," *WP*, September 28, 1987.

153. Jodi Wilogren, "The 2004 Campaign: Political Memo; Kerry's Words, and Bush's Use of Them, Offer Valuable Lesson in '04 Campaigning," *NYT*, May 8, 2004; David Stout, "Verbal Gaffe from a Senator, Then an Apology," *NYT*, August 15, 2006; David Corn, "SECRET VIDEO: Romney Tells Millionaire Donors What He REALLY Thinks of Obama Voters," *Mother Jones*, September 17, 2012, www.motherjones.com/politics/2012/09/secret-video-romney-private-fundraiser/.

154. Eleanor Randolph, "Routine Exchange on Campaign Trail Ran Out of Control for Dukakis Aides," *WP*, October 3, 1987.

155. Runkel, *Campaign for President*, 3.

156. Shrum, *No Excuses*, 181.

157. Randolph, "Routine Exchange On Campaign Trail."

158. Thomas Edsall, "Dukakis Disputes Report on Origin of Biden Tape; Staff Reportedly Compiled Clips to Hurt Rival," *WP*, September 29, 1987.

159. George J. Church, "And Then There Were Six," *Time*, October 5, 1987.

160. Andrew Rosenthal, "Two Top Aides to Dukakis Resign as One Admits Role in Biden Tape," *NYT*, October 1, 1987.

161. "Little Big Men," *Newsweek*, November 21, 1988, 55; Corrigan interview.

162. Rosenthal, "Two Top Aides to Dukakis Resign."

163. "Little Big Men," 55; George J. Church, "The Dwarfs in Disarray," *Time*, October 12, 1987.

164. Estrich interview.

165. Rosenthal, "Two Top Aides to Dukakis Resign."

166. Church, "Dwarfs in Disarray."

167. Corrigan interview.

168. "Little Big Men," 55.

169. Mickey Kaus with Howard Fineman, John McCormick, Mark Starr, and Sue Hutchinson, "Now a Dukakis Fiasco," *Newsweek*, October 12, 1987.

170. E. J. Dionne Jr., "Some Perceiving Self-Destruction for Democrats," *NYT*, October 2, 1987.

171. Andrew Rosenthal, "The Tape: What Sin?; Puzzlement at Case of Dukakis's Aide," *NYT*, October 2, 1987.

172. Estrich interview.

173. Dukakis interview.

174. Corrigan interview.

175. Shrum interview.

176. Phil Gailey, "Simon Declares, Embracing Democrats' Activist History," *NYT*, May 19, 1987.

177. Axelrod, *Believer*, 82.

178. Gailey, "Simon Declares, Embracing Democrats' Activist History."

179. Robin Toner, "Simon, Now a Credible Candidate, Still Faces an Issue of Electability," *NYT*, November 18, 1987.

180. Walter Shapiro, "Campaign Portrait, Paul Simon: Some of That Old-Time Religion," *Time*, November 16, 1987.

181. Robin Toner, "The Emerging Candidate: Who Is Senator Simon?," *NYT*, December 9, 1987; E. J. Dionne Jr., "Iowa Poll Shows Simon and Dole as Leaders," *NYT*, November 16, 1987; Toner, "Simon, Now a Credible Candidate."

182. Kenneth Pins, "Simon vs. Dole for Presidency? That's Race Iowans Favor in Poll," *Des Moines Register*, November 15, 1987.

183. Strobe Talbott, "Campaign Portrait, Al Gore: Trying to Set Himself Apart," *Time*, October 19, 1987.

184. Warren Weaver, "Nunn Rules Out Race for the Presidency," *NYT*, August 27, 1987.

185. Weaver, "Nunn Rules Out Race for the Presidency."

186. Paul Taylor, "Gore Officially Joins '88 Race; Tennessee Democrat, 39, Is Field's Youngest," *WP*, June 30, 1987. For more on Gore's background, see Maraniss and Nakashima, *Prince of Tennessee*.

187. Lieberman defeated incumbent senator Lowell Weicker (R) of Connecticut in 1988, attacking him from the right on foreign policy.

188. "Candidates Debate: National Security," C-SPAN Video, October 5, 1987, www.c-span.org/video/?3542-1/candidates-debate-national-security.

189. E. J. Dionne Jr., "Democrats Clash on Foreign Policy," *NYT*, October 9, 1987.

190. Warren Weaver, "Gore Steps Up Bid for Center in Race," *NYT*, November 7, 1987.

191. Talbott, "Campaign Portrait, Al Gore."

192. Technically there were twenty-one primaries and caucuses, as American Samoa was holding one as well.

193. Weaver, "Gore Steps Up Bid for Center in Race."

194. David E. Rosenbaum, "Gore Campaign Testing Value of Endorsements," *NYT*, January 25, 1988; Warren Weaver, "Gore Pinning Hope on Big Voting Day," *NYT*, December 10, 1987.

195. "Miracle in Michigan," *Newsweek*, November 21, 1988, 70.

196. John Margolis, "A Super-Dumb Idea from the South," *Chicago Tribune*, March 3, 1986; R. W. Apple, "Delivering the South," *NYT*, November 30, 1986.

197. Paul Taylor, "Jackson Recasting His Image: 1984 'Protest Candidate' Progressing to 'Message Candidate' in 1988," *WP*, October 5, 1987.

198. Frady, *Jesse*, 369.

199. Calculated from "Black-American Members of Congress."

200. David Rosenbaum, "Jackson Makes Formal Bid for Presidency in 1988," *NYT*, October 11, 1987.

201. Taylor, "Jackson Recasting His Image."

202. Rosenbaum, "Jackson Makes Formal Bid for Presidency"; Taylor, "Jackson Recasting His Image."

203. Rosenbaum, "Jackson Makes Formal Bid for Presidency."

204. Newport, "Americans Today Much More Accepting."

205. "Urban Issues of Concern," C-SPAN Video, January 20, 1988, www.c-span.org/video/?240-1/urban-issues-concern.

206. Robin Toner, "Women Taking Major Roles in '88 Presidential Campaigns," *NYT*, December 29, 1987.

207. Estrich interview.

208. Corrigan interview; Mary McGrory, "Dukakis' Money Machine," *WP*, September 10, 1987.

209. "Bowl," Box 34, Long Bio, Short Bio, Contra, Bowl, VHS (1988), Michael S. Dukakis Presidential Campaign Records; Dan Balz, "Credibility of Dukakis' Message about U.S. Economy Questioned," *WP*, November 8, 1987.

210. Balz, "Credibility of Dukakis' Message."

211. "Little Big Men," *Newsweek*, November 21, 1988, 55.

212. "Presidential Candidates Debate," C-SPAN Video, December 1, 1987, www.c-span.org/video/?20-1/presidential-candidates-debate.

213. David Yepsen, "Viewers: Luster Fades on Simon, Dukakis Gains," *Des Moines Register*, December 2, 1987.

214. "Little Big Men," 58.

215. "Presidential Candidates Debate," December 1, 1987.

216. "Presidential Candidates Debate," December 1, 1987.

217. Yepsen, "Viewers: Luster fades on Simon, Dukakis Gains."

218. Steven V. Roberts, "Senior Democrats Look for Alternative Candidates," *NYT*, December 2, 1987.

CHAPTER 3

1. Walter Shapiro, "Just What Is He Up To?," *Time*, September 21, 1987; E. J. Dionne Jr., "Hart Unsettles Democrats, Which Pleases Republicans," *New York Times* (hereafter *NYT*), December 16, 1987.

2. Walter Shapiro, "The Ghost of Gary Past," *Time*, December 28, 1987; E. J. Dionne Jr., "Poll Shows Hart and Jackson Leading," *NYT*, December 17, 1987.

3. E. J. Dionne Jr., "Democratic Chief Says Hart Put Own Goal over Party's," *NYT*, December 18, 1987.

4. Runkel, *Campaign for President*, 16.

5. "Dick Gephardt, 'Hyundai,'" YouTube Video, June 26, 2017, 1:00, www.youtube.com/watch?v=wiTg7zcNgP0.

6. Shrum, *No Excuses*, 185.

7. Shrum interview.

8. Shrum interview.

9. "Little Big Men," *Newsweek*, November 21, 1988, 55.

10. E. J. Dionne Jr., "Polls Find Iowa Voters More Liberal Than Nation," *NYT*, November 1, 1987.

11. Corrigan interview.

12. Robin Toner, "Dukakis, Shunning Manager Label, Incorporates Oratory of Compassion," *NYT*, January 11, 1988.

13. Robin Toner, "Politics: Shifting Style, Dukakis Turns to Emotional Heat," *NYT*, February 2, 1988.

14. "Homeless," Box 37, Golden Moments, Medicare, Health Care, Homeless (VHS), 1988, Michael S. Dukakis Presidential Campaign Records. According to the tape, these ads were made in late December, but they likely aired in January as part of the shift to a more progressive message, as their contents fit such a move.

15. Dukakis interview.

16. Corrigan interview.

17. Susan F. Rasky, "Gephardt's Iowa Campaign Resurges," *NYT*, January 19, 1988.

18. E. J. Dionne Jr., "Democrats Gentle as Hart Joins Debate," *NYT*, January 16, 1988; E. J. Dionne Jr., "Democrats in Iowa Go on the Attack," *NYT*, January 24, 1988.

19. Lucy Howard, "Campaign '88; A Conventional Wisdom Watch," *Newsweek*, January 25, 1988.

20. E. J. Dionne Jr., "Polls Show Discontent on Reagan Helps Dole Outpace Bush in Iowa," *NYT*, January 8, 1988.

21. Bill Peterson, "Gephardt Nudges Simon out of Lead in Iowa Polls," *Washington Post* (hereafter *WP*), January 22, 1988; Richard Berke, "Hart's Advisers Deny New Charges but Are Fearful of Impact," *NYT*, January 22, 1988.

22. Robin Toner, "Simon Sees Gephardt at Heels and Toughens Pitch," *NYT*, January 22, 1988; Robin Toner, "Simon Takes Off Gloves but Puts Them Back On," *NYT*, January 29, 1988.

23. "Our Views on the Candidates," *Des Moines Register*, January 31, 1988.

24. Warren Weaver, "Gephardt Hopeful on Iowa Caucuses," *NYT*, January 30, 1988.

25. Estrich interview.

26. Warren Weaver, "Gephardt Is Wary of Leader's Label," *NYT*, February 6, 1988.

27. Kenneth Pins, "Last Survey Gauges Caucus Races: Support for Simon on Upswing," *Des Moines Register*, February 7, 1988.

28. "Caucus History: Past Years' Results," *Des Moines Register*, accessed February 5, 2018, http://caucuses.desmoinesregister.com/caucus-history-past-years-results/. All primary results from Cook, *United States Presidential Primary Elections*, unless otherwise specified.

29. Paul Taylor, "Dole, Gephardt Win Iowa Caucuses; Simon and Dukakis Are Democratic Runners-up," *WP*, February 9, 1988.

30. E. J. Dionne Jr., "Politics: Twin Messages of Protest; Strength of Robertson and Gephardt Spoke to Moral Anxiety and Economic Discontent," *NYT*, February 10, 1988.

31. Taylor, "Dole, Gephardt Win Iowa Caucuses."

32. Runkel, *Campaign for President*, 16.

33. R. W. Apple, "Bush and Simon Seen as Hobbled by Iowa's Voting," *NYT*, February 10, 1988; Axelrod, *Believer*, 83.

34. Joan Vennochi, "Dukakis Looks to N.H. Governor Calls First Primary a Key to Race," *Boston Globe*, February 9, 1988. Dukakis adviser Marty Kaplan came up with the line. Estrich interview; Devine interview.

35. Walter Shapiro, "Battling for the Post-Liberal Soul," *Time*, February 22, 1988.

36. Taylor, "Dole, Gephardt Win Iowa Caucuses"; Shapiro, "Battling for the Post-Liberal Soul."

37. Devine interview.

38. David Broder, "After Iowa; Some of the Tunes Will Change," *WP*, February 10, 1988.

39. William Safire, "Essay; Revenge of the Reverends," *NYT*, February 10, 1988.

40. E. J. Dionne Jr., "After 20 Years of Infighting, the Democrats Grow Closer," *NYT*, January 17, 1988.

41. "Massachusetts Governor Moves to Stop Nuclear Plant Opening," *NYT*, September 21, 1986.

42. "New Hampshire Talks about the Dukakis Difference," Box 2, Folder 100, Michael S. Dukakis Presidential Campaign Records.

43. Runkel, *Campaign for President*, 146.

44. "Little Big Men," *Newsweek*, November 21, 1988, 60.

45. Shrum interview.

46. E. J. Dionne Jr., "Gephardt Eyes Dukakis's Backyard," *NYT*, February 12, 1988.

47. David Broder, "Bush Rebounds, Dukakis Coasts in New Hampshire; Democrat Defeats Gephardt by 16%; Simon Runs Third," *WP*, February 17, 1988.

48. Broder, "New Hampshire: A Democratic Knockout Fight; Simon and Gephardt, With Money Woes, Content for Second Place," *WP*, February 10, 1988.

49. Michael Oreskes, "Gephardt and Simon Fight for 2d Place," *NYT*, February 14, 1988.

50. Oreskes, "Gephardt and Simon Fight for 2d Place."

51. Broder, "Bush Rebounds, Dukakis Coasts in New Hampshire."

52. Michael Oreskes, "The Big Prize: Credibility; The Democrats," *NYT*, February 17, 1988.

53. All numbers except Jackson's are from Cook, *United States Presidential Primary Elections*. Jackson's percentage is from Broder, "Bush Rebounds, Dukakis Coasts in New Hampshire."

54. Michael Oreskes, "Gore in Texas Debate, Spars with Dukakis and Gephardt," *NYT*, February 19, 1988.
55. Shrum, *No Excuses*, 188; "Little Big Men," 60.
56. Shrum interview.
57. "Little Big Men," 60.
58. Corrigan interview.
59. "Little Big Men," 60.
60. James Dickerson and David Broder, "Dole Wins in S. Dakota, Gephardt, Dukakis Each Carry 1 State," *WP*, February 24, 1988.
61. Michael Oreskes, "Gephardt, Dukakis Split Two Races among Democrats," *NYT*, February 24, 1988.
62. E. J. Dionne Jr., "Bush, Stepping Up Attack, Demands Apology from Robertson," *NYT*, February 25, 1988.
63. Dickerson and Broder, "Dole Wins in S. Dakota, Gephardt, Dukakis Each Carry 1 State."
64. Steven V. Roberts, "Dole and Dukakis Are Big Winners in Minnesota," *NYT*, February 25, 1988.
65. Steven Roberts, "Simon and Kemp Pin Hopes on Caucuses in Minnesota," *NYT*, February 23, 1988; Dickerson and Broder, "Dole Wins in S. Dakota, Gephardt, Dukakis Each Carry 1 State."
66. Runkel, *Campaign for President*, 142.
67. Mickey Kaus and Eleanor Clift, "The Many Faces of Dick Gephardt," *Newsweek*, March 7, 1988.
68. "Little Big Men," 60; Corrigan interview.
69. "Little Big Men," 60.
70. Runkel, *Campaign for President*, 141.
71. R. W. Apple, "The Election Process; Super Tuesday Offers a Muddled Experiment," *NYT*, March 8, 1988.
72. Dukakis interview.
73. E. J. Dionne Jr., "Poll Finds Sharp Differences among Supporters of Presidential Candidates; Democrats Have Distinctive Bases," *NYT*, February 27, 1988.
74. E. J. Dionne Jr., "Political Memo: 2 Steady Courses to Super Tuesday," *NYT*, March 2, 1988.
75. Corrigan interview.
76. Robin Toner, "Gephardt Presses Double Theme: Nationalism and Economic Worry," *NYT*, March 3, 1988.
77. Shrum interview; "The Song of the South," *Newsweek*, November 21, 1988, 64.
78. David Rosenbaum, "Poll Shows Southern Support for Import Limits," *NYT*, March 6, 1988.
79. Shrum interview.
80. Toner, "Gephardt Presses Double Theme."
81. Jacob Lamar, "Look Away, Dixieland," *Time*, March 7, 1988.
82. E. J. Dionne Jr., "Gore Redirects Message at Workers," *NYT*, February 29, 1988.
83. Toner, "Gephardt Presses Double Theme."
84. Runkel, *Campaign for President*, 21.
85. Runkel, *Campaign for President*, 21–22.
86. Corrigan interview.
87. Warren Weaver Jr., "Gore Is Openly Challenging Jackson for Black Voters in Southern States," *NYT*, January 10, 1988.
88. Margaret Carlson, "More Than a Crusade," *Time*, March 7, 1988.

89. "The Shock of Super Tuesday," *NYT*, March 10, 1988.

90. R. W. Apple, "3-Way Muddle; Primary Vote Leaves Many Questions but No Clear Leader for Democrats," *NYT*, March 9, 1988.

91. Paul Taylor, "Bush Rolls over GOP Rivals in 'Super Tuesday' Contest as Dukakis, Jackson, and Gore Split Democratic Ballot; Tennessean's Surge Pushes Gephardt to a Poor 4th Place," *WP*, March 9, 1988.

92. Taylor, "Bush Rolls over GOP Rivals"; E. J. Dionne Jr., "Bush Routs Dole in Primaries as Dukakis, Jackson and Gore Move Far Ahead of Gephardt; 3 Democrats Lead," *NYT*, March 9, 1988.

93. Taylor, "Bush Rolls over GOP Rivals."

94. Estrich interview.

95. Dionne, "Bush Routs Dole in Primaries."

96. Taylor, "Bush Rolls over GOP Rivals."

97. David Rosenbaum, "After Super Tuesday, Blacks, Years after Selma, Share in Jackson's Victory," *NYT*, March 10, 1988.

98. Taylor, "Bush Rolls over GOP Rivals."

99. Michael Oreskes, "Jackson Is Challenging Democrats on Fairness of Delegate System," *NYT*, March 24, 1988; E. J. Dionne Jr., "Jackson Is Searching to Amend His Strategy; He Says Delegate Rules Have Been Unfair," *NYT*, May 5, 1988; Bernard Weinraub, "Party Rules Cited by Jackson Camp," *NYT*, May 18, 1988.

100. Dionne, "Bush Routs Dole in Primaries."

101. Taylor, "Bush Rolls over GOP Rivals."

102. Runkel, *Campaign for President*, 175.

103. *Decision '88: Super Tuesday*, NBC, March 8, 1988, Vanderbilt Television Archive.

104. Thomas B. Edsall and Richard Morin, "In the South: Unified GOP, Divided Democrats," *WP*, March 9, 1988.

105. Hilary Hylton, "A Texas Two-Step: When Rick Perry Backed Al Gore," *Time*, July 16, 2011.

106. Hertzke, *Echoes of Discontent*, 230.

107. R. W. Apple, "The Election Process; Super Tuesday Offers a Muddled Experiment," *NYT*, March 8, 1988.

108. Michael Oreskes, "Rivals Switch Emphasis to Electability," *NYT*, March 11, 1988.

109. E. J. Dionne Jr., "Simon Seems at Home in Last Stand," *NYT*, March 14, 1988.

110. Michael Oreskes, "3 Democrats Vie for Illinois Votes Today," *NYT*, March 15, 1988.

111. E. J. Dionne Jr., "Bush Trounces Dole Again; Simon Wins Illinois Primary over Jackson and Dukakis," *NYT*, March 16, 1988.

112. Michael Oreskes, "The Nation: Democratic Fight Seems Likely to Go the Distance," *NYT*, March 20, 1988; Oreskes, "3 Democrats Vie for Illinois Votes Today."

113. Dionne, "Bush Trounces Dole Again"; R. W. Apple, "On at Least One Thing, the Democratic Candidates Can Agree: It's Wide Open," *NYT*, March 17, 1988.

114. Dionne, "Bush Trounces Dole Again."

115. Dukakis interview.

116. James Dickerson, "Elated Gore Eases Into Northern Primary Swing: 'Our Campaign Is Going Full Blast' among Illinois Steel Furnaces," *WP*, March 10, 1988; Dionne, "Bush Trounces Dole Again."

117. Dionne, "Bush Trounces Dole Again."

118. R. W. Apple, "Michigan Race: High Risks for 2 Rivals," *NYT*, March 26, 1988.

119. Estrich interview.

120. Robin Toner, "Two U.S. Senators Endorse Dukakis," *NYT*, March 18, 1988.

121. Toner, "Two U.S. Senators Endorse Dukakis."

122. "Dukakis Is Endorsed by Senator Bradley," *NYT*, March 24, 1988.

123. Frank Phillips, "Dukakis Reverses Furlough Stand Proposes Anticrime Package, New Criminal Justice Cabinet Post," *Boston Globe*, March 23, 1988.

124. "Tightening Prison Furloughs," *Boston Globe*, October 22, 1987; Phillips, "Dukakis Reverses Furlough Stand."

125. *CBS Evening News*, December 2, 1987; *NBC Nightly News*, January 21, 1988, Vanderbilt Television Archive.

126. Robin Toner, "Dukakis Takes New Trade Message to North and Gephardt Cries Foul," *NYT*, March 23, 1988.

127. "Miracle in Michigan," *Newsweek*, November 21, 1988, 70.

128. "Miracle in Michigan," 70; Apple, "Michigan Race."

129. "Miracle in Michigan," 70.

130. R. W. Apple, "Jackson Triumph Changes Outlook of Top Democrats," *NYT*, March 28, 1988; Walter Shapiro, "Win, Jesse, Win," *Time*, April 4, 1988.

131. Jonathan Alter, "The Michigan Miracle," *Newsweek*, April 4, 1988.

132. Apple, "Jackson Triumph Changes Outlook of Top Democrats."

133. Dukakis interview.

134. Runkel, *Campaign for President*, 8.

135. Lucy Howard, "Conventional Wisdom Watch," *Newsweek*, April 4, 1988.

136. Apple, "Jackson Triumph Changes Outlook of Top Democrats."

137. Shrum interview.

138. Shrum, *No Excuses*, 191.

139. Michael Luo, "Despite Nafta Attacks, Clinton and Obama Haven't Been Free Trade Foes," *NYT*, February 28, 2008; Jennifer Steinhauer, "Both Parties Used to Back Free Trade. Now They Bash It," *NYT*, July 29, 2016.

140. E. J. Dionne Jr., "Jackson Rivals Confront Problem of How to Campaign against Him," *NYT*, March 29, 1988.

141. Walter Shapiro, "Taking Jesse Seriously," *Time*, April 11, 1988.

142. Dionne, "Jackson Rivals Confront Problem."

143. Anthony Lewis, "Abroad at Home; The Jackson Reality," *NYT*, March 31, 1988.

144. Apple, "Jackson Triumph Changes Outlook of Top Democrats."

145. Mickey Kaus with Howard Fineman, Peter McKillop, and Eleanor Clift, "Cranking Up the Mario Scenario," *Newsweek*, April 11, 1988.

146. Jeffrey Schmalz, "Cuomo Remains Unflustered at Jackson Gains," *NYT*, March 30, 1988.

147. Dukakis interview; Estrich interview; Corrigan interview.

148. "Bernie Sanders Endorses Jesse Jackson for President" (Sanders press conference that aired on "Bernie Speaks," March 31, 1988), YouTube Video, July 19, 2015, 31:42, www.youtube.com/watch?v=1PhT80FM_Yc.

149. Robin Toner, "Dukakis Outlook Remains Troubled," *NYT*, March 30, 1988.

150. "Conventional Wisdom Watch," *Newsweek*, April 11, 1988.

151. Richard Berke, "Rural Wisconsin Town Turns Out for Jackson," *NYT*, April 2, 1988; E. J. Dionne Jr., "For Wisconsin's Liberals, a Choice," *NYT*, April 1, 1988.

152. David E. Rosenbaum, "Jackson Success Brings Scrutiny of Themes That Defy Rival Views," *NYT*, April 4, 1988.

153. R. W. Apple, "Blue-Collar Contrast; Dukakis and Jackson Differ in Appeal to Wisconsin's Working-Class Voters," *NYT*, April 2, 1988; Larry Martz with Eleanor Clift, Howard Fineman, Mark Starr, and Sylvester Monroe, "Jackson's Big Takeoff," *Newsweek*, April 11, 1988.

154. E. J. Dionne Jr., "In the Other Wisconsin, Too, Jackson Has Appeal," *NYT*, April 3, 1988.

155. "Last-Minute Scuffles," *Newsweek*, November 21, 1988, 79.

156. Robin Toner, "Wisconsin Sees a Warmer Dukakis," *NYT*, April 6, 1988.

157. Robin Toner, "Dukakis Attempts to Answer Critics," *NYT*, April 1, 1988; E. J. Dionne Jr., "Wisconsin Chooses Delegates Today," *NYT*, April 5, 1988.

158. "Michael Dukakis and Wisconsin Workers," Box 2, Folder 82, Michael S. Dukakis Presidential Campaign Records.

159. Bernard Weinraub, "Gore Assails Dukakis over Jackson," *NYT*, April 4, 1988.

160. Weinraub, "Gore Assails Dukakis over Jackson."

161. Dionne, "Wisconsin Chooses Delegates Today."

162. R. W. Apple, "For Jackson, Good Will, But Not Enough Votes," *NYT*, April 6, 1988; David Broder, "Dukakis Overwhelms Jackson in Wisconsin; Gore a Distant Third; Bush Wins All 47 Delegates in GOP Primary," *WP*, April 6, 1988.

163. Apple, "For Jackson, Good Will."

164. Larry Martz with Howard Fineman, Margaret Garrard Warner, Mark Starr, Peter McKillop, and Ginny Carroll, "Score One for Dukakis," *Newsweek*, April 18, 1988.

165. *16 for '16: The Contenders*, episode 4, "The Visionaries."

166. E. J. Dionne Jr., "Dukakis Now Front-Runner after Triumph in Wisconsin," *NYT*, April 7, 1988.

167. Apple, "For Jackson, Good Will."

168. For an overall look at Jackson's life and career, see Frady, *Jesse*.

169. R. W. Apple, "Jackson Is Seen as Winning a Solid Place in History," *NYT*, April 29, 1988.

170. E. J. Dionne Jr., "Jackson Share of Votes by Whites Triples in '88," *NYT*, June 13, 1988.

171. Apple, "Jackson Is Seen as Winning."

172. Runkel, *Campaign for President*, 25.

173. Porter, *John Lewis: Good Trouble*.

174. Ronald Brownstein, "Whose Coalition Is Bigger?," *National Journal*, February 9, 2008; Newport, "Obama Dominates Clinton among College Graduates"; "ABC News 2008 Democratic Primary Exit Polls Results—Key Groups," *ABC News*, accessed August 2, 2022, https://abcnews.go.com/images/PollingUnit/08DemPrimaryKeyGroups.pdf.

175. Michael Oreskes, "Dukakis Defeats Jackson in Oregon Presidential Vote," *NYT*, May 18, 1988. Oreskes wrote, "Mr. Jackson has consistently run better among white voters in states with fewer blacks, perhaps because of less racial polarization in those states."

176. Michael Kruse, "What Jesse Taught Bernie about Running for President," PoliticoMagazine, March 15, 2019, www.politico.com/magazine/story/2019/03/15/bernie-sanders-2020-race-jesse-jackson-1988-presidential-campaign-225809.

177. *16 for '16: The Contenders*, episode 4, "The Visionaries."

178. Jonathan Alter with Eleanor Clift and Howard Fineman, "Sen. Gore's Identity Crisis," *Newsweek*, April 18, 1988.

179. "Mike Dukakis for President," Box 2, Folder 101, Michael S. Dukakis Presidential Campaign Records.

180. Joyce Purnick, "Koch Defends Attack on Jackson, Saying He Evades Issue of Israel," *NYT*, April 9, 1988. In a letter to the editor a few weeks later, Koch elaborated that the paper and others had edited his quote, which he said should read, "Jews and other supporters of Israel would be crazy to vote for Jesse Jackson." Ed Koch, "What Koch Said about Jackson and Why," *NYT*, April 27, 1988.

181. Maureen Dowd, "Jackson Conciliatory on Jewish Issue," *NYT*, April 8, 1988.

182. Horton's name does not appear in the *Los Angeles Times*, *WP*, or *NYT* articles on the debate. Nor is his name mentioned in a *NBC Nightly News* report on the debate. Robert

Shogan, "Gore, Dukakis Tangle during N.Y. Debate," *Los Angeles Times*, April 13, 1988; Paul Taylor, "Democratic Rivals Back Tougher S. Africa Sanctions," *WP*, April 13, 1988; Frank Lynn, "Pace Is Quickening in New York Race," *NYT*, April 13, 1988; *NBC Nightly News*, April 12, 1988, Vanderbilt Television Archive. Germond and Witcover also say, "Gore mentioned the prison furlough program—although not the specifics of the Willie Horton case." *Whose Broad Stripes and Bright Stars?*, 315.

183. Dukakis interview.

184. Andy Card served as George W. Bush's White House chief of staff from 2001 to 2006; James P. Pinkerton interview, Presidential Oral Histories.

185. Runkel, *Campaign for President*, 115; Sidney Blumenthal, "Willie Horton: The Making of an Election Issue," *WP*, October 28, 1988.

186. Richard Berke, "Rivals Will Be Big Spenders for the Battle of New York," *NYT*, April 7, 1988.

187. Bernard Weinraub, "Gore Backs Israeli Peace Plan Rejection," *NYT*, March 22, 1988.

188. Bernard Weinraub, "In Brooklyn, Shadow of Jackson Follows Gore," *NYT*, April 11, 1988.

189. E. J. Dionne Jr., "Jackson's Burden among Jews: Fear Overpowers Unity on Civil Rights," *NYT*, April 14, 1988.

190. Michael Oreskes, "Koch Backs Gore; New York Impact Could Aid Jackson," *NYT*, April 15, 1988.

191. Joyce Purnick, "Koch Says Jackson Lied about Actions after Dr. King Was Slain," *NYT*, April 18, 1988.

192. Laurence Barrett, "Marathon Man," *Time*, May 2, 1988.

193. David Broder and Richard Martin, "Voting Negative; Big Turnout against Jackson Builds Margin for Dukakis," *WP*, April 20, 1988.

194. Michael Oreskes, "Jackson Troops Say They Won Future," *NYT*, April 20, 1988.

195. Thomas Edsall, "Labor Split, but Moving to the Left; Race and Geography Are Factors in Choice," *WP*, April 16, 1988; Oreskes, "Koch Backs Gore."

196. E. J. Dionne Jr., "New York Gives Dukakis a Crucial Victory; Jackson Far Ahead of Gore, Who May Quit," *NYT*, April 20, 1988.

197. Jonathan Alter with Eleanor Clift and Howard Fineman, "Sen. Gore's Identity Crisis," *Newsweek*, April 18, 1988; Edward Walsh and Thomas B. Edsall, "Campaign's Legacy to Gore: Experience and Hard Feelings?," *WP*, April 21, 1988.

198. Dukakis interview; R. W. Apple, "The Look for Fall: Bush vs. Dukakis," *NYT*, April 20, 1988.

199. Maureen Dowd, "Jackson Campaign, Chastened by Recent Primary Defeats, Revises Its Goal," *NYT*, April, 28, 1988.

200. Michael Oreskes, "Jackson Pushed for 2d Spot on Ticket," *NYT*, April 21, 1988.

201. Richard Berke, "Jackson, on Stump in Ohio, Offers Criticism of Dukakis," *NYT*, May 1, 1988.

202. Bernard Weinraub, "Jackson Assails Dukakis as a Bush Twin," *NYT*, May 13, 1988.

203. Bernard Weinraub, "Democratic Candidates Spar over Budget Issues," *NYT*, May 26, 1988.

204. E. J. Dionne Jr., "Jackson Share of Votes by Whites Triples in '88," *NYT*, June 13, 1988.

205. Peter Kilborn, "On Economy, Dukakis Recasts Mold," *NYT*, May 13, 1988.

206. Runkel, *Campaign for President*, 8.

207. Estrich interview.

208. Michael Oreskes, "Bush and Dukakis Attacking Each Other after Pennsylvania's Primary," *NYT* April 28, 1988; E. J. Dionne Jr., "Poll Shows Dukakis Leads Bush; Many Reagan Backers Shift Sides," *NYT*, May 17, 1988.

209. Fuller interview.
210. E. J. Dionne Jr., "Dukakis Is Termed Extreme Liberal," *NYT*, May 20, 1988.
211. Nate Silver. "Was the Democratic Primary a Close Call or a Landslide?," Five ThirtyEight.com, July 27, 2016, https://fivethirtyeight.com/features/was-the-democratic-primary-a-close-call-or-a-landslide/.
212. Linda Wertheimer, "The Stubborn Triumph of Michael Dukakis," *WP*, June 12, 1988.

CHAPTER 4

1. William Schneider, "The Suburban Century Begins," *Atlantic*, July 1992.
2. For overall examinations of Bush's life and career, see Parmet, *George Bush*; Naftali, *George H. W. Bush*; and Meacham, *Destiny and Power*.
3. Parmet, *George Bush*, 63. The number of missions is from that page.
4. Bush, *All the Best*, 107.
5. Bush, *All the Best*, 109.
6. Bush, *Looking Forward*; Margaret Garrard Warner, "Bush Battles the 'Wimp Factor,'" *Newsweek*, October 19, 1987.
7. Al Kamen, "Bentsen Cast Bush in 1970 as Too Liberal; Democrat First Won Bitter Primary," *Washington Post* (hereafter *WP*), July 16, 1988.
8. Parmet, *George Bush*, 142–44.
9. Bernard Weinraub, "Washington Talk; Dole's Friends See Aversion to Bush," *New York Times* (hereafter *NYT*), December 10, 1987.
10. Richard Allen, "George Herbert Walker Bush; The Accidental Vice President," *NYT*, July 30, 2000.
11. Warner, "Bush Battles the 'Wimp Factor.'"
12. Warner, "Bush Battles the 'Wimp Factor.'"
13. "EXECUTIVE SUMMARY: The Leadership Gap," November 24, 1986, Box 7, The Leadership Gap—November 25, 1986 [Analysis of George Bush for 1988 campaign], Robert Teeter Collection. Emphasis in original.
14. "EXECUTIVE SUMMARY: The Leadership Gap."
15. Fuller interview.
16. Randall Rothenberg, "The Boom in Political Consulting," *NYT*, May 24, 1987; McGinnis, *Selling of the President, 1968*, 63.
17. Sherman, *Loudest Voice in the Room*.
18. Cohen et al., *Party Decides*, 208.
19. Martin Tolchin and Jeff Gerth, "The Contradictions of Bob Dole," *NYT*, November 8, 1987.
20. Helen Dewar, "Republicans Wage Verbal Civil War," *WP*, November 19, 1984.
21. Black interview.
22. See Kondracke and Barnes, *Jack Kemp*, for an overall look at his career.
23. For an overall look at the rise of the religious right in the GOP and the conservative movement, see Williams, *God's Own Party*.
24. Richard Berke, "Laxalt Rejects Bid for the Presidency," *NYT*, August 27, 1987.
25. Hedrick Smith, "Those Fractious Republicans," *NYT*, October 25, 1987.
26. "Bush and the Big A Question," *Newsweek*, June 29, 1987.
27. E. J. Dionne Jr., "Bush's Presidential Bid Shaky Despite His Lead, Poll Finds," *NYT*, July 26, 1987.
28. Bernard Weinraub, "Washington Talk: The Dole Campaign; Quarrels Abating, the Team Takes Shape," *NYT*, May 18, 1987.
29. The Iowa straw poll was held from 1979 to 2011. Kyle Cheney, "Iowa Straw Poll Pronounced Dead at 36," Politico, June 6, 2015, updated June 12, 2015, www.politico.com

/story/2015/06/iowa-gop-kills-straw-poll-118930; E. J. Dionne Jr., "Robertson's Victory in Ballot Shakes Rivals in G.O.P. Race," *NYT*, September 14, 1987.

30. Laurence Barrett, "Campaign Portrait, Robertson: His Eyes Have Seen the Glory," *Time*, September 28, 1987.
31. Dionne, "Robertson's Victory in Ballot Shakes Rivals."
32. E. J. Dionne Jr., "Michigan G.O.P. Elects Rival Slates," *NYT*, January 31, 1988.
33. Fuller interview.
34. Paul Taylor, "Unofficial Results Show Bush Wins Plurality in Michigan," *WP*, August 7, 1986.
35. E. J. Dionne Jr., "Robertson Wins Key Test over Bush in Michigan," *NYT*, September 16, 1987.
36. Don Oberdorfer and Lou Cannon, "Missile-Ban Treaty Approved 'in Principle,'" *WP*, September 19, 1987.
37. David Broder and Thomas Edsall, "Arms Agreement Improves GOP Chances in '88: Experts Feel INF Pact, Summit Can Help Party Overcome Effects of Iran-Contra Scandal," *WP*, September 20, 1987.
38. Wayne King, "Robertson, Returning to Brooklyn Home, Enters Race," *NYT*, October 2, 1987.
39. "Robertson Announcement," C-SPAN Video, October 2, 1987, www.c-span.org/video/?3191-1/robertson-announcement.
40. Barrett, "Campaign Portrait, Robertson."
41. Warner, "Bush Battles the 'Wimp Factor.'"
42. Maralee Schwartz, "Bush Jr. vs Newsweek," *WP*, October 16, 1987.
43. Fuller interview.
44. Evan Thomas, "I Called George Bush a 'Wimp' on the Cover of Newsweek. Why I Was Wrong," Yahoo News, December 5, 2018, https://news.yahoo.com/called-george-bush-wimp-cover-newsweek-wrong-140012335.html.
45. Fuller interview.
46. Howard Fineman, "The Wordsmith behind the Speech," *Newsweek*, August 22, 1988.
47. "Bush Announcement," C-SPAN Video, October 12, 1987, www.c-span.org/video/?3133-1/bush-announcement.
48. "Bush Announcement."
49. Laurence Barrett, "Where Are the Wingers?," *Time*, October 26, 1987.
50. Bob Woodward, "The Origin of the Tax Pledge," *WP*, October 4, 1992.
51. "Bush Announcement."
52. Woodward, "Origin of the Tax Pledge."
53. Richard Berke, "Campaign Finance: National Fund-Raising Eludes All but Bush," *NYT*, September 1, 1987.
54. Richard Berke, "Campaign Finance; Bush and Dukakis War Chests Bulge," *NYT*, October 17, 1987.
55. Bernard Weinraub, "Washington Talk: Presidential Politics; Compassion Becomes a Republican Theme," *NYT*, October 22, 1987.
56. Weinraub, "Washington Talk: Presidential Politics; Compassion."
57. Wolfe, *Bonfire of the Vanities*.
58. Sylvia Nasar, "The 1980's: A Very Good Time for the Very Rich," *NYT*, March 5, 1992.
59. Peter McKillop and Bill Powell, "Citizen Trump," *Newsweek*, September 28, 1987.
60. McKillop and Powell, "Citizen Trump."
61. Michael Oreskes, "Trump Gives a Vague Hint of Candidacy," *NYT*, September 21, 1987.

62. "A Trump Presidential Bid?," *NYT*, July 14, 1987.

63. Howard, *Gung Ho*; McTiernan, *Die Hard*; Zemeckis, *Back to the Future Part II*.

64. Kennedy, *Rise and Fall of the Great Powers*; Daniel Patrick Moynihan, "Debunking the Myth of Decline,"' *NYT*, June 19, 1988.

65. "There's Nothing Wrong with America's Foreign Defense Policy That a Little Backbone Can't Cure," *NYT*, September 2, 1987; John Shanahan, "Trump: U.S. Should Stop Paying to Defend Countries That Can Protect Selves," *AP*, September 1, 1987.

66. Fox Butterfield, "New Hampshire Speech Earns Praise for Trump," *NYT*, October 23, 1987.

67. Fuller interview.

68. Linda Qiu, "Is Donald Trump's 'Art of the Deal' the Best-Selling Business Book of All Time?," Politifact, July 6, 2015, www.politifact.com/factchecks/2015/jul/06/donald-trump/donald-trumps-art-deal-best-selling-business-book.

69. Katie Reilly, "Meet the Man Who Encouraged Donald Trump to Run for President in 1987," *Time*, August 12, 2016.

70. "A Firing Line Special: The Republican Presidential Candidates," YouTube video, October 28, 1987, 1:57.58, www.youtube.com/watch?v=-mQd_QgZrw8.

71. "A Firing Line Special: The Republican Presidential Candidates."

72. "A Firing Line Special: The Republican Presidential Candidates."

73. "A Firing Line Special: The Republican Presidential Candidates."

74. Michael Oreskes, "Bush Won Debate, Republicans Agree," *NYT*, October 30, 1987.

75. David S. Broder, "Round 1 Goes to George Bush," *WP*, October 30, 1987; Runkel, *Campaign for President*, 64.

76. Lucy Howard, "Debate Strategies," *Newsweek*, November 2, 1987; Alessandra Stanley, "Dole Buries His Hatchet," *Time*, November 16, 1987.

77. Thomas B. Edsall, "Dole Makes It Official; Candidacy Declared, with Stress on Austerity," *WP*, November 10, 1987.

78. "Dole Announcement," C-SPAN Video, November 9, 1987, www.c-span.org/video/?37-1/dole-announcement.

79. "Dole Announcement."

80. Bernard Weinraub, "Dole Makes His Presidential Bid Official," *NYT*, November 9, 1987; Bernard Weinraub, "Brock Is Planning a Shake-up of Dole Campaign, Aides Say," *NYT*, November 14, 1987; E. J. Dionne Jr., "Iowa Poll Shows Simon and Dole as Leaders," *NYT*, November 16, 1987.

81. Thomas B. Edsall, "Bush Defeats Robertson in Florida Republican Straw Poll," *WP*, November 15, 1987.

82. Michael Oreskes, "Organized Groups Flock to Iowa Trying to Gain Influence in '88 Campaign," *NYT*, November 21, 1988.

83. "Presidential Candidates Debate," C-SPAN Video, December 1, 1987, www.c-span.org/video/?20-1/presidential-candidates-debate; E. J. Dionne Jr., "All 12 Candidates Debate in First TV Appearance," *NYT*, December 2, 1987.

84. Jacob Lamar, "An Offer They Can Refuse," *Time*, December 14, 1987.

85. E. J. Dionne, Jr., "Arms Pact Has Major Effect on Presidential Race," *NYT*, December 6, 1987.

86. Gerald M. Boyd, "Bush's Forces Win Ruling on Michigan Delegates," *NYT*, December 5, 1987.

87. Gerald M. Boyd, "Summit Aftermath; Gorbachev's Visit Called Boon to Bush," *NYT*, December 12, 1987.

88. Bernard Weinraub, "Dole Backs Treaty, but Expects Changes," *NYT*, December 18, 1987.

89. Gerald M. Boyd, "Bush Retaliates for Dole's Criticisms," *NYT*, January 6, 1988; "Dole and Bush Leading in an Iowa G.O.P. Poll," *NYT*, December 28, 1987.

90. Robin Toner, "Political Memo; As the Preseason Ends, All Parties Take Stock," *NYT*, December 31, 1987.

91. Boyd, "Bush Retaliates for Dole's Criticisms."

92. "The Vice President's Advice," *NYT*, January 6, 1988.

93. "Republican Candidates Debate," C-SPAN Video, January 8, 1988, www.c-span.org/video/?3650-1/republican-candidates-debate.

94. "Republican Candidates Debate."

95. E. J. Dionne Jr., "Poll Finds Iowa More Liberal Than Nation," *NYT*, November 1, 1987.

96. Steven V. Roberts, "In Iowa, Tarnish on Reagan Rubs Off on Bush," *NYT*, January 18, 1988; E. J. Dionne Jr., "Candidates Already Driving Hard in Iowa for First Big Test of 1988," *NYT*, May 3, 1987.

97. Roberts, "In Iowa, Tarnish on Reagan Rubs Off on Bush."

98. Steven V. Roberts, "Robertson Seeks the Faithful in Cross-State Tour of Iowa," *NYT*, January 19, 1988.

99. Robin Toner, "G.O.P. Candidates Clash in Debate," *NYT*, January 17, 1988.

100. Richard Stengel, "Bushwacked!," *Time*, February 8, 1988.

101. Fuller interview.

102. Runkel, *Campaign for President*, 67; Peter Boyer, "Rather's Questioning of Bush Sets Off Shouting on Live Broadcast," *NYT*, January 26, 1988.

103. Bush, *All the Best*, 109.

104. Stengel, "Bushwacked!"

105. Fuller interview.

106. Runkel, *Campaign for President*, 67.

107. "Dan Rather–George Bush Showdown," YouTube video, January 25, 1988, 9:08, www.youtube.com/watch?v=FqwQw3THRvU.

108. Boyer, "Rather's Questioning of Bush."

109. "Dan Rather–George Bush Showdown."

110. "Dan Rather–George Bush Showdown."

111. Peter Boyer, "Rather Walked Off Set of CBS News," *NYT*, September 13, 1987.

112. Jonathan Alter and Howard Fineman, "The Great TV Shout-Out," *Newsweek*, February 8, 1988; Fuller interview.

113. Boyer, "Rather's Questioning of Bush."

114. Boyer, "Rather's Questioning of Bush."

115. E. J. Dionne Jr., "Bush Camp Feels Galvanized after Showdown with Rather," *NYT*, January 27, 1988; "Rather-Bush Tiff the Day After—CBS Evening News," YouTube video, January 26, 1988, 7:13, www.youtube.com/watch?v=LgwxjG7y9eE.

116. "Poll Finds Even Split on Bush-Rather Battle," *NYT*, January 29, 1988.

117. "Poll Finds Even Split."

118. Fuller interview.

119. Dionne, "Bush Camp Feels Galvanized."

120. Dionne, "Bush Camp Feels Galvanized."

121. Fuller interview.

122. Robin Toner, "Poll Finds Rather Clash Is Failing to Ease Bush's Iran-Contra Woes," *NYT*, February 2, 1988.

123. Thomas B. Edsall, "Bush Takes Lead in State Delegate Race; Backers of Robertson and Kemp Walk Out of Michigan GOP Meetings," *WP*, January 15, 1988.

124. E. J. Dionne Jr., "Victory for Bush in Michigan Fight," *NYT*, January 23, 1988; Thomas Edsall, "Robertson Says Kemp Sold Out in Michigan," *WP*, January 30, 1988;

Thomas Edsall, "Bush Wins Plurality in Michigan: GOP Bitterly Divided in First State to Pick Delegates," *WP*, January 31, 1988.

125. Black interview.

126. E. J. Dionne Jr., "Michigan G.O.P. Elects Rival Slates," *NYT*, January 31, 1988.

127. Bernard Weinraub, "Bush Aide Accuses Dole of Being 'Mean Spirited,'" *NYT*, February 4, 1988.

128. Mickey Kaus and Howard Fineman, "A Penny Ante-Game," *Newsweek*, February 15, 1988.

129. Michael Oreskes, "Bush Presses the Attack in Dole Dispute," *NYT*, February 6, 1988; David Broder, "Dole-Bush Fight Makes GOP Uneasy; Threat to Party Unity Seen if Feud Goes On," *WP*, February 8, 1988.

130. Gerald Boyd, "Dole and Bush: Dramatic Contrast of Styles . . . but There Is a Striking Similarity in Goals," *NYT*, February 7, 1988; Gerald Boyd, "Dole Makes Environment an Issue in New Hampshire," *NYT*, February 3, 1988.

131. Clifford May, "Politics; After Slow Start, Kemp's Campaign Moves with Conservatives' Support," *NYT*, February 2, 1988; T. R. Reid and Bill Peterson, "Robertson's Recruits; 'Invisible Army' Materializing," *WP*, February 8, 1988; R. W. Apple, "Robertson May Be Cause for Uncertainty in Iowa," *NYT*, February 1, 1988.

132. Black interview.

133. Fuller interview.

134. Kenneth Pins, "Last Survey Gauges Caucus Races: 2nd place: A Test of Faithful," *Des Moines Register*, February 7, 1988.

135. Bush, *All the Best*, 378.

136. Bill Peterson, "Dole, Gephardt Win Iowa Caucuses; Robertson Defeats Bush for GOP's 2nd Place," *WP*, February 9, 1988.

137. Peterson, "Dole, Gephardt Win Iowa Caucuses."

138. E. J. Dionne Jr., "Politics: Twin Messages of Protest; Strength of Robertson and Gephardt Spoke to Moral Anxiety and Economic Discontent," *NYT*, February 10, 1988.

139. E. J. Dionne Jr., "Dole Wins in Iowa, with Robertson Next," *NYT*, February 9, 1988.

140. Estrich interview.

141. "Elephants on Parade," *Newsweek*, November 21, 1988, 93.

142. Tom Morganthau with Howard Fineman, Ann McDaniel, Margaret Garrard Warner, and John McCormick, "Turmoil on the Right," *Newsweek*, February 22, 1988.

143. Meacham, *Destiny and Power*, 325.

144. Dionne, "Dole Wins in Iowa, with Robertson Next."

145. Dionne, "Dole Wins in Iowa, with Robertson Next."

146. Morganthau et al., "Turmoil on the Right."

147. Jane Norman and Thomas A. Fogarty, "Devastating Loss for the Vice President," *Des Moines Register*, February 9, 1988.

148. Dionne, "Dole Wins in Iowa, with Robertson Next."

149. Bush, *All the Best*, 378.

150. Black interview; all Iowa numbers from "Caucus History: Past Years' Results," *Des Moines Register*, accessed February 5, 2018, http://caucuses.desmoinesregister.com/caucus-history-past-years-results/.

151. Hertzke, *Echoes of Discontent*, 207–8, 206, 224, 222.

152. Hertzke, *Echoes of Discontent*, 212, 229.

153. Reed, *Active Faith*, 125.

154. Fuller interview.

155. Sununu, *Quiet Man*, 24.

156. Whipple, *Gatekeepers*, 130.

157. "Bush and Dukakis to Poll in New Hampshire," *NYT*, February 2, 1988; Bernard Weinraub, "Haig Drops Campaign for Presidency and Gives His Endorsement to Dole," *NYT*, February 13, 1988.

158. E. J. Dionne Jr., "Bush vs. Dole: Behind the Turnaround," *NYT*, March 17, 1988.

159. Michael Oreskes, "Bush Does an About-Face after Iowa," *NYT*, February 11, 1988.

160. Fuller interview.

161. Michael Oreskes, "New Hampshire's Battle on the Right," *NYT*, February 14, 1988.

162. Fuller interview.

163. "Period," Ailes Communications, 2-11-1988, OID 44069, Julian P. Kanter Commercial Archive.

164. "Elephants on Parade," 94.

165. "Elephants on Parade," 94.

166. Runkel, *Campaign for President*, 140.

167. Edward Walsh, "Dole's Campaign, Long Adrift, Runs Hard Aground," *WP*, March 16, 1988.

168. Walsh, "Dole's Campaign, Long Adrift, Runs Hard Aground."

169. "Briefing Materials for the League of Women Voters Debate," Box 5, Briefing Materials for the League of Women Voters Debate, Manchester, N.H., February 14, 1988, Copy #8, Robert Teeter Collection. Emphasis in original.

170. David Hoffman and Edward Walsh, "Bush and Dole Parry Attacks from Rivals; Front-Runners, in Final Debate before Primary, Renew Arms Dispute," *WP*, February 15, 1988.

171. James P. Pinkerton interview, Presidential Oral Histories.

172. Fuller interview.

173. Jacob Lamar, "Again the Man to Beat," *Time*, February 29, 1988.

174. Lamar, "Again the Man to Beat."

175. R. W. Apple, "The Long Fortnight of George Bush," *NYT*, February 16, 1988.

176. Lamar, "Again the Man to Beat."

177. E. J. Dionne Jr., "Bush Overcomes Dole's Bid and Dukakis Easy Winner in New Hampshire Primaries," *NYT*, February 17, 1988.

178. Edward Walsh, "Bush Rebounds, Dukakis Coasts in New Hampshire Vote; Dole 9% Behind; Kemp and DuPont Outrun Robertson," *WP*, February 17, 1988.

179. Walsh, "Bush Rebounds, Dukakis Coasts in New Hampshire Vote"; Dionne, "Bush Overcomes Dole's Bid," *NYT*, February 17, 1988. The Robertson percentage is from the Dionne article.

180. Fuller interview.

181. "Elephants on Parade," 95.

182. Runkel, *Campaign for President*, 143.

183. Lamar, "Again the Man to Beat."

184. E. J. Dionne Jr., "Bush's Move to the Front; Dole Must Now Face Hard Battles in South," *NYT*, February 18, 1988.

185. Dionne, "Bush's Move to the Front."

186. Lamar, "Again the Man to Beat."

187. Jacob Lamar, "Look Away, Dixieland," *Time*, March 7, 1988.

188. Michael Oreskes, "Gephardt, Dukakis Split Two Races among Democrats," *NYT*, February 24, 1988.

189. Runkel, *Campaign for President*, 38.

190. Steven V. Roberts, "Dole and Dukakis Are Big Winners in Minnesota," *NYT*, February 25, 1988.

191. R. W. Apple, "Bush Takes Resounding Victory in First of Southern Primaries," *NYT*, March 6, 1988.

192. Dionne, "Bush vs. Dole: Behind the Turnaround"; Bernard Weinraub, "Dole's Chairman Angrily Dismisses 2 Senior Campaign Aides," *NYT*, February 26, 1988.

193. Gerald M. Boyd, "Bush a Cautious Front-Runner Again, Avoids Attacks and Personal Campaigning," *NYT*, February 27, 1988.

194. Larry Martz with Howard Fineman, Ginny Carroll, Lynda Wright, Sylvester Monroe, and Andrew Murr, "Day of the Preachers," *Newsweek*, March 7, 1988.

195. Runkel, *Campaign for President*, 38.

196. Apple, "Bush Takes Resounding Victory."

197. "Elephants on Parade," 95.

198. Bernard Weinraub, "Frustrated Dole Struggles to Find Weapon That Will Weaken Bush," *NYT*, March 6, 1988.

199. Andrew Rosenthal, "Negative Campaign Spots Move to the Southern Airwaves," *NYT*, March 1, 1988.

200. Weinraub, "Frustrated Dole Struggles"; Michael Oreskes, "Campaign Schisms Worry the G.O.P.," *NYT*, March 6, 1988.

201. Michael Oreskes, "Bush Routs Dole in Primaries as Dukakis, Jackson, and Gore Move Far Ahead of Gephardt; Runaway in G.O.P.," *NYT*, March 9, 1988; Gerald Boyd, "After Super Tuesday, Bush Prepares to Reach Out beyond G.O.P. Voters," *NYT*, March 10, 1988.

202. Laurence Barrett, "Bush by a Shutout," *Time*, March 21, 1988.

203. Howard Fineman, "For Bush, a 'National Victory,'" *Newsweek*, March 21, 1988.

204. Maureen Dowd, "Kemp Drops Out but Drops Hint on No. 2 Spot," *NYT*, March 11, 1988.

205. William Safire, "Essay; America Turns Left," *NYT*, March 10, 1988.

206. "Bob Dole's Furies," *Newsweek*, November 21, 1988, 88; Black interview.

207. E. J. Dionne Jr., "Bush Trounces Dole Again; Simon Wins Illinois Primary over Jackson and Dukakis," *NYT*, March 16, 1988; David Broder, "Citing Unity, GOP Leaders Suggest Kansan Quit Race; Robertson Runs Far Behind," *WP*, March 16, 1988.

208. While governor of Texas, George W. Bush followed the same strategy in his 2000 presidential race, getting strong support from his fellow governors that proved instrumental to his primary victory over Senator John McCain of Arizona. Broder, "Citing Unity, GOP Leaders Suggest Kansan Quit Race."

209. Bernard Weinraub, "Dole Says Nomination of Bush Is 'Foregone,'" *NYT*, March 26, 1988.

210. Gerald M. Boyd, "Kemp, in Call for Unity, Endorses Vice President," *NYT*, March 29, 1988.

211. Bernard Weinraub, "Bush Nomination Seems Assured as Dole Leaves Republican Race," *NYT*, March 30, 1988.

212. Weinraub, "Bush Nomination Seems Assured."

213. Dionne, "Bush vs. Dole: Behind the Turnaround."

214. Dionne, "Bush vs. Dole: Behind the Turnaround."

215. Nate Silver, "Was the Democratic Primary a Close Call or a Landslide?," FiveThirtyEight.com, July 27, 2016, https://fivethirtyeight.com/features/was-the-democratic-primary-a-close-call-or-a-landslide/. I've used the popular vote totals for when the nominees still faced opponents in their race. Bush won 68 percent of overall vote, which was second-highest in that category, but much of that margin was accumulated after Dole dropped out.

216. Runkel, *Campaign for President*, 38.

217. Runkel, *Campaign for President*, 143.

218. David E. Rosenbaum, "Bush, Pennsylvania Victor, Now Has Enough Delegates to Capture the Nomination," *NYT*, April 27, 1988.

219. Gerald M. Boyd, "Bush's Success and Long-Term Hazards," *NYT*, March 19, 1988.

220. E. J. Dionne Jr., "Poll Shows Dukakis Leads Bush; Many Reagan Backers Shift Sides," *NYT*, May 17, 1988; "Satisfaction With the United States," Gallup.com, accessed March 30, 2019, https://news.gallup.com/poll/1669/general-mood-country.aspx.

221. Dionne, "Poll Shows Dukakis Leads Bush."

222. Steven Roberts, "Bush and Reagan Seem to Disagree on Noriega Talks," *NYT*, May 20, 1988.

223. Bush, *All the Best*, 387; Fuller interview.

224. Runkel, *Campaign for President*, 111; Germond and Witcover, *Whose Broad Stripes and Bright Stars?*, 157–58.

225. Runkel, *Campaign for President*, 111.

226. "Elephants on Parade," 100; Runkel, *Campaign for President*, 111–12.

227. Runkel, *Campaign for President*, 112.

228. "Elephants on Parade," 100.

229. Runkel, *Campaign for President*, 260.

230. R. W. Apple, "Despite Tie to a Popular President, Bush Faces Dukakis as Underdog," *NYT*, June 8, 1988.

CHAPTER 5

1. Jonathan Alter with Howard Fineman and Margaret Garrard Warner, "High Stakes in New Orleans," *Newsweek*, August 22, 1988.

2. "1968 Nixon vs. Humphrey vs. Wallace," The Living Room Candidate, accessed July 25, 2022, http://www.livingroomcandidate.org/commercials/1968.

3. "1968 Nixon vs. Humphrey vs. Wallace."

4. Bernard Gwertzman, "Nixon's Aide Says Peace-Plan Foes Help the Enemy," *New York Times* (hereafter *NYT*), February 8, 1972.

5. Ben Franklin, "Wallace in Race; Will 'Run to Win,'" *NYT*, February 9, 1968; "Wallace: Why I Run," *NYT*, March 1, 1972.

6. David Hoffman, "Bush: Defining Self," *Washington Post* (hereafter *WP*), June 9, 1988; Germond and Witcover, *Whose Broad Stripes and Bright Stars?*, 162.

7. Mary Meier, "School Flag Pledge Bill Ruled Unconstitutional," *Boston Globe*, May 17, 1977.

8. Dukakis interview.

9. Robert L. Turner, "State Senate Votes School Flag Pledge: A Veto Overridden, for 'All That's Holy,'" *Boston Globe*, June 17, 1977.

10. Steven V. Roberts, "Bush Intensifies Debate on Pledge, Asking Why It So Upsets Dukakis," *NYT*, August 25, 1988.

11. David Hoffman and Ann Devroy, "The Complex Machine behind Bush," *WP*, November 13, 1988.

12. Runkel, *Campaign for President*, 112–13.

13. Maureen Dowd, "Bush Paints Rival as Elitist, with 'Harvard Yard' Views," *NYT*, June 10, 1988.

14. Gerald M. Boyd, "Bush Challenges Dukakis to Explain Stand on Crime," *NYT*, June 19, 1988.

15. Robin Toner, "Dukakis Sees Support on Running Mate Issue," *NYT*, June 21, 1988.

16. Robin Toner, "Prison Furloughs in Massachusetts Threaten Dukakis Record on Crime," *NYT*, July 5, 1988.

17. Toner, "Prison Furloughs in Massachusetts."

18. Bonnie Winston, "House Investigates Furlough of Inmate Later Charged in Rape," *Boston Globe*, May 27, 1987. Jamieson, *Dirty Politics*, 26, notes that there is no proof that Horton was the actual killer.

19. Winston, "House Investigates Furlough of Inmate."

20. "Convicted Mass. Furlough Rapist Given Two Life Terms by MD. Judge," *Boston Globe*, October 21, 1987.

21. "Waving the Bloody Shirt," *Newsweek*, November 21, 1988.

22. David Rosenbaum, "Bush Talks Tough on Crime, Criticizing Prisoner Furlough Program," *NYT*, June 23, 1988.

23. *NBC Nightly News*, June 22, 1988, Vanderbilt Television Archive.

24. Rosenbaum, "Bush Talks Tough on Crime."

25. E. J. Dionne Jr., "Political Memo: Set Back in Early Skirmishes, Bush Gains with New Attack," *NYT*, July 3, 1988.

26. Walter Dellinger, "Pledge Allegiance to the Law," *NYT*, June 21, 1988.

27. Tom Wicker, "In the Nation; Bush League Charges," *NYT*, June 24, 1988.

28. "Furloughs from Common Sense," *NYT*, June 30, 1988; Toner, "Prison Furloughs in Massachusetts."

29. Sidney Blumenthal, "Willie Horton: The Making of an Election Issue," *WP*, October 28, 1988.

30. Runkel, *Campaign for President*, 117.

31. Bob Drogin, "How Presidential Race Was Won—and Lost: Michael S. Dukakis," *Los Angeles Times*, November 10, 1988.

32. Jeff Asher, "The US Murder Rate Is Up but Still Far Below Its 1980 Peak," FiveThirtyEight.com, September 25, 2017, https://fivethirtyeight.com/features/the-u-s-murder-rate-is-up-but-still-far-below-its-1980-peak/.

33. Charlie Babcock, "Fund-Raisers Gear Up for Fall Race," *WP*, June 27, 1988.

34. Dukakis interview.

35. Alexander and Bauer, *Financing the 1988 Election*, 37.

36. Estrich interview.

37. Babcock, "Fund-Raisers Gear Up for Fall Race."

38. Babcock, "Fund-Raisers Gear Up for Fall Race."

39. Richard L. Berke, "Big Money's Election-Year Comeback," *NYT*, August 7, 1988.

40. Thomas Edsall, "Soft Money Competition," *WP*, August 16, 1988.

41. Mosbacher, *Going to Windward*, 188.

42. "Last-Minute Scuffles," *Newsweek*, November 21, 1988, 82.

43. Michael Oreskes, "Jackson Says He Is Best Choice for Vice President," *NYT*, June 11, 1988.

44. Runkel, *Campaign for President*, 108; Bernard Weinraub, "Black Congressmen Exhort Dukakis to Choose Jackson," *NYT*, June 16, 1988.

45. "Last-Minute Scuffles," 82.

46. Bernard Weinraub, "Dukakis and Jackson Discuss the Vice-Presidential Spot on Ticket," *NYT*, June 22, 1988; Oreskes, "Jackson Says He Is Best Choice."

47. E. J. Dionne Jr., "Political Memo: Scouting the Vice-Presidential Field," *NYT*, June 12, 1988.

48. Dionne, "Political Memo: Scouting the Vice-Presidential Field."

49. "Last-Minute Scuffles," 82; E. J. Dionne Jr., "Dukakis Searches Capitol for a Partner," *NYT*, June 30, 1988.

50. Devine interview.

51. Bud Newman, "Democrats Approved a Pre-dawn Compromise Reached Saturday between Aides," UPI, June 25, 1988.

52. Newman, "Democrats Approved a Pre-dawn Compromise"; Devine interview.
53. Mara Liasson, "The Arc of the Democratic Race," National Public Radio, June 4, 2008, www.npr.org/templates/story/story.php?storyId=91168720.
54. "Last-Minute Scuffles," 82.
55. Michael Oreskes, "Dukakis Talks to Gephardt and Gore," *NYT*, July 6, 1988.
56. Jack White, "Bush's Most Valuable Player," *Time*, November 14, 1988.
57. E. J. Dionne Jr., "Political Memo: Set Back in Early Skirmishes, Bush Gains with New Attack," *NYT*, July 3, 1988.
58. Estrich interview.
59. E. J. Dionne Jr., "Political Memo; Dukakis Remains on Course, Dismissing Polls and Advice," *NYT*, July 11, 1988.
60. Robin Toner, "Political Memo; Dukakis and the Quest for a Running Mate: A Slow and Private Process," *NYT*, July 7, 1988.
61. "Overheard," *Newsweek*, July 25, 1988, 15.
62. "Exhaustive Search Comes Down to Late-Night Choice," *WP*, July 13, 1988.
63. "Jackson Seeks Vice Presidency; Dukakis May Choose Running Mate Today," *WP*, July 12, 1988.
64. Estrich interview.
65. Dukakis interview.
66. "Exhaustive Search Comes Down to Late-Night Choice."
67. "Last-Minute Scuffles," 82.
68. Dukakis interview.
69. "Exhaustive Search Comes Down to Late-Night Choice."
70. David Rosenbaum, "Man in the News; A Candidate Who Is More Like Bush; Lloyd Millard Bentsen Jr.," *NYT*, July 13, 1988.
71. Estrich interview.
72. Corrigan interview.
73. Devine interview.
74. Robin Toner, "Dukakis Picks Bentsen for Running Mate; Texan Adds Conservative Voice to Ticket: A Regional Balance," *NYT*, July 13, 1988.
75. Runkel, *Campaign for President*, 233.
76. Robin Toner, "Dukakis Battles Bruised Feelings in Jackson Camp," *NYT*, July 14, 1988.
77. Annetta Miller, "Conventional Wisdom Watch," *Newsweek*, July 25, 1988; Richard Stengel, "The Democrats: An Indelicate Balance," *Time*, July 25, 1988.
78. "Choice of Bentsen Called 'a Gamble'; Analysts Say Goal Is to Wrest Texas from Bush, Avoid Liberal Label," *WP*, July 13, 1988; E. J. Dionne Jr., "A Texas Gamble: Dukakis's Selection Takes a Chance on Appeal to the Right and the South," *NYT*, July 13, 1988.
79. Dionne, "Texas Gamble."
80. "Choice of Bentsen Called 'a Gamble.'"
81. Miller, "Conventional Wisdom Watch"; Stengel, "Democrats: An Indelicate Balance."
82. David E. Rosenbaum, "Unmatched Set; The Dukakis-Bentsen Ticket Has an Opinion for Anyone in the Party," *NYT*, July 17, 1988.
83. Harry Enten, "Hillary Clinton Picks Tim Kaine, Betting She Can Beat Trump Without a Splashy VP," FiveThirtyEight.com, July 22, 2016, https://fivethirtyeight.com/features/hillary-clinton-tim-kaine-vp/.
84. Toner, "Dukakis Picks Bentsen for Running Mate."
85. Toner, "Dukakis Battles Bruised Feelings in Jackson Camp."

86. Gwen Ifill, "Dukakis, Bentsen Get Cool Reception From Black Groups; Jackson Shows Anger over Selection Process," *WP*, July 14, 1988.

87. Ifill, "Dukakis, Bentsen Get Cool Reception"; Annetta Miller, "Hero's Due," *Newsweek*, July 25, 1988.

88. Toner, "Dukakis Picks Bentsen for Running Mate."

89. "MEMORANDUM FOR THE VICE PRESIDENT FROM: Bob Teeter, July 15, 1988," Subseries 10G, Box 139, Folder 1, Bush-Quayle (General Election), 1988, James A. Baker III Papers.

90. Bush, *All the Best*, 393.

91. Michael Oreskes, "Jackson Caravan Heads for Georgia," *NYT*, July 15, 1988.

92. Paul Taylor, "Jackson Tones Down Rhetoric, Speaks of Healing and Unity; Camp Set to Negotiate Platform, Fall Role," *WP*, July 16, 1988; Michael Oreskes, "Jackson's Aides Describe Goals of Partnership," *NYT*, July 16, 1988.

93. Paul Taylor, "Dukakis Arrives to Claim the Nomination; Meeting with Jackson Tops His Agenda," *WP*, July 18, 1988.

94. Runkel, *Campaign for President*, 226.

95. Bill Carter, "NBC Tightens Lead, but Networks Lose Viewers," *NYT*, April 19, 1989; Jeremy Gerard, "Networks' Changing Coverage of Conventions," *NYT*, July 16, 1988. CBS would show three hours on the final night.

96. *ABC World News Tonight*, July 18, 1988, Box 51, Democratic National Convention Coverage NBC, ABC, CBS (8 tapes) (VHS), 1988, Michael S. Dukakis Presidential Campaign Records.

97. Jacob Lamar, "The Democrats Reaching Common Ground," *Time*, August 1, 1988.

98. David S. Broder, "Dukakis-Jackson Talks Usher In Harmony as Convention Opens," *WP*, July 19, 1988.

99. Paul Taylor, "Pitching Bread-and-Butter; Convention Aims to Deliver Message of Nonideological Competence," *WP*, July 18, 1988.

100. "ABC's Convention Democratic Coverage," July 18, 1988, Box 51, Democratic National Convention Coverage NBC, ABC, CBS (8 tapes) (VHS), 1988, Michael S. Dukakis Presidential Campaign Records.

101. *ABC World News Tonight*, July 18, 1988, Box 51, Democratic National Convention Coverage NBC, ABC, CBS (8 tapes) (VHS), 1988, Michael S. Dukakis Presidential Campaign Records.

102. "ABC's Democratic Convention Coverage," July 18, 1988, Box 51, Democratic National Convention Coverage NBC, ABC, CBS (8 tapes) (VHS), 1988, Michael S. Dukakis Presidential Campaign Records.

103. "ABC's Democratic Convention Coverage," July 18, 1988.

104. David Rosenbaum, "With Palestinian Issue Put Aside, Platform Is Adopted," *NYT*, July 20, 1988.

105. *ABC World News Tonight*, July 19, 1988, Box 51, Democratic National Convention Coverage NBC, ABC, CBS (8 tapes) (VHS), 1988, Michael S. Dukakis Presidential Campaign Records.

106. Rosenbaum, "With Palestinian Issue Put Aside, Platform Is Adopted."

107. William Schmidt, "Democrats Back Palestinians at 7 State Party Conventions," *NYT*, June 23, 1988; Jack Nelson, "Dukakis Scores Platform Victory: Delegates Reject Jackson Proposal for Higher Taxes by 2–1 Margin," *Los Angeles Times*, July 20, 1988.

108. "Preliminary Speeches; Platform Speeches," C-SPAN Video, July 19, 1988, www.c-span.org/video/?3499-1/preliminary-speeches-platform-speeches; Nelson, "Dukakis Scores Platform Victory."

109. Rebecca Shimoni Stoil, "How the GOP Became a 'Pro-Israel' Party," FiveThirty-Eight.com, December 8, 2017, https://fivethirtyeight.com/features/how-the-gop-became-a-pro-israel-party/.

110. While the 2000 platform called for both parties to avoid "unilateral actions, such as a unilateral declaration of Palestinian statehood," the 2004 platform read, "We support the creation of a democratic Palestinian state dedicated to living in peace and security side by side with the Jewish State of Israel." "2000 Democratic Party Platform"; "2004 Democratic Party Platform."

111. Stoil, "How the GOP Became a 'Pro-Israel' Party."

112. "Jackson Turned Aside on 3 Platform Issues," *NYT*, July 20, 1988; *ABC World News Tonight*, July 19, 1988, Box 51, Democratic National Convention Coverage NBC, ABC, CBS (8 tapes) (VHS), 1988, Michael S. Dukakis Presidential Campaign Records.

113. "Democratic Platform Analysis," Box 6, Democratic National Convention Briefing Book—Prepared by Opposition Research, Robert Teeter Collection.

114. Estrich interview.

115. "ABC's Democratic Convention Coverage," July 19, 1988, Box 51, Democratic National Convention Coverage NBC, ABC, CBS (8 tapes) (VHS), 1988, Michael S. Dukakis Presidential Campaign Records.

116. "ABC's Democratic Convention Coverage," July 18, 1988.

117. Gwen Ifill, "Jackson Evokes Smiles, Tears; 'We Were Heard,' a Supporter Says," *WP*, July 20, 1988.

118. Edward Walsh, "Dukakis Accomplished Convention Goals," *WP*, July 23, 1988.

119. "NBC's Democratic Convention Coverage," July 19, 1988, Box 51, Democratic National Convention Coverage NBC, ABC, CBS (8 tapes) (VHS), 1988, Michael S. Dukakis Presidential Campaign Records.

120. "NBC's Democratic Convention Coverage," July 19, 1988.

121. "Jesse Jackson 1988 Convention Speech," C-SPAN-Video, July 19, 1988, www.c-span.org/video/?3504-1/jesse-jackson-1988-convention-speech.

122. Peter Boyer, "Jackson a High Point as Convention Is TV Hit," *NYT*, July 21, 1988.

123. "NBC's Democratic Convention Coverage," July 19, 1988, Box 51, Democratic National Convention Coverage NBC, ABC, CBS (8 tapes) (VHS), 1988, Michael S. Dukakis Presidential Campaign Records.

124. "ABC's Democratic Convention Coverage," July 20, 1988, Box 51, Democratic National Convention Coverage NBC, ABC, CBS (8 tapes) (VHS), 1988, Michael S. Dukakis Presidential Campaign Records.

125. Runkel, *Campaign for President*, 229–30.

126. Corrigan interview.

127. William Safire, "The Northern Strategy," *NYT*, October 13, 1988.

128. David Broder, "Voters Opt Again for a Divided Government," *WP*, November 9, 1988.

129. *ABC World News Tonight*, July 20, 1988, Box 51, Democratic National Convention Coverage NBC, ABC, CBS (8 tapes) (VHS), 1988, Michael S. Dukakis Presidential Campaign.

130. "ABC's Democratic Convention Coverage," July 20, 1988, Box 51, Democratic National Convention Coverage NBC, ABC, CBS (8 tapes) (VHS), 1988, Michael S. Dukakis Presidential Campaign Records.

131. Clinton spoke at the 1980 and 1984 Democratic conventions, but in far less prominent slots.

132. "ABC's Democratic Convention Coverage," July 20, 1988, Box 51, Democratic National Convention Coverage NBC, ABC, CBS (8 tapes) (VHS), 1988, Michael S. Dukakis Presidential Campaign Records.

133. "ABC's Democratic Convention Coverage," July 20, 1988.

134. Stephen Kurkjian and Curtis Wilkie, "Ark. Governor Winces over a Failed Nomination Speech," *Boston Globe*, July 22, 1988.

135. "ABC's Democratic Convention Coverage," July 20, 1988, Box 51, Democratic National Convention Coverage NBC, ABC, CBS (8 tapes) (VHS), 1988, Michael S. Dukakis Presidential Campaign Records.

136. Mickey Kaus with Howard Fineman, Jonathan Alter, Eleanor Clift, Margaret Garrard Warner, and Frank S. Washington, "Of 'Visibility Whips' and 'Bite Patrol,'" *Newsweek*, August 1, 1988.

137. Devine interview; Kaus et al., "Of 'Visibility Whips' and 'Bite Patrol.'"

138. Kurkjian and Wilkie, "Ark. Governor Winces"; Sam Roberts, "David Horowitz: Who Helped Make Bill Clinton a Media Darling," *NYT*, July 23, 2016.

139. Kurkjian and Wilkie, "Ark. Governor Winces."

140. "Bill Clinton: Clinton's Carson Appearance," clip from *American Experience*, season 24, episode 3, "Clinton, Part 1," aired February 19, 2012, on PBS, www.pbs.org/video/american-experience-clintons-carson-appearance/.

141. E. J. Dionne Jr., "The Democrats in Atlanta; Democrats Acclaim Dukakis and Assert Unity," *NYT*, July 21, 1988.

142. Anthony Lewis, "Abroad at Home; Waiting for Dukakis," *NYT*, July 21, 1988.

143. "ABC's Democratic Convention Coverage," July 21, 1988, Box 51, Democratic National Convention Coverage NBC, ABC, CBS (8 tapes) (VHS), 1988, Michael S. Dukakis Presidential Campaign Records.

144. "ABC's Democratic Convention Coverage," July 21, 1988.

145. "ABC's Democratic Convention Coverage," July 21, 1988.

146. Estrich interview.

147. "ABC's Democratic Convention Coverage," July 21, 1988, Box 51, Democratic National Convention Coverage NBC, ABC, CBS (8 tapes) (VHS), 1988, Michael S. Dukakis Presidential Campaign Records.

148. "ABC's Democratic Convention Coverage," July 21, 1988; "The Democrats in Atlanta; Transcript of the Speech by Dukakis Accepting the Democrats' Nomination," *NYT*, July 22, 1988; "Last-Minute Scuffles," *Newsweek*, November 21, 1988, 83.

149. "ABC's Democratic Convention Coverage," July 21, 1988, Box 51, Democratic National Convention Coverage NBC, ABC, CBS (8 tapes) (VHS), 1988, Michael S. Dukakis Presidential Campaign Records; "The Democrats in Atlanta; Transcript of the Speech by Dukakis."

150. Dukakis interview.

151. "ABC's Democratic Convention Coverage," July 21, 1988, Box 51, Democratic National Convention Coverage NBC, ABC, CBS (8 tapes) (VHS), 1988, Michael S. Dukakis Presidential Campaign Records; "The Democrats in Atlanta; Transcript of the Speech by Dukakis."

152. "ABC's Democratic Convention Coverage," July 21, 1988, Box 51, Democratic National Convention Coverage NBC, ABC, CBS (8 tapes) (VHS), 1988, Michael S. Dukakis Presidential Campaign Records.

153. "CBS's Democratic Convention Coverage," July 21, 1988, Box 51, Democratic National Convention Coverage NBC, ABC, CBS (8 tapes) (VHS), 1988, Michael S. Dukakis Presidential Campaign Records.

154. "Last-Minute Scuffles," 83.

155. "CBS's Democratic Convention Coverage," July 21, 1988, Box 51, Democratic National Convention Coverage NBC, ABC, CBS (8 tapes) (VHS), 1988, Michael S. Dukakis Presidential Campaign Records.

156. Thomas Oliphant, "Dukakis Pledge: 'A New Era' Forging of an Emotional Bond," *Boston Globe*, July 22, 1988.

157. "Special Atlanta Edition: Conventional-Wisdom Watch," *Newsweek*, August 1, 1988.

158. Corrigan interview.

159. Estrich interview.

160. Baker, *Work Hard, Study* . . . , 259.

161. Edward Walsh, "Dukakis Accomplished Convention Goals," *WP*, July 23, 1988; *16 for '16: The Contenders*, episode 3, "The Technocrats."

162. Bush, *All the Best*, 393.

163. Walsh, "Dukakis Accomplished Convention Goals."

164. Baker, *Work Hard, Study* . . . , 255.

165. "Dukakis Lead Widens, According to New Poll," *NYT*, July 26, 1988.

166. "United States Presidential Election Results," Dave Leip's Atlas of U.S. Presidential Elections, accessed July 27, 2022, https://uselectionatlas.org/RESULTS/.

167. "ABC's Democratic Convention Coverage," July 20, 1988, Box 51, Democratic National Convention Coverage NBC, ABC, CBS (8 tapes) (VHS), 1988, Michael S. Dukakis Presidential Campaign Records.

168. E. J. Dionne Jr., "Democrats, Upbeat after Atlanta, Emerge with Ambitious Strategy," *NYT*, July 24, 1988.

169. Wilkie interview.

CHAPTER 6

1. Baker, *Work Hard, Study* . . . , 249.

2. Estrich interview.

3. *16 for '16: The Contenders*, episode 3, "The Technocrats."

4. Germond and Witcover, *Whose Broad Stripes and Bright Stars?*, 359.

5. Paul Taylor, "Dukakis in a Downdraft," *Washington Post* (hereafter *WP*), August 29, 1988.

6. Estrich interview.

7. "Bill Clinton: Clinton's Carson Appearance," clip from *American Experience*, season 24, episode 3, "Clinton, Part 1," aired February 19, 2012, on PBS, www.pbs.org/video/american-experience-clintons-carson-appearance/.

8. "Johnny Carson at His Best: Introducing Clinton," *Day to Day*, broadcast January 24, 2005, on NPR, www.npr.org/templates/story/story.php?storyId=4464083.

9. "Bill Clinton on *The Johnny Carson Show* 1988," YouTube video, July 28, 1988, 12:18, www.youtube.com/watch?v=TfcKQcGg_sM.

10. The AP article appears to be reprinted on *Today*'s website as "Carson Helped Clinton Turn It Around," January 23, 2005, www.today.com/popculture/carson-helped-clinton-turn-it-around-wbna6858728; it is also quoted in Sam Roberts, "David Horowitz: Who Helped Make Bill Clinton a Media Darling," *New York Times* (hereafter *NYT*), July 23, 2016.

11. "Conventional-Wisdom Watch," *Newsweek*, August 8, 1988.

12. Baum, "Talking the Vote."

13. Estrich interview.

14. Jacob Lamar, "Reagan: Part Fixer, Part Hatchet Man," *Time*, August 15, 1988.

15. Robin Toner, "Candidates' Health Discussed," *NYT*, August 3, 1988.

16. Lamar, "Reagan: Part Fixer, Part Hatchet Man."

17. Brady, *Bad Boy*, 84.

18. Forbes, *Boogie Man*.

19. Toner, "Candidates' Health Discussed."

20. Andrew Rosenthal, "Dukakis Releases Medical Details to Stop Rumors on Mental Health," *NYT*, August 4, 1988.

21. *ABC World News Tonight*, *NBC Nightly News*, *CBS Evening News*, August 3, 1988, Vanderbilt Television Archive; Dukakis interview.

22. *CBS Evening News*, August 3, 1988, Vanderbilt Television Archive.

23. Rosenthal, "Dukakis Releases Medical Details."

24. Dukakis interview.

25. "The Ice Man Cometh," *Newsweek*, November 21, 1988, 113.

26. Bob Drogin, "How Presidential Race Was Won—and Lost: Michael S. Dukakis," *Los Angeles Times*, November 10, 1988; Corrigan interview.

27. Lucy Howard, "Conventional-Wisdom Watch," *Newsweek*, August 15, 1988.

28. Parker, *Mississippi Burning*. Many sharply criticized the film's positive portrayal of the FBI.

29. Andrew Rosenthal, "At a Fair in Mississippi, Dukakis Plays Politics in Black and White," *NYT*, August 5, 1988.

30. "Jackson Admonishes Dukakis on Civil Rights," *NYT*, August 11, 1988; "Southern Strategy," *NYT*, August 11, 1988.

31. Baker, *Work Hard, Study . . .*, 239.

32. Bob Woodward, "The Origin of the Tax Pledge," *WP*, October 4, 1992.

33. Baker, *Work Hard, Study . . .*, 244.

34. James A. Baker III interview, Presidential Oral Histories.

35. Meacham, *Destiny and Power*, 326.

36. Baker, *Work Hard, Study . . .*, 248.

37. Fuller interview with author.

38. Craig Fuller interview, Presidential Oral Histories; Fuller interview with author.

39. Larry Martz with Eleanor Clift, Howard Fineman, Ann McDaniel, Mark Starr, and Margaret Garrard Warner, "A Shaky Start," *Newsweek*, August 29, 1988.

40. Gerald Boyd, "The Republicans in New Orleans: Seeing Risks in All the Candidates, Bush Chose One with 'Star' Quality," *NYT*, August 18, 1988; "Squall in New Orleans," *Newsweek*, November 21, 1988, 103.

41. "Squall in New Orleans," 103.

42. Baker, *Work Hard, Study . . .*, 246.

43. Meacham, *Destiny and Power*, 337.

44. J. Danforth Quayle interview, Presidential Oral Histories.

45. Bob Woodward and David Broder, "Dan Quayle: The Premeditated Surprise," *WP*, January 5, 1992.

46. J. Danforth Quayle interview, Presidential Oral Histories.

47. Quayle, *Standing Firm*, 26.

48. Baker, *Work Hard, Study . . .*, 248.

49. Boyd, "The Republicans in New Orleans."

50. Gerald Boyd, "Bush Prunes Running-Mate List; Doles, Quayle, and 3 Others Stay," *NYT*, August 13, 1988.

51. Fuller interview with author.

52. James A. Baker III interview, Presidential Oral Histories.

53. Quayle, *Standing Firm*, 23-24.

54. "Squall in New Orleans," 106.

55. "Squall in New Orleans," 103-4.

56. "Squall in New Orleans," 106.

57. "Squall in New Orleans," 103.

58. Meacham, *Destiny and Power*, 337.

59. Paul Taylor and David Broder, "Reagan Hits Democrats as Liberals; Bush, in Washington, Meets with Advisers on Running Mate," *WP*, August 15, 1988.

60. Taylor and Broder, "Reagan Hits Democrats as Liberals."

61. "Letter from J. C. Willke, M.D. to Vice President of the United States," June 7, 1988, Box 140, Folder 9, Office of VP-General, 1988, James A. Baker III Papers.

62. "ABC's Convention Coverage," August 15, 1988, Box 51, Republican National Convention NBC, CBS, ABC, C-SPAN (13 tapes) (VHS), 1988, Michael S. Dukakis Presidential Campaign Records.

63. Sigmund Rogich interview, Presidential Oral Histories.

64. *ABC World News Tonight*, August 15, 1988, Box 51, Republican National Convention NBC, CBS, ABC, C-SPAN (13 tapes) (VHS), 1988, Michael S. Dukakis Presidential Campaign Records.

65. "ABC's Convention Coverage," August 15, 1988, Box 51, Republican National Convention NBC, CBS, ABC, C-SPAN (13 tapes) (VHS), 1988, Michael S. Dukakis Presidential Campaign Records.

66. "*Line of the Day*, Monday August 15, 1988," Box 7, 1988 Presidential Campaign—George Bush Line of the Day & Talking Points for Surrogates—New Orleans 1988 (Bolton), Robert Teeter Collection.

67. "ABC's Convention Coverage," August 15, 1988, Box 51, Republican National Convention NBC, CBS, ABC, C-SPAN (13 tapes) (VHS), 1988, Michael S. Dukakis Presidential Campaign Records.

68. "Squall in New Orleans," 106.

69. Quayle, *Standing Firm*, 25.

70. David Hoffman, "Bush Picks Quayle, 'Man of the Future,' as Running Mate; Senator Selected in Effort to Woo Younger Voters," *WP*, August 17, 1988.

71. Craig Fuller interview, Presidential Oral Histories.

72. Craig Fuller interview, Presidential Oral Histories; quote from Fuller interview with author; J. Danforth Quayle interview, Presidential Oral Histories.

73. Craig Fuller interview, Presidential Oral Histories.

74. "Squall in New Orleans," 102.

75. Walter Shapiro, "The Republicans: The Quayle Quagmire," *Time*, August 29, 1988.

76. Quayle, *Standing Firm*, 5-6.

77. "Squall in New Orleans," 108.

78. Fuller interview with author; "Squall in New Orleans," 108.

79. "George H. W. Bush Announces Dan Quayle as His Running Mate (1988)," YouTube Video, August 17, 1988, 18:41, www.youtube.com/watch?v=Gn00a9eDrqs&t=982s.

80. Baker, *Work Hard, Study . . .*, 251; Fuller interview with author.

81. James P. Pinkerton interview, Presidential Oral Histories.

82. Mosbacher, *Going to Windward*, 189; Thomas Edsall, "Soft Money Competition," *WP*, August 16, 1988.

83. Edsall, "Soft Money Competition."

84. Richard L. Berke, "Big Money's Election-Year Comeback," *NYT*, August 7, 1988.

85. Robin Toner, "Republicans Finish Writing a Platform," *NYT*, August 13, 1988.

86. Sununu, *Quiet Man*, 35-36.

87. "ABC's Convention Coverage," August 16, 1988, Box 51, Republican National Convention NBC, CBS, ABC, C-SPAN (13 tapes) (VHS), 1988, Michael S. Dukakis Presidential Campaign Records.

88. Reagan's Strategic Defense Initiative, popularly known as "Star Wars," for the movie.

89. "ABC's Convention Coverage," August 16, 1988, Box 51, Republican National Convention NBC, CBS, ABC, C-SPAN (13 tapes) (VHS), 1988, Michael S. Dukakis Presidential

Campaign Records. Peter Jennings referred to Kirkpatrick's speech as the first of two keynotes. Some news accounts only refer to Kean's as a keynote.

90. For more on the fall of the moderates, see Kabaservice, *Rule and Ruin*.

91. "ABC's Convention Coverage," August 16, 1988, Box 51, Republican National Convention NBC, CBS, ABC, C-SPAN (13 tapes) (VHS), 1988, Michael S. Dukakis Presidential Campaign Records.

92. "ABC's Convention Coverage," August 16, 1988.

93. "ABC's Convention Coverage," August 16, 1988.

94. "ABC's Convention Coverage," August 16, 1988.

95. Susan Rasky, "The Republicans in New Orleans: Man in the News; Baby Boomer with Right Credentials: James Danforth Quayle," *NYT*, August 17, 1988.

96. Helen Dewar and David S. Broder, "A Reagan Conservative; Hoosier Scrappy, Rich, Telegenic," *WP*, August 17, 1988.

97. Dewar and Broder, "Reagan Conservative; Hoosier Scrappy, Rich, Telegenic."

98. Lou Cannon, "Conservatives Laud Choice; GOP Strategists Skeptical," *WP*, August 17, 1988.

99. "George Bush's Turn Right," *NYT*, August 17, 1988.

100. Quayle, *Standing Firm*, 29.

101. David Hoffman, "Bush Picks Quayle, 'Man of the Future,' as Running Mate; Senator Selected in Effort to Woo Younger Voters," *WP*, August 17, 1988.

102. Runkel, *Campaign for President*, 215.

103. Estrich interview.

104. "Quayle Talking Points, 8/16/88," Box 7, Folder 446, Michael S. Dukakis Presidential Campaign Records.

105. Dukakis interview.

106. "The Republicans in New Orleans; Transcript of Debut News Conference by Bush-Quayle Ticket," *NYT*, August 18, 1988; "V.P. Announcement News Conference," C-SPAN Video, August 17, 1988, www.c-span.org/video/?3957-1/vp-announcement-news-conference.

107. "Republicans in New Orleans; Transcript of Debut News Conference"; "V.P. Announcement News Conference."

108. Baker, *Work Hard, Study . . .* , 252.

109. Quayle, *Standing Firm*, 30–31.

110. "ABC's Convention Coverage," August 17, 1988, Box 51, Republican National Convention NBC, CBS, ABC, C-SPAN (13 tapes) (VHS), 1988, Michael S. Dukakis Presidential Campaign Records.

111. "Republican Convention, August 17, 1988," YouTube video, August 17, 1988, 3:19:16, www.youtube.com/watch?v=kAWperGEUPQ&t=5s.

112. Quayle, *Standing Firm*, 34.

113. J. Danforth Quayle interview, Presidential Oral Histories.

114. Michael Kruse, "Roger Stone's Last Dirty Trick," PoliticoMagazine, January 25, 2019, www.politico.com/magazine/story/2019/01/25/roger-stone-last-dirty-trick-224217/.

115. "Donald Trump at the 1988 Republican Convention," YouTube video, August 18, 1988, 7:54, www.youtube.com/watch?v=acpmInqcuH4.

116. "Donald Trump at the 1988 Republican Convention."

117. "ABC's Convention Coverage," August 17, 1988, Box 51, Republican National Convention NBC, CBS, ABC, C-SPAN (13 tapes) (VHS), 1988, Michael S. Dukakis Presidential Campaign Records; E. J. Dionne Jr., "The Republicans in New Orleans: Republicans Acclaim Bush as Their New Leader," *NYT*, August 18, 1988; "Roll Call of States Votes and Closing," C-Span Video, www.c-span.org/video/?3836-1/roll-call-state-votes-closing.

118. Nicholas Kristoff, "The 2000 Campaign: The 1988 Campaign; For Bush, Thrill Was in Father's Chase," *NYT*, August 29, 2000.

119. Dionne, "Republicans in New Orleans: Republicans Acclaim Bush," *NYT*, August 18, 1988.

120. "Squall in New Orleans," 108.

121. Black interview.

122. "Squall in New Orleans," 108.

123. Gerald Boyd, "Defending Quayle, Bush Says His National Guard Service Will Cease to Be an Issue," *NYT*, August 21, 1988.

124. Darman, *Who's in Control?*, 190.

125. Runkel, *Campaign for President*, 209.

126. Black interview; Runkel, *Campaign for President*, 209.

127. David S. Broder and Gwen Ifill, "Bush Wins; Victory Shadowed by Questions about Running Mate's Past," *WP*, August 18, 1988.

128. Steven V. Roberts, "The Republicans in New Orleans; In Congress, Neither Loafer nor Leader," *NYT*, August 18, 1988.

129. "Note from Bob Kimmitt to James Baker," Notes and Assorted Papers, Box 140, Folder 8, 1988, James A. Baker III Papers.

130. J. Danforth Quayle interview, Presidential Oral Histories.

131. Gerald M. Boyd, "Bush's Gamble: After a Long March to Nomination, Bush Sprints to Establish Identity," *NYT*, August 21, 1988.

132. Howard Fineman, "The Wordsmith behind the Speech," *Newsweek*, August 22, 1988.

133. Bob Woodward, "The Origin of the Tax Pledge," *WP*, October 4, 1992.

134. Noonan, *What I Saw at the Revolution*, 307.

135. Woodward, "Origin of the Tax Pledge."

136. Darman, *Who's in Control?*, 192.

137. Woodward, "Origin of the Tax Pledge."

138. Woodward, "Origin of the Tax Pledge."

139. "ABC's Convention Coverage," August 18, 1988, Box 51, Republican National Convention NBC, CBS, ABC, C-SPAN (13 tapes) (VHS), 1988, Michael S. Dukakis Presidential Campaign Records.

140. "ABC's Convention Coverage," August 18, 1988.

141. Sigmund Rogich interview, Presidential Oral Histories.

142. "ABC's Convention Coverage," August 18, 1988, Box 51, Republican National Convention NBC, CBS, ABC, C-SPAN (13 tapes) (VHS), 1988, Michael S. Dukakis Presidential Campaign Records.

143. "ABC's Convention Coverage," August 18, 1988.

144. "ABC's Convention Coverage," August 18, 1988.

145. "ABC's Convention Coverage," August 18, 1988.

146. "ABC's Convention Coverage," August 18, 1988.

147. "ABC's Convention Coverage," August 18, 1988.

148. Noonan, *What I Saw at the Revolution*, 312.

149. "ABC's Convention Coverage," August 18, 1988, Box 51, Republican National Convention NBC, CBS, ABC, C-SPAN (13 tapes) (VHS), 1988, Michael S. Dukakis Presidential Campaign Records.

150. "ABC's Convention Coverage," August 18, 1988.

151. "Convention Speech Evaluation: Executive Summary," p. 6, Box 6, 1988 Presidential Campaign: Convention Speech—Evaluation/Summary—August 1988 [Prepared for George Bush for President], Robert Teeter Collection.

152. "ABC's Convention Coverage," August 18, 1988, Box 51, Republican National Convention NBC, CBS, ABC, C-SPAN (13 tapes) (VHS), 1988, Michael S. Dukakis Presidential Campaign Records.

153. Woodward, "Origin of the Tax Pledge."

154. "ABC's Convention Coverage," August 18, 1988, Box 51, Republican National Convention NBC, CBS, ABC, C-SPAN (13 tapes) (VHS), 1988, Michael S. Dukakis Presidential Campaign Records.

155. The first mention of this quote appears to be William Safire, "Bush's Gamble," *NYT*, October 18, 1992. A month later, Safire notes in a column that he "recently reported" the remark; Safire, "On Language: Growing Down Grows Up," *NYT*, November 15, 1992.

156. "ABC's Convention Coverage," August 18, 1988, Box 51, Republican National Convention NBC, CBS, ABC, C-SPAN (13 tapes) (VHS), 1988, Michael S. Dukakis Presidential Campaign Records.

157. "Memo from Senator Pete Domenici to Secretary James Baker, July 26, 1988," Box 141, Folder 7, 1988 April–July, James A. Baker Papers. This move might have been inspired by Senator Domenici, who sent Baker a memo in late July urging Bush or Reagan to ask "the delegates to rise (choreographed in advance, of course) and to recite along with him the Pledge of Allegiance." Domenici elaborated on this idea as follows: "Then one of the two should ask, 'Isn't it [true] that as Governor, Michael Dukakis vetoed a bill that would have allowed school children in Massachusetts to recite that pledge to our nation at the beginning of the school day?' Risky, perhaps, but we'll never get a better chance to get this issue in people's minds."

158. "ABC's Convention Coverage," August 18, 1988, Box 51, Republican National Convention NBC, CBS, ABC, C-SPAN (13 tapes) (VHS), 1988, Michael S. Dukakis Presidential Campaign Records.

159. James Reston, "Bush: A Hit, An Error," *NYT*, August 22, 1988.

160. Bush, *All the Best*, 395.

161. Parmet, *George Bush*, 349.

162. "Book: Bush Wrote 'I Blew It' After Picking Quayle," *Los Angeles Times*, October 5, 1997.

163. James A. Baker III interview, Presidential Oral Histories.

164. Bush, *All the Best*, 395.

165. Gallup and Gallup, "Republican Convention Boosts Bush's Candidacy."

166. J. Danforth Quayle interview, Presidential Oral Histories.

167. James A. Baker III interview, Presidential Oral Histories.

168. Baker, *Work Hard, Study...*, 248.

169. Gallup and Gallup, "Doubts about Bush's Character Allayed."

170. Lydia Saad, "Gallup Vault: What a Convention Bounce Looks Like," Gallup.com, July 20, 2016, http://news.gallup.com/vault/193826/gallup-vault-convention-bounce-looks.aspx.

171. Gallup and Gallup, "Doubts about Bush's Character Allayed."

172. Gallup and Gallup, "Doubts about Bush's Character Allayed"; "Gallup Presidential Election Trial-Heat Trends, 1936–2008," Gallup.com, accessed July 27, 2022, https://news.gallup.com/poll/110548/gallup-presidential-election-trial-heat-trends.aspx. According to Gallup polls, Bush led the rest of the way. An outlier poll here or there might have shown Dukakis with a lead at some point. For example, a Roper poll for Maryland Public Television showed the governor up in mid-September, but it was the only poll at the time that did. "Other Surveys Show Bush with an Edge. Dukakis Leads One," *NYT*, September 14, 1988.

CHAPTER 7

1. Paul Taylor, "Dukakis Returns Fire on Pledge of Allegiance," *Washington Post* (hereafter *WP*), August 24, 1988.
2. Steven V. Roberts, "Bush Intensifies Debate on Pledge, Asking Why It So Upsets Dukakis," *New York Times* (hereafter *NYT*), August 25, 1988.
3. Bill Peterson, "Bush Fans Rhetorical Six-Gun in Texas," *WP*, August 26, 1988.
4. "To: Craig Fuller, Charlie Greenleaf, Tom Collamore, Steve Hart, From: David Q. Bates, Subject: Management Meeting at Campaign," August 26, 1988, Box 14, [VP] [Campaign 88] ["Line of the Day"] [2], Stephen Hart Files.
5. "To: John, Fr: Elena, Dt: August 22, 1988, Re: Legal Background to the Pledge Veto," "Legal Background to the Pledge Veto," "To: Files, Fr: Elena, Dt: August 25, 1988, Re: SJC Advisory Opinions," Box 6, Folder 353, Michael S. Dukakis Presidential Campaign Records.
6. "From: Laurence Tribe, To: The Honorable Michael Dukakis, Paul Brountas, Susan Estrich, Jack Corrigan, Kirk O'Donnell, Chris Edley, John Podesta, Elena Kagan, Re: The Pledge of Allegiance," August 31, 1988, Box 6, Folder 353, Michael S. Dukakis Presidential Campaign Records.
7. *Meet the Press* transcript, August 28, 1988, Box 93-138/532, Transcript, "Meet the Press," Bentsen, August 28, 1988, Lloyd M. Bentsen Jr. Papers.
8. Larry Martz with Eleanor Clift, Mark Starr, and Margaret Garrard Warner, "Dukakis on the Defense," *Newsweek*, September 5, 1988.
9. Dukakis interview.
10. "Campaign '88: Self-Inflicted Injury: Dukakis Campaign Was Marred by a Series of Lost Opportunities—Ignoring Pleas to Get Tough, He Delayed Key Speeches and, in Disarray Lost," *Wall Street Journal*, November 8, 1988.
11. Corrigan interview.
12. "Abusing the Pledge of Allegiance," *NYT*, August 26, 1988.
13. "Patriotism and Democracy," *Wall Street Journal*, August 26, 1988.
14. "To: Craig Fuller, Charlie Greenleaf, Tom Collamore, Steve Hart, From: David Q. Bates, Subject: Management Meeting at Campaign," August 26, 1988, Box 14, [VP] [Campaign 88] ["Line of the Day"] [2], Stephen Hart Files.
15. Runkel, *Campaign for President*, 254.
16. "Story about Mrs. Dukakis Is Denied by the Campaign," *NYT*, August 26, 1988; Runkel, *Campaign for President*, 254; Martz with Eleanor Clift, Mark Starr, and Margaret Garrard Warner, "Dukakis on the Defense."
17. Runkel, *Campaign for President*, 60.
18. Corrigan interview.
19. "To: Craig Fuller, Charlie Greenleaf, Tom Collamore, Steve Hart, From: David Q. Bates, Subject: Management Meeting at Campaign," August 26, 1988, Box 14, [VP] [Campaign 88] ["Line of the Day"] [2], Stephen Hart Files.
20. "The Real Facts about the Boston Harbor," Box 4, Folder 225, Michael S. Dukakis Presidential Campaign Records.
21. Larry Tye, "EPA Official Says Dukakis to Blame for 6-Year Delay," *Boston Globe*, August 11, 1988. "Interviews with those involved suggest the Dukakis Administration at first did move slowly in cleaning the harbor, perhaps more slowly than other cities," wrote Larry Tye in the *Boston Globe*. "But observers also say the EPA shares the blame for delays, and the governor over the last several years has moved aggressively to end the dumping that has made Boston Harbor among the nation's filthiest."
22. Robin Toner, "Bush, in Enemy Waters, Says Rival Hindered Cleanup of Boston Harbor," *NYT*, September 2, 1988.
23. Dukakis interview.

24. "The Ice Man Cometh," *Newsweek*, November 21, 1988, 113-14; Bob Drogin, "How Presidential Race Was Won—and Lost: Michael S. Dukakis," *Los Angeles Times*, November 10, 1988.

25. Marvin Kalb writes that "60 to 65 percent" of people got their news from those broadcasts. Preface to Adatto, *Sound Bite Democracy*, 2; Mendelberg, *Race Card*, 151.

26. Bennett interview.

27. Baker, *Work Hard, Study . . .* , 266.

28. Germond and Witcover, *Whose Broad Stripes and Bright Stars?*, 404.

29. Baker, *Work Hard, Study . . .* , 268.

30. Jonathan Alter, "Getting Down and Dirty," *Newsweek*, September 12, 1988.

31. Baughman, *Republic of Mass Culture*, 211-25; O'Mara, *Pivotal Tuesdays*, 177-202; "TV's Influence on Race and Politics in the 1990s," C-SPAN Video, January 5, 2019, www.c-span.org/video/?456623-2/tvs-influence-race-politics-1990s. Kathryn Brownell's paper talks of how 1992 was a key turning point for cable.

32. "It [1988] was the last campaign where the three big networks and their local affiliates were the main tactic for communicating," Black reflected. "By the time we were running in '92, you had cables and the sitting president of the United States had to go on *Larry King* [*Live* on CNN]. Hell, you should have seen us persuade him of that! . . . After '88 there was more diffusion of media." Black interview.

33. Zev Chaffets, "Late-Period Limbaugh," *NYT*, July 6, 2008. For more on the history of talk radio, see Hemmer, *Messengers of the Right*, and Rosenwald, *Talk Radio's America*.

34. Bill Peterson, "Bush Mines for Votes in California," *WP*, September 15, 1988.

35. "The Harbor," The Living Room Candidate, accessed July 25, 2022, http://www.livingroomcandidate.org/commercials/1988/harbor#4117.

36. Richard Cohen, "Boston Harbor Is Not Radioactive," *WP*, November 18, 1988; Kathleen Hall Jamieson, "Our Appalling Politics," *WP*, October 30, 1988.

37. R. W. Apple, "State by State; Old Pros Appraise the '88 Campaign," *NYT*, November 6, 1988.

38. For more, see Turner and Isenberg, *Republican Reversal*.

39. "Iceman Cometh," 114; Robin Toner, "Dukakis Rehires Aide Who Left after Role in Ending Biden Drive," *NYT*, September 3, 1988.

40. "To: Craig Fuller, Charlie Greenleaf, Tom Collamore, Steve Hart, From: David Q. Bates, Subject: Management Meeting at Campaign," September 6, 1988, Box 14, [VP] [Campaign 88] ["Line of the Day"] [2], Stephen Hart Files.

41. E. J. Dionne Jr., "Dukakis Campaign Fights Slump with New Look and Sharper Edge," *NYT*, September 9, 1988.

42. "Iceman Cometh," 115.

43. E. J. Dionne, Jr., "Despite Squeeze on the Middle Class, a Suburb's Young Voters Like Bush," *NYT*, September 17, 1988.

44. Dionne, "Despite Squeeze on the Middle Class."

45. Dionne, "Despite Squeeze on the Middle Class."

46. Dionne, "Dukakis Campaign Fights Slump."

47. Shrum interview.

48. Estrich interview.

49. Corrigan interview.

50. Maralee Schwartz and Lloyd Grove, "TV Ads to Depict Gov. Dukakis as Coddling Criminals," *WP*, September 4, 1988. The article appeared on a Sunday and said the ad would start running on Tuesday.

51. Schwartz and Grove, "TV Ads to Depict Gov. Dukakis."

52. Schwartzapfel and Keller, "Willie Horton Revisited."

53. Martin Schram, "The Making of Willie Horton," *New Republic*, May 28, 1990, 17–18.

54. Stephen Engelberg, "Bush, His Disavowed Backers and a Very Potent Attack Ad," *NYT*, November 3, 1988; "Weekend Passes," The Living Room Candidate, accessed July 25, 2022, http://www.livingroomcandidate.org/commercials/1988/filter/ind.

55. Jane Mayer, "Attack Dog," *New Yorker*, February 5, 2012.

56. John Sides, "It's Time to Stop the Endless Hype of the 'Willie Horton' Ad," *WP*, January 6, 2016; Schram, "Making of Willie Horton," 18.

57. Adatto, *Sound Bite Democracy*, 30; Mendelberg, *Race Card*, 151; *CBS Evening News*, October 21, 1988, *ABC World News Tonight*, October 24, 1988, and *NBC Nightly News*, October 24, 1988, all at Vanderbilt Television Archive.

58. Adatto, *Sound Bite Democracy*, 8.

59. Sides, "It's Time to Stop." The first part of analysis is from Sides, and the second is my own.

60. Engelberg, "Bush, His Disavowed Backers."

61. Charlie Babcock, "FEC Split over Horton Ad Investigation," *WP*, January 16, 1992.

62. "Deposition of Roger E. Ailes," 28, 45.

63. "General Counsel's Report," 23.

64. Babcock, "FEC Split over Horton Ad Investigation."

65. Baker, *Work Hard, Study . . .* , 270–71. In interviews for a biography by Peter Baker and Susan Glasser, Jim Baker seemed to briefly suggest he regretted the use of Horton in the campaign, but he later backed off this idea. Baker and Glasser, *Man Who Ran Washington*, 582.

66. Fuller interview.

67. Estrich interview.

68. "1972 Nixon vs. McGovern," The Living Room Candidate, accessed July 25, 2022, http://www.livingroomcandidate.org/commercials/1972.

69. "Fr: Bob Boorstin, Mark Gearan, et al., To: State Directors, State Press Secretaries, Re: Talking Points for Week of 9/12," Box 4, Folder 25, Michael S. Dukakis Presidential Campaign Records.

70. Andrew Rosenthal, "Dukakis Stresses Defense, Ridicules Bush and Quayle," *NYT*, September 13, 1988.

71. Matt Bennett, "Sterling Heights, MI, 9/12, *Tank Event*," Matt Bennett Campaign Journal, November 1988, copy given to author.

72. Shobocinski and Wills, *Dukakis and the Tank*; Josh King, "Dukakis and the Tank," PoliticoMagazine, November 17, 2013, www.politico.com/magazine/story/2013/11/dukakis-and-the-tank-099119/.

73. King, "Dukakis and the Tank."

74. Bennett interview.

75. King, "Dukakis and the Tank."

76. Bennett, "Sterling Heights, MI, 9/12."

77. King, "Dukakis and the Tank."

78. King, "Dukakis and the Tank."

79. King, "Dukakis and the Tank"; Grace, *Choose Me*, 100.

80. King, "Dukakis and the Tank."

81. Bennett interview.

82. Reid, *Backfire*.

83. Bennett, "Sterling Heights, MI, 9/12."

84. King, "Dukakis and the Tank."

85. Bennett, "Sterling Heights, MI, 9/12."

86. *NBC Nightly News, CBS Evening News*, September 13, 1988, Vanderbilt Television Archive.

87. King, "Dukakis and the Tank."

88. Baker, *Work Hard, Study. . . .*, 269.

89. "To: Craig Fuller, Charlie Greenleaf, Tom Collamore, Steve Hart, From: David Q. Bates, Subject: Management Meeting at Campaign," September 16, 1988, Box 14, [VP] [Campaign 88] ["Line of the Day"] [2], Stephen Hart Files.

90. "THE MCLAUGHLIN GROUP, TAPED FRIDAY, SEPTEMBER 16, 1988, AIRED WEEKEND OF SEPTEMBER 17–18, 1988 (CAPS IN DOCUMENT)," Box 138, Folder 2, James A. Baker III Papers.

91. Robin Toner, "Dukakis Seeks to Recover His Edge," *NYT*, September 19, 1988.

92. "Fr: Estrich, To: Dukakis/Bentsen Co-Chairs, Members of Congress, Surrogates, Re: Bush's Credibility, Dt: September 16, 1988," Box 3, Folder 181, Michael S. Dukakis Presidential Campaign Records.

93. Toner, "Dukakis Seeks to Recover His Edge."

94. "Memorandum to the Vice President," September 15, 1988, Box 140, Folder 8, James A. Baker III Papers.

95. "At First for Dukakis and Now Favoring Bush, Some Voters Tell Why," *NYT*, September 20, 1988; E. J. Dionne Jr., "Crucial Bloc for Bush; Thus Far He Has Succeeded in Stemming Defections among President's Supporters," *NYT*, September 20, 1988; Paul Taylor, "Testing the Electoral College 'Lock,'" *WP*, September 18, 1988.

96. Diego Ribadaneira, "Hub Police Union Leadership Votes to Endorse Bush," *Boston Globe*, September 22, 1988.

97. Robin Toner, "As Bush Collects a Political Windfall, Dukakis Counterpunches in Boston," *NYT*, September 23, 1988; Christine Chinaland and Thomas Oliphant, "Presidential Rivals Wage Battle in Blue in Boston," *Boston Globe*, September 23, 1988.

98. Toner, "As Bush Collects a Political Windfall."

99. "Untitled Dukakis/Bentsen Press Release," Box 4, Folder 241, Michael S. Dukakis Presidential Campaign Records.

100. "Mike Dukakis, Fighting Crime, 5/18," Box 4, Folder 240; "Michael Dukakis on the Issues: A Tough, Effective Crime Fighter," Box 4, Folder 238, Michael S. Dukakis Presidential Campaign Records.

101. "To: Craig Fuller, Charlie Greenleaf, Tom Collamore, Steve Hart, From: David Q. Bates, Subject: Management Meeting at Campaign," September 23, 1988, Box 14, [VP] [Campaign 88] ["Line of the Day"] [2], Stephen Hart Files.

102. *NBC Nightly News*, September 22, 1988, Vanderbilt Television Archive.

103. Michael Oreskes, "Dukakis Camp Warned on Debates' Deadline," *NYT*, September 2, 1988; Michael Oreskes, "Dukakis Agrees to Only Two Debates with Bush," *NYT*, September 7, 1988.

104. Darman, *Who's in Control?*, 194; Baker, *Work Hard, Study . . .*, 272.

105. "To: All Concerned, From: Bob Goodwin, Date: September 21, 1988, Subject: Debate Rehearsal—The Vice President's Residence," Box 140, Folder 1, James A. Baker III Papers.

106. "Bush/Quayle Debate Book," Box 6, 1988 Presidential Campaign, Bush/Quayle Debate Book—September 17, 1988—Copy: Robert Teeter [1], Robert Teeter Collection.

107. "TO: Vice President Bush, FROM: The Debate Team, DATE: September 20, 1988, RE: Strategy for September 25, 1988 Debate," Box 140, Folder 1, James A. Baker III Papers.

108. "Memorandum, 9/18," Box 24, Folder 1278, Michael S. Dukakis Presidential Campaign Records.

109. "Lectern to Lectern," *Newsweek*, November 21, 1988, 123.

110. Estrich interview.

111. E. J. Dionne Jr., "A Third of Voters Remain Uncertain on Eve of Debate," *NYT*, September 25, 1988.

112. "Presidential Candidates Debate," September 25, 1988, C-SPAN Video, www.c-span.org/video/?4309-1/presidential-candidates-debate.

113. "Presidential Candidates Debate," September 25, 1988.

114. E. J. Dionne Jr., "Bush and Dukakis, with Anger, Debate Leadership and Issues from Abortion to Iran Contra," *NYT*, September 26, 1988.

115. "Presidential Candidates Debate," September 25, 1988.

116. "Presidential Candidates Debate," September 25, 1988.

117. "Presidential Debate Evaluation, Executive Summary," September 1988, Box 7, First Presidential Debate—9/25/88 [Prepared for Bush-Quayle '88], Robert Teeter Collection.

118. "Presidential Candidates Debate," September 25, 1988.

119. Dukakis interview; *Debating Our Destiny Documentary—Part 1*.

120. "Presidential Candidates Debate," September 25, 1988.

121. "Presidential Candidates Debate," September 25, 1988.

122. "Presidential Candidates Debate," September 25, 1988.

123. "Presidential Candidates Debate," September 25, 1988.

124. "ABC Post-Debate Comment," September 25, 1988, Box 24, Folder 1253, Michael S. Dukakis Presidential Campaign Records.

125. "Bush-Dukakis Debate (Analysis)," NBC Special for Sunday, September 25, 1988; "Bush-Dukakis Debate (Analysis)," CBS Special for Sunday, September 25, 1988, Vanderbilt Television Archive.

126. David Broder, "Dukakis Keeps His Hopes Alive," *WP*, September 26, 1988.

127. E. J. Dionne Jr., "Round One Undecisive," *NYT*, September 26, 1988.

128. R. W. Apple, "After the Debate; Dukakis Makes Headway in a Detroit Suburb, but Changes Few Minds," *NYT*, September 27, 1988.

129. "Small Lead for Bush," *NYT*, September 30, 1988.

130. Phillip Shenon, "A.C.L.U. Reports Rise in Membership in Wake of Bush's Attacks," *NYT*, September 27, 1988.

131. Gerald M. Boyd, "Bush Takes New Tack on the A.C.L.U.," *NYT*, September 30, 1988.

132. Margaret Carlson, "Spotlight on the A.C.L.U.," *Time*, October 10, 1988.

133. "Michael Dukakis and the ACLU," Box 4, Folder 215, Michael S. Dukakis Presidential Campaign Records.

134. Dukakis interview; Corrigan interview.

135. "Tony Corrado to Tad Devine, Vice Presidential Debate: Initial Planning and Logistics, September 21, 1988," Box 329-89-13/110, Debate Prep. 9/26/88, Lloyd M. Bentsen Jr. Papers.

136. Black interview.

137. J. Danforth Quayle interview, Presidential Oral Histories; Quayle, *Standing Firm*, 28, 52.

138. David Hoffman, "Bush Camp Trying to Keep Quayle out of the Limelight," *WP*, September 24, 1988; Fuller interview.

139. Richard Stengel, "Ninety Long Minutes in Omaha," *Time*, October 17, 1988; *Debating Our Destiny Documentary—Part 1*.

140. Jonathan Alter and Eleanor Clift, "The Veep Showdown," *Newsweek*, October 10, 1988.

141. Noah Bierman, "'Senator you're no Jack Kennedy' Almost Didn't Happen. How It Became the Biggest VP Debate Moment in History," *Los Angeles Times*, October 4, 2016; Devine interview.

142. E. J. Dionne Jr., "High Hopes Ride on Quayle Debate Performance," *NYT*, October 3, 1988.

143. Robert Barnes and R. H. Melton, "In Vice Presidential Debate, the Main Question May Be Quayle," *WP*, October 5, 1988.

144. Barnes and Melton, "In Vice Presidential Debate."

145. "Vice Presidential Debate Talking Points," Box 24, Folder 1254, Michael S. Dukakis Presidential Campaign Records.

146. "1988 Vice Presidential Debate—Dan Quayle and Lloyd Bentsen," YouTube Video, October 5, 1988, 1:31:21, www.youtube.com/watch?v=99-v2Farbjs.

147. "1988 Vice Presidential Debate—Dan Quayle and Lloyd Bentsen"; *Debating Our Destiny Documentary—Part 1*.

148. "Up to this point, the summer of 1988, global warming had generally been below the threshold of public attention," wrote Spencer Weart, adding later: "The break came in the summer of 1988." Weart, *Discovery of Global Warming*, 154-56.

149. Philip Shabecoff, "Global Warming Has Begun, Expert Tells Senate," *NYT*, June 24, 1988.

150. "1988 Vice Presidential Debate—Dan Quayle and Lloyd Bentsen."

151. "1988 Vice Presidential Debate—Dan Quayle and Lloyd Bentsen."

152. "1988 Vice Presidential Debate—Dan Quayle and Lloyd Bentsen."

153. Quayle, *Standing Firm*, 63.

154. "1988 Vice Presidential Debate—Dan Quayle and Lloyd Bentsen"; *Debating Our Destiny Documentary—Part 1*.

155. "Van McMurtry to Ray Bonilla, September 30, 1988, Proposed One-Liners for the Debate," Box 93-138/33A, Debate Preparation 1988, Lloyd M. Bentsen Jr. Papers.

156. "LMB Basic Answers," October 3, 1988, Box 93-138/33A, Debate Preparation 1988, Lloyd M. Bentsen Jr. Papers. This document appears to have been faxed. October 3 is the date on most pages, but the JFK page has no date or time, for whatever reason.

157. Richard Stengel, "Ninety Long Minutes in Omaha," *Time*, October 17, 1988.

158. Shrum, *No Excuses*, 194.

159. Shrum interview.

160. Estrich interview.

161. "NBC Special for Wednesday, October 5, 1988," #897225, Vanderbilt Television Archive.

162. E. J. Dionne Jr., "The Debates: Revival for Democrats," *NYT*, October 7, 1988.

163. J. Danforth Quayle interview, Presidential Oral Histories.

164. Charles Krauthammer, "Quayle Routed," *WP*, October 7, 1988.

165. George Will, "'Never Give a Child a Sword,'" *WP*, October 7, 1988.

166. "Memorandum from Julie Weeks to Robert Teeter, Fred Steener, Vince Breglio, Vice Presidential Debate Perception Test," October 7, 1988, Box 9, Vice Presidential Debate—October, 1988 [Prepared for George Bush for President], Robert Teeter Collection.

167. "To: Craig Fuller, Charlie Greenleaf, Tom Collamore, Steve Hart, From: David Q. Bates, Subject: Management Meeting at Campaign," October 7, 1988, Box 14, [VP] [Campaign 88] ["Line of the Day"] [2], Stephen Hart Files.

168. Dionne, "Debates: Revival for Democrats."

169. Dionne, "Debates: Revival for Democrats."

170. "Lectern to Lectern," *Newsweek*, November 21, 1988, 138.

171. Robin Toner, "Dukakis Seeks to Recover His Edge," *NYT*, September 18, 1988.

172. Sigmund Rogich interview, Presidential Oral Histories.

173. "Revolving Door," The Living Room Candidate, accessed July 25, 2022, http://www.livingroomcandidate.org/commercials/1988.

174. Sigmund Rogich interview, Presidential Oral Histories.
175. Runkel, *Campaign for President*, 117.
176. Sam Donaldson and Ishmael Reed both make this comment in Forbes, *Boogie Man*.
177. Estrich interview.
178. Runkel, *Campaign for President*, 121.
179. Kathleen Hall Jamieson, "Our Appalling Politics," *WP*, October 30, 1988.
180. Maureen Dowd, "Bush Portrays His Opponent as Sympathetic to Criminals," *NYT*, October 6, 1988; Martin Tolchin, "Study Says 53,000 Got Prison Furloughs in '87, and Few Did Harm," *NYT*, October 12, 1988.
181. "George Bush Debate-SNL," YouTube Video, October 8, 1988, 14:08, www.youtube.com/watch?v=N_01LySbRnY.
182. "George Bush Debate—SNL."
183. Al Franken, "My 10 Favorite 'Saturday Night Live' Political Sketches," *WP*, October 22, 2016.
184. "Tracing SNL's Political Humor," CNN.com, October 30, 2002.
185. Nguyen, *Live from New York!*
186. Melinda Henneberger and Don Van Natta Jr., "Once Close to Clinton, Gore Keeps a Distance," *NYT*, October 20, 2000; Miller and Shales, *Live from New York*, 445.
187. Robin Toner, "Dukakis Sees Heated 30 Days in Fight with a Bankrupt Foe," *NYT*, October 9, 1988.
188. E. J. Dionne Jr., "Poll Shows U.S. Voter Optimism Is Helping Bush in the Campaign," *NYT*, October 13, 1988; Runkel, *Campaign for President*, 259.
189. Dionne, "Poll Shows U.S. Voter Optimism Is Helping Bush in the Campaign."
190. "Lectern to Lectern," *Newsweek*, November 21, 1988, 138.
191. Lehrer, *Tension City*, 39.
192. Lehrer, *Tension City*, 39, 38.
193. "Presidential Candidates Debate," C-SPAN Video, October 13, 1988, www.c-span.org/video/?4256-1/1988-presidential-candidates-debate.
194. Estrich interview.
195. Corrigan interview; Bartlett, *Race for the White House*, "Bush vs. Dukakis."
196. Black interview.
197. Baker, *Work Hard, Study . . .* , 274.
198. Estrich interview.
199. Corrigan interview; Germond and Witcover, *Whose Broad Stripes and Bright Stars?*, 5.
200. Edward Walsh, "Dukakis Lashes Bush on Crime," *WP*, October 9, 1988.
201. Dukakis interview.
202. *Debating Our Destiny Documentary—Part 1*.
203. "Presidential Candidates Debate," October 13, 1988.
204. "Presidential Candidates Debate," October 13, 1988.
205. "Presidential Candidates Debate," October 13, 1988.
206. Estrich interview.
207. "1988 Presidential Debate—Closing," CBS Special for Thursday, October 13, 1988; and "1988—Presidential Debate Analysis," #881539, ABC Special for Thursday, October 13, 1988, Vanderbilt Television Archive; "Lectern to Lectern," *Newsweek*, November 21, 1988, 138.
208. David S. Broder, "Republican Scores as Rival Misses Openings," *WP*, October 14, 1988; E. J. Dionne Jr., "The Presidential Debate: Bush and Dukakis Quarrel on Pensions,

Abortion, Arms, and Campaign's Shrill Tone," *NYT*, October 14, 1988; Broder, "Republican Scores as Rival Misses Openings."

209. E. J. Dionne Jr., "Political Memo; Democrats, on the Day After, See a Long Hard Road Ahead," *NYT*, October 15, 1988.

210. "1988—Presidential Debate Analysis," #881538, #881539, ABC Special for Thursday, October 13, 1988; "1988 Presidential Debate—Closing," "1988 Presidential Debate—Analysis," "1988 Presidential Debate, Analysis Continued," CBS Special for Thursday, October 13, 1988, Vanderbilt Television Archive. NBC postdebate coverage is not available. Dionne, "Presidential Debate: Bush and Dukakis Quarrel."

211. Broder, "Republican Scores as Rival Misses Openings."

212. Edward Walsh, "While Bush Glows, Dukakis Eyes Clock," *WP*, October 15, 1988.

213. Dionne, "Political Memo; Democrats, on the Day After."

214. Walsh, "While Bush Glows, Dukakis Eyes Clock."

215. "To: Craig Fuller, Charlie Greenleaf, Tom Collamore, Steve Hart, From: David Q. Bates, Subject: Management Meeting at Campaign," October 14, 1988, Box 14, [VP] [Campaign 88] ["Line of the Day"] [2], Stephen Hart Files.

216. Estrich interview.

217. Rich Jaroslovsky, "Poll Gives Bush 55%-38% Lead over Dukakis—but Journal/NBC Survey Shows Wide Discontent with Whole Campaign," *Wall Street Journal*, October 18, 1988.

CHAPTER 8

1. R. W. Apple, "State by State: Bush-Dukakis Debate; For Workers in Texas, Little to Cheer," *New York Times* (hereafter *NYT*), October 15, 1988.

2. Apple, "State by State: Bush-Dukakis Debate."

3. Bill Peterson, "Bush Slings Toughest Words at Dukakis in Texas," *Washington Post* (hereafter *WP*), August 27, 1988.

4. "Statement of Kirk O'Donnell, August 26, 1988," Box 5, Folder 294, Michael S. Dukakis Presidential Campaign Records.

5. "Gun Control Talking Points for Dukakis Advocates, 8/26/88," Box 5, Folder 294, Michael S. Dukakis Presidential Campaign Records.

6. Apple, "State by State: Bush-Dukakis Debate."

7. Forbes, *Boogie Man*.

8. "DUKAKIS WANTS TO BAN GUNS IN AMERICA," Box 5, Folder 296, Michael S. Dukakis Presidential Campaign Records; *CBS Evening News*, October 31, 1988, Vanderbilt Television Archive.

9. R. W. Apple, "State by State; Early Euphoria on Texas Turns Sour for Dukakis," *NYT*, October 17, 1988.

10. Apple, "State by State; Early Euphoria."

11. Corrigan interview.

12. Michael Oreskes, "Dukakis Ads Aim at Wooing Blacks," *NYT*, September 29, 1988.

13. Maralee Schwartz and Lloyd Grove, "Barbara Jordan Lashes Jackson for Tepid Support of Ticket," *WP*, October 1, 1988.

14. Maureen Dowd, "Late and Loudly, Jackson Rejoins Fray," *NYT*, October 18, 1988.

15. Dowd, "Late and Loudly, Jackson Rejoins Fray."

16. Estrich interview.

17. E. J. Dionne Jr., "Political Memo; Dukakis Campaign Battling in Last Democratic Trench," *NYT*, October 20, 1988.

18. Dionne, "Political Memo; Dukakis Campaign Battling."

19. Anthony Lewis, "Abroad at Home: The Dirty Little Secret," *NYT*, October 20, 1988.
20. Estrich interview.
21. Shrum, *No Excuses*, 195; Bob Drogin, "How Presidential Race Was Won—and Lost: Michael S. Dukakis," *Los Angeles Times*, November 10, 1988.
22. Shrum interview.
23. Robin Toner, "Dukakis Gets a Needed Boost for Campaign," *NYT*, October 19, 1988.
24. Sigmund Rogich interview, Presidential Oral Histories; italics in original.
25. Josh King, "Dukakis and the Tank," PoliticoMagazine, November 17, 2013, www.politico.com/magazine/story/2013/11/dukakis-and-the-tank-099119/.
26. Chris Cillizza, "Who Really Made the Michael Dukakis 'Tank' Ad? It's Really Complicated," *WP*, August 5, 2014, www.washingtonpost.com/news/the-fix/wp/2014/08/05/who-really-made-the-michael-dukakis-tank-ad-its-complicated/.
27. Sigmund Rogich interview, Presidential Oral Histories.
28. *NBC Nightly News*, October 19, 1988, Vanderbilt Television Archive, confirms it aired the previous evening. King, "Dukakis and the Tank."
29. "Tank Ride," The Living Room Candidate, accessed July 25, 2022, http://www.livingroomcandidate.org/commercials/1988.
30. Bennett interview.
31. Bret Schulte, "Michael Dukakis: The Photo Op That Tanked," *U.S. News and World Report*, January 17, 2008.
32. Reid, *Backfire*.
33. Bennett interview.
34. "Counterpunch," The Living Room Candidate, accessed July 25, 2022, http://www.livingroomcandidate.org/commercials/1988.
35. "Meet the Press, October 23, 1988," Box 93-138/532, Transcripts of News Programs, September–October 1988, Lloyd M. Bentsen Jr. Papers.
36. Baker, *Work Hard, Study . . .* , 269.
37. "Furlough from the Truth," The Living Room Candidate, July 25, 2022, http://www.livingroomcandidate.org/commercials/1988.
38. Runkel, *Campaign for President*, 124.
39. "Talking Points for Counter Punch and Furlough from the Truth," Box 1, Folder 17, Michael S. Dukakis Presidential Campaign Records.
40. Dukakis interview.
41. Corrigan interview.
42. Dukakis interview.
43. Anthony Lewis, "What Is a Man Profited?," *NYT*, October 27, 1988.
44. *CBS Evening News*, October 31, 1988, Vanderbilt Television Archive.
45. "Bush Political Ad: He's Taller," *Saturday Night Live*, October 22, 1988, http://www.nbc.com/saturday-night-live/playlist/political-ads-collection-224931.
46. "Bush Political Ad: He's Whiter," *Saturday Night Live*, October 22, 1988, http://www.nbc.com/saturday-night-live/playlist/political-ads-collection-224931.
47. "Bush Political Ad: His Parents Were Born in America," *Saturday Night Live*, October 22, 1988, http://www.nbc.com/saturday-night-live/playlist/political-ads-collection-224931.
48. "Meet the Press, October 23, 1988," Box 93-138/532, Transcripts of News Programs, September–October 1988, Lloyd M. Bentsen Jr. Papers.
49. Meacham, *Destiny and Power*, 346.
50. Baker, *Work Hard, Study . . .* , 265.
51. Mendelberg, *Race Card*, 134–68. Mendelberg sees this as the point when the Horton ad shifted from being discussed as an element of a negative campaign to being discussed as a racial issue (152).

52. Andrew Rosenthal, "Foes Accuse Bush Campaign of Inflaming Racial Tension," *NYT*, October 24, 1988.

53. Rosenthal, "Foes Accuse Bush Campaign."

54. Maureen Dowd, "Bush Says Dukakis's Desperation Prompted Accusations of Racism," *NYT*, October 25, 1988.

55. "To: Craig Fuller, Charlie Greenleaf, Tom Collamore, Steve Hart, From: David Q. Bates, Subject: Management Meeting at Campaign," October 24, 1988, Box 14, [VP] [Campaign 88] ["Line of the Day"] [2], Stephen Hart Files.

56. Charles Krauthammer, "The Last Refuge: Cries of Racism," *WP*, October 28, 1988.

57. "A Racist Campaign," *WP*, October 25, 1988.

58. Rosenthal, "Foes Accuse Bush Campaign."

59. Runkel, *Campaign for President*, 114–16, 118.

60. Runkel, *Campaign for President*, 119.

61. Adatto, *Sound Bite Democracy*, 9; *CBS Evening News*, October 21, 1988, *NBC Nightly News*, October 24, 1988, Vanderbilt Television Archive.

62. Mendelberg, *Race Card*, 149; my research of network evening-news broadcasts from December 2, 1987, to November 8, 1988, Vanderbilt Television Archive.

63. Runkel, *Campaign for President*, 120.

64. Runkel, *Campaign for President*, 125–26.

65. Dukakis interview.

66. "Maryland Republican Flyer," Box 5, Folder 290, Michael S. Dukakis Presidential Campaign Records.

67. "White House News Summary—Monday, October 31, 1988," Box 138, Folder 3, James A. Baker III Papers.

68. Runkel, *Campaign for President*, 125–26.

69. "Two Good Men," *NYT*, October 30, 1988.

70. Albert Scardino, "The Choice of Most Dailies Is for None of the Above," *NYT*, November 4, 1988; "No Endorsement," *WP*, November 2, 1988.

71. "Thank You, Roger Ailes," *Wall Street Journal*, October 28, 1988.

72. Michael Oreskes, "TV's Role in '88: The Medium Is the Election," *NYT*, October 30, 1988.

73. Randall Rothenberg, "The Media Business: Advertising: The Disarray in Dukakis's Ad Team," *NYT*, October 20, 1988.

74. Geer, *In Defense of Negativity*, 121.

75. Adatto, *Sound Bite Democracy*, 4.

76. Adatto, *Sound Bite Democracy*, 17.

77. Fox Butterfield, "Dukakis Says Race Was Harmed by TV," *NYT*, April 22, 1990.

78. Paul Taylor and David S. Broder, "Evolution of the TV Era's Nastiest Presidential Race," *WP*, October 28, 1988.

79. Oreskes, "TV's Role in '88."

80. Devine interview.

81. Geer, *In Defense of Negativity*, 131–32; Patterson traces how the media moved toward more horse race–style coverage over time. Patterson, *Out of Order*, 53–93.

82. West, *Air Wars*, 61.

83. Richard Berke, "Lightest Turnout in 40 Years Is Seen," *NYT*, October 22, 1988.

84. *Newsweek*, October 31, 1988; E. J. Dionne Jr., "New Poll Shows Attacks by Bush Are Building Lead," *NYT*, October 26, 1988.

85. Dionne, "New Poll Shows Attacks by Bush"; "New Poll Shows Critical Groups on Bush's Side," *NYT*, October 27, 1988.

86. Lucy Howard, "Conventional-Wisdom Watch," *Newsweek*, October 30, 1988.

87. Maureen Dowd, "Bush, Illinois, Keeps Up Tough Talk," *NYT*, October 30, 1988; Robin Toner, "Dukakis Asserts He Is a 'Liberal,' but in Old Tradition of His Party," *NYT*, October 31, 1988.

88. Shrum interview.

89. Maureen Dowd, "Bush Ridicules Dukakis for Belatedly Saying That He Is a Liberal," *NYT*, November 1, 1988.

90. Drugs, Health Care, Educational Literacy, American Workmanship, Higher Education, Two Paychecks, Elderly Care, Environment (VHS), 1988, Box 37, Michael S. Dukakis Presidential Campaign Records.

91. Michael Oreskes, "Thrust of TV Campaign Ads Can Vary with the Territory," *NYT*, November 1, 1988.

92. America First (VHS), 1988, Box 35, Michael S. Dukakis Presidential Campaign Records.

93. Bernard Weinraub, "Campaign Trail; On Death Penalty, a Second Answer," *NYT*, November 2, 1988.

94. "To: Craig Fuller, Charlie Greenleaf, Tom Collamore, Steve Hart, From: David Q. Bates, Subject: Management Meeting at Campaign," November 2, 1988, Box 14, [VP] [Campaign 88] ["Line of the Day"] [2], Stephen Hart Files.

95. E. J. Dionne Jr., "2 Polls Give Bush Solid Leads," *NYT*, November 2, 1988.

96. Corrigan interview; Paul Taylor and David S. Broder, "Dukakis Electoral Strategy Set," *WP*, October 16, 1988.

97. "The Surge That Failed," *Newsweek*, November 22, 1988, 144; Estrich interview.

98. Black interview.

99. "Reagan, in the West, Asks Support of Young," *NYT*, November 2, 1988; Julie Johnson, "The Reagan Campaign Magic: He Isn't Running, but He's Winning," *NYT*, November 3, 1988.

100. "Dukakis after Dark," *Saturday Night Live*, November 5, 1988, www.nbc.com/saturday-night-live/video/dukakis-after-dark/n971.

101. Robin Toner, "Hailed by Big Crowds, Dukakis Foresees an Upset," *NYT*, November 5, 1988.

102. E. J. Dionne Jr., "Bush Still Ahead as End Nears but Dukakis Gains in Survey," *NYT*, November 6, 1988.

103. Runkel, *Campaign for President*, 9.

104. "*Face the Nation*, November 6, 1988," Box 50, Face the Nation with Lloyd Bentsen, Meet the Press (VHS), 1988, Michael S. Dukakis Presidential Campaign Records.

105. "*Meet the Press*, November 6, 1988," Box 50, Face the Nation with Lloyd Bentsen, Meet the Press (VHS), 1988, Michael S. Dukakis Presidential Campaign Records.

106. "*Meet the Press*, November 6, 1988," Box 50, Face the Nation with Lloyd Bentsen, Meet the Press (VHS), 1988, Michael S. Dukakis Presidential Campaign Records.

107. "*Meet the Press*, November 6, 1988," Box 50, Face the Nation with Lloyd Bentsen, Meet the Press (VHS), 1988, Michael S. Dukakis Presidential Campaign Records; Tom Sherwood, "Quayle Bolts From Advisers," *WP*, October 12, 1988; Richard Berke, "Quayle Role as Phantom of Campaign," *NYT*, November 7, 1988.

108. Berke, "Quayle Role as Phantom of Campaign."

109. J. Danforth Quayle interview, Presidential Oral Histories.

110. Gerald Boyd, "Bush Campaign Adds Midwest Stops," *NYT*, November 7, 1988.

111. Boyd, "Bush Campaign Adds Midwest Stops."

112. Robin Toner, "Dukakis Nears Wire in 9-State, 48-Hour Dash," *NYT*, November 8, 1988.

113. E. J. Dionne Jr., "Candidates Wage Battle to Dawn of Election Day," *NYT*, November 8, 1988.

114. "The Surge That Failed," *Newsweek*, November 22, 1988, 146.

115. Devine interview.

116. Dukakis interview.

117. "Election Night 1988 NBC News Coverage," YouTube Video, November 8, 1988, 3:45:17, www.youtube.com/watch?v=j6DuWpHmN-c&t=6222s.

118. Quayle, *Standing Firm*, 72.

119. Corrigan interview; Robin Toner, "The 1988 Elections; 'Chin Up,' Says Dukakis; ''92!' Supporters Shout," *NYT*, November 9, 1988.

120. Tom Shales, "In the Network Race, a CBS-ABC Runaway," *WP*, November 9, 1988.

121. "Election Night 1988 NBC News Coverage."

122. Margarette Leach, an elector from West Virginia, was pledged to support Dukakis but voted for Bentsen as a protest against the Electoral College.

123. Presidential numbers from "United States Presidential Election Results," Dave Leip's Atlas of U.S. Presidential Elections, https://uselectionatlas.org/RESULTS/. Obama came closest in 2008 with 52.9 percent.

124. E. J. Dionne Jr., "The Elections: Voters Delay Republican Hopes of Dominance in Post-Reagan Era," *NYT*, November 10, 1988.

125. David Broder and Paul Taylor, "Once Again, Democrats Debate Why They Lost," *WP*, November 10, 1988; Tom Wicker, "In the Nation; Medium and Message," *NYT*, November 15, 1988.

126. Adam Clymer, "Some Subtle Problems Undermine GOP Victory," *NYT*, November 14, 1988; Abramowitz and Webster, "Rise of Negative Partisanship"; Abramowitz, *Great Alignment*, 44.

127. E. J. Dionne Jr., "The Party Line Isn't So Straight Anymore," *NYT*, December 4, 1988.

128. Presidential numbers from "1988 Presidential General Election Data—National by State," Dave Leip's Atlas of U.S. Presidential Elections, https://uselectionatlas.org/RESULTS/. Senate numbers from Dendy and Anderson, *Statistics of the Presidential and Congressional Election*, 45, 44.

129. Susan Collins (R) of Maine won reelection, while Joe Biden was victorious statewide.

130. David Broder, "Voters Opt Again for a Divided Government," *WP*, November 9, 1988.

131. Abramowitz and Segal, "Beyond Willie Horton and the Pledge of Allegiance," 572.

132. Broder and Taylor, "Once Again, Democrats Debate Why They Lost."

133. Dionne, "Elections: Voters Delay Republican Hopes"; Thomas B. Edsall and Richard Morin, "Reagan's 1984 Voter Coalition Is Weakened in Bush Victory," *WP*, November 9, 1988.

134. Abramowitz and Segal, "Beyond Willie Horton and the Pledge of Allegiance," 575-76.

135. Edsall and Morin, "Reagan's 1984 Voter Coalition"; Ladd, "1988 Elections," 3.

136. Edsall and Morin, "Reagan's 1984 Voter Coalition"; E. J. Dionne Jr., "Democratic Strength Shifts to West," *NYT*, November 13, 1988.

137. Edsall and Morin, "Reagan's 1984 Voter Coalition."

138. Edsall and Morin, "Reagan's 1984 Voter Coalition."

139. Edsall and Morin, "Reagan's 1984 Voter Coalition."

140. Edsall and Morin, "Reagan's 1984 Voter Coalition"; "*New York Times* / CBS News Poll; Portrait of the Electorate," *NYT*, November 10, 1988.

141. Edsall and Morin, "Reagan's 1984 Voter Coalition"; "*New York Times* / CBS News Poll; Portrait of the Electorate."

142. Richard L. Berke, "50.16% Voter Turnout Was Lowest since 1924," *NYT*, December 18, 1988; "Voter Turnout in Presidential Elections."

143. Thomas B. Edsall, "Black Turnout Drops from 1984," *WP*, November 10, 1988.

144. As defined by Cost, "Electoral Polarization Continues under Obama," I then did my own calculations for 2016 and 2020 based on electoral data. "2016 Presidential General Election Data—National by State" and "2020 Presidential General Election Data—National by State," Dave Leip's Atlas of U.S. Presidential Elections, https://uselectionatlas.org/RESULTS/.

145. Data from 1988 to 2008 from Bishop, *Big Sort*, 10; 2016 and 2020 data from Bill Bishop, "For Most Americans, the Local Presidential Vote Was a Landslide," The Daily Yonder, December 17, 2020, https://dailyyonder.com/for-most-americans-the-local-presidential-vote-was-a-landslide/2020/12/17/.

146. DeSilver, "Growing Democratic Domination." Data from 2020 from Aaron Zitner and Dante Chinni, "How the 2020 Election Deepened America's White-Collar/Blue-Collar Split," *Wall Street Journal*, November 24, 2020.

147. Estrich interview; "1988 Presidential General Election Data—National by State," Dave Leip's Atlas of U.S. Presidential Elections, https://uselectionatlas.org/RESULTS/.

148. "1988 Presidential General Election Data—National by State," Dave Leip's Atlas of U.S. Presidential Elections, https://uselectionatlas.org/RESULTS/.

149. Dionne, "Democratic Strength Shifts to West."

150. Ronald Brownstein, "Dems Find Electoral Safety behind a Wall of Blue," *National Journal*, January 16, 2009.

151. Nate Silver, "As Nations and Parties Change, Republicans Are at an Electoral College Disadvantage," *NYT*, November 8, 2012, https://archive.nytimes.com/fivethirtyeight.blogs.nytimes.com/2012/11/08/as-nation-and-parties-change-republicans-are-at-an-electoral-college-disadvantage/; Chris Cillizza, "Democrats' Stranglehold on the Electoral College, in 1 GIF," *WP*, June 10, 2014, www.washingtonpost.com/news/the-fix/wp/2014/06/10/democrats-strangehold-on-the-electoral-college-in-1-gif/.

152. "Conventional Wisdom Watch," *Newsweek*, November 21, 1988, 18.

153. "Conventional Wisdom Watch," *Newsweek*, November 21, 1988, 18.

154. Paul Houston, "Bush, Dukakis Got Record Big Gifts: Donors of $100,000 Each Able to Exploit Legal Loophole," *Los Angeles Times*, December 10, 1988; Runkel, *Campaign for President*, 173.

155. David Wessel, "To Predict the Election, Professors Use Theories, but for Easy Selection, Just See the World Series," *Wall Street Journal*, August 24, 1988.

156. Broder, "Voters Opt Again for a Divided Government."

157. Robin Toner, "Dukakis Aides Acknowledge Bush Outmaneuvered Them," *NYT*, November 12, 1988; Estrich interview.

158. David Broder and Paul Taylor, "Once Again, Democrats Debate Why They Lost," *WP*, November 10, 1988

159. Walter Shapiro, "Are the Democrats Cursed?," *Time*, November 21, 1988.

160. Broder and Taylor, "Once Again, Democrats Debate Why They Lost."

161. "Dukakis Defeat Is Laid to Late Liberal Stand," *NYT*, November 16, 1988.

162. Runkel, *Campaign for President*, 198.

163. Runkel, *Campaign for President*, 252, 260, 221.

164. Baker, *Work Hard, Study . . .*, 258, 276.

165. Black interview.

166. Estrich interview.

167. Shrum interview.
168. Bennett interview.
169. Bai, *All the Truth Is Out*, 5.
170. James P. Pinkerton interview, Presidential Oral Histories.
171. Bennett interview; Shrum interview.
172. Dukakis interview.

EPILOGUE

1. "George Bush Inaugural Address."
2. R. W. Apple, "No Reversal, but Changes," *NYT*, January 21, 1989.
3. "A Disappointed Dukakis Wishes Bush Well," *NYT*, January 21, 1989.
4. For more on Bush and the end of the Cold War, see Engel, *When the World Seemed New*.
5. "Presidential Job Approval."
6. Allan Gold, "In Massachusetts, Dukakis Has Seen a Steady Fall since the Fall," *NYT*, May 21, 1989.
7. Jerry Berger, "Dukakis' Fall from Grace Dizzying," UPI, July 16, 1989.
8. "Dukakis Says Harm of Presidential Bid Was Unanticipated," *NYT*, January 17, 1990.
9. David Broder, "The Democrats Must Face Up to Jesse Jackson," *WP*, January 25, 1989; E. J. Dionne Jr., "New Chairman Tells Democrats to Be Tough," *NYT*, February 16, 1989; Robin Toner, "Eyes to Left, Democrats Edge toward the Center," *NYT*, March 25, 1990.
10. Richard L. Berke, "G.O.P. in Revolt on Taxes, Steps Up Criticism of Bush," *NYT*, June 28, 1990.
11. Thomas L. Friedman, "The Iraqi Invasion; Bush, Hinting Force, Declares Iraqi Assault 'Will Not Stand'; Proxy in Kuwait Issues Threat," *NYT*, August 6, 1990.
12. "President's Address to Nation on Federal Deficit and the Budget Agreement," *NYT*, October 3, 1990.
13. Dionne, *Why the Right Went Wrong*, 101–2; Mann and Ornstein, *It's Even Worse Than It Looks*, 43–58; Abramowitz, *Great Alignment*. Gingrich's campaign against Speaker of the House Jim Wright, which culminated in Wright's resignation over ethics charges in 1989, also contributed to the rising partisanship. See Zelizer, *Burning Down the House*.
14. John Yang, "Bush Says He'll Sign 5-Year Deficit Plan," *WP*, October 28, 1990.
15. Robin Toner, "Leaving Public Office, Dukakis Reflects, and Emerges Upbeat," *NYT*, January 1, 1991.
16. "The President's Popularity," *NYT*, March 5, 1991.
17. Robin Toner, "Poll Finds Postwar Glow Dimmed by the Economy," *NYT*, March 8, 1991.
18. Tom Wicker, "The Dream Ticket," *NYT*, March 6, 1991; Craig Wolf, "Gen. Powell Returns to the Bronx, and Remembers," *NYT*, April 16, 1991; Rowland Evans and Robert Novak, "Powell Politics," *NYT*, May 22, 1991.
19. Michael Oreskes, "Lee Atwater, Master of Tactics for Bush and G.O.P., Dies at 40," *NYT*, March 30, 1991.
20. Robin Toner, "Issue of Job Quotas Sure to Affect Debate on Civil Rights in the 90's," *NYT*, December 10, 1990.
21. "Dukakis on Bush Campaign: Willie Horton to 'Willie Quota,'" *WP*, June 23, 1991.
22. Andrew Rosenthal, "Reaffirming Commitment, Bush Signs Civil Rights Bill," *NYT*, November 22, 1991.
23. Clinton, "Announcement Speech, October 3, 1991."
24. Michael Decourcy Hinds, "Wofford Wins Senate Race, Turning Back Thornburgh; GOP Gains Edge in Trenton," *NYT*, November 6, 1991.

25. Buchanan, "Crossroads in Our Country's History."
26. Buchanan, "Crossroads in Our Country's History."
27. Robin Toner, "Bush Jarred in First Primary, Tsongas Wins Democratic Vote," *NYT*, February 19, 1992.
28. Richard L. Berke, "Tsongas Being Haunted by Memory of Dukakis," *NYT*, March 15, 1992.
29. Susan Estrich, "Let the Mud Fly," *NYT*, March 20, 1992.
30. Anthony Lewis, "Black and White," *NYT*, June 18, 1992.
31. Richard L. Berke, "'88 Campaign Provided Hard Lessons for Gore," *NYT*, July 10, 1992.
32. Fox Butterfield, "Dukakis Views Clinton as G.O.P.'s Worst Nightmare," *NYT*, July 10, 1992.
33. R. Drummond Ayres Jr., "Jackson Faces New Reality," *NYT*, July 15, 1992.
34. "Transcript of Speech by Clinton Accepting Democratic Nomination," *NYT*, July 17, 1992.
35. Steve Daley, "Lesson of Dukakis: Run, Don't Linger," *Chicago Tribune*, July 19, 1992.
36. David S. Broder and Dan Balz, "Campaign Hits Road Today," *WP*, July 17, 1992.
37. Gwen Ifill, "Clinton, in Houston Speech, Assails Bush on Crime Issue," *NYT*, July 24, 1992; Edward Walsh, "Clinton Charges Bush Uses Crime Issue to Divide," *WP*, July 24, 1992.
38. David Von Drehle, "A Celebration by Religious Right as Platform Panel Sees the Light," *WP*, August 18, 1992; Thomas B. Edsall, "GOP Plans a Family Values Offensive," *WP*, August 19, 1992; David E. Rosenbaum, "G.O.P. Moderates from Congress Don't Feel at Home," *NYT*, August 17, 1992.
39. Buchanan, "Culture War Speech."
40. Gwen Ifill, "Clinton Assails G.O.P. Attacks Aimed at Wife," *NYT*, August 20, 1992; Richard L. Berke, "In 1992, Willie Horton Is Democrats' Secret Weapon," *NYT*, August 25, 1992.
41. Christopher J. Georges, "The Clinton Plan (Thanks to Dukakis)," *NYT*, August 24, 1992; Gwen Ifill, "Clinton Presses Welfare Overhaul, Stressing Job Training and Work," *NYT*, September 10, 1992.
42. Robin Toner, "G.O.P. Looks at Clinton Draft Record and Spies Willie Horton," *NYT*, September 10, 1992; Black interview.
43. Andrew Rosenthal, "The Republicans; Bush Questions Clinton's Account of Vietnam-Era Protests and Trip," *NYT*, October 8, 1992.
44. "October 11, 1992 First Half of Debate Transcript."
45. Michael Kelly, "The Democrats; Clinton's Staff Sees Campaign as a Real War," *NYT*, August 11, 1992.
46. *16 for '16: The Contenders*, episode 3, "The Technocrats."
47. R. W. Apple, "The Economy's Casualty," *NYT*, November 4, 1992.
48. Sununu, *Quiet Man*, 371.
49. Staci D. Kramer, "The Gospel According to Rush," *Chicago Tribune*, November 30, 1992.
50. "Bush-Clinton-Perot Debate Cold Opening," *Saturday Night Live*, October 10, 1992, www.nbc.com/saturday-night-live/video/bush-clinton-perot-debate-cold-opening/n10302.
51. Apple, "Economy's Casualty."
52. *16 for '16: The Contenders*, episode 3, "The Technocrats."
53. Eric Schmitt and Joseph Kahn, "The China Trade Vote: A Clinton Triumph; House, in 237-197 Vote, Approves Normal Trade Rights for China," *NYT*, May 25, 2000.

54. Kathy Kiely, "Public Campaign Funding Is So Broken That Candidates Turned Down $292 Million in Free Money," *WP*, February 9, 2016, www.washingtonpost.com/posteverything/wp/2016/02/09/public-campaign-funding-is-so-broken-that-candidates-turned-down-292-million-in-free-money/.

55. Anthony Lewis, "Willie Horton Redux," *NYT*, February 26, 2000; "Inside Politics Transcript, January 13, 2000," CNN.com, http://www.cnn.com/TRANSCRIPTS/0001/13/ip.00.html.

56. Michael Kruse, "What Jesse Taught Bernie about Running for President," PoliticoMagazine, March 15, 2019, www.politico.com/magazine/story/2019/03/15/bernie-sanders-2020-race-jesse-jackson-1988-presidential-campaign-225809/. For more on links between Jackson and Sanders, as well as the legacy of the Jackson campaign, see Grim, *We've Got People*, 19–34.

57. Donald Trump, "It is outrageous what the Democrats are doing to our Country. Vote Republican now," October 31, 2018, https://twitter.com/realDonaldTrump/status/1057728445386539008/video/1.

58. Aaron Blake. "Willie Horton Is Alive, and Shame Is Dead," *WP*, November 1, 2018, www.washingtonpost.com/politics/2018/11/01/willie-horton-is-alive-shame-is-dead/.

59. Jackie Kucinich, "The Willie Horton Ad Maker Is Impressed by Trump's Latest Work," The Daily Beast, November 1, 2018, www.thedailybeast.com/the-willie-horton-ad-maker-is-impressed-by-trumps-latest-work.

60. Susan Estrich, "Don't Let Trump Get Away With His Racist Ad," *WP*, November 2, 2018.

61. Carl Hulse, "Bipartisan Criminal Justice Overhaul Is Haunted by Willie Horton," *NYT*, January 4, 2016.

62. Carl Hulse, "It Took Quite a Push, but McConnell Finally Allows Criminal Justice Vote," *NYT*, December 13, 2018.

63. Harry Enten, "George H. W. Bush Was the Most Popular Living President," December 1, 2018, CNN.com.

64. Susan Haigh, "Michael Dukakis Praises George H. W. Bush's Work to End Cold War," *Boston Globe*, December 1, 2018.

65. Peter Baker, "Bush Made Willie Horton an Issue, and the Racial Scars Are Still Fresh," *NYT*, December 3, 2018.

66. Paul Waldman. "How George H. W. Bush Exploited Racism to Win the Oval Office," *WP*, December 3, 2018; Eugene Scott, "How the Willie Horton Ad Factors into George H. W. Bush's Legacy," *WP*, December 3, 2018.

Bibliography

ARCHIVAL COLLECTIONS

James A. Baker III, George H. W. Bush White House chief of staff, secretary of state. Interviewed January 29, 2000. https://millercenter.org/the-presidency/presidential-oral-histories/james-baker-iii-oral-history-2000. Accessed March 27, 2018.

James A. Baker III. Papers. Public Policy Papers. Department of Rare Books and Special Collections, Seeley G. Mudd Manuscript Library, Princeton University, Princeton, N.J.

Lloyd M. Bentsen, Jr. Papers. Dolph Briscoe Center for American History, University of Texas at Austin.

Michael S. Dukakis Presidential Campaign Records. Archives and Special Collections, Snell Library, Northeastern University, Boston.

Craig Fuller, chief of staff to Vice President Bush. Interviewed May 12, 2004. https://millercenter.org/the-presidency/presidential-oral-histories/craig-fuller-oral-history. Accessed August 24, 2017.

Stephen Hart Files. White House Press Office. George H. W. Bush Presidential Records. George H. W. Bush Library, College Station, Tex.

Julian P. Kanter Commercial Archive. Carl Albert Center, University of Oklahoma, Norman.

James P. Pinkerton, deputy assistant to President George H. W. Bush for policy planning. Interviewed February 6, 2001. https://millercenter.org/the-presidency/presidential-oral-histories/james-p-pinkerton-oral-history. Accessed March 27, 2018.

Presidential Oral Histories, Miller Center, University of Virginia, Charlottesville (online)

J. Danforth Quayle, vice president. Interviewed March 8 and 9, 2001. https://millercenter.org/the-presidency/presidential-oral-histories/j-danforth-quayle-oral-history. Accessed August 24, 2017.

Sigmund Rogich, assistant to President George H. W. Bush, ambassador to Iceland. Interviewed March 8 and 9, 2001. https://millercenter.org/the-presidency/presidential-oral-histories/sigmund-rogich-oral-history. Accessed August 24, 2017.

Robert Teeter Collection. George H. W. Bush Library, College Station, Tex.

Vanderbilt Television Archive. Jean and Alexander Heard Library, Vanderbilt University, Nashville, Tenn.

INTERVIEWS

Bennett, Matt. Telephone interview by author, July 24, 2018.
Black, Charlie. Telephone interview by author, November 10, 2017.
Corrigan, Jack. Telephone interview by author, August 1, 2017.
Devine, Tad. Telephone interview by author, August 13, 2018.
Dukakis, Michael. Interview by author, Northeastern University, Boston, July 12, 2017.
Estrich, Susan. Telephone interview by author, June 12, 2017.
Fuller, Craig. Telephone interview by author, September 8, 2017.
Shrum, Bob. Telephone interview by author, July 22, 2017.
Wilkie, Curtis. Interview by author, Oxford, Miss., February 13, 2017.

PERIODICALS

Atlantic
Boston Globe
Chicago Tribune
Christian Science Monitor
Des Moines Register
Los Angeles Times
Miami Herald
National Interest
National Journal
New Republic
Newsweek
New York
New Yorker
New York Times
Time
U.S. News and World Report
Wall Street Journal
Washington Monthly
Washington Post

ONLINE VIDEO SOURCES

C-SPAN.org
LivingRoomCandidate.com
NBC.com
NBC Video
PBS.org
YouTube.com

WEBSITES

ABCNews.com
APNewsarchive.com
CNN.com
DailyBeast.com
Dave Leip's Atlas of U.S. Presidential Elections. https://uselectionatlas.org/RESULTS/.
FiveThirtyEight.com
Gallup.com
MotherJones.com
NPR.org
Politico.com
Politifact.com
TeachingAmericanHistory.org
Twitter.com
Yahoo.com

TELEVISION, FILMS, AND DOCUMENTARIES

Bartlett, David, dir. and writer. *Race for the White House*. Season 1, Episode 3, "Bush vs. Dukakis." Aired March 20, 2016, on CNN.

Debating Our Destiny Documentary—Part 1. MacNeil Lehrer Productions, September 24, 2000.

Forbes, Stefan. dir. *Boogie Man: The Lee Atwater Story*. InterPositive Media, 2008.

Howard, Ron, dir. *Gung Ho*. Paramount, 1986.

McTiernan, John, dir. *Die Hard*. Fox, 1988.

Nguyen, Bao, dir. *Live from New York!* NBC, June 12, 2015.

Pakula, Alan. J., dir. *All the President's Men*. Warner Brothers, 1976.

Parker, Alan, dir. *Mississippi Burning*. Orion, 1988.

Porter, Dawn, dir. *John Lewis: Good Trouble*. Magnolia, 2020.

Rabbe, William, dir. *Above the Fray: The Lessons of Dukakis '88*. December 18, 2014.

Reid, Jason, dir. *Backfire: How to Destroy a Presidential Candidate*. ESPN Films, 2016.

Shobocinski, Matthew, and Denise Wills, producers. *Dukakis and the Tank: The Making of a Political Disaster*. PoliticoMagazine, 2013. www.politico.com/video/2013/11/dukakis-and-the-tank-the-making-of-a-political-disaster-005303.

16 for '16: The Contenders. Episode 3, "The Technocrats: Mike Dukakis and Mitt Romney." Aired September 27, 2016, on PBS.

16 for '16: The Contenders. Episode 4, "The Visionaries: Gary Hart and Jesse Jackson." Aired October 4, 2016, on PBS.

Zemeckis, Robert, dir. *Back to the Future Part II*. Universal, 1989.

PUBLISHED SOURCES

Abramowitz, Alan I. *The Great Alignment: Race, Party Transformation, and the Rise of Donald Trump.* New Haven, Conn.: Yale University Press, 2018.

Abramowitz, Alan I., and Jeffrey A. Segal. "Beyond Willie Horton and the Pledge of Allegiance: National Issues in the 1988 Elections." *Legislative Studies Quarterly* 15, no. 4 (November 1990): 565–80.

Abramowitz, Alan I., and Steven Webster. "The Rise of Negative Partisanship and the Nationalization of U.S. Elections in the 21st Century." *Electoral Studies* 41 (March 2016): 12–22.

Adatto, Kiku. *Sound Bite Democracy: Network Evening News Presidential Campaign Coverage, 1968 and 1988.* Research Paper R-2 (Joan Shorenstein Barone Center on the Press, Politics and Public Policy, John F. Kennedy School of Government, Harvard University). Cambridge, Mass.: Joan Shorenstein Barone Center on the Press, Politics and Public Policy, 1990.

Alexander, Herbert, and Monica Bauer. *Financing the 1988 Election.* Boulder, Colo.: Westview, 1988.

Alterman, Eric. *Sound and the Fury: The Making of the Punditocracy.* Ithaca, N.Y.: Cornell University Press, 1999.

Axelrod, David. *Believer: My Forty Years in Politics.* New York: Penguin Books, 2015.

Bai, Matt. *All the Truth Is Out.* New York: Vintage, 2014.

Baker, James A., III. *"Work Hard, Study . . . and Keep Out of Politics!"* Evanston, Ill.: Northwestern University Press, 2005.

Baker, Peter, and Susan Glasser. *The Man Who Ran Washington: The Life and Times of James A. Baker III.* New York: Doubleday, 2020.

Baughman, James. *The Republic of Mass Culture: Journalism, Broadcasting in America since 1941.* 3rd ed. Baltimore: Johns Hopkins University Press, 2006.

Baum, Matthew A. "Talking the Vote: Why Presidential Candidates Hit the Talk Show Circuit." *American Journal of Political Science* 49, no. 2 (April 2005): 213–34.

Bennett, Matt. "Sterling Heights, MI, 9/12, Tank Event." *Campaign Journal*, November 1988.

Biden, Joe. *Promises to Keep: On Life and Politics.* New York: Random House, 2007.

Bishop, Bill. *The Big Sort: Why the Clustering of Like-Minded America Is Tearing Us Apart.* Boston: Mariner Books, 2008.

———. "For Most Americans, the Local Presidential Vote Was a Landslide." https://dailyyonder.com/for-most-americans-the-local-presidential-vote-was-a-landslide/2020/12/17. Accessed June 26, 2022.

Black, Christine, and Tom Oliphant. *All by Myself: The Unmaking of a Presidential Campaign.* Essex, Conn.: Globe Pequot, 1989.

"Black-American Members of Congress." History, Art, and Archives, U.S. House of Representatives. https://history.house.gov/Exhibitions-and-Publications/BAIC/Historical-Data/Black-American-Representatives-and-Senators-by-Congress/. Accessed July 26, 2022.

Blumenthal, Sidney. *Pledging Allegiance: The Last Campaign of the Cold War.* New York: HarperCollins, 1990.

Brady, John. *Bad Boy: The Life and Politics of Lee Atwater.* Reading, Mass.: Addison-Wesley, 1997.

Brands, H. W. *Reagan: The Life.* New York: Anchor, 2015.

Buchanan, Patrick. "A Crossroads in Our Country's History, December 10, 1991." Buchanan for President. http://www.4president.org/speeches/buchanan1992announcement.htm.

———. "Culture War Speech: Address to the Republican National Convention," Voices of Democracy, August 17, 1992. http://voicesofdemocracy.umd.edu/buchanan-culture-war-speech-speech-text.

Burnham, Walter Dean. *Critical Elections and the Mainsprings of American Politics*. New York: W. W. Norton, 1970.

Bush, George. *All the Best: My Life in Letters and Other Writings*. New York: Scribner, 1999.

———. *Looking Forward: An Autobiography*. With Victor Gold. New York: Doubleday, 1987.

Cannon, Lou. *President Reagan: The Role of a Lifetime*. New York: Simon and Schuster, 1991.

Carter, Dan T. *The Politics of Rage: George Wallace, the Origins of the New Conservatism, and the Transformation of American Politics*. New York: Simon and Schuster, 1995.

Clinton, Bill. "Announcement Speech, October 3, 1991." Bill Clinton for President. http://www.4president.org/speeches/billclinton1992announcement.htm.

Cohen, Marty, David Karol, Hans Noel, and John Zaller. *The Party Decides: Presidential Nominations before and after Reform*. Chicago: University of Chicago Press, 2008.

Cook, Rhodes. *United States Presidential Primary Elections, 1968–1996: A Handbook of Election Statistics*. Washington, D.C.: Congressional Quarterly Press, 2000.

Cost, Jay. "Electoral Polarization Continues under Obama." *HorseRaceBlog*. Real Clear Politics, November 20, 2008. www.realclearpolitics.com/horseraceblog/2008/11/polarization_continues_under_o.html.

Cramer, Richard Ben. *What It Takes*. New York: Random House, 1992.

Crespino, Joseph. *In Search of Another Country: Mississippi and the Conservative Counterrevolution*. Princeton, N.J.: Princeton University Press, 2007.

Darman, Richard. *Who's in Control? Polar Politics and the Sensible Center*. New York: Simon and Schuster, 1996.

Dendy, Dallas L., and Donnald K. Anderson. *Statistics of the Presidential and Congressional Election of November 8, 1988*. Washington, D.C.: GPO, 1989. https://clerk.house.gov/member_info/electionInfo/1988election.pdf.

"Deposition of Roger E. Ailes," August 29, 1991. MUR 3069. Federal Election Commission (FEC). www.fec.gov/files/legal/murs/3069.pdf.

DeSilver, Drew. "The Growing Democratic Domination of Nation's Largest Counties." Pew Research Center, July 21, 2016. www.pewresearch.org/fact-tank/2016/07/21/the-growing-democratic-domination-of-nations-largest-counties/.

Dionne, E. J., Jr. *Why the Right Went Wrong: Conservatism—from Goldwater to the Tea Party and Beyond*. New York: Simon and Schuster, 2016.

Draper, Theodore. *A Very Thin Line: The Iran-Contra Affairs*. New York: Hill and Wang, 1991.

Dukakis, Michael S., and Rosabeth Moss Kanter. *Creating the Future: The Massachusetts Comeback and Its Promise for America*. New York: Simon and Schuster, 1988.

Edsall, Thomas, and Mary Edsall. *Chain Reaction: The Impact of Race, Rights, and Taxes on American Politics*. New York: W. W. Norton, 1991.

Engel, Jeffrey. *When the World Seemed New: George H. W. Bush and the End of the Cold War*. Boston: Houghton Mifflin Harcourt, 2017.

Englehardt, Andrew. "Trumped by Race: Explanations for Race's Influence on Whites' Votes in 2016." *Quarterly Journal of Political Science* 14 (2019): 313–28.

Foner, Eric. *Give Me Liberty! An American History*. Brief 5th ed. New York: W. W. Norton, 2017.

Frady, Marshall. *Jesse: The Life and Pilgrimage of Jesse Jackson.* New York: Random House, 1996.

Frank, Barney. *Frank: A Life in Politics from the Great Society to Same-Sex Marriage.* New York: Picador, 2015.

Fraser, Steven, and Gary Gerstle, eds. *The Rise and Fall of the New Deal Order, 1930–1980.* Princeton, N.J.: Princeton University Press, 1989.

From, Al. *The New Democrats and the Return to Power.* New York: St. Martin's, 2013.

Gallup, George, Jr., and Alec Gallup. "Doubts about Bush's Character Allayed by GOP Convention." Gallup Poll, August 31, 1988.

———. "Republican Convention Boosts Bush's Candidacy, but Quayle Controversy Could Undermine It." Gallup Poll, August 24, 1988.

Geer, John. *In Defense of Negativity: Attack Ads in Presidential Campaigns.* Chicago: University of Chicago Press, 2006.

Geismer, Lily. "Atari Democrats." *Jacobin*, February 8, 2016. www.jacobinmag.com/2016/02/geismer-democratic-party-atari-tech-silicon-valley-mondale/.

———. *Don't Blame Us: Suburban Liberals and the Transformation of the Democratic Party.* Princeton, N.J.: Princeton University Press, 2015.

"General Counsel's Report," November 14, 1991. MUR 3069. Federal Election Commission (FEC). www.fec.gov/files/legal/murs/3069.pdf.

"George Bush Inaugural Address," January 20, 1989. The American Presidency Project. www.presidency.ucsb.edu/ws/index.php?pid=16610.

Germond, Jack W., and Jules Witcover. *Wake Us When It's Over: Presidential Politics of 1984.* New York: Macmillan, 1985.

———. *Whose Broad Stripes and Bright Stars? The Trivial Pursuit of the Presidency, 1988.* New York: Warner Books, 1989.

Gillon, Steven M. *The Democrats' Dilemma: Walter F. Mondale and the Liberal Legacy.* New York: Columbia University Press, 1992.

Grace, Arthur. *Choose Me: Portraits of a Presidential Race.* Hanover, N.H.: University of New England Press, 1989.

Greenberg, Stanley. *Middle Class Dreams: The Politics and Power of the New American Majority.* New York: Times Books, 1995.

Grim, Ryan. *We've Got People: From Jesse Jackson to Alexandria Ocasio-Cortez, the End of Big Money and the Rise of a Movement.* Washington, D.C.: Strong Arm, 2019.

Hemmer, Nicole. *Messengers of the Right: Conservative Media and the Transformation of American Politics.* Philadelphia: University of Pennsylvania Press, 2016.

Hertzke, Allen D. *Echoes of Discontent: Jesse Jackson, Pat Robertson, and the Resurgence of Populism.* Washington, D.C.: Congressional Quarterly Press, 1993.

"How Groups Voted in 1984." Roper Center. https://ropercenter.cornell.edu/how-groups-voted-1984/.

Isserman, Maurice, and Michael Kazin. *America Divided: The Civil War of the 1960s.* New York: Oxford University Press, 2000.

Jacobson, Matthew Frye. *Roots Too: The White Ethnic Revival in Post–Civil Rights America.* Cambridge, Mass.: Harvard University Press, 2006.

Jamieson, Kathleen Hall. *Dirty Politics: Deception, Distraction, and Democracy.* New York: Oxford University Press, 1992.

Judis, John B., and Ruy Teixeira. *The Emerging Democratic Majority.* New York: Scribner, 2002.

Kabaservice, Geoffrey. *Rule and Ruin: The Downfall of Moderation and the Destruction of the Republican Party, from Eisenhower to the Tea Party.* New York: Oxford University Press, 2012.

Kennedy, Paul. *The Rise and Fall of the Great Powers: Economic Change and Military Conflict from 1500 to 2000.* New York: Random House, 1987.

Key, V. O. "A Theory of Critical Elections." *Journal of American Politics* 17, no. 1 (February 1955): 3–18.

Kondracke, Morton, and Fred Barnes. *Jack Kemp: The Bleeding-Heart Conservative Who Changed America.* New York: Sentinel, 2015.

Kruse, Kevin. *White Flight: Atlanta and the Making of Modern Conservatism.* Princeton, N.J.: Princeton University Press, 2005.

"Labor Force and Unemployment Data." Mass.gov. https://lmi.dua.eol.mass.gov/LMI/LaborForceAndUnemployment/LURResults?A=01&GA=000025&TF=3&Y=1986&Sopt=Y&Dopt=TEXT. Accessed July 26, 2022.

"Labor Force Statistics from the Current Population Survey." Bureau of Labor Statistics. https://data.bls.gov/pdq/SurveyOutputServlet. Accessed January 6, 2018.

Ladd, Everett Carll. "The 1988 Elections: Continuation of the Post–New Deal System." *Political Science Quarterly* 104, no. 1 (Spring 1989): 1–18.

Lassiter, Matthew. *The Silent Majority: Suburban Politics in the Sunbelt South.* Princeton, N.J.: Princeton University Press, 2006.

Lawrence, John. *The Class of '74.* Baltimore: Johns Hopkins University Press, 2018.

Lehrer, Jim. *Tension City: Inside the Presidential Debates, from Kennedy-Nixon to Obama-McCain.* New York: Random House, 2011.

"Majority Now Says There Is a 'Great Deal' of Difference between the Republican and Democratic Parties." Pew Research Center, January 24, 2019. www.people-press.org/2019/01/24/publics-2019-priorities-economy-health-care-education-and-security-all-near-top-of-list/pp_2019-01-24_political-priorities_0-04/.

Mann, Thomas E., and Norman J. Ornstein. *It's Even Worse Than It Looks: How the American Constitutional System Collided with the New Politics of Extremism.* New York: Basic Books, 2012.

Maraniss, David. *First in His Class: A Biography of Bill Clinton.* New York: Simon and Schuster, 1995.

Maraniss, David, and Ellen Nakashima. *The Prince of Tennessee: The Rise of Al Gore.* New York: Simon and Schuster 2000.

"Massachusetts Election Statistics." William Francis Galvin, Secretary of the Commonwealth of Massachusetts. http://electionstats.state.ma.us/elections/search/year_from:1986/year_to:2018/office_id:3. Accessed July 12, 2022.

Maxwell, Angie, and Todd Shields. *The Long Southern Strategy: How Chasing White Voters in the South Changed American Politics.* New York: Oxford University Press, 2019.

McGinnis, Joe. *Selling of the President, 1968.* New York: Trident, 1969.

McGirr, Lisa. *Suburban Warriors: The Origins of the American Right.* Princeton, N.J.: Princeton University Press, 2001.

Meacham, Jon. *Destiny and Power: The American Odyssey of George Herbert Walker Bush.* New York: Random House, 2015.

Mendelberg, Tali. *The Race Card: Campaign Strategy, Implicit Messages, and the Norm of Equality.* Princeton, N.J.: Princeton University Press, 2001.

Miller, Edward H. *Nut Country: Right-Wing Dallas and the Birth of the Southern Strategy.* Chicago: University of Chicago Press, 2015.

Miller, James Andrew, and Tom Shales. *Live from New York: The Complete, Uncensored History of "Saturday Night Live."* New York: Back Bay Books, 2015.

Mosbacher, Robert. *Going to Windward: A Mosbacher Family Memoir*. College Station: Texas A&M University Press, 2010.
Naftali, Timothy. *George H. W. Bush*. New York: Times Books, 2007.
Newport, Frank. "Americans Today Much More Accepting of a Woman, Black, Catholic or Jew as President." Gallup News, March 29, 1999. https://news.gallup.com/poll/3979 /americans-today-much-more-accepting-woman-black-catholic.aspx.
———. "Obama Dominates Clinton among College Graduates." Gallup News, April 9, 2008. https://news.gallup.com/poll/106360/obama-dominates-clinton-among -college-graduates.aspx.
Noonan, Peggy. *What I Saw at the Revolution: A Political Life in the Reagan Era*. New York: Random House, 1990.
Norrander, Barbara. *Super Tuesday: Regional Politics and Presidential Primaries*. Lexington: University of Kentucky Press, 1992.
"October 11, 1992 First Half of Debate Transcript." The Commission on Presidential Debates. www.debates.org/index.php?page=october-11-1992-first-half -debate-transcript.
"October 21, 1984 Debate Transcript." The Commission on Presidential Debates. www.debates.org/voter-education/debate-transcripts/october-21-1984-debate -transcript/.
O'Mara, Margaret. *Pivotal Tuesdays: Four Elections That Shaped the Twentieth Century*. Philadelphia: University of Pennsylvania Press, 2015.
Osborne, David. *Laboratories of Democracy*. Boston: Harvard Business School Press, 1988.
Parmet, Herbert. *George Bush: The Life of a Lone Star Yankee*. New York: Scribner, 1997.
Patterson, Thomas E. *Out of Order*. New York: Alfred Knopf, 1993.
Perlstein, Rick. *Before the Storm: Barry Goldwater and the Unmaking of the American Consensus*. New York: Hill and Wang, 2001.
———. *The Invisible Bridge: The Fall of Nixon and the Rise of Reagan*. New York: Simon and Schuster, 2014.
———. *Nixonland: The Rise of a President and the Fracturing of America*. New York: Scribner, 2008.
———. *Reaganland: America's Right Turn, 1976–1980*. New York: Simon and Schuster, 2020.
Phillips-Fein, Kim. *Invisible Hands: The Making of the Conservative Movement from the New Deal to Reagan*. New York: W. W. Norton, 2009.
Pitney, John, Jr. *After Reagan: Bush, Dukakis, and the 1988 Presidential Election*. Lawrence: University Press of Kansas, 2019.
Ponce de Leon, Charles. *That's the Way It Is: A History of Television News in America*. Chicago: University of Chicago Press, 2015.
"Presidential Job Approval." The American Presidency Project. www.presidency.ucsb .edu/statistics/data/presidential-job-approval. Accessed January 6, 2018.
"Public Trust in Government, 1958–2021." Pew Research Center, May 17, 2021. www .pewresearch.org/politics/2021/05/17/public-trust-in-government-1958-2021/.
Quayle, Dan. *Standing Firm: A Vice-Presidential Memoir*. New York: HarperCollins, 1994.
Reed, Ralph. *Active Faith: How Christians Are Changing the Soul of American Politics*. New York: Free Press, 1996.
Reeves, Richard. *President Reagan: The Triumph of Imagination*. New York: Simon and Schuster, 2005.
Rieder, Jonathan. *Canarsie: The Jews and Italians of Brooklyn against Liberalism*. Cambridge, Mass.: Harvard University Press, 1985.

Rolph, Stephanie. *Resisting Equality: The Citizens' Councils, 1954–1989*. Baton Rouge: Louisiana State University Press, 2018.

Rosenfeld, Samuel. *The Polarizers: Postwar Architects of Our Partisan Era*. Chicago: University of Chicago Press, 2018.

Rosenwald, Brian. *Talk Radio's America: How an Industry Took Over a Political Party That Took Over the United States*. Cambridge, Mass.: Harvard University Press, 2019.

Runkel, David R., ed. *Campaign for President: The Managers Look at '88*. Dover, Mass.: Auburn House, 1989.

Schattschneider, E. E. *The Semisovereign People: A Realist's View of Democracy in America*. New York: Holt, Rinehart and Winston, 1960.

Schlesinger, Arthur, Jr. *The Cycles of American History*. Boston: Houghton Mifflin, 1986.

Schwartzapfel, Beth, and Bill Keller. "Willie Horton Revisited." The Marshall Project, May 13, 2015. www.themarshallproject.org/2015/05/13/willie-horton-revisited.

"September 25, 1988 Transcript." The Commission on Presidential Debates. www.debates.org/voter-education/debate-transcripts/september-25-1988-debate-transcript/.

Sherman, Gabriel. *The Loudest Voice in the Room*. New York: Random House, 2014.

Shrum, Robert. *No Excuses: Concessions of a Serial Campaigner*. New York: Simon and Schuster, 2007.

Simon, Roger. *Road Show*. New York: Farrar, Straus and Giroux, 1990.

Sundquist, James L. *Dynamics of the Party System: Alignment and Realignment of Political Parties in the United States*. Washington, D.C.: Brookings Institution, 1973.

Sununu, John H. *The Quiet Man: The Indispensable Presidency of George H. W. Bush*. New York: Broadside Books, 2015.

The Tower Commission Report: The Full Text of the President's Special Review Board. New York: Bantam Books, 1987.

Turner, James Morton, and Andrew Isenberg. *The Republican Reversal: Conservatives and the Environment from Nixon to Trump*. Cambridge, Mass.: Harvard University Press, 2018.

"2000 Democratic Party Platform." The American Presidency Project. www.presidency.ucsb.edu/documents/2000-democratic-party-platform. Accessed July 26, 2022.

"2004 Democratic Party Platform." The American Presidency Project. www.presidency.ucsb.edu/documents/2004-democratic-party-platform. Accessed July 26, 2022.

"Voter Turnout in Presidential Elections." The American Presidency Project. http://www.presidency.ucsb.edu/data/turnout.php. Accessed July 26, 2022.

Waterhouse, Benjamin. *Lobbying America: The Politics of Business from Nixon to NAFTA*. Princeton, N.J.: Princeton University Press, 2014.

Weart, Spencer. *The Discovery of Global Warming*. Cambridge, Mass.: Harvard University Press, 2003.

West, Darrell. *Air Wars: Television Advertising and Social Media in Election Campaigns, 1952–2016*. Thousand Oaks, Calif.: Congressional Quarterly Press, 2018.

Whipple, Chris. *Gatekeepers: How the White House Chiefs of Staff Define Every Presidency*. New York: Crown, 2017.

Wilentz, Sean. *The Age of Reagan: A History, 1974–2008*. New York: Harper, 2008.

Williams, Daniel K. *God's Own Party: The Making of the Christian Right*. New York: Oxford University Press, 2010.

Wolfe, Tom. *The Bonfire of the Vanities*. New York: Farrar, Straus and Giroux, 1987.

Zelizer, Julian. *Burning Down the House, Newt Gingrich, the Fall of a Speaker, and the Rise of the New Republican Party*. New York: Penguin, 2020.

Index

Italic page numbers refer to illustrations.

ABC World News Tonight (television show), 45, 56, 146
abortion, 7, 11, 19, 97, 101, 148, 168. See also *Roe v. Wade*
Abramowitz, Alan, 244
adultery. *See* sex scandals
Afghanistan, 11, 111
AFL-CIO, 52, 123, 225. *See also* labor unions
African Americans. *See* Black community
After Reagan (Pitney), 269n8
Aid to Families with Dependent Children (AFDC), 36
Ailes, Roger: background of, 99; on campaign ads, 94, 122, 197-98, 233, 234; campaign strategy of, 20, 114-15, 122, 124, 135, 166, 180, 199, 262-63; criticisms and praise of, 235; on Dukakis, 190, 250; on Dukakis tank ride and ad, 201, 228; on electability of Dukakis, 250; in Group of Six, 99; on Horton issue, 197-98, 233-34; on *Newsweek* "Wimp Factor" cover, 104; on "no new taxes" pledge, 180; on Pledge of Allegiance, 135, 190; Quayle and, 166, 178, 209, 210; on Rather interview, 114-15; on "Straddle" ad, 122; television work of, 263
Albright, Madeline, 199-200
Alexander, Herbert, 139
Allen, George, 56
Allen, Richard, 97
All the President's Men (film), 40
Alter, Jonathan, 87-88, 193
American Civil Liberties Union (ACLU), 33, 51, 137, 138, 189, 204, 206, 208-9, 217, 220, 225, 235
American Enterprise Institute, 51
American Newspaper Publishers Association, 43
Americans for Bush (organization), 196, 197
Americans for Tax Reform, 106

anti-establishment rhetoric, 64, 67, 70, 74
antiwar sentiment, 6, 7, 10, 133, 191-92. *See also* flag-burning; Vietnam War
Apple, R. W., 46, 76, 79, 80, 117, 131, 253
Arab American Institute, 148
Arab Americans, 80
Arafat, Yasser, 83, 88
Armandt, Lynn, 40
Armed Services Committee, 25
The Arsenio Hall Show (television show), 161, 162
The Art of the Deal (Trump), 109
Atari Democrats (term), 17
Atwater, Lee: G. W. Bush and, 20, 177; on campaign ads, 94, 122; death of, 257, 263; on Democratic ticket, 144, 149; and Dukakis mental health story, 163; on Dukakis tank ride, 201-2; on end of election, 232, 239; in Group of Six, 98-99; on Horton issue, 89, 137, 138, 141, 196, 233-34, 257, 266; on Mondale, 13; on "no new taxes" pledge, 106, 179; on Pledge of Allegiance, 135; political background of, 20; on Quayle, 189-90, 214; on Rather interview, 116; on "Revolving Door" ad, 215; on Sasso's return, 194; on "Straddle" ad, 122
Austin, Gerald, 86
Axelrod, David, 32, 58, 63, 69
Ayres, R. Drummond, 260

Babbitt, Bruce, 18, 21, 63
Babcock, Charlie, 139, 197
baby-boomer politicians, 5-6, 52, 159, 171, 181
Baker, James: on campaign ads, 197, 198, 201, 234; on campaign offensive strategy, 193, 202, 214, 222, 230, 232; on Democratic National Convention, 156; on Dukakis tank ride and ad, 201, 228, 230; on G. W. Bush, 177; on Horton issue, 197-98, 234; on legacy of Quayle selection, 185-86; on liberalism, 250;

331

Baker, James (*continued*)
position on Bush campaign, 156, 165, 172; on reasons for Bush victory, 250; on Shaw death penalty question in debate, 219-20; on vice- presidential pick, 159, 166, 167, 170, 171, 172, 176, 178, 179, 184, 185, 186, 214
Baldwin, Alec, 217
Balz, Dan, 2
Barber, James, 86
Barbour, Haley, 22, 78
Barnes, Robert, 210
Barrett, Laurence, 89, 106
Bayh, Birch, 174, 176
Beckel, Bob, 140
Bennett, Matt, 192-93, 199-201, 219, 229, 251
Bentsen, Lloyd, *213*; on Bush's negative campaign, 240-41; in campaign ad, 238; Democratic National Convention speech by, 153; discussion of in first presidential debate, 207; as Dukakis's running mate, 133, 140, 142-45; on Horton issue, 232; impact in Texas during race, 228; political ideology of, 143-44; and Quayle debate, 209-14; *Saturday Night Live* satire of, 240; senate race of against Bush in 1970, 96
Berke, Richard, 241
Berlin Wall, 254
Bernstein, Carl, 40
Biden, Jill, 55
Biden, Joe, *55*; 1988 presidential campaign of, 3-4, 32-33, 49-50, 52-53; "Blue Wall" and, 248; plagiarism scandal of, 53-55, 63; as senator, 18, 52-54; as vice president, 92-93; as victim of media revolution in campaigns, 55-57
birther campaign, 237
Black, Charlie: on Dukakis tank ride and ad, 201, 229-30, 232, 250; on electability of Dukakis, 250; and Kemp campaign, 100, 103, 116, 117, 119, 127; on Quayle, 178, 209; on Reagan's role in Bush campaign, 239; on Shaw death penalty question in debate, 219
Black, Merle, 233
Black community: 1988 election campaign and, 4, 12; Bush and, 227-28, 232-33; Dukakis and, 224, 226-27, 246; housing discrimination against, 96; political participation of, 60-61, 64-65, 86-87; political rights of, 6; racism against, 61-62; school desegregation and, 101; on Jackson's presidential campaign, 60, 61, 75, 76, 80. *See also* civil rights movement; Jackson, Jesse
Blake, Aaron, 266
"Blue Wall," 6, 224, 248, 264
Bode, Ken, 53, 150
Boland, Edward, 26
Bond, Julian, 87
Bond, Rich, 116, 139, 222
The Bonfire of the Vanities (Wolfe), 107
Bork, Robert, 52-53, 54, 190
Boston Harbor, 192-94, 235, 306n21
Boston Police Department, 203
Boston Police Patrolmen's Association, 203
Boyd, Gerald, 167
Bradley, Bill, 18, 20, 72, 79, 140, 265
Brady, Nicholas, 98-99, 166
Brazile, Donna, 87
Breaux, John, 24
Brinkley, David, 151, 184
Broadhurst, Billy, 40
Brock, Bill, 119
Broder, David, 25, 69, 103, 110, 174, 208
Brokaw, Tom, 1, 38, 63, 124, 150, 208, 212, 242
Brountas, Paul, 139, 140, 142, 215
Brown, Floyd, 196, 197, 266
Brown, Ron, 145, 146, 150, 255
Brown Brothers Harriman, 95
Bruno, Hal, 45
Buchanan, Pat, 18, 109, 202, 258, 261, 264
Buckley, William F., 49, 50
Buford, Anne Gorsuch, 192
Bumpers, Dale, 18, 56
Burnham, Walter Dean, 226
Bush, Barbara, 95, 121
Bush, George H. W., *105*, *123*, *171*, *184*, *219*; 1988 election success of, 1, 6, 242-49; 1988 primary race of, 101-31; 1992 election loss of, 2, 262-63; background of, 19, 95-97; budget agreement of 1990 and, 255-56; campaign rhetoric of, 4, 7-8, 202-3, 220-21; criminal justice policies of, 183, 195, 196, 203, 204, 207, 218; criticisms of campaign by,

215–16, 229–35, 239–41; death of, 266; and Dukakis debates, 204–8, 218–23; economic policies of, 179–80, 183, 255–56; education policies of, 98, 105, 117; environmental policies of, 98, 105–6, 189, 194; Iran-Contra scandal and, 26–31, 99, 112–15; legacy of campaign by, 252–59, 264–67; post-election analysis on, 248–51; Rather's interview of, 114–16; Republican National Convention speech by, 160, 179–80, 181–84; Richards on, 146, 147; running mate nomination by, 159–60, 165–68, 175–76, 185–87, 207; swearing-in ceremony of, 252–53, *253*; television ads by, 193–94, 196–98, 215, 228–29, 230–33; as vice president, 97–98; Watergate and, 97

Bush, George W.: father's campaign and, 102, 104, 147, 177; presidential campaign of, 247, 265, 293n208; presidential term of, 20; *SNL* satire of, 217; trade policies of, 264

Bush, Jeb, 127–28

Bush, Prescott, 95, 262

Bush-Dukakis presidential race (1988), 91–93, 133–242, *219*. *See also* Bush, George H. W.; Dukakis, Michael

campaign-finance system, 5, 138, 172, 249, 265. *See also* campaign fundraising

campaign fundraising: by Democrats, 45, 49, 52, 57, 63, 74, 76, 80, 83, 132, 138–39, 265; by Republicans, 102, 106, 111, 171–72. *See also* soft money

campaigning, negative, 2, 215–16, 229–42, 246, 260, 261. *See also* television advertisements; *names of specific ads*

Campbell, Carroll, 20, 125

Cannon, Lou, 103

Canzeri, Joe, 209

capital punishment. *See* death penalty

Card, Andy, 89, 121, 134, 191, 286n184

Carlson, Margaret, 209

Carrick, Bill, 56, 73, 77

Carson, Johnny, 152, 160–61, *162*

Carter, Jimmy: economic policies of, 179–80; election success of, 7, 142, 243; foreign policies of, 198; negative perception of, 14–15, 180–81, 182, 195,

203, 207, 238, 251; political coalition of, 11, 101; on southern primary, 22

Carvey, Dana, 216

Carville, James, 263

Casey, Bob, 257

Casey, Susan, 39

Castro, Fidel, 83

Catholic Americans, 227

cell-phone video recordings, 56

Chafee, John, 244

Chancellor, John, 150

Chaney, James, 164

Chase, Chevy, 217

Cheney, Dick, 175

Chiles, Lawton, 21

China, 109

Christian, George, 226

Christian Broadcasting Network, 101

Christian Coalition, 5, 95, 120. *See also* Christians, evangelical

Christians, evangelical, 11, 95, 100–101, 117, 121, 124, 125; and Christian Coalition, 5, 95, 120

Christian conservatism, 5, 11, 19, 119–20, 168. *See also* Robertson, Pat

CIA (Central Intelligence Agency), 97

citizenship policies, 21

Civil Rights Act (1964), 6, 24, 61, 96

civil rights movement, 6, 7, 10, 60, 96, 150. *See also* Black community

class-based politics, 62, 228, 246, 255, 265. *See also* racism

Clifford, Clark, 15

climate change, 6, 189, 211–12, 311n148. *See also* environmental policies

Clinton, Bill, *162*; 1988 election and, 3, 51–52, 132–33, 163, 214, 231; 1992 election and term of, 2, 258–64; 1996 election of, 265; "Blue Wall" and, 248; campaign rhetoric of, 4, 5, 249–50, 257, 259–64; criminal justice policies of, 264; Democratic National Convention speech in 1988 and recovery from,151–52, 160–63, 260; as DLC chair, 255; economic policies of, 37, 50, 261–62; on Horton, 261; Jackson and, 151, 259; negative attacks against, 237; sex scandals of, 32, 44, 46, 51–52, 63, 162–63, 258; on *SNL* satire, 217; soft money and, 265; television

Index · 333

Clinton, Bill (*continued*)
    performances by, 153, 160-62, 193; trade policies of, 50, 264; Vietnam-era draft and avoidance of, 185, 258, 262
Clinton, Hillary, 65, 81, 87, 141
CNN (Cable News Network), 55, 145
Cobble, Steve, 266
Coehlo, Tony, 254
The Colbert Report (television show), 162, 189
College Republicans, 20
Collins, Susan, 317n129
Committee for the Study of the American Electorate, 246
compassion rhetoric, 30, 106-7, 117, 220
Compton, Ann, 218
Congressional Black Caucus, 140, 144
conservatism, 10, 193. *See also* Christian conservatism
Conservative Caucus, 111
contras (Nicaragua). *See* Iran-Contra scandal
Conventional Wisdom Watch (CW), 67-68, 81, 84, 143, 152, 155, 161, 184, 238, 248
Conyers, John, 144
Corrections Compendium (journal), 216
Corrigan, Jack: Biden tape scandal and, 57; on campaign ads, 67, 72, 74; on Democratic National Convention, 150-51, 155-56; on Dukakis decision to run, 37; on Dukakis general election strategies, 190, 191, 196, 209, 219-20, 226, 230, 242; on Dukakis mental health story, 164; on electability of Dukakis, 250; on Jackson, 150-51; on Pledge of Allegiance, 190; on primaries, 46, 52, 58, 62, 67, 70, 72, 74, 75, 80; on Reagan's impact on campaign, 218; on Shaw death penalty question in debate, 219-20; on vice-presidential pick, 142-43, 226
crack-cocaine epidemic, 6
credibility gap, 39-40
criminal justice policies: of Clinton, 264; on death penalty, 6, 88, 133, 137, 188, 195, 203, 207, 218-20; on drugs, 6, 129; on furlough program, 79-80, 88-89, 130, 132, 135-38, 196-97, 207, 215-16; of Nixon, 6-7, 133; political divisions on, 10

Cruz, Ted, 120
C-SPAN, 32, 55
cultural populism, 49, 109, 134, 195-96
Cuomo, Mario, 13, 16, 25, 28, 51, 62, 64, 83, 89, 147, 230-31
The Cycles of American History (Schlesinger), 29

The Daily Show (television show), 162, 189
"Daisy" advertisement, 236
Daley, Steve, 260
Daniels, Mitch, 23, 178
Darman, Richard, 178, 180, 204, 222
Daschle, Tom, 72
Dean, Howard, 128
death penalty, 6, 88, 133, 137, 195, 203, 207, 218-20. *See also* criminal justice policies
debates: Bush-Dukakis, 204-8, 218-23; of Democratic primary, 60, 67; Dole-Mondale, 204; Ford-Carter, 204; Kennedy-Nixon, 204; Quayle-Bentsen, 209-14; Reagan-Carter, 204; Reagan-Mondale, 204
de Cordova, Fred, 160-61
defense budget, 50, 56, 61
defense policies, 26-31, 99, 103, 199
Dellinger, Walter, 137
Democratic Leadership Council (DLC), 21, 22, 47, 81, 255, 271n44
Democratic National Committee (DNC), 18, 21, 65, 79, 229, 238, 255, 265
Democratic National Convention, 5, 16, 34, 66, 79, 133, 145-58, 169
Democratic nomination (1988), 28-29, 32-33, 47, 65, 90, 92-93
Democratic Party. *See names of specific politicians*
Democratic primary race (1987-88), 32-93. *See also names of specific candidates*
Devine, Tad: on Clinton 1988 convention speech, 152; on final hours of campaign, 242; on Iowa caucus outcome, 69; on negative advertising and legacy of 1988 election, 236; on political campaigns, 69, 143, 152; preparation for vice presidential debate, 209-10; on proportional representation reforms in primaries, 140-41

334 • Index

Dewar, Helen, 174
Dewey, Thomas, 173
Dickenson, James R., 22
Diller, Barry, 219
Dionne, E. J.: on 1988 campaign, 1, 8; on Democratic primary, 28-29, 69; on GOP and tax agreement, 255-56; on Hart, 44; on Iran-Contra scandal, 30, 31; on Republican primary, 102, 127, 129; on senate race, 23
Dirksen, Everett, 24
discrimination, 10
distrust, 39-40
Doak, David, 56
Dodd, Chris, 79
Dole, Bob, *123*; 1988 campaign of, 101-31; 1996 campaign of, 265; background of, 99; at Bush's funeral, 266; Bush's vice presidential selection process and, 166-68, 170; campaign rhetoric of, 4, 20; campaign successes and failures of, 1, 27, 28, 99-100, 248; on Iran-Contra, 30-31; political ideology of, 20, 100, 109, 110, 117, 128; as RNC chair, 97
Dole, Elizabeth, 167
Domenici, Pete, 167, 305n157
Donaldson, Sam, 43, 147, 149, 177, 200, 208
Donilon, Tom, 205
Doonesbury (cartoon), 19
Dorsen, Norman, 208
Dorsey, James, 33-34
Dowd, Maureen, 53, 226
Downey, Jim, 217
draft avoidance, 185, 258. *See also* military service
drug policies, 6, 129. *See also* criminal justice policies
Dukakis, Kitty, 36, 37, 67, 188, 191, 194, 218, 222, 238, 254, 263
Dukakis, Michael, *155, 200, 219*; 1988 presidential election loss of, 1, 2, 6, 8, 242-49; background of, 33, 36, 38; Biden tape controversy and, 56-58; Black community and, 224, 226-27; "Blue Wall" and, 6, 224, 248, 264; and Bush debates, 204-8, 218-23; on Bush's foreign policy, 267; campaign-finance system by, 5; campaign rhetoric of, 4, 37-39, 49-50, 51, 52, 62-63, 66-67, 217, 240; campaign successes of, 25, 33-34, 71, 73, 76, 83; on Clinton, 259-60; criminal justice policies of, 6, 79-80, 88-89, 130, 132, 135-38, 188, 196-97; Defense Week, 198-202; at Democratic National Convention, 145-58; Democratic National Convention speech by, 154-56; economic policies of, 35-37, 83-84, 254; education policies of, 130, 134-35; environmental policies of, 155, 192; as governor of Massachusetts, 33-38; on gun control, 143, 183, 195, 225, 227; on Iran-Contra scandal, 28; Kirkpatrick on, 172-73; legacy of campaign by, 252-59, 264-67; mental health of, 163-64, 165; party nomination of, 32, 65, 90, 92-93; on Pledge of Allegiance, 134-35; political ideology of, 4-5, 7-8, 18, 34-35, 51, 132, 220-21, 238, 245; postelection analysis on, 248-51; running mate nomination for, 139-45, 207; tank ride and ad of, 199-202, 228-29; television ads of, 66-68, 72-74, 215, 228, 229, 230; trade policies of, 50, 80
Dukakis, Olympia, 153-54
Dunbar, William, 107
du Pont, Pierre "Pete," IV, 101, 110, 119, *123*, 124
Durbin, Dick, 266

Eagleton, Thomas, 163, 178
East Germany, 254
Eastland, James, 24
Ebersol, Dick, 217
Eckhart, Dennis, 210
economic inequality, 64, 83-84
economic nationalism, 38, 61, 64, 81, 238
economic policies: of Bush, 179-80, 183; of Carter, 179-80; of Clinton, 257, 261-62; of Dukakis, 35-37, 83-84; of Kemp, 100; of Mondale, 13-14, 16, 180; of Reagan, 13-14, 20-21, 63, 72, 120, 150, 152, 180, 240; of Simon, 63. *See also* taxation; trade policies
economic populism, 49, 61, 92, 134
economic recession, 9. *See also* inflation; taxation
"economic violence," 61, 84, 150
Edsall, Thomas, 103

Index · **335**

education policies: of Bush, 98, 105, 117; of Dukakis, 130, 134–35. *See also* schools and politics
Ehrenhalt, Alan, 34
Eichel, Larry, 249
Eisenhower, Dwight D., 15, 18, 100, 131, 173
Eizenstat, Stuart, 249
Electoral College, 6, 25, 157, 166, 203, 227, 239, 242, 243, 247, 257, 248, 264
electroshock treatment, 163
Employment and Training Choices (ET Choices) program, 36–37
England, Gordon, 200
enterprise zones, 107
environmental policies: of Bush, 98, 105–6, 189, 194; of Dole, 117; of Dukakis, 155, 189, 192; of Reagan, 117, 192. *See also* global warming
Environmental Protection Agency (EPA), 117, 155, 192, 306n21
Equal Rights Amendment (ERA), 11, 19, 40, 97, 101
Estrich, Susan: on campaign ads, 196, 198, 215, 240; on Clinton, 163; on closing strategy, 228, 230, 239, 247; on Democratic platform, 149; on Dukakis convention speech, 153, 156; on Dukakis as liberal, 91, 141, 149; on Dukakis mental health story, 164; on electability of Dukakis, 250; on Horton issue and furloughs, 138, 153, 215, 230, 233, 264, 266; on Jackson, 83, 91, 142, 143, 227; lessons of defeat, 250, 266; positions on Dukakis campaign, 47, 62; on presidential debates, 202, 205, 219, 221, 222; on primaries, 47, 66, 68, 73, 76, 79, 81, 85; on Quayle selection, 175; on Reagan's impact on campaign, 131, 250; on Robertson campaign, 118; on Sasso resignation, 57; on Tsongas, 259; on vice-presidential debate, 213, 214, on vice-presidential picks, 142, 143, 175; on working relationship with Dukakis, 57, 160, 249
extramarital affairs. *See* sex scandals

Face the Nation (television show), 240
Fair, Ray, 249
Fairness Doctrine, 193

Falwell, Jerry, 11, 101, 261
Family Ties (television show), 245
farm economy, 48, 72
Farmer, Bob, 62, 139, 265
Farrakhan, Louis, 88
Federal Communications Commission (FCC), 193
Federal Election Commission (FEC), 197–98
feminist politics, 3, 10, 16, 40, 46, 49, 261
Ferraro, Geraldine, 12–13, 37
Ferrell, Will, 217
Fey, Tina, 217
Fiedler, Tom, 41–42
Fineman, Howard, 41
Firing Line (television show), 49, 109
flag-burning, 191–92. *See also* antiwar sentiment
Flowers, Gennifer, 46, 162, 258
Flynn, Ray, 203
Foley, Tom, 47
Foner, Eric, 2
food stamps program, 100
Ford, Gerald, 18, 19, 97, 99, 173, 204, 217
Fournier, Joseph, 136
Fox News, 20, 99, 145, 263
Frank, Barney, 35, 82–83, 194
Franken, Al, 216
Friedman, Milton, 17
From, Al, 47
Fuller, Craig: on Bush-Reagan roles, 98, 129–30; on debates, 124; on Dukakis, 91; on G-6, 99; on Goldwater, 123; on Horton ad, 198; on Iran Contra, 27, 29; on messaging strategy, 30, 104, 122, 198; on *Newsweek* "Wimp Factor" cover, 104; position in Bush administration, 27; on primaries, 103, 117, 121; on Rather interview, 114, 115, 116; vice presidential pick and, 165–66, 167, 170, 171, 209
fundraising. *See* campaign fundraising
furlough program, 6, 79–80, 88–89, 130, 132, 135–38, 183, 196, 203, 207, 215–16, 230, 232, 233, 234, 245, 265. *See also* criminal justice policies

Gans, Curtis, 246
gay rights movement, 10
Gaza Strip. *See* Israeli-Palestinian conflict

GE (General Electric), 38
Geer, John, 236
gender gap, 246
Georges, Christopher, 261
Gephardt, Dick: Biden tape scandal and, 56, 58, 64; campaign rhetoric of, 4, 66-69, 258; Dukakis using his message, 194, 195, 224; on Gore, 59; on Horton issue, 257; as House majority leader, 93, 254; legacy of campaign, 64, 81; political ideology of, 21, 47, 48-49; presidential campaign of, 47, 63, 68-81; tax reform by, 20; trade policies of, 38, 48-49, 50-51, 66, 81, 264; and vice presidential selection process (1988), 141, 142, 144
Gergen, David, 1, 250
Germany, 254
Germond, Jack, 2, 134, 193
Gingrich, Newt, 30, 91-92, 100, 101, 255, 319n13
glasnost policy, 21
Glenn, John, 12, 22, 190, 199, 226; as part of vice-presidential selection process (1988), 140-44
globalization, 4, 49, 81, 264
global warming, 6, 211-12, 311n148. *See also* environmental policies
Goldwater, Barry: Bush and, 120, 123-24; on Civil Rights Act, 61, 96; party nomination of, 96; political ideology of, 18, 19, 24; presidential campaign of, 10, 18, 120, 157, 236, 248
Goodman, Andrew, 164
Gorbachev, Mikhail, 21, 65, 103, 112, 130, 169, 175, 198, 254, 267
Gore, Al: campaign rhetoric of, 71, 72, 74, 75, 77, 78, 85; campaign successes and failures of, 32, 76, 248; as Clinton's running mate, 259; defense politics of, 63; Horton issue and role in it, 88, 265; political ideology of, 59; presidential campaign of, 58-60, 64, 70, 79, 84, 86, 87-90, 92; *SNL* satire of, 217; and Super Tuesday, 60, 70, 75, 76, 77, 78; as vice president, 92-93; and vice-presidential selection process (1988), 141-42
Graham, Bob, 18, 21, 22, 63
Graham, Kay, 104
Grassley, Charles, 118

Great Depression, 9, 10
Great Society, 13, 17, 18, 34, 91, 179, 227
Greek Americans, 33, 36, 38, 49, 80, 88, 258-59
Greenberg, Stanley, 15-16, 90, 259
Greenfield, Jeff, 146, 168-69
Gregg, Donald, 114
Grenada, 59
Group of Six, 98-99, 130
gun control, 143, 183, 195, 225, 227

Haig, Al, 72, 101, 111, 119
Haldeman, H. R., 133
Hamilton, Lee, 141, 142
Hammond, Darrell, 217
Hanks, Tom, 216
Hansen, James, 211
Harris, Louis, 235, 262
Harris County Republicans, 96
Harrison, Tubby, 68
Hart, Gary, 44; 1984 presidential campaign of, 12; 1988 presidential campaign of, 16, 25, 28, 29, 39, 41, 45, 65-66, 68, 70, 76; campaign rhetoric and political ideology of, 17-18, 257; on Iran-Contra scandal, 30, 31; on media scrutiny, 46-47, 258; sex scandal of, 3, 32, 39, 40-46, 51-52, 63, 251
Hart, Peter, 15
Hatcher, Richard, 86-87
Hayek, Friedrich, 17
Heinz, John, 257
Helms, Jesse, 25
Herbers, John, 18
Heston, Charlton, 181, 189
Hickman, Harrison, 201
Hispanic Americans, 89
Hoffman, David, 129
Holtzman, Paul, 199
Hooks, Jan, 216
Horowitz, David, 160-61
Horton, William, 6, 8, 79-80, 88, 136-37, 138, 141, 153, 196, 216, 266. *See also* furlough program; "Weekend Passes" advertisement
hostages, American, in Lebanon (1986), 26-27, 30, 31, 114
housing discrimination, 96
Huckabee, Mike, 120
Hulse, Carl, 266

Index · 337

Hume, Brit, 174, 184, 212
Humphrey, Hubert, 7, 13, 18, 24, 34, 49, 54, 58, 70, 131
Hussein, Saddam, 255
Hyundai advertisement, 66, 68

immigrant background of politicians, 13, 33, 36, 38, 52, 65, 88, 154, 206, 208, 258-59. *See also* Greek Americans
immigration policies, 21
Immigration Reform and Control Act (1986), 21
inflation, 9, 11, 128, 182, 194, 249. *See also* economic policies
intermediate-range nuclear forces (INF) treaty, 103, 110, 130
internet, 73, 193
interventionism, 59
Iran, 11, 26, 27, 108, 113, 155, 198. *See also* Iran-Contra scandal
Iran-Contra scandal, 26-31, 99, 112-15
Iranian hostage crisis (1979-81), 11, 198
Iranian Revolution, 11
Iraq, 56, 108, 255, 256
Iraq War, 56
isolationism, 59
Israeli-Palestinian conflict, 5, 80, 84, 88, 132; Democratic Party position on, 147-49, 298n110
Ivins, Molly, 226

Jackson, Henry "Scoop," 59
Jackson, Jesse, 82; 1988 campaign of, 4, 12, 41, 47, 60-62, 64, 72-92; 1992 campaign and, 255, 259-60; agreement with Dukakis, 146, 151; bid for vice presidential nomination by, 139-40, 142, 143, 144; campaign successes of, 65, 69-70, 76-77, 83-85; at Democratic National Convention (1988), 145, 149-51; Dukakis and, 165, 226-27; on Horton, 232; legacy of campaign by, 4, 65, 86-87, 92, 140-41, 151, 265; on Palestinian self-determination, 80, 84, 88, 132, 147-49; political ideology of, 61, 84-85; Rainbow Coalition of, 259, 265
Jamieson, Kathleen Hall, 2, 216, 231-32
Japan, 48, 51, 61, 64, 66, 107-8, 109, 194, 195, 238
Jaroslovsky, Rich, 223

Javits, Jacob, 24
Jennings, Peter, 45, 56, 146, 149, 151, 168, 184, 206
Jewish Americans, 88, 89, 90, 147-48
Job Training Partnership Act (1982), 175
John Birch Society, 96
John Hancock Insurance, 215
Johnson, Lyndon B., 10, 61, 91, 131, 157, 167
Jordan, Barbara, 226
judicial nominations, 20, 209

Kagan, Elena, 190
Kasich, John, 256
Kaus, Mickey, 57
Kean, Tom, 168, 173-74
Kemp, Jack, *123*; 1988 campaign of, 28, 50, 101-28; political ideology of, 100; position in Bush's cabinet, 254; taxation policies of, 20, 100, 179; and vice-presidential selection process (1988), 166, 167, 168, 170
Kennedy, Edward "Ted": Democratic National Convention speech by, 149, 221; Kean and Reagan on the speech, 169, 174; legislation by, 175; political ideology of, 11, 24, 250; presidential campaign of, 69; role in Sasso resignation, 57; scandal of, 40, 46
Kennedy, John F.: election of, 10; extramarital affairs of, 32, 40, 41; Quayle's comparison to, 212-14
Kennedy, John F., Jr., 149
Kerry, John, 56, 57, 185, 248
Keynesian economics, 11
Kilborn, Peter, 91
Kimmitt, Robert, 165-68, 178
King, Ed, 35, 36
King, Martin Luther, Jr., 60, 89, 150
Kinnock, Neil, 53-54
Kirk, Paul, 21, 23, 66
Kirkpatrick, Jeanne, 172-73
Kissinger, Henry, 209
Klein, Joe, 51
Koch, Ed, 88, 89, 285n180
Kohut, Andrew, 209
Koppel, Ted, 65
Krauthammer, Charles, 214, 233
Kristol, Irving, 100
Kuwait, 255, 256

labor unions, 10, 16, 34, 48, 225. *See also* AFL-CIO
Lacy, Bill, 125, 126, 128
Ladd, Everett Carll, 245
Laffer, Arthur, 100
Lamar, Jacob, 23, 24
Larouche, Lyndon, 163
Larry King Live (television show), 162, 176-77, 193, 262
Late Show with David Letterman (television show), 162
"law and order" rhetoric, 6-7, 133. *See also* criminal justice policies
Laxalt, Paul, 101
"Leadership Gap" (1986 document), 98
Leahy, Patrick, 79
Lebanon: American hostages in (1986), 26-27, 30, 31, 114
Lehrer, Jim, 205
Lewinsky, Monica, 46, 163
Lewis, Anne, 75
Lewis, Anthony, 42, 83, 153, 227, 231
Lewis, John, 87
liberalism: of Dukakis, 4-5, 34-35, 51, 132, 238, 245; rise of, 10-11; of Simon, 58
libertarianism, 17
Lieberman, Joe, 59, 279n187
Limbaugh, Rush, 193
Lockhart, Joe, 201
Lovitz, Jon, 216, 240
Lubber, Mindy, 201

MacNeil/Lehrer NewsHour (television show), 38
Macomb County, Mich., 16, 199, 208
malaise speech (Carter), 11
Manafort, Paul, 204
Maraniss, David, 51
Margolis, John, 211
Martin, Fred, 75
Martin Luther King Jr. Day, 100
Martz, Larry, 191
"Massachusetts Miracle," 37, 38, 50, 52, 62, 67, 71, 73, 193, 204, 254
Massachusetts Police Association, 203
Massachusetts Police Chiefs Association, 203
mass incarceration, 264. *See also* criminal justice policies
Mayer, Jane, 197

mayoral campaigns, 61
McAuliffe, Terry, 74
McCain, John, 120, 185, 186, 265
McCain-Feingold bill (2002), 265
McCarthy, Joseph, 95, 133, 196, 262
McCarthy, Larry, 124, 196
McConnell, Mitch, 99, 172
McDougal, Malcolm, 194
McGee, Jim, 41-42
McGee, Tommy, 35
McGovern, George, 7, 8, 34, 79, 92, 100, 198, 237
McGovern-Fraser reforms, 79, 92
McLaughlin, John, 202
McLaughlin Group, (television show), 197, 202
media institutions, 55-56, 145-46, 161-62, 192-93, 307n32. *See also names of specific companies and networks*
medical records, 163-64
Meese, Ed, 27
Meet the Press (television show), 168, 190, 229
Melton, R. H., 210
mental health, 163-64, 165
Metzenbaum, Howard, 228
Miami Herald (newspaper), 41-43
Michael, Terry, 66
Michaels, Lorne, 217
midterm elections: of 1974, 17; of 1982, 9; of 1986, 22-26; of 2018, 266
Mike Douglas Show (television show), 99
Mikulski, Barbara, 79
military arms policies, 26-31, 99, 103, 199
military service: of Bentsen, 142; of Bush, 19, 95; as campaign issue, 6; Clinton and, 258; of Dukakis, 33; of Gore, 59; of Kerry, 185; of McCain, 185; Quayle and, 159, 167-68, 176, 178, 180, 184-85; Trump and, 185. *See also* draft avoidance; patriotism
military spending, 50, 56, 61
Mills, Wilbur, 46
Miranda v. Arizona, 133
Mississippi Burning (film), 164, 301n28
Mississippi Freedom Democratic Party (MFDP), 150
Mitchell, Andrea, 214, 218
Mitchell, George, 147

Index · 339

Mondale, Walter: 1984 Democratic primary, 12–13; 1984 presidential election and explanation for defeat, 9, 13–16, 270n6; campaign rhetoric of, 13; on Dukakis-Bentsen, 146; economic policies of, 13–14, 16, 180; on Jackson, 84; political ideology of, 13; political support for, 12; similarities to Dukakis, 50, 132, 155, 250; trade policies of, 48
Moral Majority, 11, 101, 120
Morganthau, Tom, 12
"Morning in America" rhetoric, 9, 14, 182
Morton, Bruce, 164, 201
Mosbacher, Bob, 99, 130, 139, 167, 171–72, 177
Moynihan, Daniel Patrick, 23
MSNBC, 145
MTV, 193
Mudd, Roger, 40
murder rate, 138
Muskie, Edmund, 27, 30

NAACP, 144
NASA, 211
National Democratic Issues Convention, 34
National Guard service, 159, 167, 176, 178, 180, 184–85
National Rifle Association (NRA), 206, 225, 227
National Right to Life, 111, 168
National Security Council (NSC), 26, 29
National Security Political Action Committee, 196–98, 233
National Sheriffs' Association, 137
Nation of Islam, 88
NBC Nightly News (television show), 38, 137, 204
Nealon, Kevin, 216
neoconservatism, 59, 100, 172
neoliberal (term), 17, 34
Netanyahu, Benjamin, 148
New Deal coalition, 10–18, 34, 36, 58, 91, 134, 246, 248
Nicaragua. *See* Iran-Contra scandal
Nightline (television show), 144, 161
Nixon, Richard: Ailes and, 99; Bush and, 96–97; campaign rhetoric of, 7, 49, 132, 133, 134, 198, 249; on dissent, 133; election success of, 7, 10, 18; resignation of, 17; Watergate scandal of, 9, 20, 40, 97
"no new taxes" pledge, 106, 179–80, 183, 255, 258
Noonan, Peggy, 104, 179, 180, 182–83
Noriega, Manuel, 129
Norquist, Grover, 106
North, Oliver, 26, 206
North American Free Trade Agreement (NAFTA), 81, 264
Novak, Bob, 163, 202
nuclear power plants, 49, 70, 71
nuclear weapons, 103, 110, 147, 236
Nunn, Sam, 21, 25, 30, 59, 140, 142–43

Obama, Barack: "Blue Wall" and, 6, 248; campaign rhetoric of, 81; Jackson's 1988 campaign and, 4, 65, 70, 86–87, 92, 140–41; legacy of, 2; negative attacks against, 237; presidential election of, 4, 65, 70, 141
Oberdorfer, Don, 103
O'Donnell, Kirk, 225
Oliphant, Tom, 44, 155
O'Neill, Tip, 16, 23
Operation Desert Shield, 255, 256
Operation Desert Storm, 256
Operation PUSH, 60, 78, 83
Oreskes, Michael, 78, 90, 226, 235–36

Packwood, Bob, 210
Palestine, 5, 80,132, 147–49, 298n110
Palestinian Liberation Organization (PLO), 84, 88
Palin, Sarah, 186, 217
Panama, 129
Paramus focus group, 130
Parks, Rosa, 150
Parmet, Herbert, 184
patriotism, 6–7, 189, 190–91, 206, 233, 262, 264. *See also* military service; Pledge of Allegiance
Peña, Frederico, 147
perestroika policy, 21
Perot, Ross, 162, 193, 260, 264
Persian Gulf War (1990–91), 193, 252
"personal is political" scandals, 3, 40–46, 63. *See also* sex scandals
Peters, Charlie, 17

Peterson, Bill, 68
Phillips, Howard, 111
Phillips, Kevin, 25
Pinkerton, Jim, 51, 89, 106, 123, 130, 134, 138, 171, 179, 191, 204, 251
Pins, Kenneth, 118
plagiarism scandal, 53–55
Pledge of Allegiance, 8, 130, 132, 134–35, 137, 156, 157, 183, 189–92, 195, 202, 203, 204, 206, 207, 209, 225, 232, 235, 236, 245, 249, 262. *See also* patriotism; schools
Podesta, Tony, 192
Poindexter, John, 26, 27
poverty, 10
Powell, Colin, 256
Powell, Lewis, 52
prayer in schools, 96, 100–101, 106, 109, 183. *See also* schools and politics
presidential debates, 204–8, 218–23
presidential elections. *See names of specific candidates*
primary races (1988): Democratic Party, 64–93; Republican Party, 94–131
pro-choice politics. *See* abortion
pro-life politics. *See* abortion
proportional representation system, 76–77, 140–41
Proposition 13 (Calif.), 11
protectionism, 49, 66, 74
psychiatric treatment, 163–64
public distrust of government, 39–40

Quayle, Dan, *171*; and Bentsen debate, 209–14; Bush's nomination of, 159, 165–68, 170–71; descriptions of, 174–76, 218; discussion of in first presidential debate, 207; impact of candidacy, 186, 189, 218, 240, 241, 251; legacy on vice-presidential process, 5–6, 185–86, 259; and National Guard service, 6, 159, 167–68, 176, 178–80, 184–85, 258; political ideology of, 174–75; on Reagan, 31; Republican National Convention speech by, 180–81

racism, 61–62, 82–83, 96, 164, 232–34, 265, 266. *See also* class-based politics; Horton, William

Rainbow Coalition, 259, 265
Rasky, Susan, 174
Rather, Dan: interview with Bush, 114–16
Raytheon, 38
Reagan, Nancy, 183
Reagan, Ronald: 1984 presidential election, 9, 13–15; 1986 midterm elections and, 23–24; at 1988 Republican National Convention, 169; arms-control agreement with Soviet Union, 103; Bush as vice president of, 97–98; Bush's 1988 success and, 1, 121, 124–25, 127, 130–31, 217–18, 239, 244–45, 251; campaigning for Bush in 1988, 239; criminal justice policies of, 216; criticism of, 29–30; on Dukakis's health, 163–64; economic policies of, 13–14, 63, 72, 120, 150, 152, 180, 240; election successes of, 7, 8, 9, 18; furlough program of as governor of California, 135, 216; Iran-Contra scandal and, 26–27, 30, 31, 99; legacy of, 2; legislative successes of, 20–21; mental acuity of, 15; and Soviet Union, 14, 19, 21, 103, 110, 130, 198; televised debates of, 204
Reagan Democrats, as group, 7–8, 130, 137, 151, 154, 178, 179, 190, 208, 224–25, 262
Reaganomics, 13–14, 63, 72, 120, 150, 152, 225, 240
Reed, Ralph, 120, 261
Regan, Don, 27
Reich, Robert, 91, 262
religious right. *See* Christian conservatism
reproductive rights. *See* abortion
Republican National Committee (RNC), 19, 20, 22, 97, 257
Republican National Convention, 7, 97, 103, 106, 112, 116, 160, 168–86, 188, 261
Republican Party. *See names of specific politicians*
Republican primary race (1988), 94–131, 293n215. *See also names of specific candidates*
"Revolving Door" advertisement, 215–16, 231, 233, 236
Rice, Donna, 40–45, 240, 251
Richards, Ann, 146–47, 221
Ridley, Timothy, 53, 54

Riegle, Donald, 80
Rivlin, Alice, 91
Road to the White House (television show), 55
Robb, Charles, 16, 21
Roberts, Steven, 29, 179
Robertson, Pat, *119, 123*; 1988 campaign of, 95, 101–27, 131; background of, 100, 101; campaign success of, 5, 69; political power of, 148, 168, 261; on Quayle, 174
Robinson, Will, 72, 80
Rockefeller, Nelson, 18, 99
Rockefeller Republicans, 19, 173, 177
Roe v. Wade, 11, 101. *See also* abortion
Rogich, Sid, 181, 215, 228
Rollins, Ed, 127, 146
Romney, Mitt, 56
Roosevelt, Franklin D.: economic policies of, 36, 49; extramarital affairs of, 40, 41; influence on Sanders, 265; judicial nominations by, 20; political coalition of, 10; and Works Progress Administration, 58
Roosevelt, Theodore, 192, 194
Rosenbaum, David, 61, 144, 147
Rosenthal, Andrew, 56, 57
Rostenkowski, Dan, 47
Roth, William, 100
Rudman, Warren, 261
Russert, Tim, 145

Sabato, Larry, 106
Safire, William, 70, 126–27
Sampson, Ruby, 36, 154, 221
Sanders, Bernie, 62, 81, 83, 87, 149, 265–66
Sandinistas, 26
Santorum, Rick, 120
Sargent, Francis, 33, 135
Sasser, Jim, 244
Sasso, John: campaign strategies of, 28, 62–63, 73, 139, 202, 215, 226; Ferraro and, 37; on Jackson, 226, 255; position on Dukakis campaign, 28, 36, 37, 194, 255; resignation of over Biden tape, 56–58; on vice-presidential pick, 232
Saturday Night Live (*SNL*, television show), 6, 189, 216–17, 231, 240, 263
Saudi Arabia, 255
Savage, James, 43

Scammon, Richard, 16
Schieffer, Bob, 193, 208
Schlafly, Phyllis, 18, 261
Schlesinger, Arthur, Jr., 29, 248
Schneider, Bill, 51, 53, 205, 227, 239
school desegregation, 101
schools and politics: and Pledge of Allegiance, 8, 130, 132, 134–35, 156, 183, 189–92; and prayer, 96, 100–101, 106, 109, 183. *See also* education policies
Schultz, George, 26, 129
Schumer, Charles, 148
Schwerner, Michael, 164
Scowcroft, Brent, 27
Seabrook nuclear power plant, 49, 70, 71
Segal, Jeffrey, 244
Serafin, Barry, 149
"Seven Dwarfs," 47, 50, 92
sex scandals: of Clinton, 32, 44, 46, 51–52, 63, 162–63, 258; of Hart, 3, 32, 39, 40–46; of Kennedy, 32, 40
Shabecoff, Philip, 211
Shales, Tom, 217
Shapiro, Walter, 9, 39, 65, 249
Shaw, Bernard, 188, 218, 220, 222, 238, 263
Shrum, Bob: on Dukakis closing message, 195, 228, 238, 250–51; on electability of Dukakis, 250–51; and Gephardt campaign, 48, 56, 58, 66, 71, 72, 74, 75, 81; positions on political campaigns, 32, 34; role in "You're no Jack Kennedy" line, 213
silent majority (term), 7
Simon, Paul: campaign successes of, 50, 64, 78; political ideology of, 58; presidential campaign of, 58, 63, 66, 67, 68–69, 71–73, 78, 84, 86, 92, 118
Simpson, Alan, 167, 168
Simpson-Mazzoli Act (1986), 21
Sister Souljah, 259
60 Minutes (television show), 46, 162
Smith, Alfred E., 248
Social Security, 217, 221
soft money, 5, 138–39, 171–72, 248–49, 265. *See also* campaign-finance system; campaign fundraising
"Somersault" ad, 74
Somoza, Anastasio, 26
Southern Legislative Conference (SLC), 22

Southern Primary Republican Project, 22
Southern Strategy, 7, 269n14
South Korea, 66
Soviet Union: GOP politics on, 19; invasion of Afghanistan by, 11, 111; Reagan's policies on, 14, 19, 21, 103, 110, 130, 198. *See also* Gorbachev, Mikhail
Spencer, Stuart, 209
Squier, Bob, 249
stagflation, 11. *See also* inflation
Stahl, Lesley, 155, 225, 240
Star Wars (Strategic Defense Initiative), 67, 106, 144, 173, 302n88
Stengel, Richard, 143
Stennis, John, 24-25
Stephanopoulos, George, 262
Stevenson, Adlai E., 144
Stone, Roger, 137, 176
"Straddle" ad, 94, 122-24, 128
Strategic Defense Initiative (SDI). *See* Star Wars
Summers, Larry, 91, 262
Sununu, John, 121, 122, 124, 127, 172, 263
superdelegates, 77, 79, 140-41
Super Tuesday (1988), 60, 64, 70, 72, 73, 75-79, 125-26, 271n44; development of, 21-22
supply-side economics, 11, 19, 20, 100
surveillance, 41-42
Swaggart, Jimmy, 125-26
Symms, Steve, 191

Taft, Robert, 18
talk radio, 8, 193
Talmadge, Herman, 24
"Tank" event and ad, 199-202, 228-30
taxation, 11; Bush on, 179-80, 183, 255-56; Dukakis on, 35, 254; Kean on, 173-74; Kemp-Roth cuts, 20, 100; Reagan on, 13-14, 97. *See also* economic policies; inflation; supply-side economics
Tax Reform Act (1986), 20-21
Taylor, Paul, 44, 69
Tea Party, 256
Teeley, Pete, 97, 114, 115
Teeter, Bob, 13, 99, 130, 144, 166, 170, 180, 222, 241
televangelism, 101. *See also* Robertson, Pat

television, cable, 55, 73, 162, 193
television advertisements: of Bush, 122, 124, 193-94, 196-98, 215, 228-29, 230-33; of Dukakis, 66-68, 72-74, 215, 228, 229, 230; of Gephardt, 75; by Gore, 89; by Johnson, 236; as pivotal to campaign, 76, 235-36; Trump and, 266
This Week with David Brinkley (television show), 43, 168
Thomas, Evan, 15, 104
Thomason, Harry, 152-53, 160-61
Thomason, Linda, 152-53
Thompson, Jim, 127
Thornburgh, Dick, 257-58
"three strikes and you're out" laws, 264
Thurmond, Strom, 20, 202
Toner, Robin, 52, 83-84, 112, 136
The Tonight Show Starring Johnny Carson (television show), 5, 153, 160-62, 162
Tower, John, 27
Tower Commission, 28, 29, 30, 31, 113
trade policies: of Dukakis, 50, 80; of Gephardt, 48-49, 50-51, 66, 81, 264; of Mondale, 48; of Trump, 108, 109. *See also* economic policies
Trager, John, 22
Trans-Pacific Partnership (TPP), 81
Tribe, Laurence, 190
Trippi, Joe, 66, 75
Truman, Harry S., 10, 29, 49, 58, 59, 142, 238, 239, 240, 246, 256
Trump, Donald: 1988 election and, 3, 95, 107-9, 131, 176-77; *The Art of the Deal*, 109; draft avoidance by, 185; early political rhetoric of, 5; exploratory presidential campaign of, 81, 248, 258; interest in vice presidency, 165; political ad and, 266; political ideology of, 108-9; *SNL* satire of, 217
Tsongas, Paul, 258-59
Tully, Paul, 52, 56-57
Turner, Nina, 266

unemployment, 9, 35, 260, 263
United Press International (UPI), 33
urban riots, 6, 10
U.S. House of Representatives, 9, 15, 22-25, 55, 244. *See also names of specific representatives*

Index · 343

U.S. Senate, 9, 15, 22–25, 244. *See also* names of specific senators
USSR. *See* Soviet Union

Van Buren, Martin, 1, 20, 243
vice-presidential debate, 209–14
video revolution in politics, 55–56. *See also* media institutions
Vietnam War, 6, 59, 159, 252–53. *See also* antiwar sentiment
Viguerie, Richard, 19, 111, 116, 241
Volcker, Paul, 9
voter registration, 60, 64–65, 146, 164, 227
Voting Rights Act (1965), 6, 24, 61, 100

Wallace, Chris, 201, 204, 229, 241
Wallace, George, 7, 18, 85, 133, 226
Warner, Margaret, 104, 218
Watergate scandal, 3, 9, 17–18, 20, 26, 32, 40, 43, 46, 55, 97, 132, 138, 172, 249, 265. *See also* Nixon, Richard
Waters, Maxine, 144
weapons policies, 26–31, 99, 103
"Weekend Passes" advertisement, 196–98, 215, 257, 266. *See also* campaigning, negative
Weeks, Jack, 199–200
Weeks, Julie, 214
Weems, Dana, 41
Weicker, Lowell, 25
Weinberger, Caspar, 26
welfare system reform, 36–37, 100, 152, 153–54, 257, 274n26
Wertheimer, Fred, 172

Wertheimer, Linda, 92
West Bank. *See* Israeli-Palestinian conflict
West Germany, 48, 254
West Virginia State Board of Education v. Barnette, 134, 190
White, Teddy, 2
Whitney, Craig, 56
Whose Broad Stripes and Bright Stars? (Germond and Witcover), 2
Wicker, Tom, 16, 42, 137
Wilkie, Curtis, 158
Wilkins, Roger, 259
Will, George, 151, 153, 214
Willkie, J. C., 168
Willkie, Wendell, 173
"Wimp Factor," 104, *105*, 110, 116, 186
Winston, Bonnie, 136
Wirthlin, Richard, 15, 122
Witcover, Jules, 2, 134, 193
Wofford, Harris, 257
Wolfe, Tom, 107
Woodruff, Judy, 38
Woodward, Bob, 40
World Trade Organization (WTO), 264
Wright, Betsy, 51–52
Wright, Jim, 148, 254, 319n13

Yarborough, Ralph, 96
Yepsen, David, 53
Young, Coleman, 80
"You're no Jack Kennedy" (Bentsen debate line), 212–14
YouTube, 56

Zogby, James, 148

www.ingramcontent.com/pod-product-compliance
Lightning Source LLC
Chambersburg PA
CBHW031433230426

43668CB00007B/513